Intelligence and Espionage: An Analytical Bibliography

Also of Interest

Terror and Communist Politics: The Role of the Secret Police in Communist States, edited by Jonathan R. Adelman

Military Development in Africa: The Political and Economic Risks of Arms Transfers, Bruce E. Arlinghaus

Latin America and the U.S. National Interest: A Basis for U.S. Foreign Policy, Margaret Daly Hayes

National Security Crisis Forecasting and Management: From Basic Research to Operational Use, edited by Gerald W. Hopple, Stephen J. Andriole, and Amos Freedy

Communist Nations' Military Aid, John F. Copper and Daniel S. Papp

The U.S. Government Response to Terrorism: In Search of an Effective Strategy, William Regis Farrell

* *Managing U.S.-Soviet Rivalry: Problems of Crisis Prevention,* Alexander L. George and Contributors

Secure Communications and Asymmetric Cryptosystems, edited by Gustavus J. Simmons

Arms Control and Defense Postures in the 1980s, edited by Richard Burt

** *The Military Balance 1981–1982,* International Institute for Strategic Studies

* *Arms Control and Security: Current Issues,* edited by Wolfram F. Hanrieder

Arms Transfers to the Third World: The Military Buildup in Less Industrial Countries, edited by Uri Ra'anan, Robert L. Pfaltzgraff, Jr., and Geoffrey Kemp

Expert-Generated Data: Applications in International Affairs, edited by Gerald W. Hopple and James A. Kuhlman

Quantitative Approaches to Political Intelligence: The CIA Experience, edited by Richards J. Heuer

* *U.S.-Soviet Relations in the Era of Détente,* Richard Pipes

Verification and SALT: The Challenge of Strategic Deception, edited by William C. Potter

Words and Arms: A Dictionary of Security and Defense Terms: With Supplementary Data, Wolfram F. Hanrieder and Larry V. Buel

* *World Power Trends and U.S. Foreign Policy for the 1980s,* Ray S. Cline

The Military and Security in the Third World: Domestic and International Impacts, edited by Sheldon W. Simon

* Available in hardcover and paperback.
** Available in paperback only.

About the Book and Author

Intelligence and Espionage:
An Analytical Bibliography
George C. Constantinides

This pioneering work, based on many years of reading and research and ranging mainly from the seventeenth century to the present, breaks new ground in intelligence bibliography. It is the most comprehensive and thorough bibliography of English-language nonfiction books on intelligence and espionage to date. The in-depth analytical annotations deal with the accuracy and reliability of each book cited, the significance of the material covered in the book, and the degree of thoroughness evidenced by the investigation of the subject matter. Mr. Constantinides draws attention to items and portions that spotlight errors and myths, that cover historically significant exploits, and that address subjects representative of larger issues. Subjects needing further study are identified, and events whose interpretation should await further research or the judgment of history are carefully delineated.

Among the events and periods covered in the works included are the American Revolution and the Civil War, World War I, the Bolshevik Revolution and the subsequent rise of the Soviet Union, World War II, and the post-war era. Constantinides has paid particular attention to the principal aspects, processes, and means of the intelligence function—from collection to the use of intelligence information and from espionage and counter-espionage to modern means of technical collection and unconventional warfare. His comments are supplemented by excerpts from assessments by other analysts. The text is liberally cross referenced and fully indexed.

George C. Constantinides retired from the U.S. government after almost twenty-five years of national security and intelligence-related assignments, both in Washington and abroad. Since retirement, he has served as a consultant with Ketron, Inc., of Arlington, Virginia, and as an independent contractor on national security subjects. He has completed a number of studies for the U.S. intelligence community.

To Artie

For One of Life's Supreme Gifts—
A Happy Marriage

Intelligence and Espionage: An Analytical Bibliography

George C. Constantinides

Westview Press / Boulder, Colorado

Published in 1983 in the United States of America by
Westview Press, Inc.
5500 Central Avenue
Boulder, Colorado 80301
Frederick A. Praeger, President and Publisher

Library of Congress Cataloging in Publication Data
Constantinides, George C.
Intelligence and espionage.
Includes indexes.
1. Intelligence service—Bibliography. 2. Espionage—Bibliography. I. Title.
Z6724.I7C66 1983 [UB250] 016.3271'2 83-3519
ISBN 0-86531-545-0

Printed and bound in the United States of America

Contents

Acknowledgments

When I agreed to the publisher's suggestion that I write this bibliography, I did so with the comfortable awareness that I would be able to rely on support from and access to experts and to specialized literature beyond my own resources. However, the foundation for the study of the five-hundred-odd works that make up this volume was my own records and notes. For these, much of the credit goes to CIA's Historical Collection Division, whose holdings I had access to while I was a federal employee and after my retirement when I was on contract to various agencies, including CIA, on behalf of Ketron, Inc., and when I was working as an independent consultant. Mary Christine Flowers, formerly of that division, was particularly helpful because of her amazing archival and substantive knowledge of writings in the areas of intelligence and espionage. I also had access to two other major holdings in these fields, the Russell Bowen Collection at Georgetown University and the collection of Walter Pforzheimer, the former curator of the Historical Intelligence Division of CIA.

In addition to these libraries and their rich collections of specialized literature, I benefited from the ready availability of opinions and knowledge from those whose familiarity with the literature and whose professional credentials are enviable. Walter Pforzheimer not only let me use his books and his files but also shared with me his vast knowledge of the backgrounds of published works, of their authors, and of the nuances of many events and personal relationships in modern intelligence history. Colonel Bowen was eager to advise on works I should include; his enthusiasm for intelligence history is contagious. Raymond Rocca gave me the benefit of his wide reading and numerous areas of expertise, and he patiently answered my many questions. Samuel Halpern contributed greatly on many subjects dating back to OSS. Norman Smith and John Carroll are two others with a wide knowledge of the literature who were always available for consultation. Beyond these are a number of retired intelligence officials who were most helpful but who choose to remain anonymous.

With due recognition to all listed above, I must still single out my wife, Artie, for her contributions. She is the most important factor behind the publication of this work. She not only spent many hours typing and editing the manuscript but also provided constant encouragement, first for undertaking the project and then for having the patience and tenacity to see it completed. My thanks are also due to the staff of Georgetown's Special Collections, under George M. Barringer, and to Constance Walker of the Davis Memorial Library in Bethesda, Maryland, for their help in making my research easier and more pleasant. Finally, Carol Rasmussen, who edited the manuscript for Westview Press, made me a confirmed believer in the value, to any author, of a good editor.

G.C.C.

Introduction

The Need for an Analytical Bibliography

In 1955, Sherman Kent, whose writings and career were to have an impact on U.S. intelligence, observed that intelligence was not merely a profession—it had taken on the aspects of a discipline. He believed, however, that what the field still lacked was a literature.

What may have been true a quarter of a century ago cannot be said to be the case today. For a number of reasons—the passage of time, changes in rules concerning the timing of the release of classified records, access through freedom of information laws, changing attitudes toward security and secrecy regulations, and the urge to tell a particular side of a story—there has been a marked increase in the number of books devoted to espionage and intelligence. This growth has been nurtured in part by a public interest in, and almost a fascination with, these subjects.

The attitude of Americans toward intelligence and espionage is similar to their attitude toward monarchy: they approve the institution only for others but are still addicts on the subject and enormously enjoy its displays. Films and fiction have been the most obvious beneficiaries of this fascination, but nonfiction has been given an impetus, too.

One need not be an expert to note that not only has the literature grown, but also as events have receded into the past, books have appeared revealing many innermost secrets: Ultra, the reading of German and Axis ciphers, and the double-cross system that controlled German espionage in Britain in World War II, to name but a few. Works on deception in that war have multiplied and now include the memoirs of those who were members of the intelligence and deception organizations. The events perhaps most symbolic of the more open treatment of matters formerly secret were the declassification and release in 1976 of the official OSS history and the publication in 1980 of the official history of British intelligence. The authors of the latter were permitted access to most official records; and with the reports of the U.S. Senate Select Committee (the Church committee) in 1975–1976, their chronicle of British intelligence represents the culmination of a trend of official release of intelligence-related material that dates back to publication in the 1960s of the history of the SOE in France.

Unfortunately, reference books on intelligence works of nonfiction designed to help students and researchers have not kept pace with the flood of other types of publications to the extent needed. Of course, some useful bibliographies have appeared and partially filled the void. But before 1981 only one encyclopedia had been published about the intelligence field, and that one was a poor start that dissipated much energy that could have been better spent. Existing bibliographies serve as indexes to books and manuscripts in print and to works in particular categories of intelligence, serve an archival purpose, and offer some descriptive annotation of the contents. Even those few that have gone further do not adequately meet the need for a bibliography that includes analytical, evaluative comments of sufficient depth and length to help the researcher in the field of intelligence deal with this arcane world.

The need for a more thoroughly annotated and more analytical bibliography has long been recognized. In *Intelligence and National Security: A Bibliography with Selected Annotations* (1968), the author, William R. Harris, comments on the need for such an in-depth work though its compilation must be a "painful task," and also observes that in many fields, but especially in intelligence and espionage, "authors utilize dubious materials serenely and reviewers commend their work uncritically. The process is deleterious to scholarship." Because the very nature of intelligence and espionage imposes restrictions on access to anything connected with them, writers on these topics are perhaps more prone to error and perpetuation of misinformation than writers on any other subject. Though the situation has improved somewhat in recent years, the basic problem still remains: it is difficult for the intelligent layman to judge what works or portions of works are reliable. Some works that have been elevated to virtually authoritative status perpetuate certain myths and may contain important central mistakes or untruths. M.R.D. Foot and J. M. Langley (both well versed in intelligence) note that too many authors who deal with facets of intelligence have been swept away by the excellent stories they have heard and have "woven fine-spun narratives" that do not always adhere to the verifiable truth.[1] David Martin, who in his first attempt to tackle an intelligence subject proved sensitive to its nuances, writes that "the amount of misinformation that has appeared in print and then [been] elevated to history through constant repetition is appalling."[2] A telling example of the extent of this quagmire of misinformation is the fact that only recently research by scholars, especially that of Edwin C. Fischel, has raised serious questions about literature on Civil War intelligence.

My undertaking the compilation of a bibliography to go beyond those available really came about only after Fred Praeger of Westview Press discussed with me his wish to publish a bibliography that scholars, writers, and students could use as a guide to intelligence literature. I responded because I was excited by the idea of breaking new ground in intelligence bibliographies and thus establishing additional criteria for their usefulness. I make no claim, though, that this work is comprehensive or definitive. If in the future it is regarded as innovative and a standard for future works of its type, that will be reward enough.

My decision to take up the project was also influenced by a conviction that the time for a work such as this had truly arrived and that the need had never been greater. Whatever neglect of the intelligence process by scholars had been the case in the past, this situation was changing; more and more

1. *MI 9,* 1979.
2. *Wilderness of Mirrors,* 1980.

people in academia were beginning to accord the study of intelligence its rightful attention. The revelation of Ultra, for example, as much as anything focused attention on the fact that the writing of the history of World War II was incomplete without examination of the intelligence factor. Intelligence as a determinant of human events and national security policy may or may not, in a particular instance, be vital; but it cannot be ignored as it has been in the past. One is ruefully reminded of the attitude of some cavalry generals after World War I who refused to recognize even the reality of tanks or of those U.S. political scientists who, as David Dallin points out, for some twenty years paid scant attention to Soviet intelligence and security despite the fact that Soviet affairs cannot be adequately understood without them. We must not make a mistake of like magnitude about the importance of intelligence.

The Organization of This Bibliography

In compiling this analytical bibliography with descriptive and evaluative commentaries, I have tried to cover all principal aspects of the intelligence process and to include as many periods and events of intelligence history as I felt important. The bulk of the entries represent those works that I have read over the years without any product like this in mind; consequently, readers will, without a doubt, spot what seem to be significant omissions. Nevertheless, I believe that this bibliography does contain the majority of the more important sources available in English. (It is an unfortunate fact that many deserving foreign-language titles have not been translated into English—the World War II memoirs of General Amé of Italian SIM and of Paul Paillole of French Intelligence being examples in this regard.)

In putting together this volume, I have tried to adhere to the following guidelines:

1. Since this reference is intended for those familiar with English, all books included except one are available in English. (The sole exception is Bertrand's *Enigma,* which I regard as too important to the field to leave out.)

2. In certain categories in which the literature is extensive, I have chosen to include mainly those works that deal with the subject from a particular vantage point. For instance, of the many titles on resistance and escape and evasion (E&E) in World War II, I list those that describe these activities as seen from the point of view of intelligence headquarters rather than from the view of the individual field operatives, those that are general surveys, and those that deal with some important network.
3. Congressional committee reports and Royal Commission studies are included only as references. When such works have been published commercially, however, I have relaxed this rule; e.g., the Karalekas history of CIA. Periodical articles also appear only as references.
4. Works in the categories of terrorism and political assassination and kidnapping are included only when the directing authorities of these activities were intelligence services. The books by Khokhlov and Tinnin, for example, are in this category.
5. Books on military or paramilitary operations in which the primary objective was intelligence or intelligence support or in which the operation was controlled by an intelligence service are part of the bibliography. So it is that Gallagher's *Assault on Norway* will be found here while his *X-Craft Raid* will not. The same criterion excluded Borghese's history of the Italian torpedo men.
6. Analytical and evaluative comments are my own except where otherwise indicated. My annotations are not meant to be exhaustive in the manner of a scholarly research paper or lengthy review. Rather, they are designed to serve as general guides to the usefulness and accuracy of the material and the reliability and thoroughness with which the authors have dealt with the principal matters in their publications. Literary quality is appraised only when it is of particular interest.
7. Individual items are spotlighted for a variety of reasons: to note where something of significance is discussed; to call attention to little-known or forgotten facts, events, or individuals; to cite errors; to focus on myths that need to

be put to rest; to use details as examples of larger matters; and to stimulate research.

8. I presume that most readers interested in this bibliography already have a certain familiarity with intelligence terminology and interest in the technical details of matters like intelligence tradecraft. Consequently, I have not defined most intelligence terms common to the field when they are used in the text; rather, a glossary primarily of organizational titles appears after the list of annotated entries for the reader's reference.
9. I quote from published book reviews with which I am familiar when I feel those reviews enhance understanding of a work or underscore a judgment of it—whether or not that judgment agrees with my own.
10. In selecting books relating to security, I have emphasized those works dealing with counterintelligence (CI) and counterespionage (CE) rather than with security per se.
11. One final note: comments from DIS's *Bibliography* are from the fifth edition (1977).

About the Author

It is only natural for the reader to want to know my qualifications for tackling the formidable task of assembling this volume. First, I have been reading books on intelligence-related subjects and keeping notes on them for most of my adult life. Second, I have spent almost a quarter of a century in the U.S. government largely in intelligence and national security work. Third, my work during those years, especially when it was intelligence related, has given me the enviable advantages of having been immersed in this particular environment and of having acquired knowledgeable contacts and what I like to think of as a sensitivity for the subject of intelligence and how it should be treated. Fourth, since my retirement in 1974, I have worked as a consultant on a number of national security studies for Ketron, Inc., and also as an independent contractor. If this background predisposes me toward a particular view or set of values, I have nevertheless tried as much as is humanly possible to be fair. The reader should also be aware that I take seriously my obligation to guard privileged information not declassified. Wherever it is not possible for me to be categoric, I remain silent or comment so generally as to adhere to my responsibility to protect classified data.

Final Comments

I stated earlier that this work is in no way definitive. The use of this adjective to describe any study is precarious, but to apply the word to anything in intelligence is fatuous as well. Experience teaches that in this field secrets spill out, now in droplets, now in gushes, which modify and at times alter entirely our previous comprehension of particular events. This process of transformation is true of matters and works on which I will herein comment; and, of course, future works will be more accurate and improve still further our knowledge and understanding. In the final stages of completing this volume a new development in the Alexander Szek story reminded me of both this process of constant revision and the corollary need for tolerance and humility in dealing with the world of intelligence. For some sixty years, the story of Alexander Szek, the purported British agent in Brussels in 1914 who, it was said, had provided British naval intelligence with German codes, was considered a canard—rejected by most authorities in Britain and by most experts in intelligence. In 1981, thanks to Stephen Roskill, we learned that the story actually may very well be true.

George C. Constantinides
Potomac, Maryland
November 1, 1981

Intelligence Category Index

Air Intelligence (See also **Photographic Intelligence**)

Barker, R. *Aviator Extraordinary*
Clayton, A. *The Enemy is Listening*
Jones, R. *The Wizard War*
Peskett, S. *Strange Intelligence*
Smith, T. *Air Intelligence Activities*
Streetly, M. *Confound and Destroy*
Taylor, J., & Mondey, D. *Spies in the Sky*
Winterbotham, F. *The Nazi Connection*
Winterbotham, F. *Secret and Personal*

American Intelligence—General

Bryan, G. *The Spy in America*
Cline, R. *Secrets, Spies and Scholars*
Corson, W. *The Armies of Ignorance*
Powe, M., & Wilson, E. *The Evolution of American Military Intelligence*

American Intelligence—Post-American Revolution to World War II

Bakeless, J. *Spies of the Confederacy*
Bates, D. *Lincoln in the Telegraph Office*
Corson, W. *The Armies of Ignorance*
Dorwart, J. *The Office of Naval Intelligence*
Freese, J. *Secrets of the Late Rebellion*
Lester, R. *Confederate Finance and Purchasing in Great Britain*
Mashbir, S. *I Was an American Spy*
Smith, T. *Air Intelligence Activities*
Stern, P. *Secret Missions of the Civil War*
Taylor, C. *The Signal and Secret Service of the Confederate States*

American Intelligence—World War II

Van Der Rhoer, E. *Deadly Magic*
Welch, R. *The Life of John Birch*
Wohlstetter, R. *Pearl Harbor*
Zacharias, E. *Secret Missions*

American Intelligence—Post-World War II

Agee, P. *Inside the Company*
Ambrose, S. *Ike's Spies*
Archer, J. *Superspies*
Armbrister, T. *A Matter of Accountability*
Borosage, R., & Marks, J. *The CIA File*
Burleson, C. *The Jennifer Project*
Cline, R. *Secrets, Spies and Scholars*
Colby, W., & Forbath, P. *Honorable Men*
Copeland, M. *The Game of Nations*
Corson, W. *The Armies of Ignorance*
De Silva, P. *Sub Rosa*
Elliff, J. *The Reform of FBI Intelligence Operations*
Eveland, W. *Ropes of Sand*
Felix, C. *The Spy and His Masters*
Freedman, L. *U.S. Intelligence and the Soviet Strategic Threat*
Karalekas, A. *History of the Central Intelligence Agency*
Kim, Y. *The Central Intelligence Agency*
Kirkpatrick, L. *The Real CIA*
Kirkpatrick, L. *The U.S. Intelligence Community*
Lasby, C. *Project Paperclip*
McChristian, J. *The Role of Military Intelligence 1965–67*
McCoy, A. *The Politics of Heroin in Southeast Asia*
McGarvey, P. *CIA: The Myth and the Madness*
Marchetti, V., & Marks, J. *The CIA and the Cult of Intelligence*
Marks, J. *The Search for the "Manchurian Candidate"*
Martin, D. *Wilderness of Mirrors*
Meyer, C. *Facing Reality*
Meyer, K., & Szulc, T. *The Cuban Invasion*
Phillips, D. *The Night Watch*
Powers, F. *Operation Overflight*
Powers, T. *The Man Who Kept the Secrets*
Ransom, H. *The Intelligence Establishment*

Robbins, C. *Air America*
Roosevelt, K. *Countercoup*
Rositzke, H. *The CIA's Secret Operations*
Sihanouk, N. *My War With CIA*
Smith, J. *Portrait of a Cold Warrior*
Smith, T. *The Essential CIA*
Snepp, F. *Decent Interval*
Stockwell, J. *In Search of Enemies*
Sullivan, W. *The Bureau*
Szulc, T. *Compulsive Spy*
Troy, T. *Donovan and the CIA*
Tully, A. *CIA*
Tully, A. *Inside the FBI*
Varner, R., & Collier, W. *A Matter of Risk*
Walters, V. *Silent Missions*
Wise, D., & Ross, T. *The Espionage Establishment*
Wise, D., & Ross, T. *The U-2 Affair*
Wohlstetter, R. *Cuba and Pearl Harbor*
Wyden, P. *Bay of Pigs*

American Revolution

Augur, H. *The Secret War of Independence*
Bakeless, J. *Turncoats, Traitors and Heroes*
CIA. *Intelligence in the War of Independence*
Currey, C. *Code Number 72*
Ford, C. *A Peculiar Service*
Fryer, M. *Loyalist Spy*
Grendel, F. *Beaumarchais*
Hall, C. *Benjamin Tallmadge*
Howe, J. *A Journal Kept by Mr. John Howe*
James, C. *Silas Deane*
Mathews, H. *Frontier Spies*
Pennypacker, M. *General Washington's Spies on Long Island and in New York*
Sellers, C. *Patience Wright*
Van Doren, C. *Secret History of the American Revolution*

Anthologies

Dulles, A. *Great True Spy Stories*
Eisenberg, D., Dan, U., & Landau, E. *The Mossad*
Foot, M. *Six Faces of Courage*
Maclean, F. *Take Nine Spies*
Newman, B. *Spy and Counterspy*
Piekalkiewicz, J. *Secret Agents, Spies and Saboteurs*
Rowan, R. *The Story of Secret Service*
Strong, K. *Men of Intelligence*
Whitehouse, A. *Espionage and Counterespionage*

Australian Intelligence

Bialoguski, M. *The Case of Colonel Petrov*
Hall, R. *The Secret State*
Lord, W. *Lonely Vigil*
Thwaites, M. *Truth Will Out*

Bibliographies

Blackstock, P., & Schaf, F. *Intelligence, Espionage, Counterespionage and Covert Operations*
Defense Intelligence School. *Bibliography of Intelligence Literature*
Devore, R. *Spies and All That*
Galland, J. *An Historical and Analytical Bibliography of the Literature of Cryptology*
Harris, W. *Intelligence and National Security: A Bibliography*
Library of Congress. *Soviet Intelligence and Security Services*
Shulman, D. *An Annotated Bibliography of Cryptography*
Smith, M. *The Secret Wars: A Guide to Sources in English*

British Intelligence—General

Bulloch, J. *M.I.5*
Deacon, R. *A History of the British Secret Service*
Haswell, J. *British Military Intelligence*
Scotland, A. *The London Cage*

British Intelligence—Through World War I

Aston, G. *Secret Service*
Cobban, A. *Ambassadors and Secret Agents*
Cockerill, G. *What Fools We Were*
Dukes, P. *The Story of 'ST25'*
Engle, A. *The Nili Spies*
Ewing, A. *The Man of Room 40*
Fraser, P. *The Intelligence of the Secretaries of State*
Hill, G. *Go Spy the Land*
Hobman, D. *Cromwell's Master Spy*
Howe, J. *A Journal Kept by Mr. John Howe*
Hoy, H. *40 O.B.*
James, W. *The Eyes of the Navy*
Landau, H. *All's Fair*
Landau, H. *Secrets of the White Lady*
Landau, H. *Spreading the Spy Net*
Lawrence, T. *Seven Pillars of Wisdom*
Lawson, J. *Tales of Aegean Intrigue*
Le Caron, H. *Twenty-Five Years in the Secret Service*
Lockhart, R. *Ace of Spies*
Lord, J. *Duty, Honor, Empire*
Mackenzie, C. *Aegean Memories*
Mackenzie, C. *First Athenian Memories*
Mackenzie, C. *Greek Memories*
Mathews, H. *Frontier Spies*
Mitchell, H. *The Underground War Against Revolutionary France*
Parritt, B. *The Intelligencers*
Reilly, P. *Britain's Master Spy*
Van Doren, C. *Secret History of the American Revolution*
Willert, A. *The Road to Safety*
Winstone, H. *Captain Shakespear*

British Intelligence—Interwar and World War II

Agar, A. *Baltic Episode*
Agar, A. *Footprints in the Sea*

Masterman, J. *The Double-Cross System*
Masterman, J. *On the Chariot Wheel*
Minshall, M. *Guilt-Edged*
Montagu, E. *Beyond Top Secret Ultra*
Montagu, E. *The Man Who Never Was*
Moss, W. *Ill Met by Moonlight*
Muggeridge, M. *The Infernal Grove*
Neave, A. *The Escape Room*
Ogilvy, D. *Blood, Brains and Beer*
Sansom, A. *I Spied Spies*
Stafford, D. *Britain and European Resistance, 1940–1945*
Stevenson, W. *A Man Called Intrepid*
Sweet-Escott, B. *Baker Street Irregular*
Trenowden, I. *Operations Most Secret*
Walker, D. *Lunch With a Stranger*
Whitwell, J. *British Agent*
Winterbotham, F. *The Nazi Connection*
Winterbotham, F. *Secret and Personal*
Winterbotham, F. *The Ultra Secret*

British Intelligence—Post-World War II

Boyle, A. *The Climate of Treason*
Cockerill, A. *Sir Percy Sillitoe*
Cookridge, E. *The Many Sides of George Blake, Esq.*
Lucas, N. *Spycatcher*
Page, B., Leitch, D., & Knightley, P. *The Philby Conspiracy*
Philby, K. *My Silent War*
Pincher, C. *Inside Story*
Pincher, C. *Their Trade Is Treachery*
Sillitoe, P. *Cloak Without Dagger*
Strong, K. *Intelligence at the Top*
Trevor-Roper, H. *The Philby Affair*
West, R. *The New Meaning of Treason*
West, R. *The Vassall Affair*
Wynne, G. *Contact on Gorky Street*

Canadian Intelligence

Sawatsky, J. *Men in the Shadows*

Censorship and Economic Warfare

Communications Intelligence, Cryptology, and Signals Intelligence

Counterespionage, Counterintelligence, and Security

Covert Action, Political Warfare, and Special Operations
(See also **Unconventional Warfare and Resistance, World War II,** and **Unconventional Warfare, World War I**)

Deriabin, P., & Gibney, F. *The Secret World*
Eisenberg, D., Landau, E., & Portugali, M. *Operation Uranium Ship*
Eveland, W. *Ropes of Sand*
Harel, I. *The House on Garibaldi Street*
Hoettl, W. *The Secret Front*
Johnson, H. *The Bay of Pigs*
Kaznacheev, A. *Inside a Soviet Embassy*
Kim, Y. *The Central Intelligence Agency*
Khokhlov, N. *In the Name of Conscience*
Kofos, E. *Greece and the Eastern Crisis, 1875–1878*
Lawson, J. *Tales of Aegean Intrigue*
Lockhart, R. *Ace of Spies*
MacDonald, E. *Undercover Girl*
Mackenzie, C. *Greek Memories*
Marchetti, V., & Marks, J. *The CIA and the Cult of Intelligence*
Meyer, K., & Szulc, T. *The Cuban Invasion*
Mitchell, H. *The Underground War Against Revolutionary France*
Moss, W. *Ill Met by Moonlight*
Phillips, D. *The Night Watch*
Reilly, P. *Britain's Master Spy*
Roosevelt, K. *Countercoup*
Seale, P., & McConville, M. *The Hilton Assignment*
Shackley, T. *The Third Option*
Smith, J. *Portrait of a Cold Warrior*
Stafford, D. *Britain and European Resistance, 1940–1945*
Steven, S. *Operation Splinter Factor*
Stockwell, J. *In Search of Enemies*
Strik-Strikfeldt, W. *Against Stalin and Hitler*
Szulc, T. *Compulsive Spy*
Tinnin, D. *The Hit Team*
Tully, A. *CIA*
Wyden, P. *Bay of Pigs*
Zeman, Z., & Scharlau, W. *The Merchant of Revolution*

Cuban Intelligence

Castro Hidalgo, O. *Spy for Fidel*

Czech Intelligence

Bittman, L. *The Deception Game*
Frolik, J. *The Frolik Defection*
Moravec, F. *Master of Spies*

Deception and Disinformation

Army Times Editors. *The Tangled Web*
Bailey, G. *The Conspirators*
Barkas, G. *The Camouflage Story*
Bittman, L. *The Deception Game*
Blackstock, P. *Agents of Deceit*
Blackstock, P. *The Secret Road to World War II*
Burleson, C. *The Jennifer Project*
Cave Brown, A. *Bodyguard of Lies*
CIA and Mathtech. *Covert Rearmamment in Germany 1919–1939*
CIA and Mathtech. *Deception Maxims*
CIA and Mathtech. *Thoughts on the Cost-Effectiveness of Deception and Related Tactics in the Air War 1939–1945*
Chester, L., Fay, S., & Young, H. *The Zinoviev Letter*
Clarke, D. *Seven Assignments*
Colvin, I. *The Unknown Courier*
Cruickshank, C. *Deception in World War II*
Delmer, S. *Black Boomerang*
Delmer, S. *The Counterfeit Spy*
Giskes, H. *London Calling North Pole*
Handel, M. *Perception, Deception and Surprise*
Hartcup, G. *Camouflage*
Haswell, J. *The Intelligence and Deception of the D-Day Landings*
James, M. *I Was Monty's Double*
Kaznacheev, A. *Inside a Soviet Embassy*
Kerr, W. *The Secret of Stalingrad*
Maskelyne, J. *Magic—Top Secret*
Masterman, J. *The Double-Cross System*
Minott, R. *The Fortress That Never Was*
Montagu, E. *Beyond Top Secret Ultra*

Montagu, E. *The Man Who Never Was*
Mure, D. *Master of Deception*
Mure, D. *Practice to Deceive*
Owen, D. *Battle of Wits*
Peis, G. *The Mirror of Deception*
Perrault, G. *The Secrets of D-Day*
Reit, S. *Masquerade*
Streetly, M. *Confound and Destroy*
Walker, D. *Lunch With A Stranger*
Whaley, B. *Codeword Barbarossa*
Whaley, B. *Strategem*
Wheatley, D. *The Deception Planners*
Wheatley, D. *Stranger than Fiction*
White, J. *The Big Lie*
Wingate, R. *Not in the Limelight*
Wynne, B. *Count Five and Die*

Defectors

Barron, J. *MiG Pilot*
Bentley, E. *Out of Bondage*
Bialoguski, M. *The Case of Colonel Petrov*
Brook-Shepherd, G. *The Storm Petrels*
Castro Hidalgo, O. *Spy for Fidel*
Chambers, W. *Witness*
Chavez, J. *Defector's Mistress*
Frolik, J. *The Frolik Defection*
Gouzenko, I. *The Iron Curtain*
Kaznacheev, A. *Inside A Soviet Embassy*
Khokhlov, N. *In the Name of Conscience*
Krivitsky, W. *In Stalin's Secret Service*
Massing, H. *This Deception*
Monat, P. *Spy in the U.S.*
Morros, B. *My Ten Years as a Counterspy*
Myagkov, A. *Inside the KGB*
Petrov, V., & Petrov, E. *Empire of Fear*
Poretsky, E. *Our Own People*
Sigl, R. *In the Claws of the KGB*
Thwaites, M. *Truth Will Out*

Weinstein, A. *Perjury*
West, R. *The New Meaning of Treason*
X, Mr. *Double Eagle*

Double Agents

Delmer, S. *The Counterfeit Spy*
Giskes, H. *London Calling North Pole*
Huminik, J. *Double Agent*
Masterman, J. *The Double-Cross System*
Montagu, E. *Beyond Top Secret Ultra*
Morros, B. *My Ten Years As a Counterspy*
Neligan, D. *The Spy in the Castle*
Peis, G. *The Mirror of Deception*
Popov, D. *Spy Counterspy*
Sergueiev, L. *Secret Service Rendered*
Young, G. *The Cat With Two Faces*

Dutch Intelligence

De Beus, J. *Tomorrow at Dawn!*

Encyclopedias

Seth, R. *Encyclopedia of Espionage*

Escape and Evasion

Caskie, D. *The Tartan Pimpernel*
Crawley, A. *Escape From Germany*
Darling D. *Secret Sunday*
Foot, M., & Langley, J. *MI 9*
Hutton, C. *Official Secret*
Langley, J. *Fight Another Day*
Neave, A. *The Escape Room*

Espionage (See also **Soviet Intelligence and Espionage**)

Accoce, P., & Quet, P. *A Man Called Lucy*
Agee, P. *Inside the Company*
Altavilla, E. *The Art of Spying*

Moravec, F. *Master of Spies*
Mosley, L. *The Cat and the Mice*
Moyzisch, L. *Operation Cicero*
Neligan, D. *The Spy in the Castle*
Newman, B. *Spy and Counterspy*
Page, B., Leitch, D., & Knightley, P. *The Philby Conspiracy*
Penkovsky, O. *The Penkovsky Papers*
Pennypacker, M. *General Washington's Spies on Long Island and in New York*
Perrault, G. *The Red Orchestra*
Persico, J. *Piercing the Reich*
Philby, K. *My Silent War*
Pilat, O. *The Atom Spies*
Pincher, C. *Inside Story*
Pincher, C. *Their Trade Is Treachery*
Rado, S. *Codename Dora*
Seale, P., & McConville, M. *Philby*
Seth, R. *The Art of Spying*
Seth, R. *Secret Servants*
Silber, J. *The Invisible Weapons*
Snow, J. *The Case of Tyler Kent*
Stern, P. *Secret Missions of the Civil War*
Sutherland, D. *The Fourth Man*
Trepper, L. *The Great Game*
Van Doren, C. *Secret History of the American Revolution*
Vassall, J. *Vassall*
Weinstein, A. *Perjury*
Whiteside, T. *An Agent in Place*
Whiting, C. *The Spymasters*
Willoughby, C. *Sorge*
Wynne, G. *Contact on Gorky Street*

Estimates and Indicators; Analysis and Evaluation

Cline, R. *Secrets, Spies and Scholars*
Critchley, J. *Warning and Response*
De Beus, J. *Tomorrow at Dawn!*
Freedman, L. *U.S. Intelligence and the Soviet Strategic Threat*

Godson, R. *Intelligence Requirements for the 1980's: Analysis and Estimates*
Hilsman, R. *Strategic Intelligence and National Decisions*
Kent, S. *Strategic Intelligence for American World Policy*
Kerr, W. *The Secret of Stalingrad*
Kirkpatrick, L. *Captains Without Eyes*
Knorr, K. *Foreign Intelligence and the Social Sciences*
Minott, R. *The Fortress That Never Was*
Thorpe, E. *East Wind Rain*
Whaley, B. *Codeword Barbarossa*
Wohlstetter, R. *Cuba and Pearl Harbor*
Wohlstetter, R. *Pearl Harbor*
Zuckerman, S. *From Apes to Warlords*

Failures, Intelligence Flaps, and Causes Célèbres

Armbrister, T. *A Matter of Accountability*
Best, S. *The Venlo Incident*
Burleson, C. *The Jennifer Project*
Chapman, G. *The Dreyfus Trials*
Chester, L., Fay, S., & Young, H. *The Zinoviev Letter*
El-Ad, A. *Decline of Honor*
Ennes, J. *Assault on the "Liberty"*
Golan, A. *Operation Susannah*
Johnson, H. *The Bay of Pigs*
Kirkpatrick, L. *Captains Without Eyes*
Marks, J. *The Search for the "Manchurian Candidate"*
Minott, R. *The Fortress That Never Was*
Pearson, A. *Conspiracy of Silence*
Powers, F. *Operation Overflight*
Szulc, T. *Compulsive Spy*
Thorpe, E. *East Wind Rain*
Tinnin, D. *The Hit Team*
Trevor-Roper, H. *The Philby Affair*
Varner, R., & Collier, C. *A Matter of Risk*
Wise, D., & Ross, T. *The U-2 Affair*
Wohlstetter, R. *Pearl Harbor*
Wyden, P. *Bay of Pigs*

French Intelligence

Bertrand, G. *Enigma, 1939–1945*
Chapman, G. *The Dreyfus Trials*
De Vosjoli, P. *Lamia*
Stead, P. *Second Bureau*
Thomson, B. *The Allied Secret Service in Greece*

German Intelligence—to World War II

Felstead, S. *German Spies at Bay*
Flicke, W. *War Secrets in the Ether* (Vol. 1, Parts 1 & 2).
Nicolai, W. *The German Secret Service*
Rintelen, F. *The Dark Invader*
Sykes, C. *Wassmuss, 'The German Lawrence'*
Zeman, Z., & Scharlau, W. *The Merchant of Revolution*

German Intelligence—World War II and Post-World War II

Bleicher, H. *Colonel Henri's Story*
Brissaud, A. *Canaris*
Brissaud, A. *The Nazi Secret Service*
Carter, C. *The Shamrock and the Swastika*
Colvin, I. *Chief of Intelligence*
Eppler, J. *Operation Condor*
Farago, L. *The Game of the Foxes*
Flicke, W. *War Secrets in the Ether* (Vol. 2, Part 3)
Gehlen, R. *The Service*
Giskes, H. *London Calling North Pole*
Hoettl, W. *The Secret Front*
Höhne, H., & Zolling, H. *The General Was a Spy*
Irving, D. *Breach of Security*
Kahn, D. *Hitler's Spies*
Leverkuehn, P. *German Military Intelligence*
Mosley, L. *The Cat and the Mice*
Moyzisch, L. *Operation Cicero*
Schellenberg, W. *The Labyrinth*
Schulze-Holthus, B. *Daybreak in Iran*
Trevor-Roper, H. *The Philby Affair*

Illegals

Aldouby, Z., & Ballinger, J. *The Shattered Silence*
Bulloch, J., & Miller, H. *Spy Ring*
Carr, B. *Spy in the Sun*
CIA. *The Rote Kapelle*
Donovan, J. *Strangers on a Bridge*
Dukes, P. *The Story of 'ST25'*
Khokhlov, N. *In the Name of Conscience*
Lonsdale, G. *Spy*
Lotz, W. *The Champagne Spy*
Orlov, A. *Handbook of Intelligence and Guerrilla Warfare*
Perrault, G. *The Red Orchestra*
Rado, S. *Codename Dora*
Trepper, L. *The Great Game*

Intelligence History

Blackstock, P. *The Secret Road to World War II*
Bryan, G. *The Spy in America*
FitzGibbon, C. *Secret Intelligence in the Twentieth Century*
Haldane, R. *The Hidden War*
Haswell, J. *Spies and Spymasters*
Rowan, R. *The Story of Secret Service*
Starr, C. *Political Intelligence in Classical Greece*
Thompson, J., & Padover, S. *Secret Diplomacy*

Intelligence Services—General and Allied

Ambrose, S. *Ike's Spies*
Ind, A. *Allied Intelligence Bureau*
Strong, K. *Intelligence at the Top*
Strong, K. *Men of Intelligence*
Wise, D., & Ross, T. *The Intelligence Establishment*

Israeli Intelligence

Aldouby, Z., & Ballinger, J. *The Shattered Silence*
Dan, U., & Ben-Porat, Y. *The Secret War*
Davenport, E., Eddy, P., & Gillman, P. *The Plumbat Affair*

Deacon, R. *The Israeli Secret Service*
Dekel, E. *Shai*
Eisenberg, D., Dan, U., & Landau, E. *The Mossad*
El-Ad, A. *Decline of Honor*
Golan, A. *Operation Susannah*
Harel, I. *The House on Garibaldi Street*
Lotz, W. *The Champagne Spy*
Lotz, W. *A Handbook for Spies*
Steven, S. *The Spymasters of Israel*
Tinnin, D. *The Hit Team*

Italian Intelligence

Maugeri, F. *From the Ashes of Disgrace*

Japanese Intelligence

Seth, R. *Secret Servants*

Military Intelligence

Butler, E. *Mason-Mac*
Haswell, J. *British Military Intelligence*
Hunt, D. *A Don at War*
Kirkpatrick, L. *Captains Without Eyes*
Koch, O. *G-2*
Lord, W. *Lonely Vigil*
McChristian, J. *The Role of Military Intelligence 1965–67*
Parritt, B. *The Intelligencers*
Powe, M., & Wilson, E. *The Evolution of American Military Intelligence*
Strong, K. *Intelligence at the Top*
Strong, K. *Men of Intelligence*
Wagner, A. *The Service of Security and Information*

Naval Intelligence

Beesly, P. *Very Special Admiral*
Beesly, P. *Very Special Intelligence*
Blair, C. *Silent Victory*

Bywater, H., & Ferraby, H. *Strange Intelligence*
Campbell, R. *The Luciano Project*
Deacon, R. *The Silent War*
Dorwart, J. *The Office of Naval Intelligence*
Farago, L. *The Tenth Fleet*
Grant, R. *U-Boat Intelligence, 1914–1918*
Green, J. *The First Sixty Years of the Office of Naval Intelligence*
Holmes, W. *Double-Edged Secrets*
James, W. *The Eyes of the Navy*
Lord, W. *Lonely Vigil*
McLachlan, D. *Room 39*
Maugeri, F. *From the Ashes of Disgrace*
Miles, M. *A Different Kind of War*
Minshall, M. *Guilt-Edged*
Montagu, E. *Beyond Top Secret Ultra*
Zacharias, E. *Secret Missions*

Operational Support

Agar, A. *Baltic Episode*
Agar, A. *Footprints in the Sea*
Alcorn, R. *No Bugles For Spies*
George, W. *Surreptitious Entry*
Hamilton, A. *Wings of Night*
Hampshire, A. *The Secret Navies*
Lovell, S. *Of Spies and Strategems*
MacCloskey, M. *Secret Air Missions*
Robbins, C. *Air America*
Sigl, R. *In the Claws of the KGB*
Slater, L. *The Pledge*
Smith, T. *The Essential CIA*
U.S. War Dept. *War Report of the OSS* (Vol 1)

Photographic Intelligence (See also **Air Intelligence**)

Babington-Smith, C. *Air Spy*
Barker, R. *Aviator Extraordinary*
Brookes, A. *Photo Reconnaissance*
Heiman, G. *Aerial Photography*

Klass, P. *Secret Sentries in Space*
Powers, F. *Operation Overflight*
Taylor, J., & Mondey, D. *Spies in the Sky*
Wise, D., & Ross, T. *The U-2 Affair*

Polish Intelligence

Listowel, J. *Crusader in the Secret War*
Monat, P. *Spy in the U.S.*
Woytak, R. *On the Border of War and Peace*
X, Mr. *Double Eagle*

Psychological Warfare

Cruickshank, C. *The Fourth Arm*
Delmer, S. *Black Boomerang*
Lockhart, R. *Comes the Reckoning*
MacDonald, E. *Undercover Girl*
Owen, D. *Battle of Wits*
White, J. *The Big Lie*

Science and Technology

Burleson, C. *The Jennifer Project*
Garlinski, J. *Hitler's Last Weapons*
Goudsmit, S. *Alsos*
Johnson, B. *The Secret War*
Jones, R. V. *The Wizard War*
Lasby, C. *Project Paperclip*
Leasor, J. *Green Beach*
Marks, J. *The Search for the "Manchurian Candidate"*
Millar, G. *The Bruneval Raid*
Paine, L. *The Technology of Espionage*
Pash, B. *The Alsos Mission*
Peskett, S. *Strange Intelligence*
Price, A. *Instruments of Darkness*
Richardson, C. *Uranium Trail East*
Streetly, M. *Confound and Destroy*
Varner, R., & Collier, W. *A Matter of Risk*

Soviet Intelligence and Espionage—General

Soviet Intelligence and Espionage—Pre-World War II

Soviet Intelligence and Espionage—World War II and Post-World War II

Swiss Intelligence

Theory and Organization

Godson, R. *Intelligence Requirements for the 1980's: Elements of Intelligence*
Hilsman, R. *Strategic Intelligence and National Decisions*
Kent, S. *Strategic Intelligence for American World Policy*
Kirkpatrick, L. *The U.S. Intelligence Community*
Pettee, G. *The Future of American Secret Intelligence*
Ransom, H. *The Intelligence Establishment*
U.S. Army Security Agency. *The Origin and Development of the Army Security Agency 1917–1947*
U.S. Counter Intelligence Corps School. *Counter Intelligence Corps History and Mission in World War II*
U.S. War Dept. *War Report of the OSS* (Vol 1)
Zlotnick, J. *National Intelligence*

Tradecraft and Techniques

Carr, B. *Spy in the Sun*
Copeland, M. *Without Cloak or Dagger*
Dulles, A. *The Craft of Intelligence*
Felix, C. *The Spy and His Masters*
George, W. *Surreptitious Entry*
Harel, I. *The House on Garibaldi Street*
Lewis, D. *Sexpionage*
Lotz, W. *A Handbook for Spies*
McLachlan, D. *Room 39*
Masterman, J. *The Double-Cross System*
Monat, P. *Spy in the U.S.*
Orlov, A. *Handbook of Intelligence and Guerrilla Warfare*
Rositzke, H. *The CIA's Secret Operations*
Sun Tzu *The Art of War*
Wade, A. *Spies To-day*

Unconventional Warfare—World War I

Hall, W., & Peaslee, A. *Three Wars With Germany*
Landau, H. *The Enemy Within*
Lawrence, T. *Seven Pillars of Wisdom*

Rintelen, F. *The Dark Invader*
Sykes, C. *Wassmuss, 'The German Lawrence'*

Unconventional Warfare and Resistance—World War II

Alsop, S., & Braden, T. *Sub Rosa*
Amery, J. *Approach March*
Auty, P., & Clogg, R. *British Policy Towards Wartime Resistance in Yugoslavia and Greece*
Bergier, J. *Secret Weapons*
Buckmaster, M. *Specially Employed*
Buckmaster, M. *They Fought Alone*
Collier, R. *Ten Thousand Eyes*
Cooper, M. *The Phantom War*
Davidson, B. *Special Operations Europe*
Deakin, F. *The Embattled Mountain*
Fielding, X. *Hide and Seek*
Foot, M. *Resistance*
Foot, M. *Six Faces of Courage*
Foot, M. *SOE in France*
Ford, C. *Donovan of OSS*
Fourcade, M. *Noah's Ark*
Fuller, J. *Born For Sacrifice*
Fuller, J. *The German Penetration of SOE*
Gallagher, T. *Assault in Norway*
Garlinski, J. *Poland, SOE and the Allies*
Gilchrist, A. *Bangkok Top Secret*
Hamilton-Hill, D. *SOE Assignment*
Hampshire, A. *On Hazardous Service*
Hampshire, A. *The Secret Navies*
Haukelid, K. *Attack on Telemark*
Howarth, P. *Undercover*
Hutchinson, J. *That Drug Danger*
Johnson, S. *Agents Extraordinary*
Lampe, D. *The Last Ditch*
Macksey, K. *The Partisans of Europe in the Second World War*

Marshall, B. *The White Rabbit*
Martelli, G. *Agent Extraordinary*
Masson, M. *Christine*
Maugeri, F. *From the Ashes of Disgrace*
Miles, M. *A Different Kind of War*
Millar, G. *The Bruneval Raid*
Molden, F. *Exploding Star*
Moss, W. *Ill Met By Moonlight*
Peers, W., & Brelis, D. *Behind the Burma Road*
Persico, J. *Piercing the Reich*
Petrow, R. *The Bitter Years*
Stafford, D. *Britain and European Resistance, 1940–1945*
Sweet-Escott, B. *Baker Street Irregular*
Thomas, J. *The Giant Killers*
Trenowden, I. *Operations Most Secret*
Wighton, C. *Pin-Stripe Saboteur*

World War I

Aston, G. *Secret Service*
Boucard, R. *Revelations from the Secret Service*
Boucard, R. *The Secret Services of Europe*
Brownrigg, D. *Indiscretions of the Naval Censor*
Bywater, H., & Ferraby, H. *Strange Intelligence*
Cockerill, G. *What Fools We Were*
Dukes, P. *The Story of 'ST25'*
Engle, A. *The Nili Spies*
Ewing, A. *The Man of Room 40*
Felstead, S. *German Spies at Bay*
Friedman, W., & Mendelsohn, C. *The Zimmermann Telegram*
Grant, R. *U-Boat Intelligence, 1914–1918*
Gylden, Y. *The Contribution of the Cryptographic Bureaus in the World War*
Hall, W., & Peaslee, A. *Three Wars with Germany*
Hill, G. *Go Spy the Land*
Hoy, H. *40 O.B.*
James, W. *The Eyes of the Navy*
Landau, H. *All's Fair*
Landau, H. *The Enemy Within*

Annotated List of Entries, by Author

A

Accoce, Pierre, and Quet, Pierre. A MAN CALLED LUCY. New York: Coward-McCann, 1967. 248 pp., bibliog., no index [London: W. H. Allen. *The Lucy Ring*].

The two French journalists who authored this volume said that they came upon the story of the Lucy ring in Switzerland in World War II during their investigation of Switzerland's history in that war. After they discovered the intriguing story of the Lucy operation, they wrote this book, claiming to adhere always to the facts. However, questions subsequently were raised about certain important claims they had made and aspects of the case that they had described that they could not substantiate to the critics' satisfaction. Consequently, experts have concluded that their work is not a reliable source on the subject. Soviet agent Sandor Rado, a principal in the Lucy operation, strongly denounced the book and was particularly critical of what he interpreted to be the book's thesis—that the Swiss group rather than the Red Army won the war.

Agabekov, Georges. OGPU: THE RUSSIAN SECRET TERROR. Westport, Conn: Hypernion Press, 1975. 277 pp., no index [New York: Brentano, 1931].

Agabekov served in the OGPU for some ten years (1920–1930) and defected in Paris. He specialized in the Near East, serving in Persia and Afghanistan, and was the illegal resident at Constantinople. In addition, he held the position of chief of the Eastern Section of the OGPU. He provides in this work valuable material on and a rare vantage point of Soviet intelligence organization, activities, modus operandi, and infighting in the 1920s and particularly good information on Soviet intelligence activities in the countries in which he served. The book was first published in Berlin in 1930; the 1975 English version is a reprint of the 1931 English edition, and its language, like that of original English edition, is stilted and awkward.

In 1930 Agabekov's work was a revelation. But now, although some will still find of interest his insider's description of the self-serving, careerist attitude and opportunism of the OGPU personnel and his testimony to the cynical conversion of the OGPU to an organization for dictatorial control at home and for forwarding Soviet interests abroad, much of the book is of primarily historical value. What may strike the current reader as impressive is the list of professional accomplishments of the OGPU that he recounts: humint ("agent") penetrations of governments, security and military services, foreign embassies, and émigré groups; political action; psychological warfare; pouch intercepts; subversion; and even communications intelligence successes abound and offer evidence of the quickly developed professionalism of this new service.

Agabekov disappeared in Belgium in 1938 and is believed to have been the victim of Soviet vengeance for his defection. Most students of Soviet intelligence consider his book an important document on Soviet intelligence of the 1920s, and some classify it the *most* important for the period covered. One dissenter is Lyman Kirkpatrick, formerly of CIA and later at Brown University. In his *Soviet Political Warfare Techniques* he states that Agabekov's account is "detailed but contains some questionable material" without specifying what is questionable. See also Gordon Brook-Shepherd's *The Storm Petrels* for more insights into Agabekov, his life, and his personal reasons for defecting.

Agar, Augustus. BALTIC EPISODE: A CLASSIC OF SECRET SERVICE IN RUSSIAN WATERS. London: Hodder and Stoughton, 1963. 255 pp., no index.

Agar was commanding officer of British navy coastal motor boats (CMBs) in Finnish waters in 1919. This book is the absorbing account of his actions and activities in these waters while on secret assignment to the British SIS during this period, an account he compiled between 1928 and 1935 but could not publish then because the British Admiralty objected and had the authority to stop publication while Agar was on active duty.

Not only is the account absorbing, it is incredible and instructive at the same time. Agar was assigned secretly to Finland to provide communications links using the CMBs with Sir Paul Dukes, chief of British intelligence in Russia acting as an illegal and dodging the Cheka. Despite this and without specific orders, Agar attacked and sank a Soviet cruiser, for which he subsequently received the V.C.; later he participated in naval attacks against Kronstadt. From an intelligence point of view, his actions were questionable though admittedly brave. He was aware that his military activities jeopardized the security of his primary mission—that of running couriers in and out of Russia and of eventually extricating Dukes. His account leaves no doubt that he sank the Russian cruiser two weeks before the British cabinet approved any naval action other than blockade against the Bolshevik regime. See also his *Footprints in the Sea.* Sir Paul Dukes's memoirs are a necessary complement to this book.

Agar, Augustus. FOOTPRINTS IN THE SEA. London: Evans Bros., 1959. 328 pp., index.

It was in this autobiography that Agar, who won the V.C. while operating navy coastal motor boats (CMBs), first published an account of his secret service assignment during 1919 in the Baltic and the circumstances of how he attacked a Soviet warship there. A fuller version of this service and his involvement in armed attacks on Soviet naval units appeared four years later in *Baltic Episode* (above). Though both accounts of the event generally match, they differ on what role the British naval commander, Cowan, played in Agar's decision to attack the Russian warship *Oleg.* In this book Agar relates that Cowan told him that he could not possibly direct him to attack the *Oleg* but that if Agar did, he could count on his support, and then wished him "good luck." In *Baltic Episode,* Agar says that since there was no time to go to Admiral Cowan for a specific order, he had to make the decision to attack the *Oleg* himself.

Agar here also relates the story of his World War II command of the cruiser *Emerald,* which secretly shipped British gold holdings to North America. Included is a chapter on his assignment to direct an operation called Lucid, a highly secret plan to tow tankers to French channel ports and use them as fire ships against German 1940 invasion barges.

Agee, Philip. INSIDE THE COMPANY: CIA DIARY. New York: Stonehill, 1975. 640 pp., no index [London: Allen Lane].

Of those CIA officers who published works critical of that agency up to 1981, Agee stands apart. He was the only ideological Marxist convert among them, the only one whose purpose was to neutralize CIA's activities and expose its personnel in order to destroy it as an effective organization, and the only one considered a defector to the opposition for all intents and purposes. Agee made no effort to disguise his Marxist ideological orientation or his purpose in writing this reconstructed diary covering his twelve years as an agency officer with service in Washington, Ecuador, Uruguay, and Mexico. Allegedly provided in the text and appendixes are details of CIA operations, of the functioning of CIA stations abroad, and the names of CIA personnel and agents and of organizations supported by or used by that agency in its operations. Purported penetration operations for intelligence, liaison activities, covert action, counterespionage, and counterintelligence work of various types are all laid out, allowing the reader to see them both as isolated operations and as part of the team effort of a CIA station. At the time of its publication, this book was unique and unparalleled for its claimed revelations and for its close-up of CIA training, activities, and personnel seen through the eyes and mental filter of the operations officer. However, one should be aware of the following. First, there is the polemical quality of his writing that reflects on the reliability of what he writes and also shows its ideological bias. CIA, for example, he calls the "biggest and most powerful secret service that has ever existed"—a statement that will surprise the KGB. Next, there are errors in the book that justify caution regarding Agee's infallibility: he claims CIA set up the Greek junta and associates CIA with the coup attempt in Indonesia in 1965 and the slaughter that followed; and he flatly accuses CIA of being the party that arranged for the assassination of Trujillo. Third, he does not explain adequately his conversion to Marxism or his relations with the Cubans after he left CIA. The *New York Times* reviewer found it hard to believe the details Agee set down were possible to remember without notes, as he claims, and speculated that some of Agee's material had been provided by Cuban intelligence. Agee admits that in going to Cuba for material he knew his book would have to be "politically acceptable" to the Cubans. The same review, which philosophically sympathized with Agee's criticism of CIA's covert actions, made a fourth and telling point: Agee always pictures Americans as one dimensional without any noble or patriotic motives, and Agee's world never includes "disruptive acts by Cuban or Soviet agents, though bombings, strikes and guerrilla warfare were being promoted by their Communist agents." Phillips in *The Night Watch* gives first-hand information on CIA's intelligence of Agee's travels to Cuba and of CIA's damage-limiting measures in reaction to Agee's disclosures. For a refutation of Agee's intimations of CIA complicity in torture in Latin America, see Colby's *Honorable Men.* The November 1975 report of the Senate Select Committee to Study Government Operations with Respect to Intelligence Activities (Church committee) entitled *Alleged Assassination Plots Involving Foreign Leaders* deals with the Trujillo assassination question.

Alcorn, Robert Hayden. NO BUGLES FOR SPIES: TALES OF THE OSS. New York: David McKay, 1962. 209 pp., no index [London: Jarrolds, 1963].

Alcorn was an early recruit of General Donovan, serving first in COI, the predecessor of OSS, and later in positions such as administrative officer for the Research and Analysis (R&A) branch and as executive officer to the chief, OSS for the European theater of operations. While in London, he was also special funds officer, "the one man responsible for the financing of all secret operations on the continent." It is in the section of the book in which he discusses the importance of finances for operations and the security problems involved in the acquisition of foreign currencies to be used operationally that Alcorn has the most to contribute. The book does not give the names of the operations discussed or of the OSS agents involved. Alcorn is so careful about names that persons of later prominence, such as William Casey, are not mentioned. The few tidbits on the problems of catering to some of the academic prima donnas who staffed R&A are the only places he digresses from his uncritical portrayal of anything having to do with OSS and talks about personnel selection and security screening in COI. Alcorn is most at home telling administrative and support stories. The U.S. War Department's *War Report of the OSS* contains sections on OSS financing arrangements and practices.

Aldouby, Zwy, and Ballinger, Jerrold. THE SHATTERED SILENCE. New York: Lancer Books, 1971. 426 pp., bibliog., notes, index [New York: Coward, McCann and Geoghegan].

This book is the story of the Eli Cohen espionage operation run by the Israeli service Mossad against Syria. Cohen, an Israeli assuming the role of an Arab expatriate from Argentina, established high-level entrée into Syrian ruling circles to acquire intelligence on Syrian military, political, and diplomatic matters. Finally caught, he was executed by the Syrians in 1965 despite strenuous Israeli efforts to save him.

Cohen's information certainly must have been of great value, though an understanding of how vital must await evidence beyond that provided by the authors. Accomplished writers and journalists, they have given the fullest account in English of the Eli Cohen affair, and an insight into Israeli use of talent available to run an effective illegal operation into a denied area. The work is marred, however, by the tendency of the authors to insert what seems to be propaganda against the Syrians and other Arabs. The courage and heroism of Eli Cohen needs no such extraneous comment. Whether, too, all the facts of the case as presented are essentially correct must also await release of further information by the Israelis and the Syrians. How Cohen was caught is still not certain; in 1979 the American Robert Axelrod, in a scholarly article on surprise, wrote that the Syrians may have been alerted by the Israelis, who used Cohen's intelligence for propaganda by broadcasting a number of secret Syrian cabinet decisions. According to Eisenberg, Dan, and Landau in *The Mossad,* Cohen was captured by the use of radio direction finding with Soviet assistance.

Alsop, Stewart, and Braden, Thomas. SUB ROSA: THE OSS AND AMERICAN ESPIONAGE. New York: Harcourt, Brace and World, 1964. 264 pp., no index.

This work originally was published in 1946 by Reynal and Hitchcock, shortly after the authors, two veterans of OSS, left the service. By the 1964 edition, they had become well-known journalists and members of the Washington press corps with excellent entrée into U.S. national security and intelligence structures. The 1946 edition was one of the first of the postwar books on OSS. It was also regarded by some as part of the budding debate on the structure of U.S. intelligence after the war. Braden's new introduction in the later edition contains a description of the authors' meeting with General Donovan to tell him of their intent to write this book that does not bear out the view that the book was inspired by Donovan and OSS. Alsop's postscript to this edition is about the CIA, successor to OSS. It still reads rather accurately after so many years and indicates how well connected into the CIA and intelligence community Alsop was. Of special interest is the fact that he revealed, in a general way, the existence of

CIA-subsidized and -controlled front organizations. Later, this revelation was to cause a furor when the subsidies and their specifics were exposed in U.S. media.

As for the core of this book, a few OSS operations and missions are outlined in *True Adventure* style. The intelligence collection and resistance operations covered are not significant in themselves because subsequent writings have offered much more, and no attempt is made to correct factual errors in the original version: errors, for example, about secrecy of the North African landing of 1942 and the purported success of the so-called Dakar portion of the deception plan for the same invasion. There is no evidence to support the authors' story of the claimed success of "Billy's" deceptive information resulting in the German dispositions to Holland. As to the OSS personalities named, this book was the second in which the name William Colby appeared within one year of the end of the war.

Altavilla, Enrico. THE ART OF SPYING. Englewood Cliffs, N.J.: Prentice-Hall, 1967. 199 pp., no index [London: Robert Hale, 1968].

The author, an Italian journalist, states that in writing this work dealing with "today's espionage," he turned to those whose job it was to fight spies—the counterintelligence men. He claims to have talked to various knowledgeable officials in the West, the British excepted. He concludes by saying that an official of a counterespionage service described him as the first journalist who understood the world of real espionage. Judging Altavilla solely on the basis of this effort, that remark was unjustified flattery. Reading the book, one has the feeling of taking a true-or-false test. The text alternates little-known facts and trenchant observations with erroneous and even preposterous ones. For example, his description of illegals is not correct, and therefore he does not deal with this increasingly significant method of Soviet espionage. With greater diligence and effort the writer might have produced a more reliable work. As it stands, it could serve as an end-of-course assignment on post–World War II espionage in which students are assigned the task of identifying errors in the text.

Ambrose, Stephen E., with Richard H. Immerman. IKE'S SPIES: EISENHOWER AND THE ESPIONAGE ESTABLISHMENT. Garden City, N.Y.: Doubleday, 1981. 322 pp., bibliog., notes, index.

Ambrose, a historian, worked as an editor of the official papers of Eisenhower and published works on the general's role as commander of the Allied forces. Those undertakings led to this book, in which the authors picture Eisenhower as the beneficiary of the efforts of Allied intelligence (by which they really mean the British) during the war, as "the center of a successful deception program" against the Germans, and as commander of "a series of covert operations" that contributed crucially to victory. As a result, runs the authors' thesis, when Eisenhower became president, he encouraged and directed the growth and expansion of CIA as a necessary weapon against the Soviets, with consequences that are still debated.

The principal fault of this book is the authors' exaggeration of Eisenhower's direct role and first-hand participation in intelligence matters as distinct from his general responsibilities as commander and president. To picture him during the war as having "first-hand knowledge" of clandestine operations—knowing how to set them up, control them, and direct them—is excessive and misleading. Little evidence is produced to show that he took more than a normal leader's interest in intelligence operations and techniques (as we know Churchill did); in fact, the authors tell us that Ike spent more of his own preinvasion time and energy on security than on deception. They have more evidence of Eisenhower's role during his presidential tenure in crucial decision making in intelligence matters (there is a good chapter on the U-2). But, as the discussion of the assassination plots shows, the exact role a president plays in some intelligence decisions, as it can be derived from records, is less clear than his role in other matters where operations rather than overall policy and organization are involved. The reader may be tempted during the first ten pages to stop reading this book because of an avalanche of errors, but performance gets better. Among the initial mistakes: SOE is placed under SIS; SIS rather than SOE is called the service responsible for the North Pole disaster in Holland; the Allies are presented as certain in 1942 that German atomic research was misdirected; there are wrong details on Enigma and Bletchley Park. Later, the authors quote the mistaken testimony of Howard Hunt concerning Boris Pash and his postwar role without rectifying it with Pash's denial, and they have Frank Wisner, the former head of CIA's Clandestine Services and long dead, testifying before the Church committee. These and other errors, which should cause the reader to be cautious, are offset by some good passages, such as the comments on the poor judgment shown in risking Torch by sending a clandestine mission to North Africa before the invasion, the conclusions on the murder of Admiral Darlan, and the sorting of some of the charges of responsibility for the bad estimate of a German National Redoubt in 1945.

Amery, Julian. APPROACH MARCH: A VENTURE IN AUTOBIOGRAPHY. London: Hutchinson, 1973. 456 pp., index.

The first volume of an autobiography, this book stops in 1950. Amery, whose *Sons of the Eagle* (1948) is about his experiences in Albania in World War II, has provided here an important and interesting contribution to our knowledge of British covert and resistance operations in that war. His coverage of his activities in Bulgaria, Yugoslavia, Albania, China, Cairo, and London with D Section and later with SOE is not merely informative but candid. A man with social and political connections, Amery has the self-confidence to be unabashedly frank about events and his role in them. He throws light on SOE ties with political parties in the Balkans in the early years of the war and on the role of that organization in developments leading to the Yugoslav coup, among other things. His eye for sizing up people and situations adds to the value of this personal narrative, making it one of the better books on SOE and particularly on British operations in the Balkans, even for those who do not accept his political judgments and opinions. A number of other works provide a wider look at the period covered and at British operations in the Balkans, among them Auty and Clogg's *British Policy Towards Wartime Resistance in Yugoslavia and Greece* and Barker's *British Policy in South-East Europe in the Second World War.*

Archer, Jules. SUPERSPIES: THE SECRET SIDE OF GOVERNMENT. New York: Delacorte Press, 1977. 235 pp., bibliog., index.

This is more a political tract than anything else. Archer, primarily a writer of books for children and young adults, has also written on matters such as Watergate, treason, and the police state. This is a poor piece of work that can probably be explained as the product of the time of its publication, when the pendulum of feeling about the intelligence and security community had swung rather widely toward opposition. The chapters on CIA are loaded with errors, and the cut-and-paste quality of the book is manifest. Archer's expertise is brought into question by such statements as that Dulles was the first head of CIA or that the Castro revolution provided the model for Nasser's overthrow of the Egyptian monarch; and any feeling that he tried to deal with the problem of secrecy in a balanced way vanishes when he calls on the reader to join an organization against "government spying."

Armbrister, Trevor. A MATTER OF ACCOUNTABILITY: THE TRUE STORY OF THE PUEBLO AFFAIR. New York: Coward-McCann, 1970. 402 pp., no index.

Armbrister, an American journalist, has produced a first-rate piece of work considering the relatively short time between the event he describes and the book's appearance.

The work has the distinction of identifying and spelling out the errors and omissions in the planning for this intelligence mission that ultimately led to considerable loss of U.S. intelligence data and equipment. Until an account of this affair is written that includes more precise information on the "damage assessment" in regard to intelligence-related material, this is probably the best book by a nonparticipant on the intelligence aspects and lessons learned. But, Armbrister should have attempted to discover how the lessons learned from the attack on the *Liberty* in 1967 affected the planning for this mission. There is no index.

***Army Times* Editors. THE TANGLED WEB: TRUE STORIES OF DECEPTION IN MODERN WARFARE. Washington, D.C.: Robert E. Luce, 1963. 183 pp., bibliog., index.**

Many works on deception in World War II have appeared since the publication of this popular treatment. *The Tangled Web,* which treats examples of ruses de guerre going back to the American Civil War, merits special mention, however, for two reasons. It was still, in 1980, one of the few works listed under the heading "Deception in Warfare" in the Library of Congress catalog. It is also the first work published in English after 1945 devoted to military deception that covers more than one conflict or the particular operations of a single war. It may have the added minor distinction of being one of the first works to mention the name of John Bevan, the head of LCS, the British deception committee in World War II.

Aside from the absence of notes and references, there are a number of shortcomings. There is an odd asymmetry in the research of historical examples of deception. Of the 142 works cited in the bibliography 25 concern Norway in 1940, which is covered by only 11 pages of text. Even then, no mention is made of the important German deception that succeeded in drawing the British fleet away from Norway as the Germans prepared to invade the country. There are chapters on German sabotage in the

United States and on Big Bertha in World War I and on psychological warfare in World War II, subjects that do not fall into the category of deception. The recounting of the U.S. deception plan for the attack on the St. Mihiel salient in 1918 does not mention the strong suspicions of German intelligence that a deception plan was in the works. Finally, the naval deceptions treated are strategically less important than many others, such as those covered in Admiral William James's 1956 biography of Admiral Hall, *The Eyes of the Navy*. To the authors' credit, they show no scholarly pretensions about this work.

Aston, Sir George. SECRET SERVICE. London: Faber and Faber, 1930. 308 pp., index [New York: Cosmopolitan Book Corp.].

A Royal Marines officer who rose to the rank of brigadier, Sir George was an original staff member and a pioneer of British Naval Intelligence when it was established in 1887. During most of World War I he was involved in security work connected with the protection of British naval installations, having left military service in 1914 for reasons of health. This book is a collection of stories of secret service, partly derived from personal experience. The book would have had greater historical value had Aston written more from first-hand experience and knowledge rather than attempting to provide a partial account of the work of the British intelligence services in World War I, a subject covered by others before and after him. He might thus have given us more than a glimpse of the early years of British naval intelligence while avoiding errors such as those he makes about the German intelligence instructor in Belgium, Fräulein Schragmüller, AKA "Mademoiselle le Docteur" (the result of his reliance on erroneous accounts of Schragmüller written by Richard Rowan). Credit must be given to Sir George for his recognition of the importance of security and counterintelligence and for his provision of many examples of their vital role in the success or failure of military operations. His description, too, of deception in the Middle East in World War I is one of the earliest accounts of the work of Meinertzhagen, although it does not mention that name.

Augur, Helen. THE SECRET WAR OF INDEPENDENCE. New York: Duell, Sloan and Pearce; Boston: Little, Brown, 1955. 341 pp., bibliog., index [Westport, Conn.: Greenwood Press, 1976].

Experts on the American Revolution recommend this as one of the better books on the history of the secret war in that conflict. Scholars find it to be thoroughly researched, utilizing the best secondary sources and manuscript collections, as well as reliable and marked by good judgment. One expert regarded it as likely to stand for some time as authoritative. The author herself considered that she was addressing what she calls the "commercial-diplomatic complex," features of which she felt had been neglected or suppressed. Among them were war profiteering, gun running, blockade running, and privateering. Other aspects she discusses, such as the Deanes's feud with Franklin or British intelligence penetration of American offices in Europe, have been covered in other works. Only the secret war in Europe is treated (and treated very well), not that in other areas; consequently, the title is somewhat misleading. But Augur fulfills her claim of having restored a balance between the "military and the maritime-commercial aspects of the conflict."

Auty, Phyllis, and Clogg, Richard, eds. BRITISH POLICY TOWARDS WARTIME RESISTANCE IN YUGOSLAVIA AND GREECE. London: Macmillan, 1975. 308 pp., bibliog., index.

This represents the proceedings of a 1973 conference organized by the University of London School of Slavonic and East European Studies. Included are papers, statements, and transcripts of discussions of the participants, all but one of whom were involved in the actual events discussed. SOE is heavily represented; in fact, the majority of participants were with SOE. They were the "stars" of British operations in the Balkans. Fascinating new material on British intelligence and resistance operations, capabilities, and relationships emerges from the proceedings, including some rare first-hand glimpses of tensions, relations, and thinking within SOE, between SOE-London and SOE-Cairo, and between intelligence and the Foreign Office. One learns of the attempt within SOE to sabotage the assignment of Fitzroy Maclean to Yugoslavia and how Ultra was or was not disseminated to SOE both in London and Cairo. Although by 1973 most of the participants had written books on their experiences and the role of British departments in wartime resistance and policy disputes, these papers show that things were left unsaid. Similarly, Davidson's *Special Operations Europe,* published in 1980, has additional behind-the-scenes revelations not mentioned by Davidson or any other participant in the conference. Valuable as this book is, therefore, to the history of British intelligence in the Balkans in World War II (and it is valuable), there are probably other very pertinent facts on the subject still to see the light of day. The fact, too, that the Foreign Office view is not as well represented as are those of the intelligence organizations deprives the book of a valuable additional perception of British intelligence activities and policy. Barker's *British Policy in South-East Europe* is a useful companion, though Yugoslavia and Greece are not its central topics

B

Babington-Smith, Constance. AIR SPY: THE STORY OF PHOTO INTELLIGENCE IN WORLD WAR II. New York: Harper and Bros., 1957. 259 pp., index [London: Chatto and Windus, 1958. *Evidence in Camera*].

Considering the importance of photographic intelligence to total intelligence in World War II, there have been, comparatively speaking, few books published on this aspect of intelligence. Babington-Smith's is to be prized for this reason and also for being one of the earliest postwar works on the subject. With access to official records, she has produced a mixture of personal experiences and observations and a wider treatment. The work is not exactly what the subtitle implies, but rather the history of Allied photo reconnaissance and interpretation in Europe and the Mediterranean, largely from the British vantage point. A skilled photo interpreter, Babington-Smith takes great pride in the accomplishments of British and later Allied photo interpreting. Her claim that the war was won by the side with the best photo reconnaissance (as the German General von Fritsch predicted in the 1930s) will be contested, especially with the revelation of the Ultra successes. In her judgment, the role of photo intelligence in dealing with German V weapons was more modest; according to her, kept secret, except for a few allusions, until the appearance of this book. There are only glimpses of certain areas, such as the shortcomings of German photo reconnaissance and interpretation. Her version of the early collaboration of Sidney Cotton and Winterbotham needs to be supplemented with the latter's version in his *The Nazi Connection* and Barker's *Aviator Extraordinary.* Jones's *The Wizard War* needs to be referred to for the role of photo intelligence and interpretation against German V weapons, as well as other contributions not fully addressed here. See also Brookes's *Photo Reconnaissance.*

Bailey, Geoffrey. THE CONSPIRATORS. New York: Harper and Bros., 1960. 269 pp., bibliog., notes, index [London: Gollancz, 1961].

Bailey is a pseudonym; some people believe there may have been more than one author of this story of Soviet intelligence operations. The book covers two famous cases, connected by a section entitled "Interlude" on the kidnapping of Aleksandr Kutyepov. The first part, on the Trust, is by and large a useful presentation of facts and interpretation. The point of view is that of the promilitary émigrés. Experts believe this is one of the best treatments of that Soviet operation, even though it is not the whole or definitive story and it includes some errors, such as the equating of Boris Savinkov with the precise Soviet effort against the Trust and some uncertainty about which Western powers were targets. The bibliography on the Trust is considered one of the best available.

The segment on the Tukhachevsky affair is not of the same quality. Specialists consider it quite unreliable. Blackstock wrote in his bibliography that the book was "sensational and journalistic" and that the author used spurious sources such as the Litvinov diary. Although Blackstock had his own preferences for sources on the Trust, his criticism of the book was apparently meant mainly for the Tukhachevsky treatment, which represents its major flaw.

Bakeless, John. SPIES OF THE CONFEDERACY. Philadelphia: J. B. Lippincott, 1970. 391 pp., notes, index.

Bakeless, the author of a book on espionage in the American Revolution (below), devoted more than ten years to this opus. He was assiduous in uncovering and presenting information on Civil War intelligence that, he states, was not known to exist before his research. Confining his work to spies, i.e., those primarily concerned with collecting military information, he is fully aware of the difficulty of evaluating such sources because, as he put it, agents are inclined to exaggerate. Despite this caution and his commendable effort, his results must be questioned. Even with the plethora of new information he claims to have uncovered, the fact is that the principal means of confirming many postwar claims is missing: Confederate secret intelligence records were destroyed in 1865 during the evacuation of Richmond. Bakeless also attributes without qualification some important developments to intelligence despite his claim that he does not do so if he cannot find confirmation. The purist will object to the inclusion of combat intelligence personnel in a book with "Spies" in the title. The space given to their efforts might better have been devoted to other intelligence activities, such as those of Confederate agents abroad, which are not addressed.

Bakeless, John. TURNCOATS, TRAITORS AND HEROES. Philadelphia: J. B. Lippincott, 1959. 365 pp., bibliog., index.

Bakeless's interest in the subject undoubtedly stemmed partly from his service in U.S. military intelligence. He produced in this book a history of espionage in the main theater of war in the American Revolution. Calling it a thorough study of espionage, counterespionage, and other military intelligence on both sides, he believed that a large proportion of the material he presented was new. This was the most complete work on the intelligence war in the North American theater at the time of publication, although the work of the British Northern Department is not discussed. But for the area of operations covered, it is one of the best works available; and it should be required reading for all U.S. officers as consumers or producers of intelligence for two reasons. First, it gives a vivid picture of General Washington's interest in intelligence and deception and the value he placed on effective intelligence. Second, it will dispel any notion that Americans lack a talent for or a tradition of intelligence operations. Much operational tradecraft will be found here: secret writing, couriers and cutouts, letter drops, deceptive chickenfeed, and counterintelligence techniques (to name a few). Bakeless's belief that the American agent Enoch Crosby was the model for James Fenimore Cooper's Harvey Birch was not accepted by all students of the American Revolution. Nor was his research on the British agent John Howe complete, judging by later findings. Frank E. McKone in Volume 1 of *General Sullivan: New Hampshire Patriot* (New York: Praeger, 1977) identified Howe as one of the aliases of the British agent John Hall who served England faithfully in four wars and was a link in the defection of Benedict Arnold.

Barkas, Geoffrey, in collaboration with Natalie Barkas. THE CAMOUFLAGE STORY: FROM AINTREE TO ALAMEIN. London: Cassell, 1952. 216 pp., no index.

Geoffrey Barkas was head of Britain's camouflage organization in the Middle East in World War II, beginning in January 1941. Natalie, his wife and collaborator in this book, worked in British censorship. The work covers the period through the battle of El Alamein, dealing with both defensive and offensive visual deception employed against Axis forces. Interesting as is the description of defensive measures, such as those employed in the defense of Tobruk, it is the section of the book dealing with offensive deception that is the most fascinating. Barkas reveals how poorly prepared the British were in the field of camouflage at the start of the war (the British army neglected it completely between the wars). Consequently, the progress shown by the end of the book is both interesting and impressive. His surprising failure to mention Jasper Maskelyne's role in camouflage in the Middle East theater of war was only partially explained with the appearance of David Mure's *Master of Deception*.

Barker, Elizabeth. BRITISH POLICY IN SOUTH-EAST EUROPE IN THE SECOND WORLD WAR. London: Barnes and Noble, 1976. 268 pp., bibliog., notes, index.

A product of high quality can be expected from Barker. On this subject, she has the qualifications of an area expert reinforced by wartime service in PWE; she followed or participated in the events chronicled here. The countries covered are those in the Balkans and Hungary. Greece and Yugoslavia are deliberately given less treatment than British interest in them merited because Barker felt Britain's relations with these two had already been amply documented. British policy and activities, including much on SOE and resistance operations, are put in perspective and given a balanced account. Her main source was the Public Record Office holdings of official documents, and these she rounded out with first-hand records by British and non-British participants in the events. She produces new material and insights, particularly on British unofficial and intelligence contacts with various organizations and individuals in the area during the war. A review in *RUSI* praised this book as thorough, penetrating, and well written; only "thorough" seems inappropriate. Barker herself advises that many documents in the Public Record Office were withheld at the time of her research. Auty and Clogg's *British Policy Towards Wartime Resistance in Yugoslavia and Greece* rounds out the picture

Barker, Ralph. AVIATOR EXTRAORDINARY: THE SIDNEY COTTON STORY. London: Chatto and Windus, 1969. 289 pp., index.

In *Air Spy* Babington-Smith declared that at the start of World War II Cotton's methods in photo reconnaissance succeeded where orthodox methods had failed. R. V. Jones said Cotton had a genius for getting things done. This is his story, as he told it to Ralph Barker, of his photo reconnaissance career from shortly before the war to the fall of France. He describes the innovations in British photo reconnaissance and interpretation in which he was involved or for which he says he was responsible and the bureaucratic and interservice rivalries that impeded him and that he thinks finally succeeded in removing him from active duty. Cotton's great contributions are supported by researchers such as Brookes in *Photo Reconnaissance.* However, Winterbotham in *The Nazi Connection* must be consulted for his account of Cotton and for a different perspective on who was responsible for some new methods. Winterbotham gives more reasons for the end of Cotton's role in 1940; for more on this question, see Cave Brown's *Bodyguard of Lies,* which does not, however, indicate the source of its information. Whatever the circumstances, R. V. Jones reminds us that Geoffrey Tuttle, who worked for Cotton, succeeded him, and became an air marshal, thought Cotton the greatest leader he ever met (see *The Wizard War*).

Barron, John. KGB: THE SECRET WORK OF SOVIET SECRET AGENTS. Pleasantville, N.Y.: Reader's Digest Press, 1974. 415 pp., bibliog., notes, index [London: Hodder and Stoughton].

The KGB and its predecessors, their central role in maintaining the Soviet regime, and their long history of espionage and covert action abroad have been documented in many ways. Yet there have been comparatively few full-length studies published in English of the organization and operations, both at home and abroad, of this important, nay vital, support of the Soviet system, without which that system would collapse. Barron brings together more information about certain KGB collection and action operations and more up-to-date data on its organization and reveals more names of operatives on all levels than have ever before been collected in one book. His conviction, and that of his colleague Kenneth Gilmore, is "that it is impossible to understand the Soviet Union without understanding the KGB," a conclusion with which few would argue. Main emphasis is on the KGB's activities abroad, with chapters describing individual espionage operations and giving the identities of the KGB operatives. The KGB's organizational structure at headquarters and field levels is outlined, and there is a short section on its internal security function within the Soviet Union. Hugh Trevor-Roper's statement in his *New York Times* review that this internal function, supported by great effort and resources, is what makes the KGB sinister is his way of indicating an imbalance in Barron's treatment.

From the range, pervasiveness, and persistence of the KGB efforts abroad that Barron describes, the KGB warrants the description as the largest in scope and most sinister foreign intelligence operation in history. Examples of collection, agents of influence, disinformation, political and other kinds of warfare, sabotage, assassination ("wet affairs"), and aid to terrorist operations abound. Chapters on the departments of the KGB responsible for sabotage, assassination, and disinformation reveal many valuable facts for the first time. The short chapter on satellite services is concerned mainly with one Cuban agent.

Barron had two primary sources of original data: Soviet defectors and Western security and intelligence services; the majority of the data came from private individuals. He could not have produced such a detailed and revealing study without access to Western security and intelligence organizations—he acknowledges, for instance, the editorial help of the chief of DIA's counterintelligence department for the final version of his chapter on Sergeant Robert Lee Johnson, one of the significant cases in the book. This help gives the work a more authoritative status and greater authenticity. The Western services' willingness to be forthcoming was probably inspired by several motives: the wish to expose Soviet activities and operatives as a counter to the ongoing Soviet campaign to discredit Western, and especially U.S., intelligence and to reveal the identities of Western intelligence personnel; the wish to differentiate between the two sides; and the desire to put Soviet activities in their proper perspective.

There were a few other criticisms of the book. Trevor-Roper disliked Barron's style, calling it journalistic with an excess of dramatic reconstruction. The *RUSI* reviewer thought Barron should have used more material from reports of government commissions and trials of KGB agents—which only proves that the study was in no way comprehensive. Source identification and documentation are superior to those of the typical journalistic work, and the bibliography is fairly complete. Serious if not scholarly, this is very nearly a textbook on the subject.

Barron, John. MIG PILOT: THE FINAL ESCAPE OF LIEUTENANT BELENKO. Pleasantville, N.Y.: Reader's Digest Press, 1980. 217 pp., index [New York: McGraw-Hill, 1980].

Largely an accurate account of the Soviet flyer's defection to the West in his MiG-25 in September 1976. Belenko's defection brought to the West the Foxbat aircraft that was the object of intense interest to U.S. and other Western intelligence services. Possession of it helped dispel a great number of errors and misperceptions concerning its makeup and performance. Barron exaggerates when he describes Belenko as "probably the most knowledgeable military man to flee since WWII." He also perpetuates the erroneous Soviet charge that U.S. SR-71s on reconnaissance missions off the Soviet coast "taunted and toyed with the MiG-25's" as if this were deliberate and authorized policy or practice.

Barron's account is valuable not so much in describing the whys and hows of a defector but rather in focusing attention on Western intelligence errors connected with this Soviet weapons system. His analysis and description of the reasons for Western self-deception and misperception may or may not be the complete story. There is a chance that the Soviets may have actively encouraged these misperceptions by measures other than those of strict security, a factor Barron does not weigh.

Bates, David Homer. LINCOLN IN THE TELEGRAPH OFFICE: RECOLLECTIONS OF THE U.S. MILITARY TELEGRAPH CORPS DURING THE CIVIL WAR. New York, London: D. Appleton-Century, 1939. 425 pp., index.

Richard Rowan in *The Story of Secret Service* calls to our attention the fact that the invention of telegraphic wire tapping occurred in the American Civil War, making it an American development in military intelligence. The author of this book, first published in 1907, was manager of the U.S. War Department Telegraph Office and a cipher-operator during the years 1861–1866. He was one of the first four operators in this office, involved in both cryptographic and cryptanalytic duties. Unfortunately only some four chapters are devoted to codes, ciphers, and cryptologic matters and to Union counterintelligence—using deciphered messages against Confederate agents. What Bates reveals only whets the appetite for more. Still, we learn that the Confederates failed to break higher-level Union cryptographic systems while the Union had greater success. A historical gem is his description of President Lincoln's personal interest in the breaking of enciphered Confederate messages.

In David Kahn's monumental *The Codebreakers,* a chapter is partly based on this work. Taylor's *The Signal and Secret Service of the Confederate States* tells a little of what has come down to us about the Confederate cryptologic effort.

Beesly, Patrick. VERY SPECIAL ADMIRAL: THE LIFE OF ADMIRAL J. H. GODFREY, C. B. London: Hamish Hamilton, 1980. 336 pp., bibliog., index.

Captain Stephen Roskill, in the foreword, says this is two books in one. The one pertinent to this bibliography is on Godfrey's work in British naval intelligence in World War II, which Beesly paints with rather a broad brush. This section is not as good as the author's earlier *Very Special Intelligence,* perhaps because, as Roskill reveals, Beesly was for some reason denied access to the monographs Godfrey wrote on his wartime NID work. We are given a picture of the admiral's contributions to the effective organization of the NID and his leadership of it for almost four years. There are also some wonderful anecdotes and revelations. Especially enthralling are some seven pages on the confusion that existed at one stage on responsibility for the security of British naval ciphers. What seems to be lacking is a feel for Godfrey's role in operational matters, similar to that of Admiral Hall in World War I. A better picture of that role would allow us to judge whether Godfrey's reputation rests on more than administrative talents. The reasons Beesly gives for Godfrey's transfer in the midst of the war may be the full story; on the other hand, future works may throw further light on what seems a petty and potentially damaging decision for the Allied war effort. Future works may also help explain Roskill's remark, "Some well-informed readers will probably disagree with Beesly on certain controversial points." McLachlan's *Room 39* and Montagu's *Beyond Top Secret Ultra* are necessary supplements to this biography.

Beesly, Patrick. VERY SPECIAL INTELLIGENCE: THE STORY OF THE ADMIRALTY'S OPERATIONAL INTELLIGENCE CENTER 1939–1945. London: Hamish Hamilton, 1977. 262 pp., bibliog., index [Garden City, N.Y.: Doubleday, 1978].

A fine book on intelligence in World War II and one of the finest on the naval intelligence aspects as seen from the British side. Beesly served in the OIC, the Admiralty's Operational Intelligence Center, which collated, evaluated, and disseminated all intelligence on enemy navies. His own wartime experiences and knowledge, British public records, and interviews with knowledgeable veterans of the war are combined to produce this first-rate product. It is not the definitive work on the OIC, as Ewen Montagu calls it in *Beyond Top Secret Ultra,* for one reason: Beesly's version does not deal with the Pacific or Mediterranean. The author, a serious and honest writer, has tried to place the role of communications intelligence and Ultra in proper perspective as an aid in winning the naval war, particularly against German submarines. The book clarifies the question of when communications intelligence flowed and when it did not. It is informative on both general and specific matters—we learn, for instance, of the system of special Y parties on German ships. One hopes someone will write a similar book on the war in the Mediterranean, which, Beesly writes, deserves a separate study.

Two minor points. The jacket on the Doubleday edition states that the OIC was so secret until 1975 that nobody not connected with it had ever heard of it. However, McLachlan wrote about it in 1968 in *Room 39.* Also, Beesly's evaluation of the role of cryptanalysis in the destruction of the German battleship *Bismarck*—that it played only a minor part—is not universally accepted (see Calvocoressi's *Top Secret Ultra*).

Bell, Ernest L. AN INITIAL VIEW OF ULTRA AS AN AMERICAN WEAPON. Keene, N.H.: TSU Press, 1977. 110 pp., no index.

This could more accurately have been entitled "An Initial Glimpse." It reproduces censored versions of three Ultra documents released to the author under the U.S. FOIA. Considering the existence of some half a million such documents, according to NSA's information, this publication gives only bits on the organization within U.S. intelligence for the secure handling and dissemination of Ultra in the War Department, elsewhere in Washington, and in the field. It is interesting to learn of the tight controls on Ultra dissemination even within the War Department and to make mental comparisons with more current practices. We learn something else from the author. He had a most difficult time in getting material from NSA, which relented and released segments only after appeal. Therefore, this is a pioneer work for the U.S., which has much to do to catch up with the extent and quality of works written by the British on Ultra.

Bennett, Ralph. ULTRA IN THE WEST: THE NORMANDY CAMPAIGN 1944–5. London: Hutchinson, 1979. 266 pp., notes, index [New York: Scribners, 1980].

Another giant step in the effort to evaluate the role of Ultra in the events and important decisions of World War II. Bennett worked at Bletchley Park from February 1941 to the end of the war as a member of Hut 3, which received army and air decodes. He reveals more than any previous author about how broken messages were annotated, evaluated, and distributed to commanders. His study is based on Ultra signals released for scholars beginning in October 1977, and he is careful to indicate what he was not able to see—Ultra messages called teleprints with comments as footnotes. He states he set out to do what had not been attempted before: to portray the Allied campaign in 1944–1945 solely through the intelligence provided by Ultra, to show how forecasts of enemy action were derived from it, and to deduce Ultra's contribution to victory. He does not claim that this is a history of Ultra or Bletchley Park. The publisher, however, has provided a misleading subtitle, for this book treats much more than the Normandy fighting of 1944. The impression, too, given by Bennett that all Ultra was derived solely from Enigma decrypts may be unintentional.

Beyond his own evaluation of Ultra's impact on past histories of the war, Bennett provides us with some interesting and even startling revelations on what Ultra intelligence was available before Arnhem, the Ardennes counteroffensive, the National Redoubt fear, and the Normandy invasion. His findings will force a revision, or at least a qualification, of previous judgment on the efficacy of the deception operation Copperhead, the "Monty's double" ploy using the actor Clifton James.

Because of the author's unique qualifications for tackling this task and his care and scholarly approach, the book deserves the accolade "well done." It is required follow-up reading to Lewin's *Ultra Goes to War.* Calvocoressi's *Top Secret Ultra* supplies additional facts on the organization and functioning of Bletchley Park.

Bentley, Elizabeth. OUT OF BONDAGE. New York: Devin-Adair, 1951. 331 pp., no index [London: R. Hart-Davis, 1952].

Bentley is famous in espionage history as the Soviet agent, colleague of the Soviet principal agent Jacob Golos, whose revelations led to the uncovering of a number of Soviet agents in the United States (especially in the U.S. government) in the 1930s and 1940s. This personal narrative gives a picture of the Soviet espionage operations she was familiar with or involved in, especially of the exploitation of Communist sympathizers or party members. Bentley explains the Soviet spotting and recruiting methods used, some of the tradecraft employed, and something of the relations between the party and the Soviet intelligence service. The reader will be struck by the very sloppy operating methods, which, according to David Dallin, led to the crisis between the Soviets and the party's principal agents. Bentley, in dealing with the issue of Soviet takeover of the nets and the heavy-handed insistence on compartmentation, cites her and Golos' opposition to Soviet plans as looming large in her eventual defection, along with her New England conscience. Her treatment of this important point is not altogether convincing. According to David Martin's recent *Wilderness of Mirrors,* an FBI memo suggests that she feared the FBI was already on to her and that she was simply trying to save herself. Pilat in *The Atom Spies* also comments on Bentley's curious failure to mention in this book Miriam Moskowitz's triumph over her in 1947 when Miriam managed to keep Gold and Brothman from attacking each other under the stress of imminent exposure as Soviet agents. Although Dallin also spoke of slight inaccuracies in this book, he judged it as significant and as a good description of the gradual development of a Soviet secret agent. All these comments seem to point to the need for further works on Bentley's life as a Soviet agent.

Bergier, Jacques. SECRET WEAPONS—SECRET AGENTS. London: Hurst and Blackett, 1956. 184 pp., no index.

A translation of the French edition of 1955. The author was a leader of the French network Marco Polo (later called Promontoine) under the name Verne. Caught by the Germans, he spent the rest of World War II in a concentration camp. There is little here to recommend this book. It is outdated and vastly surpassed in accuracy and quality by later books on the subject of German secret weapons, especially the V weapons. Its style is confusing, and the author's aim is equally so. He alternates between talking about his net and describing the contributions he claims the French resistance made to the defeat of German secret weapons. The many errors and unsubstantiated claims weigh against the book. Neither R. V. Jones nor Garlinski, writing on German V weapons, nor M.R.D. Foot, on resistance, mentions Bergier.

Bertrand, Gustave. ENIGMA 1939–1945. Paris: Librairie Plon, 1973. 295 pp., no index.

This is one of the most important works yet published on the history of Allied cryptologic successes against Enigma. Despite its value, and perhaps because of certain doubts that existed about the author's claims and the accuracy of his account, it has never been translated into English. That failure is now inexcusable in light of the latest evidence, which supports the author's story. Bertrand was chief of the French cryptologic section in 1939–1940; his work in this sphere extended back into the 1930s. After the war, he served in the French service SDECE as deputy chief until 1950.

There are two segments. One is on Enigma and the cryptographic service's work until 1942, partly under the German occupier's nose; the other is on Bertrand's resistance work, capture, and escape. Giving the Poles the main credit for the early successes against the Enigma machine, he also credits the aid provided by French intelligence, whose agent Asche was an employee of the German cryptographic service in the 1930s.

Ronald Lewin in *Ultra Goes to War* describes Bertrand's account of his career as overblown and quotes a leading French historian to the effect that Bertrand was boastful in this work. He also points out that all those associated with Bertrand—Poles, British, and French—agree that he made a genuine contribution, but none agree with his own large claims. More recently, Hinsley's *British Intelligence in the Second World War* contains an appendix on Enigma that appears to support many of Bertrand's claims. The testimony of General Henri Navarre, who worked with Bertrand in the 1930s, is called to our attention by Calvocoressi in *Top Secret Ultra.* Whatever the final verdict, he was still one of those few French officers who knew of the Allied cryptanalytical success and guarded it, no small input to victory in itself. David Kahn, in a review of Francis Winterbotham's work, accepts Bertrand's version of how Enigma was broken.

Best, S. Payne. THE VENLO INCIDENT. London and New York: Hutchinson, 1950. 255 pp., no index.

The Venlo incident was the kidnapping of two SIS officers in Holland by German intelligence, specifically the Sicherheitsdienst (SD). The luring of Captain Best, the author and chief of one of the SIS organizations in Holland, and Major Stevens, the Hague SIS station chief, was a unique event in the intelligence war of World War II. It had a precedent in World War I, according to Captain Henry Landau (see *The Enemy Within*), when the Germans kidnapped two French intelligence agents on Dutch soil. More important was the incident's effect on future British contacts with German dissidents, since the British officers were lured in the belief that they were making such a contact. Psychologically, the consequences of the German operation were almost strategic.

The title is misleading because only twenty pages concern the incident and little is provided of the background found in such other works as *The Labyrinth* by Walter Schellenberg (who was involved on the German side) and Farago's *The Game of the Foxes.* The rest of the book is on Best's five-and-a-half years of imprisonment. There is nothing of any length or substance on the interrogation the officers underwent, although it is pictured as disorganized and amateurish. Even after more than forty years, the full story from the British side has yet to be told, and it will not be for quite a while longer; Hinsley tells us in *British Intelligence in the Second World War* that certain Foreign Office files on the matter are closed until 2015 because of references to individuals and technical matters. Best does give us the information that the SIS organization in Holland had been penetrated since 1935 and that this did not become known until the Venlo incident. A version of the German penetration of the British in Holland can be found in Farago's work, mentioned above. Immediate damage to British intelligence interests resulted, according to Foot quoting the Dutch historian DeJong, because Stevens had on him at the moment of the kidnapping a list of the people he must make sure to get out of Holland. DeJong also claims that the officers' interrogation by the Germans unraveled numerous SIS links in Holland and in Czechoslovakia. Stafford (*Britain and European Resistance, 1940–1945*) tells us that the British regarded any contacts with German dissidents with deep distrust after Venlo. See also Whiting's *The Spymasters.*

Bialoguski, Michael. THE CASE OF COLONEL PETROV: HOW I WEANED A HIGH MVD OFFICIAL FROM COMMUNISM. New York: McGraw-Hill, 1955. 238 pp., no index [London: Heinemann, 1955. *The Petrov Story*].

A Polish-born Australian physician, Bialoguski served as an agent of Australian security and as the intermediary in the defection of Petrov, the MVD chief in Australia, in 1954. The defection led to that of Petrov's wife shortly thereafter in dramatic circumstances. This is a questionable version of those events and the author's role in them. Petrov himself in the appendix to his own *Empire of Fear* stated that Bialoguski's account is inaccurate and misleading on a number of points, enumerating eight of them, including the extent of his knowledge and his role, his claim to know the names of Petrov's agents, and his downgrading of the role of Dr. Beckett to give himself credit for single-handedly persuading Petrov to defect. Petrov described Bialoguski's role in the defection as simply that of an intermediary.

These are not the only questionable matters. There is the author's claim that he was slated to become the chief MVD illegal and head of Soviet espionage in Australia in the event of a rupture of Soviet-Australian relations. His boast that he had penetrated Petrov's activities to the extent that Petrov's defection did not have any consequences from an espionage point of view is also suspect. Instead of being instructive as to Petrov's motives and past, Petrov's wife, and the role the death of Stalin may have played in events, Bialoguski unwittingly gives insights into another aspect of agent operations. He provides a case study of the problems faced by a service in handling agents such as Bialoguski. Perhaps this is why no Australian of official status wrote an introduction to the book. For Australian security's view of his role, see Thwaites's *Truth Will Out.*

Bittman, Ladislav. THE DECEPTION GAME: CZECHOSLOVAK INTELLIGENCE IN SOVIET POLITICAL WARFARE. Syracuse, N.Y.: Syracuse Univ. Research Corp., 1972. 240 pp., index.

In recent years there has been a great increase in public knowledge of and interest in Soviet deception operations and efforts to cause dissension in the non-Communist world. Bittman is uniquely expert on these matters because he actually was involved in these efforts. With Czech intelligence for fourteen years (1954–1968), he was in 1964 deputy chief of its special operations department, also known as the disinformation/active measures section. Bittman defines and describes what the Soviets and their allies call special operations—disinformation, black propaganda, and influence operations—as well as explaining the Czech organizations for conducting them and their role in the overall Communist intelligence efforts. He is careful to note that what he says of such Soviet operations he deduced from Czech operations as they were guided by the Soviets. This is probably the best available treatment on Soviet and Czech deception operations on a tactical level in peacetime. It could have been even more thorough had the author written less on the events of 1968 in Czechoslovakia and more on such matters as agent of influence operations. His unqualified conclusion that the Soviet intervention in Czechoslovakia in 1968 was an example of top-level Soviet strategic deception and surprise is debatable.

Blackstock, Paul W. AGENTS OF DECEIT: FRAUDS, FORGERIES AND POLITICAL INTRIGUE AMONG NATIONS. Chicago: Quadrangle Books, 1966. 286 pp., notes, index.

A collection of case studies of frauds and forgeries either of Russian origin or concerning Russia, from the "Testament of Peter the Great" in the early nineteenth century to Soviet forgeries in the 1960s. Blackstock, with experience in army intelligence and as a Russian expert and translator (he translated one of Solzhenitsyn's books), evaluates the effect of these forgeries as weapons in covert action and brings to bear his background in psychological warfare. He also analyzes and tries to judge the authenticity of documents, including some that are still subjects of controversy. The results are surprisingly extreme. There is an excellent and early rejection of the Penkovsky papers' origins and claims. In his penetrating look at these claims, he joins the critics who rejected explanations about the papers at the time of their publication (see Oleg Penkovsky, *The Penkovsky Papers*) and was perceptive in discerning probable authorship and reasons for publication. There is an appendix by George F. Kennan on the Sisson Documents of 1917–1918 that adds substance to this work. (The documents purported to prove that the leaders of the Bolsheviks were at one time paid agents of the German General Staff.) At the other extreme, Blackstock's theory that the Zinoviev Letter was "a perfect example of Soviet provocation" lacks similar analytical quality or evidence. He comes to the overall conclusion that it is hard to make any general statements about the use of forgeries for political warfare since there is a small basis of documents for such covert operations. William R. Harris, in his notation on this book, calls it "sensationalistic but occasionally informative" but provides no explanation of this judgment.

Blackstock, Paul W. THE SECRET ROAD TO WORLD WAR II: SOVIET VERSUS WESTERN INTELLIGENCE 1921–1939. Chicago: Quadrangle Books, 1969. 384 pp., bibliog., index.

Of Blackstock's published products, this was subjected to the greatest criticism, on a number of grounds. One is that the author's title and approach to the subject imply that it was the battles between the secret services that led to war. This is not an unfair comment; Blackstock also does not prove that the battles themselves were not reflections of the policies of the sponsoring governments or that they were undertaken or engaged in without the governments' knowledge or consent. Another criticism is that the book contains a number of errors and is insufficiently critical of the sources it uses. Blackstock shows that he is not unaware of the problem of the reliability of sources when he mentions, for instance, the entrenchment of the story of the Trust in historical myth and legend and the impossibility of "stripping some layers to the core of reality." He also acknowledges that all sources on the Trust (the account of which covers almost a third of the book) "must be used with caution." In his catch-all final chapter, there is a cautionary lead-in that speaks of the tentative value of judgments drawn from incomplete data. The reader is wise to keep these caveats by the author in mind, along with the reservations of the critics. Those interested in Soviet penetration, manipulation, deception, and violence against Russian émigré organizations and their allies, particularly the Trust, may still find some merit in his treatment of aspects of these operations that are not well known. Those aspects should become known because of their technical and professional interest as well as their long-term consequences in the intelligence war.

Blackstock, Paul W. THE STRATEGY OF SUBVERSION: MANIPULATING THE POLITICS OF OTHER NATIONS. Chicago: Quadrangle Books, 1964. 321 pp., notes, index.

The late Blackstock attempted here to describe and analyze covert operations, feeling there were gaps in scholarly and serious writings covering the subject. He was aware that at the time of writing rigorous standards of data gathering and documentation were not possible due to the nature of the subject. The thrust of his arguments is against such operations despite his belief that his aim in writing was neither to promote their use nor to call for their abandonment. He regarded them as oversold as to capabilities and a major threat to peace. Support for his views was drawn from recent covert political operations. The book's principal shortcoming is that Blackstock uses the perspective and the criteria "derived from a specialized study of both Czarist Russian and Nazi German covert operations." The example of Russian operations in Bulgaria in the 1870s is repeatedly used. Soviet examples, however, with their extensive, sophisticated, and persistent qualities, are hardly mentioned. As a result, we are not offered these and more meaningful criteria for the period studied. This is representative of some of the product of its time—the post–U-2 and –Bay of Pigs era, when covert operations were beginning to be scrutinized and debated as tools of a nation's foreign policy. For the record, the reason given here for the removal in 1955 of General Arthur Trudeau from G-2 is incorrect.

Blackstock, Paul W., and Schaf, Frank L. INTELLIGENCE, ESPIONAGE, COUNTERESPIONAGE AND COVERT OPERATIONS: A GUIDE TO INFORMATION SOURCES. Detroit: Gale Research Co., 1978. 229 pp., index.

When it appeared, this work was the most comprehensive annotated bibliography of its type yet published. The authors had excellent professional and academic credentials for the task: both had served in U.S. military intelligence, and the late Blackstock had specialized in various aspects of intelligence, especially in Soviet activities and covert action. The authors regarded this as a highly selective bibliography designed "primarily for the general American public," and it is restricted mainly to books and articles in English. However, they also saw it as possibly of use to political analysts and students of international and foreign affairs. The book is divided into a number of intelligence and geographic categories and contains a selected bibliography of fifty titles, a general critique of the literature, and a chapter on general bibliographic resources.

This very useful breakdown results in an individual work's sometimes being listed under different categories—for example, two of Deacon's books are listed in a total of five categories. Introductory essays are helpful to the lay reader. However, readers may not find acceptable the failure to differentiate adequately between authorized disclosures of a country such as the USSR and those of a U.S. Senate committee in the section titled "General Critique," and they will spot a questionable item about George Blake's having been ordered by British intelligence to work for the Soviets.

Despite its many praiseworthy qualities, among which must be mentioned some good judgmental annotations of certain books, this work contains a number of errors on particular books. It refers to Foot's *SOE in France* as a definitive work, ignoring Foot's own catalog of the limitation to his research; Krivitsky's spurious rank is repeated and his memoirs only called fairly reliable; the designation "definitive" is used more than it should be, as in the case of Lasby's *Project Paperclip;* McCoy's *The Politics of Heroin in Southeast Asia* is called carefully documented, which is not the case; McChristian's *The Role of Military Intelligence 1965–1967* is described as comprehensive, which, since it is unclassified, it obviously is not, as DIS's *Bibliography of Intelligence Literature* pointed out. Cookridge's *The Many Sides of George Blake* certainly is not "the full story." To call Cave Brown's *Bodyguard of Lies* "the single best source of information on intelligence and deception operations in World War II" misses the many serious and basic faults of the book; Young's *Rutland of Jutland* is not "excellent" because the author missed material of critical importance; Stevenson's *A Man Called Intrepid* does not receive the sharp criticism it deserves. The same is true of Deacon's *A History of the British Secret Service,* which is only called "an important work." The annotation for Scotland's *The London Cage* is incorrect, and John Schwarzwalder, the author of *We Caught Spies,* is called Schwarzelder. Blackstock and Schaf are not aware of the errors in Wighton's *Pin-*

Stripe Saboteur cited in Foot's *SOE in France.* The major shortcomings of Winterbotham's *The Ultra Secret* are not mentioned, and neither are those of Copeland's *Without Cloak or Dagger.* Kim's *The Central Intelligence Agency* is described as a collection of essays on secrecy when it actually ranges beyond that. Farago's *The Game of the Foxes* and *The Broken Seal* also escape any of the adverse comments that have been leveled against them by others. The verdict on Seth's *Encyclopedia of Espionage* is incomplete; it is called "a remarkable compilation" despite Blackstock and Schaf's awareness of its gaps. The shortcomings of Pinto's *Spy-Catcher* are not indicated, and Rowan's work, though prodigious, is hardly "exhaustive," as it is described.

Blair, Clay, Jr. SILENT VICTORY: THE U.S. SUBMARINE WAR AGAINST JAPAN. Philadelphia: J. B. Lippincott, 1975. 1072 pp., bibliog., index [Toronto: Bantam, 1976].

A massive study of U.S. submarine operations in the Pacific in World War II. Within it are scores of references to the role of cryptanalysis in that particular naval war. When it appeared, this was probably the most extensive treatment of the cryptologic war and its contribution to the successes of U.S. submarines in the Pacific. Blair is an ex-submariner and writer on submarine warfare. Deprived of access to classified documents and unit histories connected with the code-breaking effort in the war, he resorted to acquiring such information from interviews with and letters from unnamed persons involved in or familiar with it. Other sources of such material were not only published works and congressional hearings but patrol reports and war diaries that, he says, inadvertently referred to such intelligence. Obviously, a more comprehensive and more reliable account of the intelligence contribution will be forthcoming once Blair or another writer gains full access to official records.

Bleicher, Hugo. COLONEL HENRI'S STORY: THE WAR MEMOIRS OF HUGO BLEICHER, FORMER GERMAN SE-

CRET AGENT. London: William Kimber, 1954. 200 pp., no index.

The German edition of this personal narrative was published under the authorship of Erich Borchers. Bleicher was the celebrated sergeant with the Abwehr in France who became one of the best-known CI operatives of that side in World War II. It is obvious that Bleicher does not give a full story of the operations he does treat and leaves others obscure. Gordon Young, in his book on the double agent "the Cat," said Bleicher wrote how he uncovered the net of which the Cat was a member but did not discuss her or her actions. Ian Colvin, editor of this English edition, added explanatory and expansionary notes to the text and corrections on matters concerning the Allies about which he felt Bleicher was not well informed; there is a patronizing quality in Colvin's comments. Other British writers also expressed reservations about Bleicher's overall accomplishments. Foot, in *SOE in France,* said that Bleicher's importance in the affairs of SOE had been considerably exaggerated. He also said that Bleicher included versions of unrecorded conversations. Bleicher, however, provides some valuable views of the counterintelligence war from the other side of the hill despite shortcomings or debatable opinions (such as the importance he attaches to Peter Churchill and Odette Sanson).

Bondy, Ruth. THE EMISSARY: A LIFE OF ENZO SERENI. Boston: Atlantic Monthly Press and Little, Brown, 1977. 265 pp., bibliog., notes, index [London: Robson Books, 1978].

A translation of the original Hebrew edition. Sereni, an Italian Jew, was an early Zionist; he migrated to Palestine and subsequently worked on behalf of the Zionist cause in Germany and the United States. During World War II he was employed by the British in propaganda against the Italians. He was parachuted into northern Italy; there he was caught and executed by the Germans. All these activities are described, as is Sereni's involvement in the smuggling of arms and Jews to Palestine from Iraq in the midst of the war. The segments on intelligence activities and relationships are of interest primarily when they concern the Jewish Agency operations with which Sereni was connected. Bondy's revelation of the atmosphere of distrust that prevailed during the war in relations between British intelligence and the Jewish Agency is one of the more valuable contributions. Allied intelligence operations get no real treatment because the focus is elsewhere. According to Steven's *The Spymasters of Israel,* Sereni's widow was later connected with Jewish arms procurement efforts in Italy after World War II.

Borosage, Robert L., and Marks, John, eds. THE CIA FILE. New York: Grossman, 1976. 228 pp., notes, no index.

Under the sponsorship of the Center for National Security Studies, a two-day conference was held in 1974 on CIA covert operations. This is a collection of the essays presented and some later complementary pieces. The editors characterize the participants as "generally critical" of such covert-action operations. In fact, the conference and the papers were made up by what might be called the anti-intelligence establishment. Besides the editors, such well-known critics of CIA as Marchetti, Halperin, Ross, Congressman Harrington, Raskin, Ellsberg, Branfman, and Barnet either were present, presented papers, or addressed the conference. Reading this collection helps one capture some of the mood of the times in certain circles toward intelligence. Barnet expressed this mood frankly in his essay when he observed that "in the climactic year of Watergate it is not hard to make a strong case against secret intelligence operations." William Colby's remarks and the question-and-answer session following his talk vividly provide further proof of the atmosphere of hostility to secret operations and to CIA in particular that prevailed at the conference. The attitudes toward intelligence held by the majority at this meeting influenced popular and political attitudes in the United States toward CIA and secret intelligence for the next half decade. Thus, the student of intelligence needs to be familiar with the philosophical and other underpinnings of the participants' positions.

Boucard, Robert. REVELATIONS FROM THE SECRET SERVICE: THE SPY ON TWO FRONTS. London: Hutchinson, 1930. 173 pp., no index.

Boucard says he was a member of the "Mixed Bureau," composed of British, French, and Belgian intelligence officers during World War I. This organization, located on English soil, again according to the author, served as a permanent liaison center for these secret services and the place where information was pooled and intelligence planning undertaken in common. Shulman's notes in his *An Annotated Bibliography of Cryptography* state Boucard "saw service" with the famous Admiral Hall of Room 40 fame as a member of that liaison unit. Presumably, then, Boucard writes as a knowledgeable insider and a person privy to the secrets he writes about. Yet this story of a successful French double agent who penetrated the circle of an unnamed German prince has no authoritative corroboration. The first section, which deals primarily with the Zimmermann Telegram, includes pure speculation on Kitchener's death. The remainder of his version of the Zimmermann affair is now dated except for what he says of Alexander Szek. This material assumes a new relevance in light of new information revealed by Stephen Roskill in his 1981 biography, *Admiral of the Fleet Earl Beatty* (New York: Atheneum). See Boucard's *The Secret Services of Europe* for other information on the Szek case.

Boucard, Robert. THE SECRET SERVICES OF EUROPE. London: Stanley Paul and Co., 1940. 252 pp., index.

This English edition eliminated a number of names that appeared in the French edition because of English libel laws. A chapter cut by the censor was replaced by one written by the translator, who also wrote the first chapter as an introduction. Appearing just as World War II started, the book is mostly outdated. Boucard's allegations of German intelligence successes in Russia either have been refuted or have never been substantiated (he claims Rasputin, the Russian War Minister Soukhomlinoff, and his aide Myasoedov were German agents—see Rowan's *The Story of Secret Service* for refutation on the latter two). His description of the scope of the German secret services is pure speculation, and his account of the intelligence reasons for the outcome of the Battle of Tannenberg is not only incorrect but surprising, considering it was written a quarter-century after the event. There are a few segments on the French services and some of their operations in World War I. The version of a story that also appears in his 1930 book differs from the earlier account in a way that could be significant. He now claims it was the "Mixed Bureau" (explained above) that stole the German political code in Brussels. Since, according to Stephen Roskill, it may be true that Alexander Szek acquired it (a version previously denied by the British), we must await further disclosures to see if Boucard's version of the Mixed Bureau's role was correct.

Boyle, Andrew. THE CLIMATE OF TREASON: FIVE WHO SPIED FOR RUSSIA. London: Hutchinson, 1979. 452 pp., bibliog., notes, index [New York: Dial/James Wade. ***The Fourth Man: The Definitive Account of Kim Philby, Guy Burgess and Donald Maclean and Who Recruited Them to Spy for Russia.*** **London: Coronet Books and Hodder & Stoughton].**

Both the original British and the U.S. edition appeared prior to the official naming of Anthony Blunt as the "fourth man" and should be passed up for the revised version put out by Coronet Books. In it, Boyle was able to include the name of Blunt and material on his life and career, which he could not do earlier. At the same time, some minor slips are corrected. The persistence of some factual errors and the criticisms by certain reviewers that Boyle's effort is marred by lack of evidence in support of particular facts, allegations, or opinions need to be kept in mind. Allen Weinstein, the author of *Perjury: The Hiss-Chambers Case,* was particularly hard on Boyle for using what he called "anecdotal evidence uncritically and without corroboration." Boyle has, in fact, an unfortunate tendency to present some facts, both large and small, with a certainty that is better avoided. For instance, he states that Philby was not able to pass on to the Soviets anything of value while he was with MI6 other than the names of British agents in the Soviet Union and Eastern Europe in 1941–1943.

Despite these criticisms, Boyle's descriptions of these Soviet agents and of British attitudes toward them—official, personal, and class—are perhaps the best to date. The implicit trust, lack of effective vetting, and failure to report to proper authorities crucial knowledge or reservations are still as instructive and difficult to comprehend as ever, despite Boyle's detailed recounting of security attitudes and procedures that are classic examples of a sort. The *Economist* as late as 1979 still called these cases of Soviet espionage and the British handling of them a history of bungling and coverup. As for Boyle's allegations that there are two or three others involved and that a fifth man was an American double agent (denied by one individual), one must refer to Pincher's *Their Trade Is Treachery* for further revelations or allegations and for confirmation of Boyle's prediction that "Britain has not heard the last of the Cambridge conspiracy." This warning that more could be expected makes the U.S. edition's subtitle ("The Definitive Account") all the harder to understand and all the more inappropriate. *Foreign Affairs* was also hasty in calling the book as full an account of the Soviet spy ring as we were likely to get without full access to internal documents. It would be more prudent to call Boyle's work a new and important landmark in the literature of these cases.

Brissaud, André. CANARIS: THE BIOGRAPHY OF ADMIRAL CANARIS, CHIEF OF GERMAN MILITARY INTELLIGENCE IN THE SECOND WORLD WAR. London: Weidenfeld & Nicolson, 1970. 331 pp., notes, index [New York: Grosset and Dunlap, 1974].

The translation and editing of the original French edition was done by Ian Colvin, the author of a much earlier biography of Canaris. The *Economist* review praised Brissaud for "a masterly study" that seemingly consulted every available source. Brissaud, a journalist and the author of a number of works on the Nazis and the Nazi era, has written a fairly well-researched biography. Colvin found the research painstaking and scholarly and did not take issue with the rejection of the old Colvin theory that Canaris might have been a British agent. For Colvin, there was nothing "inherently impossible" in this work.

Yet this work is concerned mainly with Canaris's attitude toward and connections with conspiracies against the Nazi state. This aspect is emphasized more than his intelligence activities, accomplishments, and failures even though Brissaud himself remarks early that many historians forget Canaris was the head of an intelligence service and not merely a drawing-room conspirator. Though he does not completely neglect Canaris's intelligence work, Brissaud has not produced a work that treats Canaris the intelligence officer adequately. Mathtech, in its study on German rearmament, considered the book surprisingly weak on Canaris's career before his taking over the Abwehr in 1935, and the *Economist* thought Brissaud resorted too frequently to direct quotations for which there are no verbatim records. One may add that Brissaud is not quite clear in his mind on the exact meaning of some of Canaris's activities. At one point he insists Canaris was never guilty of treason in giving information on German military moves to the enemy, but earlier he relates how Canaris warned the Polish military attaché in August 1939 of the date of the impending German attack on Poland. The final and exact picture of Canaris's opposition role is still to be drawn and is not to be found in this work.

Brissaud, André. THE NAZI SECRET SERVICE. New York: W. W. Norton, 1974. 309 pp., bibliog., index [London: The Bodley Head].

The journalist in Brissaud is much more evident here than in *Canaris.* This book covers a series of events in the history of the SD up to 1940 rather than giving a history of that organization. There are chapters on such matters as the Venlo incident, the murder of Röhm, the Tukhachevsky deception operation, the Polish agent Sosnowski, and the bombing of the Munich beer hall in 1939. The author interviewed many individuals, some of whom, like Schellenberg, were long dead by the time the French edition appeared in 1972. He states many of these requested anonymity. Another matter for concern is the author's habit of giving direct quotes despite the unlikelihood of their having been perfectly recalled by the participants or secondary sources. Perhaps Brissaud's caution to the reader is the best judgment of the book itself: much has yet to be learned about the SD, "too many questions remain open, too many documents undiscovered, too many witnesses remain silent."

Brookes, Andrew J. PHOTO RECONNAISSANCE. London: Ian Allan Ltd, 1975. 240 pp., index.

The title should more properly have been "British Photo Reconnaissance." What was started as a squadron history became a well-researched book devoted largely to the British experience, especially in World War II. German photo reconnaissance is treated in a few short sections, and the Americans get brief mention. The contribution of photo reconnaissance (PR) at important junctures of the war is made clear, and the fullest tribute is paid to the PR units whose dangerous work of intelligence collection has not been given the recognition it deserves. More attention to the contribution PR made to intelligence and a bit less to administrative and organizational matters would have been preferable. Besides some minor technical errors cited by British reviewers, there are features of this book that will provoke comment and some differences of opinion. Some may believe that the author is too uncritical in his description of Sidney Cotton's role. Second, there is no mention of Ultra and its contribution to identifying and pinpointing PR targets. Third, any future history of the subject meant to be more all-embracing would need to give more treatment to the U.S. contribution. Fourth, the same fuller coverage would need to be devoted to the partial dependence of PR on ground intelligence, which the author acknowledges in his story of the search for the German V weapons. The final chapter on postwar PR systems contains some very interesting and revealing information. But it demonstrates the hazards of predicting the future of PR in concluding that reconnaissance satellites were invulnerable "for the foreseeable future." For the early and war years, consult both Babington-Smith's *Air Spy* and Barker's *Aviator Extraordinary*.

Brook-Shepherd, Gordon. THE STORM PETRELS: THE FIRST SOVIET DEFECTORS 1928–1938. New York: Harcourt Brace Jovanovich, 1978. 257 pp., index [London: Collins, 1977].

The value of Soviet defectors for the intelligence and insights they impart is now taken for granted. This suspenseful and instructive book reminds us it was not always so. It recounts the case of the Soviet defectors Boris Bajanov, Stalin's secretary, whom the author interviewed at length; Gregory Bessedovsky, the chargé in Paris; Georges Agabekov (see his *OGPU*); Walter Krivitsky; and Alexander Orlov. We learn of the incredible lack of judgment and appreciation of what could be acquired from defectors by reading of the reaction of the British Indian government in 1928 when Bajanov requested asylum. Brook-Shepherd's book is a rarity in English on the early history of Soviet defections. But it is still only an introduction to the subject and to the errors that occurred in handling these valuable sources of information on the Soviets. One will quickly spot the absence of Poretsky's comments on Krivitsky's career and rank or the lack of more than surface knowledge about subjects like Orlov and Bessedovsky; for more on the defectors, see Poretsky's *Our Own People* and Orlov's *Handbook of Intelligence and Guerrilla Warfare*. Brook-Shepherd performed a service in reminding us how much the story of the early Soviet defectors had been neglected.

Brownrigg, Admiral Sir Douglas. INDISCRETIONS OF THE NAVAL CENSOR. New York: George H. Doran, 1920. 286 pp., index [London: Cassell].

The author, by reason of his experience and positions, should have produced an interesting and revealing work;

but he did not. Head of British naval censorship in World War I and an officer with previous experience in British naval intelligence, he had worked closely with people like Admiral Hall, the genius of British naval intelligence in that war. He also had access to much classified information. Writing on the heels of the conflict, he was obviously constrained, for in his "P.S." he confesses that he wished he could have told the whole truth. There is little to hold attention beyond a few interesting war stories on censorship and related matters and fleeting looks at some of the famous figures of that period. Not a single success of counterintelligence or economic warfare is provided; any contribution of his office to intelligence and economic warfare will not be found here.

Bryan, George S. THE SPY IN AMERICA. Philadelphia: J. B. Lippincott, 1943. 243 pp., bibliog., index.

Bryan says this was written for the general reader, and the style conforms with the intent. Covering the period from the American Revolution up to and including World War I, the author gives "enlivening tales of hardihood and courage." These stories of derring-do are presented with a certain sense of awe, the only exception being the last chapter on German espionage and sabotage in the United States in World War I. Bryan's indignation at such German doings is without doubt explained by the time of writing. This only provides some entertaining reading and is obviously not to be relied on for thoroughness or total accuracy. Bryan does not question many of the Civil War stories he retells and obviously is not conscious of many other aspects of American espionage in the years of peace.

Buckmaster, Maurice J. SPECIALLY EMPLOYED: THE STORY OF BRITISH AID TO FRENCH PATRIOTS OF THE RESISTANCE. London: The Batchworth Press, 1952. 200 pp., no index.

This was the first of the author's two books on the operations of the SOE's F Section during World War II.

Head of this section and an officer who gained some fame because of his work with French resistance, Buckmaster was in a position to provide much more information than he did. He admits at the start that he does not claim that incidents he relates are completely and factually accurate, to which Foot in *SOE in France* adds the comment, "quite so." The author tells of some of the SOE agents' operations in France but very little of his own and his section's work. What he does relate on recruitment, training, and communications of agents, as well as methods of infiltration and exfiltration, is also minimal. This is another instance where constraints of various sorts were at work, especially so shortly after the war. They were so strong that Buckmaster goes to great pains not to reveal the names of the persons discussed or even to mention SOE by name. Many other works deal more comprehensively with the subject than this volume (Foot's being one), and in others Buckmaster is described and his work discussed. In Foot's *Resistance* F Section and Buckmaster get a condensed treatment.

Buckmaster, Maurice J. THEY FOUGHT ALONE: THE STORY OF BRITISH AGENTS IN FRANCE. New York: W. W. Norton, 1958. 245 pp., no index [London: Odhams].

An improvement over the author's first book on SOE F Section's operations into France in World War II. Buckmaster gives a hint of the political problems the British found in dealing with de Gaulle and the Free French in London. There is still a reluctance to speak frankly of these difficulties and those with SOE's RF Section in sufficient detail, which few could supply with first-hand authority and accuracy. He provides one explanation for the absence of many important facts about his stewardship of F Section during most of the war: the section, he informs us, did not keep complete or proper records, and he was too busy to do so. Further, he was little inclined to think of the historian while the war was on. Another improvement over the earlier book is his inclusion of a number of humorous anecdotes that enhance the interest of a well-paced narrative. Foot's comment in *SOE in France* is that there is no claim that this new book is completely accurate.

Bulloch, John. AKIN TO TREASON. London: Arthur Barker, 1966. 183 pp., index.

Bulloch attempts to analyze the motives of Britons who committed acts "akin to treason" from the Boer War to the present. He also writes of the actual trials and sentences and the British legal provisions dealing with them. Individuals and cases he examines are varied, with names now famous in espionage or other activities on behalf of a foreign power included: Casement, Amery and Joyce, Philby and Blake. Bulloch is as much at home in dealing with espionage and counterintelligence as he is with the general history of the many cases about which he writes. He is also inclined to perpetuate errors or to indulge in unrewarding speculation. This series of essays lacks source notes and suffers from the author's tendency to combine fact, opinion, and speculation. Bulloch accepts as proven the story about the treachery of the Dutch double agent King Kong (the failure at Arnhem in 1944); he is certainly not fully conversant with Blake's history, connections, and activities. On Philby, his speculations are a bit odd and off the mark. Studies such as Rebecca West's *The New Meaning of Treason* deal much more exhaustively with certain cases he covers, but his treatment of lesser-known cases of British collaboration in World War II is of value. Even here we find omissions, such as no mention of the British fascist who infiltrated the SIS and the French resistance organization Alliance as a German double agent during the 1939–1945 war. His judgment that the British security service is "a mixture of efficiency and inefficiency" brings him closer to the view in *Spy Ring* than to the picture in his history of MI5 (below) but appears consistent with his belief that there were many loopholes in the British security system.

Bulloch, John. M.I.5: THE ORIGIN AND HISTORY OF THE BRITISH COUNTER-ESPIONAGE SERVICE. London: Arthur Barker Ltd, 1963. 206 pp., index.

The contents are far less comprehensive than the title suggests. This book appeared at a time of adverse publicity and lowered esteem for MI5 stemming from cases such as that of George Blake and scandals like the Profumo affair. Vernon Kell, the first head of the security service, looms large and occupies much space in this account. One reason is undoubtedly the author's reliance on Kell's widow for some of his material, which also may partly account for the strong pro-Kell views. The work is especially skimpy on the period of World War II and after. MI5 failures against Soviet espionage do not get the attention they deserve, giving the book the appearance of being a selective account. Bulloch fails to provide sources for much of what he writes, adding to the criticism that this book can in no way be considered even to begin to deal with the history of the organization. A clue to the work's quality is its failure to dispose of the Scapa Flow spy story by a full account of the supposed operation.

Bulloch, John, and Miller, Henry. SPY RING: THE FULL STORY OF THE NAVAL SECRETS CASE. London: Secker and Warburg, 1961. 224 pp., no index.

A fairly competent treatment of what is known as the Portland spy case in Britain, this book was written shortly after the completion of the trial of Gordon Lonsdale, the Krogers (the Cohens), Harry Houghton, and Ethel Gee, which found them guilty of espionage. These Soviet agents and illegals, their methods of operations (modus operandi [m.o.]), their capture, and their trial are recounted along with some very astute and professional (from an intelligence point of view) observations on the case. The last chapter is a particularly good summary of the lapses in the British security system that permitted this Soviet success. The fact that the British, along with the Americans, made every effort to counter the effects of the U-2 setback is brought out. The book is marred by the authors' statements on certain Soviet matters, statements not supported by any evidence or else incorrect. Example: how do they know that Lonsdale was head of all Soviet agents in London and southern England? Or that Russian agents in 1961 in most countries, including Britain, were small fry? (We have since learned this was not the case.) Or exactly what Soviet intelligence needed when it planned the Portland operation? The authors are quite wrong in claiming that the Soviet m.o. in this operation established something new, i.e., the use of illegals with their own system of communications. At the time of writing, they were not in a position to know the full and correct story on all aspects of the operation, from recruitments to discovery and the break-up of the net; consequently the subtitle ("The Full Story") is hardly on target.

Burleson, Clyde W. THE JENNIFER PROJECT. Englewood Cliffs, N.J.: Prentice-Hall, 1977. 179 pp., index [London: Sphere Books, 1979].

The purported story of the CIA's ship *Glomar Explorer* and of the operation to raise a sunken Soviet G-class submarine at the bottom of the Pacific. The objective was the acquisition by the United States of important intelligence from salvaged Soviet weapons, equipment (including cryptographic), and documents. Burleson has no credentials in intelligence work, and his previous writings were fiction. His principal contention is that CIA did succeed in the purpose of the entire operation but has attempted to disguise the truth. William Colby in *Honorable Men* calls such accounts nonsense. There are other things in this book that make one hesitate to accept its reliability. First, Chapter 12, on the history of CIA, is full of errors, many of them egregious. Second, sources cited are newspapers, magazines, or unidentified persons said to have been connected with the crew or the operation. We are not offered any first-hand or more authoritative sources than that. This probably accounts for qualifiers that Burleson uses with certain items—openers such as "It is likely," "There is reason to believe," "It is possible that." Readers interested in researching the *Glomar Explorer* operation are better advised to consult Varner and Collier's *A Matter of Risk.*

Butler, Ewan. AMATEUR AGENT. New York: W. W. Norton, 1963. 234 pp., index [London, Toronto: George G. Harrap].

In 1962, the British government seriously considered forbidding the publication of this book on security grounds. Reading it, one realizes how security standards have changed, even in Britain. Butler was a *London Times* correspondent in New York and Berlin before World War II who was recruited into SOE. He served in Cairo in charge of black propaganda for the Balkans and the Middle East and then in Stockholm as head of the German section of SOE. What he reveals cannot be considered of either great sensitivity or great significance to the history of intelligence of that war. There are a few anecdotes, including some on the early activities of OSS in Sweden and of OSS-SOE liaison there. Knowledgeable Americans found fault with some of his versions of OSS activities and conduct, however. As for accomplishments, he tells us he managed to insert seven Danes into northern Germany to collect intelligence at the end of the war. This was not exactly SOE's main responsibility, and sabotage and morale operations from Stockholm that he may have conducted do not stand out. Foot in *SOE in France* thought this book was useful in conveying the flavor of SOE.

Butler, Ewan. MASON-MAC: THE LIFE OF LT. GENERAL SIR NOEL MASON-MACFARLANE. London: Macmillan, 1972. 230 pp., index.

The subject of this biography served in a number of military intelligence assignments, among which was the post of military attaché in Berlin before World War II. He also was chief of intelligence in the British Expeditionary Force in France. These assignments, not to speak of that of heading the British Military Mission to Russia should have provided Butler, an old friend, with considerable material on Mason-Macfarlane's intelligence work. He gives, however, only snippets of intelligence interest, one of the most notable being Mason-Mac's toying with the idea of assassinating Hitler. Butler does touch on a little-known event that almost affected the Mincemeat deception operation in 1943. This was the shooting down of a British aircraft carrying a British officer to Gibraltar to brief Mason-Mac, then the governor, on planned Operation Torch, the invasion of Africa. The body and the "eyes only" sealed envelope were handed over to the British by the Spaniards intact, though there was no certainty at the time that the envelope had not been opened. This incident is also discussed by Colvin in *The Unknown Courier* and by Darling in *Sunday at Large.* Butler appears mistaken when he accuses Mason-Macfarlane of going off on his own to deceive the Germans prior to the invasion of North Africa. According to Wheatley in *The Deception Planners,* his actions were part of the deception plan.

Bywater, Hector, and Ferraby, H. C. STRANGE INTELLIGENCE: MEMOIRS OF NAVAL SECRET SERVICE. London: Constable, 1931. 292 pp., index.

Bywater and Ferraby, described as writers on naval subjects, seem to have derived motivation to write this volume from books about intelligence that held such work up to derision. Feeling that detractors knew little of what British naval intelligence had accomplished (Compton Mackenzie is prominently named as an example), they wrote this paean of praise to British naval intelligence. This service is described as one that succeeded during the whole of World War I and the four years preceding it in great feats of information gathering on German naval developments; it was, according to them, an indispensable factor in winning the war and a prime factor in the defeat of the German U-boat. The only source given for these sweeping judgments and fulsome praise are some 1930 articles in the London *Daily Telegraph.* They qualify their remarks by saying that the book is a partial record of British naval intelligence for the period covered and that much more was contained in confidential files. Knowing what we now do of the accomplishments of Admiral Hall and British naval intelligence, we can assume the authors were made privy to some inside information, although Hall does not figure here at all. The chapter on the Battle of Jutland does not mention the mistakes committed by the British in their use of Room 40 decrypts and is reflective of the less-than-central treatment accorded this strategic intelligence success. The successes the authors claim for naval intelligence of the prewar period seem exaggerated in the light of later evidence. It would be better to rely on William James's *The Eyes of the Navy.* Grant's study, *U-Boat Intelligence,* calls *Strange Intelligence* a mix of fact and fiction.

C

Caldwell, Oliver J. A SECRET WAR: AMERICANS IN CHINA 1944–45. Carbondale: Southern Illinois Univ. Press, 1972. 214 pp., index.

Born and educated in China, and having been a teacher there, Caldwell was a natural recruit for OSS service. Elizabeth MacDonald in her personal history of her days in OSS refers to him as the most unforgettable of the four missionaries in OSS she writes about and the one "who most readily assumed the cloak and dagger." There is comparatively little written on the intelligence history in China in World War II, especially of OSS there, so Caldwell might have contributed something of significance on the subject. This is not the case, despite the fact that Caldwell had the perspective of over a quarter-century. We do get his views on the differences between OSS and Captain Miles of SACO (the U.S.-Chinese intelligence arrangement), on SACO and Miles, on Tai Li and his control of Chinese intelligence, on differences between Tai Li and OSS, and on some other matters; but nothing is discussed in any depth. Caldwell tells some anecdotes from his OSS work in psychological warfare operations, and he touches on one counterintelligence case. If he has more knowledge of intelligence matters, however, he neglects to share it. His judgments of personalities and events are subjective, with no references to authoritative writings or documents. When he writes of the Hurley-Miles "clique" against General Stilwell, for example, he also admits he does not know what connection there was between these two. Caldwell's sections on the differences among U.S. intelligence organizations in China reflects the predominant OSS point of view. For another perspective, Miles's *A Different Kind of War* is very useful.

Calvocoressi, Peter. TOP SECRET ULTRA. London: Cassell, 1980. 127 pp., index [New York: Pantheon Books].

Calvocoressi served as an RAF intelligence officer at Bletchley Park (BP) between 1940 and 1945. He was the second British officer who worked on substantive matters at BP to write on the subject of Ultra, trying to give some account of "what Ultra was, how it was got and what its uses were." With first-hand knowledge of some of the things he writes, he has made an important additional contribution to the growing literature and knowledge of this strategic cryptologic success. Calvocoressi gives information about the organization and workings of BP that supplements that found in Bennett's *Ultra in the West.*

Of the many items of value, one is of considerable importance to scholars and writers. Calvocoressi makes it clear that much material on the huts at BP is not to be found among the Public Record Office material cleared for public scrutiny. His appendix on this point is the most precise and revealing that has appeared. The researcher is alerted that works dealing with Ultra based solely or overwhelmingly on PRO records cannot automatically be considered the final word on a particular matter. He illustrates this by citing the report he coauthored on signals intelligence available to the Allies prior to the German 1944 attack in the Ardennes, which is not to be found in the PRO records. This fact may account for this book's differences from Lewin's treatment of the intelligence aspects of this major attack (*Ultra Goes to War*).

Calvocoressi also touches upon the British means for passing to the Soviets in disguised form intelligence derived from Ultra traffic. Hinsley's second volume of *British Intelligence in the Second World War* (London: Her Majesty's Stationery Office, 1981), which appeared too late to be included in this bibliography, throws light on this matter and clarifies any confusion resulting from remarks by Edward Crankshaw, one of the channels named by Calvocoressi. Hinsley also mentions the Air Operational Watch. Calvocoressi might have discussed in more depth the role of Ultra in the Battle of Britain. Pincher's *Their Trade Is Treachery* mentions, incidentally, the existence of a Soviet penetration of the air section of BP. Most difficult to reconcile is Calvocoressi's seeming equation of Ultra only with decrypted Enigma traffic, a matter of basic importance that, it is to be hoped, future disclosures will clarify.

Campbell, Rodney. THE LUCIANO PROJECT: THE SECRET WARTIME COLLABORATION OF THE MAFIA AND THE U.S. NAVY. New York: McGraw-Hill, 1977. 282 pp., bibliog., index.

After World War II, reports circulated and periodicals published stories of alleged U.S. Navy or U.S. government arrangements to use the Mafia during the war. Campbell based this book on the 1954 Herlands Report that was made to Governor Dewey of New York, who had ordered it as a means of ascertaining the facts about the cooperation of Mafia figure Lucky Luciano with the U.S. armed forces. At the request of the U.S. Navy, the Herlands Report was kept secret. Not until 1976 was the wish of the Office of Naval Intelligence reviewed and overruled.

Campbell does a fine piece of work in tracing events connected with this cooperative arrangement, which was designed to result in intelligence and security benefits for the United States. The Axis' sabotage and intelligence threat to U.S. East Coast ports turns out to have been greatly exaggerated. Campbell does well in analyzing the rationale and means used by U.S. officials in disavowing the cooperation. Lacking access to U.S. Navy and other U.S. departmental records, Campbell never really answers certain questions—for example, what, if any, intelligence on Italy was actually produced via this strange partnership, the precedent for more controversial postwar Mafia contacts with CIA.

Carpozi, George, Jr. RED SPIES IN THE U.S. New Rochelle, N.Y.: Arlington House, 1973. 250 pp., index.

Carpozi's book was his third on Soviet espionage; it was written without the assistance of the FBI, unlike the first two, due to a change in FBI policy after J. Edgar Hoover's death. Carpozi gives no sources except when he quotes from an official announcement or indictment. Cases he writes of include the Morros-Sterns-Foster-Soble group, which takes up the bulk of the book; the Harris-Safford involvement with Soviet espionage; the Krogers (Cohens); and a few others. The results are mixed. Carpozi is able to uncover significant or interesting facts, but he carelessly includes incorrect or unsubstantiated remarks. He tells us of the characters and personalities of Martha Dodd Stern and Jane Foster, discusses Boris Morros's motives in revealing to the FBI his work for the Soviets, and identifies the problem of Soviet illegals in the United States. Oddly, he asserts that Martha Dodd performed the Soviets' first mission of subversion in the United States, that Harry Houghton was the top Soviet spy in Britain, that the Kremlin concentrated on British naval installations in Britain because of the extreme security of U.S. ones, that the Zlatovskis were in Czechoslovakia, that George Zlatovski was in OSS, that Pawel Monat identified the existence of a Soviet network in a British naval base, and that the Krogers (Cohens) had been chosen by the Soviets to succeed the Rosenbergs—all mistakes, guesses, or unsupported claims. Most serious of all the assumptions is the linking of the Morros-Sterns-Soble group with the Rosenbergs, Fuchs, and even Abel. Carpozi's message about Soviet espionage as a continuing, resolute effort was out of tune with contemporary popular U.S. attitudes toward national security questions.

Carr, Barbara. SPY IN THE SUN: THE STORY OF YURIY LOGINOV. Cape Town, S. Afr.: Howard Timmins, 1969. 224 pp., no index.

Yuriy Loginov is the Soviet illegal arrested by the South African security police in 1967. This account is based on South African records, including interrogation reports, that were supplied Carr for the writing of a book on the case. A journalist making no claims to knowledge of intelligence matters, she wrote this in semifictional form "to make a true situation more interesting." Not only is it based on official records, it often reads as such. Worse, it reads like a propaganda effort inspired by those wishing to identify internal discontent with Communist and Soviet inspiration. The many faults and shortcomings overshadow one of the lengthier and more complete expositions of Soviet illegal modus operandi, which stands up if particular details do not.

Carr is not the person to discern errors or to make any significant observations on the case. She does not go into how Loginov was captured or the reasons for his conduct. She is not able to ask such questions as: Was Loginov's version of his activities over a period of years (including his training) exactly and wholly the truth? Was it likely he was assigned to South Africa to perform duties not really requiring an illegal? What explanation did intelligence experts provide for portions of the Loginov story that were questionable? That Carr did not comment on the silliness of the story of American code clerks' being guarded as are Soviet code clerks, is a good example of her inadequacy on intelligence and security subjects. The epilogue is of no intelligence relevance. The Loginov case needs more competent treatment than this.

Carter, Carolle J. THE SHAMROCK AND THE SWASTIKA: GERMAN ESPIONAGE IN IRELAND IN WORLD WAR II. Palo Alto, Calif.: Pacific Books, 1977. 250 pp., bibliog., index.

Carter's effort is far from the final word on the subject. It relies largely on German sources, obviously the prime choice since it is concerned with German espionage; but the absence of access to Irish and British files makes it less than comprehensive. With such files unavailable, Carter got the story of the Irish side principally from an individual, now deceased, who assisted Irish military intelligence. The tale of Irish intelligence officers working with the British to thwart the Nazis, is one of the great twists in intelligence history, considering the violence of the past Irish-British intelligence war. The author is best when she writes of the failures and the incredible ineptitude of the German intelligence services, both the Abwehr and the SD, in their

Irish operations; the book is loaded with instructive examples of bad intelligence planning and practice. David Kahn in a review believed the work did not give the sum of the effect of German espionage in Ireland in the war.

Caskie, Donald C. THE TARTAN PIMPERNEL. London: Oldbourne, 1957. 270 pp., no index.

Caskie, who served as pastor of the Scottish Church in Paris in 1940, became involved in escape and evasion work (E&E) as part of the Ian Garrow organization in 1940–1941 and was one of the early pioneers of British E&E in France. One needs to read later works, such as Darling's *Secret Sunday* and Langley's *Fight Another Day,* to get a more complete view of the Garrow organization and the reasons for its collapse. Caskie did not know that the Germans and the Vichy authorities were aware of all moves by Garrow, nor was he aware when he wrote this book that London had failed to pass to the group derogatory information it had on the British traitor responsible for the betrayal of the author, Garrow, and others (see Langley). An interesting item of historical interest is his disclosure that the U.S. consul in Marseilles was used by the British to supply new identity papers to British soldiers in the E&E pipeline, documenting them as civilians. Whether this was done with the knowledge and approval of the consul's superiors in Vichy or Washington is not indicated.

Castro Hidalgo, Orlando. SPY FOR FIDEL. Miami: E. A. Seemann, 1971. 110 pp., no index.

This is the first book on Cuban intelligence written by an officer of that service. Castro Hidalgo was an officer of the DGI, the Cuban General Directorate of Intelligence, the foreign intelligence service. While stationed in Paris in 1969, he defected to the Americans. He provides first-hand information on the DGI's organization, training, personnel, modus operandi, and targets. The appendix, entitled "A Brief History of the DGI," is especially useful as a resumé and contributes to the main text. Cuban interest in Africa is here exposed long before Cuban involvement, including ties of intelligence, attracted world attention. The author could have been more specific on dates of events and could have elaborated more on many points. Brevity was overdone.

Cave Brown, Anthony. BODYGUARD OF LIES. New York: Harper and Row, 1975. 828 pp., bibliog., notes, index [London: W.H. Allen].

Deception in World War II attracted the attention of researchers and writers relatively late. Cave Brown's enormous book stimulated interest by focusing on this subject. Stupendous research taking some seven years produced the story of the Allied deception organization and operations connected with the 1944 invasion of Europe, culminating in the greatest of them designed to mislead the Germans. A potentially great study and reliable reference work on the subject, this has been severely criticized by knowledgeable British personalities. Reviews by Sir Dennis Wheatley, Hugh Trevor-Roper, and Michael Howard not only refute the book's central thesis on deception but also cite some errors that so mar it as to render it untrustworthy as history, according to Trevor-Roper. Sir Dennis, a member of the London Controlling Section (LCS), the body that coordinated and directed Allied deceptions in London, wrote in *RUSI* that Cave Brown's book was a source of "historical misinformation" and agreed with Trevor-Roper's judgment that it was "a congeries of stories united only by a thesis which gravely distorts the truth." Trevor-Roper's detailed review in the *New York Review of Books* makes a number of critical points among which are the following. Its thesis that the deception program and all British intelligence were controlled by MI6 is wrong; too much initiative is ascribed to LCS; the most striking successes were not by LCS but by deception specialists in the war theaters or by B1A of MI5; Menzies, the head of MI6, was not the hero of the intelligence war; and it was Ultra that was central to intelligence operations and successes, not MI6. The association of Menzies and Canaris, the head of the Abwehr, and the identification of the latter as a source for MI6 are called "purest fantasy." So, too, is his story of the reason for the assassination of Heydrich. Wheatley calls the stories of Menzies's relations with Canaris "complete nonsense." Howard in the *Times Literary Supplement* judges Cave Brown to be a journalist writing popular history, not a serious historian. He finds the book lacking in discrimination on accuracy of accounts and says "facts, gossip, rumor, irrelevancies, [and] speculation" are all included. Some errors he felt were dangerously misleading. These criticisms seem justified, and the list can be expanded.

A work like this that stimulates research has its shortcomings revealed as new material becomes available. New findings have shown up Cave Brown's sections on Ultra, the Coventry raid, the extent of forewarnings of German intentions, and the exact role of Ultra in the sinking of the *Bismarck*. Insistence that the Germans "had consistently broken into every Russian cryptosystem from the highest commands down to battalion" is contrary to other evidence and is not ascribed to a source; neither is his story that Colonel Fellers of the U.S. Army was used for deception by the British. The use of such material as was available did not prevent errors of detail, such as making it appear that William Friedman was in charge of the 1920s Black Chamber or mistaking the intelligence consequences of the loss of the courier just before the Torch invasion. The exact role of the agent King Kong in Holland is still being debated. It is a paradox that in his wish to be encyclopedic on the subject of deception operations, Cave Brown produced a history of many Allied and especially British intelligence operations in the war in certain theaters that can be used as a reference on particular operations only if it is used as a starting point and further research is pursued on the matter elsewhere. Mure in *Practice to Deceive* supports Cave Brown on his controversial version of Allied deception in connection with peace feelers by the German satellites.

Cave Brown, Anthony, ed. THE SECRET WAR REPORT OF THE OSS. New York: Berkley, 1976. 570 pp., bibliog., no index.

This is a reprint of the declassified official history of the U.S. Department of War's *War Report of the OSS,* rearranged, edited, and abridged by Cave Brown. He has also added certain material and deleted the Far East segment, thus confining it to European and North African operations. The commentaries of Cave Brown add to the understanding of a number of events and identify a number of individuals involved. The latter change is particularly helpful since the official history made it a rule to exclude most names of OSS personnel. Thus he identifies Malcolm Muggeridge, Frank Wisner, and many others; there are also some observations like the one that this history reveals for the first time ever the financial organization and methods of a secret service.

All the same, the reader and researcher must be on the lookout for a number of errors and controversial statements in these commentaries. There is the old rejected story of Scapa Flow and Albert Oertel; Cave Brown confuses some of James Angleton's biographical details with those of his father; he credits Menzies and MI6 for organizing the Yugoslav coup in 1941; he tries to make General Donovan a tool of Cardinal Spellman, Catholic interests, and Kermit Roosevelt; he is not aware that David Bruce did rush ashore in Normandy as did Donovan in Sicily; he maintains the French resistance nets around Paris in 1943 were used as pawns in a deception scheme, or that small European resistance movements were used "ruthlessly" for strategic deception; he also claims that the Anglo-American intelligence alliance against the Soviets and their allies was "super-successful"; his version of why Foot's *SOE in France* was released takes no account of British criticisms of SOE performance in France; he says Tom Karamassines was in SI when he really was in X-2; he says General Donovan demanded that OSS recruit only monarchists among Italians, when it actually recruited

Italians of all political persuasions; many veterans of OSS do not recall or have trouble confirming the accuracy of his story of the American OSS agent who infiltrated Albania toward the end of the war and vanished; OSS may have been parsimonious in some sections, as he says, but was generous in others since separation pay was usually determined by each commanding officer; EAM (the communist-dominated resistance organization) and its army ELAS in Greece were under the control of the Greek communists from the start. There are undoubtedly others that experts would be able to spot.

Central Intelligence Agency. INTELLIGENCE IN THE WAR OF INDEPENDENCE. Washington, D.C.: CIA, 1976. 40 pp., no index.

This short work was published by CIA as an employee orientation handbook. Timed as a bicentennial work, it also commemorates the two hundredth anniversary of Nathan Hale's death. It represents the contribution of the Historical Intelligence division of CIA, which had on its staff some very knowledgeable students of the history of American intelligence and especially of the Revolution and the earlier years of the republic. The handbook touches on the general categories of organization, techniques, and personalities. Within these, it gives short examples of cover, disguise, secrecy, secret writing, communications interception, CI, deception, foreign intelligence, special operations, covert action, political action, and intelligence analysis and estimates. Reading this will quickly dispel the thought that Americans have no tradition or talent for intelligence work and lead to the realization that virtually all intelligence techniques and methods have ancestors. A quick, commendable introduction to the subject. A reviewer of other books in the *New York Times,* referred to this one as "kid stuff," an opinion that reflected the prevailing climate toward intelligence and particularly CIA as much as the predisposition of the reviewer.

Central Intelligence Agency. THE ROTE KAPELLE: THE CIA'S HISTORY OF SOVIET INTELLIGENCE AND ESPIONAGE NETWORKS IN WESTERN EUROPE 1936–1945. Washington, D.C.: University Publications of America, 1979. 390 pp., no index.

This study was made under the direction and with the participation of some of the agency's most knowledgeable analysts in counterintelligence. It was previously classified and deposited in the U.S. National Archives. It will remain the measure of other works on the subject until new information is discovered and released by others, particularly the Swiss. Drawing chiefly from radio messages deciphered by the Germans, it helps to offset sensationalistic works (such as Accoce and Quet's *A Man Called Lucy*) or self-serving or political volumes (Trepper's *The Great Game* or Rado's *Codename Dora*). As a good CI study should, it readily recognizes and admits gaps in its knowledge and takes care to distinguish fact from speculation. It is loaded with fascinating items in both categories and presents one of the best and most reliable pictures available on the intricacies and operating procedures of Soviet espionage at that time. Left unanswered are a number of questions. Among them are: What was the exact role of Swiss intelligence? How was intelligence from Germany passed to Lucy? What were the identities of all of the German sources? What was Trepper's true role after his capture by the Germans? Editing would have improved the organization and the content, originally tailored for a specialized and somewhat knowledgeable audience. To read this with some ease, some prior knowledge of the Soviet networks is needed. An index would be helpful in future editions.

Central Intelligence Agency and Mathtech. COVERT REARMAMENT IN GERMANY 1919–1939: DECEPTION AND MISPERCEPTION. Washington, D.C.: CIA, Office of Research and Development, March 1979. 241 pp., bibliog., no index.

The authors deal with a subject not only of historical interest but also of considerable relevance to current questions of arms control. There is no claim this is anything but a preliminary effort to cover a story never fully told. Based on overt material, the study provides some valuable insights, lists a number of lessons, and makes a start in exploring an important subject. However, it is, at the same time, handicapped by its sources in answering a central question: to what extent exactly Allied intelligence services, particularly those of France and Great Britain, knew of German evasions of disarmament provisions. The answer would allow the reader to judge conclusions reached in this study with greater confidence, especially the conclusion that even on-site inspection by dominant powers furnishes no guarantee that arms evasion will be detected. The authors, in commenting on a 1954 book by Georges Castellan, produce contrary evidence. Castellan's work was based entirely on French intelligence records, and to the authors of this study it "demonstrates the very intensive coverage and general accuracy of the [French] Deuxieme Bureau's intelligence on this subject." Similarly, there is the problem of reconciling one of the study's seven main lessons, that political leaders tend to ignore awkward intelligence, with the conclusion that there is no guarantee of evasion detection. Either there was good intelligence that was ignored (as is implied by the Castellan findings), or there was not. A definite statement on this point would show whether deception or misperception (or self-deception) was the more important ingredient in Allied policy toward covert German evasions.

Central Intelligence Agency and Mathtech. DECEPTION MAXIMS: FACT AND FOLKLORE. Washington, D.C.: CIA, Office of Research and Development, January 1980. 48 pp., bibliog., no index.

A part of an ongoing research program staffed by CIA and Mathtech, with Barton Whaley, the student of and writer on deception, as one of the team. The attention given to deception reflects increased interest in it as an intelligence and political/military weapon in recent years. One stimulant has undoubtedly been the revelations of the great Allied deception successes against the Germans in World War II. This is a commendable piece of work, high in quality and presented in language devoid of any pretension or scholarly jargon. The ten maxims discussed represent the synthesis of a number of historical case studies. The project is to provide intelligence analysts aid in dealing with the problem of deception by opposition forces. There is no claim that the maxims listed are immutable or the study exhaustive; it is, rather, a pathfinding work.

Central Intelligence Agency and Mathtech. THOUGHTS ON THE COST-EFFECTIVENESS OF DECEPTION AND RELATED TACTICS IN THE AIR WAR 1939 to 1945. Washington, D.C.: CIA, Office of Research and Development, March 1979. 166 pp., index.

The title is too sweeping. The air war that is covered is really the RAF bomber offensive in Europe and in essence just night bombing. The authors are more precise in delineating the limitations of the study. It is said to be a preliminary analysis with only initial observations. The task of designing a cost-benefit model is candidly described as possible but formidable. The method used is explained as "two shortcuts that give rough but convincing answers." Keeping in mind these qualifications, one can accept the study as having an admirable objective, with conclusions and lessons that seem reasonable. The main objective is to create an awareness of the potential of deception and to show the need for "counterdeception inquiry." The main conclusion and lesson, that wartime deception was cost-effective, is equally applicable to current military conflicts. Follow-up efforts along this line need to delve more deeply into certain matters. For example, research could determine more exactly how many personnel were assigned to deception activities prior to the June 1944 landing in Normandy, a number that is guessed at here.

Chambers, Whittaker. WITNESS. Chicago: Henry Regnery, 1952. 799 pp., index [New York: Random House. London: A. Deutsch, 1953].

Witness, which was an immediate best-seller, is regarded as a milestone book. According to Dallin in *Soviet Espionage,* U.S. public opinion had its turning point on Soviet espionage following Chambers's revelations and the resultant congressional and legal proceedings. Meyer in *Facing Reality* believed the subsequent Hiss case gave public opinion another shove in the direction of suspicion of Soviet designs, where it had first been directed by the Gouzenko case. After disclosures by defectors like Elizabeth Bentley, there was also a turn in U.S. public and official attitudes toward communism that led to a major crackdown against U.S. communists.

Chambers's account of his work for the communist cause and for the Soviets includes interesting details of Soviet clandestine methods of operating and of penetration of intelligence targets. There are the lessons to ponder, such as the almost ten-year delay in the CI exploitation of what he had divulged. It was and is what *Nation* called a fascinating grab bag: an autobiography, an account of Chambers's underground work, and a religious tract. Most reviewers also agreed it was written by a man with rare literary talents, although those who rejected the political and other lessons injected by Chambers rejected him as a writer of prose. His version of clandestine activities substantially stands after three decades and should be read as an evocation of the temper of a particular time in intelligence history and as a first-hand account of a Soviet apparat in the United States. Though much has been written on the Hiss case, Weinstein's *Perjury: The Hiss-Chambers Case* gives the most up-to-date analysis based on new material and additional insights into Chambers and his version of events.

Chapman, Guy. THE DREYFUS TRIALS. New York: Stein and Day, 1972. 273 pp., bibliog., index [London: B. T. Batsford].

No bibliography of espionage and intelligence would be complete without including something on this famous case. Chapman's book is one of the latest efforts to deal with the many facets and complexities of the affair. This updating of his 1955 *Dreyfus Case: A Reassessment* (New York: Reynal) takes advantage of new material.

The Dreyfus case is fascinating and instructive in a number of ways. First, though surpassed by others when judged by the strategic damage and consequences of the espionage itself, it is surpassed by none as a political and intelligence cause célèbre. Second, it is a showcase, a horror showcase if you will, of how individuals in an intelligence organization, even in a democracy, can abuse their trust. Third, the performance of French counterintelligence was of the lowest quality when dealing with the investigation and arrest of Dreyfus. It is an object "how-not-to" lesson in CI. (On the other hand, the performance of a later CI section was both professional and courageous.) Fourth, it shows that just as there were intelligence officers guilty of errors and illegal or dishonest acts, so it was an intelligence officer who was honest and courageous enough to blow the whistle on an injustice. Fifth, it highlights the dangers that follow when intelligence officers approach an investigation with prejudice, bias, or a closed mind. These lessons are well brought out by Chapman, though some experts felt his 1955 book was too kind to Dreyfus's accusers and some may feel the same about this work. For a good, brief rendition of the French cryptanalytical work in connection with the case and of the French successes against Italian codes, see Kahn's *The Codebreakers.*

Chavez, Judy. DEFECTOR'S MISTRESS: THE JUDY CHAVEZ STORY. New York: Dell, 1979. 267 pp., no index.

When he defected to the United States, Arkady Shevchenko was the highest-ranking Soviet diplomat to have done so: he was the senior Soviet official in rank working at the United Nations in 1978. Chavez is an admitted prostitute with whom Shevchenko took up after his defection. She gives only bits and pieces of intelligence-connected matters: Shevchenko's views of the KGB, of the Soviet system, and of his possible role of some sort in intelligence prior to his flight. She does provide some glimpses of the handling, security, and resettlement procedures of the FBI and CIA in regard to defectors. Chavez's account falls far short of providing what the reader could hope to learn. Chavez, first of all, is not familiar enough with intelligence questions to do them justice. Second, her attitude is frankly and obviously hostile to Shevchenko, making the book unreliable as a case study of the psychological problems and reactions of defectors. Chavez was also not a trusted, inner cog in the government machinery handling the defector. Her allegations and sensational revelations on U.S. television led to questions to President Carter at a press conference about U.S. government funds' being used to pay for Chavez's sexual services to Shevchenko—probably the first time questions of this kind were ever put to a president. Persons familiar with the Shevchenko-Chavez affair say Chavez's reasons for this damaging portrayal of Shevchenko, who in the meanwhile has remarried, are not completely explained in the book.

Chester, Lewis; Fay, Stephen; and Young, Hugo. THE ZINOVIEV LETTER. Philadelphia: J. B. Lippincott, 1968. 195 pp., bibliog., index [London: Heinemann, 1967].

These British journalists called this the story of a successful conspiracy or series of conspiracies that led to the defeat of the Labor government in 1924. The release of the famous Zinoviev Letter also came at the moment a British-Soviet trade treaty was to be signed. Based on the original article written in the London *Sunday Times,* this piece of investigative journalism has lumped together the British intelligence services, the Conservative party Central Office, the British Foreign Office, and segments of the British press as being involved in these conspiracies. The authors' attempt to make their points and their case is not fully successful or convincing. The authors readily allow that even with the new documents they claim to have discovered, the evidence is still not complete. They admit that some areas of their story on the role of the secret services and of the politicians are "totally undocumented." Lastly, they allow they were sometimes obliged to speculate, though such speculation is clearly labeled as such. Their new version of the alleged forgery of the Zinoviev Letter is based on the evidence of one witness, the widow of one of the White Russians originally accused by the Soviets. Confidence in the authors' use of sources may be shaken by their uncritical acceptance of Winfried Lüdecke's writings on the role of Sidney Reilly in the case; Lüdecke's book is full of errors, and his charge that Reilly was the man who passed the Zinoviev Letter to the Foreign Office is not the solid evidence these authors wish to consider it. Lüdecke gave no source for his charge, and Reilly's wife called the segment of Lüdecke's *Behind the Scenes of Espionage* devoted to Reilly "abounding in inaccuracies." Additional support for Reilly's involvement in the Zinoviev Letter will be found in the writings of Robin Bruce Lockhart. For a minority theory that the letter originated with the Soviets, see Natalie Grant's article in *Soviet Studies* of October 1967; that view is also developed by Blackstock in *Agents of Deceit.*

Clark, Ronald William. THE MAN WHO BROKE PURPLE: THE LIFE OF THE WORLD'S GREATEST CRYPTOLOGIST,

COL. WILLIAM F. FRIEDMAN. London: Weidenfeld and Nicolson, 1977. 262 pp., index [Boston & Toronto: Little, Brown].

The first biography of Friedman. David Kahn had much to say about him in *The Codebreakers,* as did others, and Kahn's verdict that "Friedman was the world's greatest cryptologist" is accepted by Clark. Written with Friedman's widow's help, this book has been judged by many as a good outline of Friedman's career. Critics have noted the lack of source credits as well as the absence of a bibliography, but these are usually regarded as something to regret rather than a major shortcoming. Some critics have had serious reservations about parts of this work and about some of its major conclusions. They noted that because Clark did not have access to all Friedman's classified work, he perpetuated errors on Friedman's career and gave the wrong picture of the areas to which Friedman made unique contributions. The verdict of these critics has been that Clark's biography is not the full and accurate treatment the subject deserved. For this and other reasons, it would be prudent to heed the reviewer of the *USNI Proceedings,* who cautioned there is more to be said about this remarkable man than Clark told. That Friedman was a complex personality with amazing talents is not in dispute. What has yet to be determined is how his talents were applied, what exactly he accomplished, what his unique and abiding contributions to cryptography and cryptanalysis were, and finally what his style was.

Clarke, Dudley. SEVEN ASSIGNMENTS. London: Jonathan Cape, 1948. 262 pp., no index.

Field Marshal Wavell had a career-long interest in deception. It was he who had Clarke assigned to the Middle East, where Clarke organized a deception section. Clarke's work in deception and that of his A Force have received mention in certain books (such as Cave Brown's *Bodyguard of Lies*), but it was David Mure who would focus attention on him as the pioneer and genius in deception in World War II (see particularly *Master of Deception*). For those expecting to learn more of Clarke's deception work, this book will be a disappointment. It ends at the moment he assumes staff duties in the Middle East. Only in the introduction by Wavell do we get some hint of these duties. Wavell tells us that Clarke was involved in less orthodox services, "the story of which cannot yet be told," and that Clarke was good for work in misleading and mystifying opponents. Mure states that in 1953 Clarke wanted to publish a book on his deception work to counter bad publicity the British services had received from books on the Cicero and North Pole operations, but he was refused official approval to do so. Mure also qualifies Clarke's belief that he alone conceived and helped found the commandos.

Clayton, Aileen. THE ENEMY IS LISTENING. London: Hutchinson, 1980. 338 pp., notes, bibliog., index.

In *Ultra Goes to War,* Lewin wrote that the story of Y Service, responsible for maintaining a watch on the enemy's traffic, "is a triumph yet untold." Calvocoressi in *Top Secret Ultra* called interception the basis for the entire Ultra achievement, while R. V. Jones in *The Wizard War* and McLachlan in *Room 39* describe some of the work done by the naval and air intercept services of the British and acknowledge their vital contributions. Clayton, the first British WAAF to have been commissioned for intelligence duties, is the first specialist of any service to write on a portion of the Y Service. Her wartime memoir provides more details than have ever been published before on the RAF Y Service—its personnel, problems, and organization as well as its operational work. RAF intercept work in England in the early years of the war is described, but the focus is on the Middle East and North Africa. The distribution of intercept work among services, types of traffic and signals, forms of intercept, interservice coordination, functions relative to Bletchley Park, and the use of Ultra to facilitate Y Service work are all explained, as are the complications of the command structure. Clayton gives many examples of security or poor security on both sides and discloses tricks of the trade that facilitated the work of the code breakers; meaconing, jamming, and interference are also explained and illustrated. All this supplements information in R. V. Jones's account of the air and signals war. More than a story of the technical achievements of the RAF's Y Service, the book is, as the foreword says, about the qualities of individuals needed for its successes. Her story ends abruptly in early 1944; Clayton is frank in telling us that "lack of space and an ingrained sense of security" preclude her from covering all facets.

Cline, Ray S. SECRETS, SPIES AND SCHOLARS: BLUEPRINT OF THE ESSENTIAL CIA. Washington, D.C.: Acropolis Books, 1976. 272 pp., notes, index.

The *New York Times* review called this short history of CIA combined with autobiographical narrative the most authoritative book to date on CIA and the best explanation of the elements that made up modern intelligence production processing and distribution. Sir Maurice Oldfield, the scholarly former head of the British SIS, was quoted posthumuously in the *London Times* as calling this one of his four favorites on espionage and intelligence. Blackstock and Schaf's bibliography, *Intelligence, Espionage, Counterespionage and Covert Operations,* and DIS's bibliography, agreed with the praise, but *Library Journal* thought it an apologia for CIA, a retelling of tales of that organization with no noteworthy revelations.

Cline himself called this his account of the development of the role and functions of central intelligence in the United States. The illustrative materials were his own or those of colleagues with first-hand knowledge. Thirty years in U.S. intelligence in OSS, CIA, and the Department of

State gave Cline authority and first-hand experience on much of what he wrote about. But there was a slip here and there along with an occasional debatable judgment. The Berlin Tunnel operation was betrayed by the Soviet agent George Blake long before it was "discovered" by the Soviets; James Angleton disputed Cline's assurances that CIA paid for the 1956 Khrushchev speech; the U.S. Navy was not a participant in the Black Chamber of the 1920s; and the claim that the United States in 1960 or 1965 possessed the world's best intelligence system is open to debate.

Cline provided a modicum on the important and critical U.S. intelligence and policy discussions and studies on Vietnam up to 1966, and his very brief account of OSS operations made no mention of those into the Reich itself. Not everyone agreed fully with him on how good U.S. intelligence estimates have been. Still, it is difficult to understand the charge that Cline only retold old stories. His first-hand accounts were valuable confirmations or variations of other versions. He gave a first-hand picture of the U.S. estimative machinery; of cooperation in intelligence with the British when he served in London; and of many intelligence personalities, especially those on the U.S. intelligence estimates and analysis side. There is the larger perspective. He included a frank appraisal of the U.S. covert action operations in Iran and Guatemala in the 1950s and of the weakness in covert paramilitary action. He confirmed the use of U-2 planes flown by Taiwanese pilots over the People's Repulic of China prior to the use of satellites and revealed the inside debate on what to do with the 1956 Khrushchev speech. His recommendation to consolidate the main analytical staffs reflected the author's main experience and expertise. In regard to the charge the whole book was an apology for CIA, the reader should keep in mind that Cline wrote at a time of great turmoil and criticism of that agency. His opinion that respect for scholarship has given CIA a superiority in intellectual quality over the Soviet KGB and other totalitarian intelligence services will be widely accepted.

Cobban, Alfred. AMBASSADORS AND SECRET AGENTS: THE DIPLOMACY OF THE FIRST EARL OF MALMESBURY AT THE HAGUE. London: Jonathan Cape, 1954. 218 pp., bibliog., notes, index.

A most impressive work on secret service. Cobban's basic belief and premise was that little had been written on the role of secret service activities in British diplomacy. The situation in the 1780s in Holland, about which he wrote, presented an excellent case study for his conviction, quoted halfway through the book, that "there are situations in which secret maneuvers are the real heart of the diplomatic game." Utilizing official documents and the letters of the principals, he gives a fascinating picture of the secret intelligence, propaganda, and political war waged in the Dutch Republic in the 1780s by the English and the French. Though the activities of the British minister to The Hague, Sir James Harris, and of the British generally get the major coverage, the French are not neglected. Cobban tells of the involvement of Harris in the recruitment and handling of secret agents and of his plotting with Dutch political factions. French and British covert subsidies are named, the British support to the Prince of Orange not being omitted. There are a number of interesting parallels with recent history to be found in the events of this period. One is the secret dispatch of French troops in mufti to the Dutch Republic and the importance of the issue of whether the French had established a camp on the Meuse to stage such movement into Holland—reminiscent of the 1979 Soviet brigade issue in Cuba. The complaints that the French embassy at The Hague was really two embassies, one composed of agents and covert activists, also have a familiar ring. Sir William Eden appears peripherally as the envoy to Paris, but Cobban says nothing of his past intelligence work.

Cockerill, A. W. SIR PERCY SILLITOE. London: W. H. Allen, 1975. 216 pp., bibliog., index.

This biography of the man who headed MI5 between 1946 and 1950 is disappointing because the author has included very little on Sillitoe's MI5 tenure. It is largely on the subject's police career with only one chapter on the MI5 stage, and that is composed of generalities. Sillitoe, according to Hugh Trevor-Roper, was imposed on MI5 by Herbert Morrison of the Labor party in preference to "the intelligent Guy Liddell." Cockerill partly explains the void in his coverage of Sillitoe's security service by explaining that Sillitoe left little in writing. However, he claims that he was provided information by a number of MI5 personnel who to a man were unwilling to be identified. Either Cockerill was not told anything significant or he was inhibited by the Official Secrets Act. He informs us, too, that the Home Office refused to clear Sillitoe's first draft of his autobiography, *Cloak Without Dagger,* written in 1953, and deleted everything about MI5 that was of interest. Cockerill fails to deal adequately with the question of Sillitoe's performance in MI5. He observes that while other writers have, without exception, dismissed Sir Percy's work in MI5 as insignificant, he does not accept this judgment; but he does not succeed in producing evidence to refute it. He was unaware that Deacon in *A History of the British Secret Service* called Sillitoe a shrewd, competent administrator, often still underrated.

Cockerill, Sir George. WHAT FOOLS WE WERE. London: Hutchinson, 1944. 169 pp., index.

That Brigadier General Sir George Cockerill wrote this in the midst of World War II may be one reason that so much is left unsaid or unclarified. In World War I Sir George held the title of director of special intelligence of the general staff of the British War Office. His pre–World War I intelligence experience included service in the Indian Army's intelligence branch and in the War Office's Special Intelligence Sub-Division after the Boer War. In this latter position he studied such matters as censorship of cables, the security of ciphers, CI against sabotage and espionage, and the need for a censorship organization in wartime. Among the lessons he says he was taught by the Boer War was the need for an expert staff to undertake cryptanalysis; he claims he worked diligently to improve British ciphers before World War I. He then became head of the special intelligence section until 1908. At the start of the 1914 war, he provided War Office direction to the intelligence and security services about press, cable, and postal censorship. He has written only in general terms of his earlier posts and concentrated on economic warfare and the blockade in the war period. These latter events relied on censorship and propaganda, weapons he claims were forged in his directorate. Even so, only one-third of the book is concerned with World War I. Details on the workings of his special intelligence section are lacking; the author seems to have been less concerned with supplying them than with laying a claim to a place in history for certain innovations.

Colby, William, and Forbath, Peter. HONORABLE MEN: MY LIFE IN THE CIA. New York: Simon and Schuster, 1978. 474 pp., index [London: Hutchinson].

Colby has written, in conjunction with Forbath, about more than his life in CIA. The autobiography spans his years in OSS as well, when he survived dangerous missions into France and Norway. His philosophy about operations and the role of an intelligence service in a democratic society are the book's most significant features. They are doubly significant: not only are they the thoughts and memoirs of the former head of CIA, they were written at a time of debate in the United States on the place of intelligence in the governmental fabric.

Attacks on CIA were at their height during Colby's tenure, and his handling of the agency's response and its defense became the most controversial part of his stewardship. He reveals not only his side of the story but also his operational outlook on intelligence and the underlying philosophy on which it is based. His confidence that in his dealings with Congress and the White House he was sure of the Constitutional grounds for his actions surprised his predecessor, Richard Helms. His service in Vietnam with ambassadorial rank is another controversial part of his career, particularly with antiwar elements, and his version of events there and of his role should raise the debate to a more dispassionate level even if it does not end the controversy. The same can be said of his treatment of Chile and other matters.

By definition, a book such as this, written by a service chief, must be selective in content. Colby's operating and managerial outlook, his relations with senior colleagues, his manner of handling Congress and the demands for access to CIA secrets—these and other issues are still being debated, as are the completeness and accuracy of some of the accounts he gives. There are certainly points on which Colby's recall may not be infallible. John Bruce Lockhart, the former member of the British SIS, wrote in his review of *Honorable Men* that the book was unlikely to increase the status or reputation of its author. Interesting as this foreign view is, it would be fairer and more accurate to allow time to give greater perspective.

The work's publication, in itself, has had legal consequences that exacerbated the debate between critics and supporters of intelligence. According to congressional testimony and one point of view, this book was not properly submitted for CIA security review. Complaints were raised about dual standards of justice and about basing the decision to apply legal sanctions on a book's position on CIA or the intelligence community. CIA veterans agreed on the following: the book faithfully reflected Colby's preference and understanding of action operations, which mirrored the man's strong missionary and reformist strain, and the author was candid about his understanding of counterintelligence. For inside views from a senior level in CIA during Colby's stewardship, see Cord Meyer's *Facing Reality* and Phillips's *The Night Watch.*

Collier, Richard. TEN THOUSAND EYES. New York: E. P. Dutton, 1958. 314 pp., no index [London: Collins].

Collier, a British journalist, here wrote the exciting story of one of the networks in France during the German occupation in World War II. This network, concentrated in Normandy, collected intelligence on the German forces in the Atlantic wall as part of the overall Century network under Passy and the French BCRA in London. Collier had some access to French archives and drew upon both the memoirs and the memories of Passy and Colonel Remy (G. Renault-Roulier). This network acquired and forwarded to London the detailed plans for the German Atlantic wall, the system of fortifications and the defenses against invasion. M.R.D. Foot testifies that these plans were invaluable to the Allies, a testimony based on personal experience at Combined Operations headquarters (see *Resistance*). When this work was written, Collier was not familiar with the assignments of all personnel to various organizations operating in France, for he mistakenly puts F.F.E. Yeo-Thomas, who was really in the RF section of SOE, in the F section. There is, too, the question of whether he gives Passy too much credit for conceiving a system of having agents on the spot in occupied territories (compared with dispatching agents into and out of areas of intelligence interest). These are minor flaws in a book that is well written and that honors an effective network.

Colvin, Ian. CHIEF OF INTELLIGENCE. London: Victor Gollancz, 1951. 223 pp., bibliog., no index [New York: McGraw-Hill. *Master Spy*].

Winston Churchill wrote in *The Gathering Storm* that Colvin was a British journalist who before World War II had "plunged very deeply into German politics and established contacts of a most secret character with some of the important German generals." Wheeler-Bennett described him as a channel to the British of General Beck, leader of the German opposition. Such credentials increased interest in this book on Admiral Canaris of the Abwehr, as did Colvin's device of posing the question of whether

Canaris had been a British agent. (Colvin left the answer to the judgment of the reader.) In a series of essays on Canaris and German intelligence, the author tried to describe Canaris's character, his views, his role in the Abwehr and in German intelligence, and his place in German opposition to Hitler. Views of various individuals were inserted throughout. One of the earliest postwar works in English on Canaris, the book is obviously dated, contains a number of errors, and misdirects attention by posing the wrong central question. Colvin jumped to conclusions on the basis of the evidence available at the time: he judged precisely how Canaris encouraged opposition movements against Hitler and assumed Canaris knowingly passed intelligence to the Allies after the Polish campaign. Colvin also implies that Canaris's intelligence failures were designed to help the enemy. The author's style leads to statements subject to misinterpretation, such as the one that Cicero, the German agent in Turkey, got "the outline of Operation Overlord." Brissaud's *Canaris* deals largely with the admiral's opposition to the Nazi regime and rejects the agent theory. Trevor-Roper's *The Philby Affair* contains an essay on Canaris and a harsh conclusion about the effectiveness of the Abwehr as an intelligence organization.

Colvin, Ian. THE UNKNOWN COURIER. London: William Kimber, 1953. 206 pp., no index.

This is Colvin's somewhat disjointed and at times elliptical account of his search for the story of the Mincemeat operation, which involved the use of a corpse laden with deceptive documents to mislead the Germans and Italians on the true objective of the Allies following the North African campaign in 1943. The story of this operation was treated more authoritatively and completely by Montagu in *The Man Who Never Was.* Colvin's book, however, is not to be ignored by those interested in the operation and in the subject of deception. In researching the book Colvin was confused for a time by the discovery that there were *two* instances of corpses with documents washing ashore in Spain. The earlier incident occurred at the time of Torch and was not a deception operation; the body was that of a courier who was carrying highly secret documents to brief the governor of Gibraltar on the plans for the North African invasion. The existence of this other corpse was first mentioned in the memoirs of Sir Samuel Hoare. Subsequent to Colvin, the incident was touched upon by Butler in *Mason-Mac.* Montagu does not mention it. Colvin calls attention to some weaknesses in the planning and the documentation carried by the Mincemeat corpse. Darling's *Sunday at Large* has good coverage of the incident of the first courier.

Cookridge, E. H. THE MANY SIDES OF GEORGE BLAKE, ESQ.: THE COMPLETE DOSSIER. New York and Princeton, N.J.: Vertex, 1970. 254 pp., no index [London: Hodder, 1970. *George Blake: Double Agent*].

The life and career of SIS officer and Soviet agent George Blake and the many questions surrounding him have never been adequately tackled. The effort of Cookridge (real name Edward Spiro) does not do the job. An enlarged version of his 1962 book, it is lacking in source notes, unreliable on many central matters, and speculative on others. Foot in *SOE in France* called the 1962 version's references to SOE "wild." The net effect is to confuse what Blake really was, how he got where he did, and why. Cookridge's central thesis, that Blake was a double agent of the British service who finally chose the Soviets, is repeated throughout. Yet he pictures Blake as converting to communism while a prisoner in Korea, before he assumed this double agent role, and offers no evidence to support his claim. He ties in Blake with a variety of other cases, such as that of Czech agent Alfred Frenzel; he is either speculating or wrong. He describes General Gehlen as a senior Abwehr officer and Allen Dulles as the successor to Donovan as head of OSS. He was correct in saying that Blake betrayed the Berlin Tunnel to the Soviets; that fact was admitted years later by CIA retiree Harry Rositzke in his *The CIA's Secret Operations.*

Coon, Carleton S. A NORTH AFRICA STORY: AN ANTHROPOLOGIST AS OSS AGENT, 1941–1943. Ipswich, Mass: Gambit, 1980. 141 pp., index.

The late Harvard anthropologist wrote of his activities as first a COI and then an OSS operative in North Africa shortly after the events. The book covers the period 1942–1943; the postscript on Coon's OSS services after that is only four pages. Written in the form of a postaction report, it discusses the wide range of activities Coon had to perform and shows U.S. intelligence in the early stage of learning its craft. The author had to perform in a variety of ways: as trainer, collector of intelligence, CI officer, smuggler of arms via the diplomatic pouch, communicator, and organizer of subversive groups in Spanish Morocco. As if those were not sufficient, he was used in actual combat situations. Lessons learned for the future on cover, relations with the State Department, and the proper use of OSS are made clear in his report. There are a number of interesting vignettes and observations on State Department attitudes towards espionage, on personnel and attitudes of British SOE and SIS personnel, on the hectic days before the invasion of North Africa by the allies, and on the security of some U.S. generals on Gibraltar just prior to the landing. One wishes Coon had provided current comments as did the editors who give the historical setting for each segment. The historian would have appreciated hearing what the author had to say about Fernand de la Chapelle, a student of Coon's training school at the time he assassinated Admiral Darlan. Cave Brown's *The Secret War Report of the OSS* contains annotations that expand on the official text on the killing of Darlan and on de la Chapelle's connection with the Allied training school.

Cooper, Mathew. THE PHANTOM WAR: THE GERMAN STRUGGLE AGAINST SOVIET PARTISANS 1941–1944. London: MacDonald and Jane's, 1979. 194 pp., bibliog., notes, index [New York: Stein and Day. *The Nazi War Against Soviet Partisans 1941–1944*].

Cooper had previously written on the German army between the years 1939 and 1945; this volume is the result of research done in completing that book. It deals with German security policy in the USSR and the partisan war there, primarily from the German point of view. Acknowledging reliance on particular works (he names three), Cooper traces the history of German policy, its racial origins, and the results, which drove the populace to oppose the Germans. He is especially good on German organization and efforts to defeat or at least control the partisan threat and does not neglect German dissent to official policy, which correctly saw the official line as self-defeating. Estimates given on German casualties from partisan activity are a healthy contribution to the literature on the subject, which has relied up to now largely on Soviet claims.

There is, unfortunately, little on the intelligence war, though that little and the author's general comments about the subject are correct. Cooper has nothing on how the Germans used communications intelligence, though he speaks of radio communications between partisan headquarters and units in the field. Calvocoressi says in *Top Secret Ultra* that Soviet signal security was quite bad and as a result the Germans read a good deal of Soviet traffic. The author's reliance on only a few works for his segments on the Soviet partisans is a matter of concern, though the description of official Soviet neglect of planning and delays in organizing, coordinating, and supplying the partisans is probably correct and another healthy antidote to official Soviet versions. Cooper fails to cite sources for German casualties beyond General Jodl. There will be some debate on his estimate of the effect of the Soviet partisans.

Copeland, Miles. THE GAME OF NATIONS. New York: Simon and Schuster, 1969. 300 pp., bibliog., index [London: Weidenfeld and Nicolson].

Copeland, who served in the Middle East in the 1950s with CIA, defined the "game of nations" as what results when "all nations in their respective self-interest pursue their national goals by means—any means—short of war." What he calls "cryptodiplomacy" is the use of nonovert and abnormal channels of diplomacy to conduct relations and to pursue a nation's interests. This book describes and explains the "game" and its hidden side as practiced in the Middle East, concentrating on Egypt from the 1950s under Nasser to the Six-Day War of 1967. Copeland served in official and nonofficial positions during part of the period covered and presumably was in a position to tell accurately of many behind-the-scenes events in Egypt and Syria. That he saw Nasser frequently up to one point, as he claims, is a fact. Eveland, however, who Copeland testified was involved in some events, in his own book on his experiences with CIA in the area, *Ropes of Sand,* warned that Copeland may not always have been so accurate. He wrote that on more than one occasion he had evidence of Copeland's tendency to exaggerate. As for this work, Eveland remarked that Copeland credited Kermit Roosevelt of CIA with the "peaceful revolution" that allowed King Farouk to abdicate and said that Roosevelt had agreed to the military coup of Nasser and his followers even though he, Eveland, knew that CIA was caught by surprise when the coup took place. Eveland's observations tend to agree with the consensus of those familiar with events: that, perceptive as some of Copeland's writing on Nasser and his regime and on regional developments may be, Copeland's versions of behind-the-scenes events about which he learned later, and even those in which he said he was a participant, cannot be accepted automatically as reliable and accurate. Experts' opinion that he tended to be inaccurate (for example, Roosevelt did not know Nasser before the coup) make circumspection necessary.

Copeland, Miles. WITHOUT CLOAK OR DAGGER: THE TRUTH ABOUT THE NEW ESPIONAGE. New York: Simon and Schuster, 1974. 336 pp., index [London: Weidenfeld and Nicolson. *The Real Spy World*].

Copeland says in his foreword that "the flood of misinformation on spies and counterspies that is poured out to the public" was what tempted him to write on these subjects. The result is that he himself has contributed to the confusion and the errors. Responsible and knowledgeable former intelligence officers have had difficulty in reconciling much of what he writes with their knowledge and understanding of such matters. Equally unsupported are his version of his intelligence relationships and his claims or implications of having had access to classified information as a result of such relationships in the years preceding the publication of this book. He advises that he did not submit the work for CIA security review. Considering that agency's criteria for deletion of items, explained by Colby in *Honorable Men*—that errors and opinions could not be treated as classified—this book would have been returned to him virtually untouched had he submitted it. The reader is well advised not to consider the work a reliable reference about the "new espionage" or many other matters it touches upon.

The number of mistakes on even the simplest questions of organization show how divorced Copeland is from the actual facts. He continues to speak of OSO in CIA when it ceased to exist some twenty years earlier and to assure us that CIA desk officers are groomed to replace their respective chiefs of station. Copeland uses terms that are never heard in CIA (such as "marines") and repeatedly mentions a component of CIA that did not exist. He confuses clandestine and covert operations in a manner surprising for someone who claims long and continuous connections with or service in intelligence, and he makes errors even on matters of public knowledge, such as CIA's and the State Department's respective retirement benefits. The KGB he refers to as the KVD. Certain of his pronouncements on Soviet operational philosophy and methods of operating are misleading for 1974.

Other errors indicate that some reviewers who thought it an apologia for CIA or an authorized work did not read it carefully or else did not know much about the subject. Mistakes that discredit CIA include the description of a supposed CIA stable of former Nazi intelligence officers used to conduct foreign liaison and the statement that CIA ran operations in British labor and student groups. More serious are his allegations or intimations that CIA covered up or "disposed of" hostile penetrations into that organization. It is difficult to identify many cases he cites as examples of various operational techniques, so one is better advised to ignore them, even in those couple of better chapters where conventional espionage and counterespionage means are treated. There he shrewdly guesses that had Kim Philby cooperated with British authorities when he was discovered to be a Soviet agent, he might have been allowed to live out his life on a pension, a treatment close to that later known to be accorded Anthony Blunt. For comments on Copeland and his remarks on alleged CIA operations in Britain, see Cord Meyer's *Facing Reality.*

Corson, William R. THE ARMIES OF IGNORANCE: THE RISE OF THE AMERICAN INTELLIGENCE EMPIRE. New York: Dial Press/James Wade, 1977. 599 pp., bibliog., index.

A pioneer attempt at writing a history of U.S. intelligence, this work includes an examination of the factors that went into the formation of the U.S. intelligence establishment and a survey of its functioning beginning with the period just prior to Pearl Harbor. An "outsider-insider" of U.S. intelligence, Corson is well qualified for the enormous task. The historical portions are placed at the beginning and end; the afterword is concerned with the exploits of U.S. spies from the American Revolution to World War I. The rest of the book covers the political and legal bases, the struggles for control, the incessant political and bureaucratic quarrels and maneuvering, and the evolving relationships within the intelligence community and between it and the executive branch and Congress since World War II. It includes recommendations for the future.

Corson uses newly available material and interviews knowledgeable sources; he used much of the overt literature. The result, according to a review in *American Historical Review,* by Lyman Kirkpatrick, the intelligence scholar and former CIA official, is a more comprehensive tracing of the evolution of the U.S. system than can be found in previous studies. Kirkpatrick points out that Corson is weakest in areas where no documentation exists, i.e., interpersonal relations, and that exception could be taken to some of the material selected and events emphasized. One serious omission: *The Armies of Ignorance* fails to deal adequately with the full range of U.S. intelligence gathering and covert action between the Revolution and World War II. Corson does not give a full and accurate picture of the activities of U.S. presidents in intelligence history. Thus, his bibliography fails to list Wriston's *Executive Agents in American Foreign Relations.* Likewise, while properly emphasizing the legacy of General Ralph Van Deman, he fails to mention the U.S. organizations under John Franklin Carter (Jay Franklin) and Colonel John Grombach, though there are seeming hints of the latter. Sixty percent of the appendix chapter is devoted to Civil War intelligence and agents. Some of the accounts are of doubtful authenticity (see the reference to Fischel's article on the mythology of Civil War intelligence in the comments to Stern's *Secret Missions of the Civil War*).

The errors include the reference to the supposed role of Israeli intelligence in the discovery of Burgess, Maclean, and Philby; the explanation for the removal of James Angleton from CIA; the account of the Iranian coup; the reliance on Winterbotham for the refuted story of the bombing of Coventry; and the story that British officials had informed General Donovan of Churchill's decision to sacrifice Coventry to protect Ultra.

For the latest and most painstaking research on Donovan

and the creation of OSS and CIA, including mention of the Carter and Grombach organizations, see Troy's *Donovan and the CIA*. See also Kirkpatrick's *The Real CIA* on Grombach's group.

Crawley, Aidan. ESCAPE FROM GERMANY: A HISTORY OF RAF ESCAPES DURING THE WAR. London: Collins, 1956. 308 pp., index [New York: Simon and Schuster].

Crawley was asked by the British Air Ministry to write a history of RAF escapes from German POW camps in World War II. This is an abbreviated version of that history. Its focus is on escape from camps, with evasion getting only secondary treatment. Crawley, a POW himself, admits this is in no way a complete record. Part 4, which recounts the saga of the freedom and evacuation of POWs, is not really connected with the subject of the book but is more a part of the general history of RAF POWs.

Though interesting, the book fails to tell the full story of the combined effort that went into the planning, preparation, and support for escape and evasion, which can be learned from other works. Among them is Hutton's *Official Secret*, published five years after this book, which revealed the existence of escape aids and told how they were produced and made available to POWs. More recently, there has been the excellent *MI 9* by Foot and Langley. These works impart a fuller picture of the outside aid that went into escape efforts, though some secrets were still withheld as late as 1979. Intelligence officers will applaud Crawley's rule that "the basis of escape is intelligence." They may not agree that escape is a military operation.

Critchley, Julian. WARNING AND RESPONSE: A STUDY OF SURPRISE ATTACK IN THE 20TH CENTURY AND AN ANALYSIS OF ITS LESSONS FOR THE FUTURE. London: Leo Cooper, 1978. 121 pp., notes, no index.

Critchley was a Conservative M.P. when he wrote this, with a wide knowledge of and experience in defense matters. The central thesis is that there is now increased danger of Soviet surprise attack. His conclusion recognizes secrecy, deception, and self-deception in bringing about surprise, but his analysis of historical examples emphasizes self-deception and human failure to deal properly with intelligence warnings because of preconceptions. His view of surprise is closer to Roberta Wohlstetter's than to Barton Whaley's; active deception measures and means do not get the attention such operations warrant. This fixed gaze on self-deception (and on the secrecy of Soviet society) misses investigation of active Soviet measures to mislead. Only in Critchley's discussion of détente does he come close to confronting what some suspect to be a possible Soviet disinformation effort.

Cruickshank, Charles G. DECEPTION IN WORLD WAR II. Oxford and New York: Oxford Univ. Press, 1979. 221 pp., bibliog., notes, index.

The title is misleading: this is not a study of all such operations but rather of Allied and mainly of British operations in Europe, the Mediterranean, and the Middle East. It is the first try at writing such a history by making use of official documents and transcending the work of any one component; Masterman's *The Double-Cross System* covered only the work of the XX Committee. In a reversal of the policy laid down in 1945 on deception records, these documents were released for the first time in 1977 and 1978. Cruickshank touchs on the main deception plans and operations beginning with the 1940 defensive stage and ending with the Normandy invasion. He does not hesitate to give evaluations of the success or failure of the major deception operations and of the contributions of those operations or of particular means. Some of these assessments will be contested because the author has not developed sufficient support or evidence. We are not sure whether he has relied wholly on documents or whether he has consulted with knowledgeable individuals for further analysis and testing of his conclusions. He gives a bit more on the organization of deception in the Allied camp, but here again more interest in and consultation with experts would have given Cruickshank a better feel for the role of the London Controlling Section and that of other units. Some opinions that will not go unchallenged are his assumption that deception is not of much use to the side on the defense and his evaluation of the Sicilian deception's exact contribution.

Brief, and somewhat hastily done, this book may be. But it does open for reexamination and further research a number of cases where the success of deception had become accepted as conventional wisdom. It also provides a most comprehensive list of code names for Allied operations in deception. The seven pages on German deception are obviously too few to do more than scratch the surface, but the chapter on the performance of the Soviets in support of Allied deception plans finally examines a neglected subject.

Cruickshank, Charles G. THE FOURTH ARM: PSYCHOLOGICAL WARFARE 1938–1945. London: Davis-Poynter, 1977. 190 pp., bibliog., index.

A concise history of the organization, operations, and the experiences of Allied and especially British psychological warfare in the years covered. The *Economist* review characterized it as the first published account of the work of the British Political Warfare Executive (PWE), participant autobiographies aside. Relying on documents available in Britain and the United States, Cruickshank was able to cull a number of items of intelligence interest: the British policy of denying to Allied governments in exile that black radios were run by PWE; the creation of a Greek black radio in 1942 to serve long-range political objectives in Greece; the compromise of Britain's most secret black radio in 1941 to a British publication by a former member of PWE (showing that generalities about national traits of security consciousness do not always stand up); the quarrels and wrangling among organizations (including intelligence) involved in such operations; the spreading of rumors in deception operations. PWE's intelligence activities are covered; Hinsley's first volume on the history of British intelligence in World War II cites two of the chapters in *The Fourth Arm* on the subject. One of these, "Market Research—Intelligence," deals with the collection of intelligence and its problem for propaganda. The author's conclusions on the effectiveness of black radios and black propaganda have been shared by others.

The weakest part of this whole effort is Cruickshank's refusal to tap the memory of those still living because of his conviction that such recollections are unreliable, a conviction that shows a surprisingly excessive faith in the accuracy of documents and an equally excessive reluctance to double-check personal memories. Reliance on documents also forces this work at times to veer in the direction of what records were available rather than to consider what was important. Finally, psychological warfare, including covert aspects, was conducted in neutral countries, and any complete history of the subject must address this area.

Currey, Cecil B. CODE NUMBER 72: BEN FRANKLIN: PATRIOT OR SPY. Englewood Cliffs, N.J.: Prentice-Hall, 1972. 322 pp., bibliog., notes, no index.

Currey developed a thesis that Franklin may have been a British agent while serving in Paris. Using documents of the British secret service wherein Franklin is referred to as Number 72, he paints a picture of his subject that one reviewer characterized as unrelieved in its derogation of any act by Franklin. Critics of Currey's work agreed he failed to produce conclusive evidence that Franklin was a British spy. There was also criticism that the author made practically everything Franklin did appear sinister; the impression created was of an effort to interpret facts to fit a theory. The author would have been better advised to let the record of known British intelligence activities in Europe against the American colonies speak for themselves. British penetration, deception, defamation, and covert-action operations of that period have an eternal and absorbing quality that makes them worth reading about. Currey, however, has not even handled some of these well. Without solid evidence, he accuses Silas Deane of having been recruited as a British agent by the known agent Bancroft. The same is true of his remarks about the British ties of William Carmichael. In view of the author's handling of evidence, intelligence historians are wise to use caution with this work. In 1981 Currey's credibility in general was compromised by the discovery that he had used a pen name and claimed credentials he did not possess as the author of a book on the U.S. Army.

D

Dakin, Douglas. THE GREEK STRUGGLE IN MACEDONIA 1897–1913. Salonika, Greece: Institute for Balkan Studies, 1966. 477 pp., bibliog., index.

This would have been even more massive in size had the long footnotes, which take up half a page at times, been incorporated in the text. Dakin, of the University of London, used mainly Greek sources to produce this scholarly study on the military, political, diplomatic, and covert activities and events associated with the Macedonian issue. Though he felt he did not get all details on covert support by the Greek government of the Greek side of the struggle, he still managed to uncover a wealth of material on this topic and on the covert aid provided by a Greek committee obviously set up for this purpose. Dakin gives particulars on the intelligence, assassination, and support networks set up by the Greek side to fight the Bulgarians and the Comitadjis for control of Macedonia. The work of Greek consulates in Salonika and elsewhere in organizing information-collection nets and fighter bands and in supplying arms is set out. The excellent Greek system of penetrating and bribing Turkish governmental and police authorities is pictured as part of the unified, well-planned effort. So, too, is the cooperation between the Greeks and Turks to defeat the Internal Macedonian Revolutionary Organization (IMRO), cooperation that included unofficial Turkish assistance to Greek bands and the passage of intelligence by the Greeks to the Turks on their rivals. The Greek government's covert role in directing and supporting the Greek Macedonian Committee and through it Greek bands may one day be made even clearer by further research.

Dallin, David J. SOVIET ESPIONAGE. New Haven, Conn.: Yale Univ. Press, 1955. 510 pp., notes, index [London: Oxford Univ. Press, 1956].

One of the more important contributions of Dallin's study was that it put a scholarly spotlight on the subject covered. The expert on Soviet affairs became a missionary, driven by the conviction that U.S. political science's neglect had caused the United States to minimize the significance of Soviet espionage for two decades and equally that the Soviets could not be adequately understood without an understanding of the role of Soviet espionage. It is hard to say how profound and lasting was the effect of Dallin's observation that Soviet intelligence was "one of the most remarkable phenomena of our times." *Soviet Espionage* did not deal with Soviet operations against émigrés and defectors, a topic the author meant to cover in a second volume devoted to what he called Soviet police operations abroad.

Dallin was of the view it was impossible for one man to deal with anything but the most important areas due to the "global dimensions of Soviet intelligence." But that opinion did not explain his choice or emphasis of material; the perspective of the last twenty-five years, as well as new knowledge, allows us to make observations on Dallin's choices, to spot errors, and to question some judgments. There is little on the Gouzenko case despite its importance and known effect on U.S. and Western postwar perceptions of the Soviets and Soviet espionage. Krivitsky is not treated; in fact, he is mentioned only twice in passing. Dallin fails to delve into the Sorge case. Conversely, some two hundred pages are devoted to the Lucy and Red Orchestra networks. By comparing this section to the CIA's *The Rote Kapelle* we can identify errors and areas in which Dallin was weak. His view that the Soviet intelligence services were qualitatively inferior to other services is not supported by the record of espionage success he provided. He did not discuss how good the Soviet evaluative and estimative machinery was. An early try to deal with an important subject, this book must nevertheless be regarded as dated and hardly definitive, as the *Kirkus* review at the time called it.

Dan, Uri, and Ben-Porat, Y. THE SECRET WAR: THE SPY GAME IN THE MIDDLE EAST. New York: Sabra Books, 1970. 243 pp., no index.

Two journalists' account of a number of Israeli, Egyptian, and Soviet espionage cases in the Middle East, instances of espionage either for or against Israel. The two cases that receive the lengthiest treatment are those of Israel Beer and Wolfgang Lotz. The Beer case is particularly of interest because it involved a high-level Soviet penetration of the Israeli national security structure due to Beer's positions as military commentator, journalist, teacher, and adviser on strategy and geopolitics. It has not been studied and analyzed to the extent it probably should be, making whatever is revealed about it all the more useful. In regard to Lotz, the authors' version of what was raised about Lotz's citizenship at his trial is different from that in Lotz's own book, published two years later (*The Champagne Spy*). The other well-known cases they describe, such as the Cherbourg missile boat caper or the stealing of the Mirage airplane plans, are treated (some in greater detail) in other works. The authors include little-known cases of Israeli and Egyptian agents. They present the facts without indicating sources, except infrequently in the text. The introduction, which discusses Soviet intentions in the Middle East, seems to have been attached specially for a U.S. audience. There are a number of errors in their treatment of other intelligence services and their roles.

Darling, Donald. SECRET SUNDAY. London: William Kimber, 1975. 208 pp., index.

Code-named "Sunday," Darling was head of MI9's Gibraltar Office in 1940–1944. MI9 was the British War Office section that was responsible for escape and evasion

(E&E). Darling informs us that he was with the operational side of MI9 and that this side (P15) did not identify its agents to MI9, which was concerned with E&E matters in general. The evasion side, i.e., the recovery of persons evading capture, was the principal occupation of men such as Darling. *Secret Sunday* is one of the first books on British E&E written by an officer operating from a field office and is to be read in conjunction with works such as Neave's *The Escape Room,* Foot and Langley's *MI9,* and Langley's *Fight Another Day.* Darling is good in describing how an E&E operation was conducted and is quite informative on intelligence-embassy relations. He reveals the British neglect to provide to those concerned derogatory information that was available on the British deserter and German informer Harold Cole, who betrayed British E&E operations. Still, according to some familiar with Darling's work, he has not told all.

Darling, Donald. SUNDAY AT LARGE. London: William Kimber, 1977. 174 pp., index.

Neave described Darling in *The Escape Room* as the man who brought imagination and humor to his newsletters from Gibraltar. The humor is still evident in this pleasant collection of anecdotes from Darling's days on Gibraltar. They span a variety of experiences, of both an intelligence and a nonintelligence nature. The intelligence ones, which illustrate the big and little events in an intelligence officer's life, would make a good collection for a training course. In addition to a good chapter on Italian frogmen, there are two chapters on deception. One relates details of the case of the document-laden British officer's body washed ashore in Spain just prior to the invasion of Africa in 1942 (see Butler's *Mason-Mac*). Humorous examples of German ineptness in intelligence reveal Keystone Kops–like features in the Germans' performance. Darling's account and his joyful approach will support the theory that humor is an attribute of a good intelligence officer and that lack of it and too much earnestness is the opposite.

Davenport, Elaine; Eddy, Paul; and Gillman, Peter. THE PLUMBAT AFFAIR. Philadelphia and New York: J. B. Lippincott, 1978. 184 pp., bibliog., index [London: André Deutsch].

Three intelligence stories are told in *The Plumbat Affair,* all linked, according to the authors, by the same ship's being used in two and the same Israeli operative's being involved in two of the three. The authors include two members of the London *Sunday Times* Insight Team; the first version of this book was a series in that paper. It is basically the story of the Israeli operation to transfer illegally two hundred tons of uranium from Belgium to Israel in November, 1968. In 1973, after the mistaken Israeli assassination of an Arab in Norway, one of the Mossad (Israeli intelligence) agents caught gave away the story of the Israeli uranium operation. That operation and the famous dash of the missile boats out of Cherbourg, another Israeli operation described, are linked not only by the use of the same ship but also by the involvement of the captured Mossad agent, who was used in the earlier uranium operation to cover the ship. As far as is known, this is a fairly good account of the events examined; any errors, such as in certain names, are not crucial. The investigative team's claim to have undertaken more than two-hundred interviews seems supported by the amount of accurate material uncovered. The handling of the loss of the uranium by Euratom is well described by the authors, who also provide an interesting refinement on a previous account of an Israeli intelligence operation. They see the appearance at the last minute of the hit team in Norway as a deliberate security measure, not an unplanned replacement of the original assassination squad. For a fuller account of the Norway affair, see *The Hit Team* by Tinnin and Christensen.

Davidson, Basil. SPECIAL OPERATIONS EUROPE: SCENES FROM THE ANTI-NAZI WAR. London: Victor Gollancz, 1980. 278 pp., bibliog., index.

Much of what is recounted here has been described or covered by others with similar backgrounds and experiences in resistance operations during World War II. But the new revelations Davidson provides on behind-the-scenes maneuvering within British intelligence are fascinating and throw new light on certain events and decisions. Davidson served in Hungary, Cairo, Yugoslavia, and finally Italy with D Section and subsequently with SOE. We have the best first-hand account of the split in SOE-Cairo over whom to support since he headed the operations section for Yugoslavia at one point. Davidson was a strong supporter of the partisans in Yugoslavia and was regarded as having leftist views on European resistance developments during the conflict. He reveals his involvement with Brigadier Keble, head of operations for SOE-Cairo, and then with Captain F. W. Deakin in a maneuver, backstage, to further their views on the Yugoslav issue. It was they who brought to Churchill's attention their views on Tito and the situation in Yugoslavia which led to the dispatch of the first liaison mission to Tito. Davidson also fills in details of the Keble attempt to sabotage the assignment of Fitzroy Maclean to Yugoslavia, previously brought out in Auty and Clogg's *British Policy Towards Wartime Resistance.* Of less historical moment but interesting and entertaining are his experiences in D Section and SOE at the start of the war when amateurishness was rampant.

Deacon, Richard. THE BRITISH CONNECTION: RUSSIA'S MANIPULATION OF BRITISH INDIVIDUALS AND INSTITUTIONS. London: Hamish Hamilton, 1979. 262 pp., bibliog., index.

This book was recalled by the publisher following a suit brought by one of the persons named as a Soviet agent by Deacon, who thought the man had died. Its withdrawal may allow Deacon the opportunity to research the subject more comprehensively and provide more evidence on many startling matters he raises. Deacon names alleged Soviet agents, mistaken idealists, and agents of influence. Persons previously regarded simply as progressives or as known communists are alleged by Deacon (for the first time) to have been Soviet agents. He leaves the possible agent status of others undetermined. There seem to be too great liberties taken in labeling people and not enough separation of wheat from chaff in his attempt to prove extensive and intensive Soviet influence in Great Britain. On subjects about which something is known, such as the Lucy ring, the Krivitsky case, and the Balkan section of SOE, the shortcomings of his presentation are obvious. Anthony Blunt is not even one of those identified as a Soviet agent. Deacon presents again the earlier theory of the use of Lucy to pass Ultra to the Russians as almost a certainty, again without convincing support. Occasionally Deacon startles with a little-known, closely guarded bit of information that points to his having access to some knowledgeable sources. One example is his identification of the family relationship of George Blake and Henri Curiel, not well known at the time of writing.

Deacon, Richard. A HISTORY OF THE BRITISH SECRET SERVICE. London: Frederick Muller, 1969. 416 pp., bibliog., index [New York: Taplinger, 1970].

Traces the development of the British intelligence and counterintelligence services since the time of Henry VII, although the title with its singular "Service" might mislead one to think it dealt with the SIS and its predecessors. This is the author's first major sally into the field of intelligence writing where he has gained the reputation of an indefatigable and prodigious (though not always accurate) writer. *The Times Literary Supplement* review said this contained what it called a reasonably sober selection of stories from the time of the Tudors to Victoria (about a quarter of the book). The rest was of a different quality—the reviewer found his stories on Reilly, Zaharoff, Sikorski, and others "outside of reality." To these faults one can add a few more representative examples: the author's mistakes and speculation about the Lucy ring in Switzerland during World War II; his "certainty" that Alexander Foote had all along been a British agent and thus a penetration of the Soviet service; his acceptance of the discredited story of the nonexistent German spy at Scapa Flow, Oertel, as the provider of the intelligence that sank the battleship *Royal Oak.* Deacon had no idea of the real scope of the work of British counterintelligence and the XX Committee in controlling all German agents and persons such as Owens and his "group." He was also quite wrong in saying that no historian had ever mentioned the Russian ambassador Vorontzov as the possible source of intelligence to the British on the secret clauses of the Treaty of Tilsit; Thompson and Padover did in *Secret Diplomacy,* which he listed in his bibliography. However, Deacon has probably turned out to be right about the work of Alexander Szek in World War I (though he fingers Admiral Hall rather than Admiral Oliver as the one who ordered the action against him). Note too that he wrote of Bletchley Park and its work. It is inevitable that a writer undertaking a history such as this without access to official records and thus reliant on secondary sources or war stories will end up with a work that is selective of material and spotty in reliability.

Deacon, Richard. THE ISRAELI SECRET SERVICE. London: Hamish Hamilton, 1977. 300 pp., bibliog., notes, index [New York: Taplinger, 1978].

The Israeli secret services make attractive copy for journalist and adventure-story writers because of their dramatic successes (or occasional failures), which have caught the imagination of the world and the respect and envy of many, including Israel's opponents. One ingredient of this success has been security. Strict security and censorship regulations control the information available on how these services are organized and on the details of their past performances. This restrictiveness is combined with a dose of public relations. Thus, at best it is difficult for even a serious student of Israeli intelligence and security to write with confidence on these matters due to the absence of authoritative source material. Deacon's book is not troubled by these constraints. It depends upon newspaper accounts and a few published memoirs plus some books by persons no more privy to Israeli secrets (to quote the reviewer in *Choice*) than the author himself. There is a journalistic treatment of a number of well-known episodes described elsewhere, usually in greater detail.

One problem is that Deacon speculates on large and small matters without qualification or hesitation and without bothering to indicate whether there is support for his assertions. For instance, his chapter on the Six-Day War contains a number of statements concerning a supposed secret, joint war plan between CIA and the Israeli secret services; purported CIA help to Israel on technical matters connected with the nuclear field; various "highly secret meetings between CIA area representatives in the Middle East and members of the Israeli Secret Service"; and other supposed occurrences of considerable import without one identification of a source—the whole chapter contains only one footnote.

Deacon does not express reservations about many of the things he speculates on or has picked up from somewhere. He is positive about contacts between the Saudi and Israeli intelligence services and about CIA liaison arrangements with the Israelis. He states that the Israelis had a U.S. officer as an agent to pass requirements to the Germans and tells how, supposedly, Eli Cohen was discovered by the Syrians to be an agent. He repeats errors, like the story of Jack Nissenthal and the Dieppe raid in which he fails to point out the mistake in designating Nissenthal as the person to be shot in case of capture; there is the supposed presence of an FBI agent on the mission. There was wisdom in the *Choice* comment that the book should be reserved for those well enough acquainted with the subject to recognize the guesswork when they see it.

Deacon, Richard. THE SILENT WAR: A HISTORY OF WESTERN NAVAL INTELLIGENCE. Newton Abbot, Eng.: David

and Charles, 1978. 244 pp., bibliog., index [New York: Hippocrene Books].

The title is ambitious and not exactly descriptive of the contents. "Western" includes France and Italy along with other nations; but the book has little on France and nothing on Italy. Easy to read, the book must be approached with caution because it is a mixture of good sections or treatment and weak ones, with debatable and (at times) sweeping conclusions. The best segments are those on world wars I and II, for which Deacon taps the pool of fine published works on naval warfare and naval intelligence. Even here we find errors, such as making the U.S. Navy a participant in Yardley's Black Chamber. For some reason, after Midway naval intelligence in the Pacific no longer concerns Deacon, and this omission is accompanied by a failure to come up with later findings on some points. Poorest are the initial chapter and those dealing with the post–World War II era; here he obviously must rely mainly on journalistic sources. The tendency to make sweeping conclusions and generalizations manifests itself in such matters as his interpretation of the appointment of Admiral Turner as director of central intelligence as denoting a presidential emphasis on naval intelligence or his sections on Benjamin Franklin and Yardley as directly related to naval intelligence. His view that the Soviets only began to develop deception and disinformation after World War II is wrong. And there should be no perpetuation of the error that the Admiralty's Room 39 was the World War II equivalent of Room 40 of World War I.

Deakin, F. W. THE EMBATTLED MOUNTAIN. New York and London: Oxford Univ. Press, 1971. 268 pp., bibliog., notes, index.

This was to be only a prelude to a future professional study, according to the author. One of the players in the Yugoslav drama of World War II, he has been relatively slow in giving us the benefit of his knowledge of many developments. Deakin is important because he was a commander of the first British mission to Tito. His account of the months spent in Yugoslavia is interesting, if at times complicated and even confusing; even he describes it as "elusive and protean in shape." There are a number of anecdotes or items of intelligence interest, but perhaps two are of significance. The first is his categoric statement that the British in 1942 and early 1943 had a picture of what was happening in Yugoslavia primarily from German intercepts. This is another of those early tip-offs of the existence of Ultra. The second is his version of events that culminated in the British mission to Tito. We have since learned from Davidson's *Special Operations Europe* that there was more to those happenings than what Deakin imparts in this account. Davidson's version is one of a planned end run around existing authority and policy to get to Churchill the side of the story on Yugoslavia that Deakin and others supported. Deakin was one of the three SOE officials involved in this maneuver, which used his friendship with Churchill to achieve its purpose. See Sweet-Escott's *Baker Street Irregular* on why Deakin was sent to Yugoslavia and on his knowledge of partisan strength from special intelligence (read Ultra) before his departure.

Deakin, F. W., and Storry, G. R. THE CASE OF RICHARD SORGE. New York: Harper and Row, 1966. 351 pp., bibliog., notes, index [London: Chatto and Windus].

According to DIS's *Bibliography,* Allen Dulles thought this the most authoritative book on one of the greatest spy rings in modern history. He had every reason to speak so highly of it. It is by and large an accurate account that makes use of oral histories and other important pieces of information known at the time. Deakin researched the German end of the story and compiled his and Storry's Japanese segments. Storry, the Japanese expert, worked on Japanese material and did the Japanese interviews. This effective partnership tackled Japanese material (including the judicial proceedings) and unpublished German reports and interviewed for three years.

The authors acknowledge that not all questions on the case are answered. They do not give a satisfactory reason for the German failure to properly vet Sorge, an old communist, and they do not expose the identities of Soviet agents and informers in China; nor do they discuss the relative effectiveness of Sorge's nets compared to others in Japan (a question that only the Soviets can answer), Sorge's personal reaction to the Nazi-Soviet Pact, or exactly how Sorge got his job as a journalist. However students of Soviet intelligence will find in this a rare published account of the General Lyushkov defection of 1938. As good a feel as the authors have for intelligence operations, they either were not sufficiently knowledgeable or did not wish to spend time making any comments or observations on the many professional and technical flaws in the Sorge organization. Rereading this excellent account, one is still struck by the fact that despite its many faults in methods of operation, Sorge's net was so successful. Schellenberg's *The Labyrinth* must be consulted for his version of the case. The authors discuss Schellenberg's claims that Sorge was connected with German intelligence, which explained his position as a journalist and the extent of his security check by the Germans. They conclude that they cannot prove or disprove Schellenberg's version.

De Beus, J. G. TOMORROW AT DAWN! New York: W. W. Norton, 1980. 179 pp., bibliog., index.

The author was a secretary of the Dutch legation in Berlin at the start of World War II. He served there until the German invasion of Holland in May 1940. This is his account of how Colonel Hans Oster, a senior German Abwehr officer, provided the Dutch military attaché to Berlin, Major Sas, information on Hitler's plans to attack in western Europe following the destruction of Poland. The story is based on personal knowledge brought up to date by research in postwar works. The Dutch Parliament Commission of Inquiry report is one of the sources cited.

Sas has long been known as the channel for Oster's warnings, and he is mentioned in many works. De Beus contributes a picture of the reactions of the Dutch and Belgians and their inability to deal with the warnings once the first such warnings of attack were not borne out. After many changes in Hitler's plans, Sas's source and intelligence lost any semblance of credibility with his superiors. Their confidence was not even established when Oster gave accurate information on the planned invasions of Norway and Denmark. Deception by the Germans was suspected by Dutch analysts, and this perception affected their judgment until the last moment. An interesting case study of intelligence misperception without any external effort to deceive or to precondition the target of a deception, this book is also a case study of the failure of intelligence analysts to ask the right questions. Deception is not achieved with eighteen false alarms by the deception channel. The security and means of communication between Oster and Sas and between Sas and Dutch officials are matters the reader will find interesting for the many vulnerabilities. The author has not seen fit to comment on these or to ask certain questions, such as why two trained intelligence officers like Oster and Sas made no effort to explain past warnings to Sas's superiors in a way that would dissipate the suspicions that they, as intelligence officers, knew were inevitable. For those interested in the intelligence problem of surprise, there is much to ponder in this work. In 1951 Colvin's *Chief of Intelligence* revealed the near compromise of Oster due to the insecure communications between Holland and the Dutch embassy in Berlin.

Defense Intelligence School. BIBLIOGRAPHY OF INTELLIGENCE LITERATURE: A CRITICAL AND ANNOTATED BIBLIOGRAPHY OF OPEN SOURCE INTELLIGENCE LITERATURE. Washington, D.C.: Defense Intelligence School, October 1977. 71 pp., no index. 7th ed. April 1981. 78 pp., no index. Rev. ed. August 1981.

The bibliography of the U.S. Defense Intelligence School was conceived in the early 1970s as "a reasonably comprehensive listing of the most significant books in English on intelligence and related topics." A groundbreaking work in postwar intelligence scholarship, it was not a typical bibliography. The annotations of more than two hundred books and reports of the U.S. congressional committees and royal commissions were meant to be descriptive, evaluative, or both. The 1981 edition has forty-eight new book listings while omitting thirty-four from the previous edition. This newest edition improves on earlier ones in a number of ways. First, the annotations for the new books tend to be more extended. Second, the selection of works for inclusion is much better and reflects the continuing examination of criteria for inclusion. Third, annotations are beginning to include citations of additional references. The 1977 edition contained certain questionable statements or judgments in connection with the works of Accoce and Quet, Schellenberg, Whitehouse, Pratt, Foote, and Yardley, that needed to be examined. All except the Pratt and Yardley items were repeated in the latest edition. Aside from these points, the book has been the most reliable single guide to the significance and accuracy of works included and consequently serves as a necessary supplement to other intelligence bibliographies by Blackstock and Schaf, Devore, Harris, and Myron Smith.

Dekel, Efraim. SHAI: THE EXPLOITS OF HAGANA INTELLIGENCE. New York and London: Thomas Yoseloff, 1959. 369 pp., no index.

Shai was the security and intelligence section of Hagana, the underground Jewish army during the mandate in Palestine. It was founded in 1921 and was one of the ancestors of the present Israeli intelligence community. Dekel himself was at one time its chief. He has written mainly about its exploits and successes. The author proudly relates them: the penetration of the British governmental and security organization in Palestine; the creation of hidden arms caches and underground arms factories whose security was protected by Shai; intelligence and CI support to illegal immigration; penetration of the Arab community; aid in the illegal acquisition of arms; CI work for Hagana; the protection of illegal radio broadcasts; the monitoring of British communications; and the deciphering of encrypted British messages. Dekel does not neglect to include Shai's duties of execution of informers working for their opponents or of Germans in Palestine who were believed to be Nazis. The litany of accomplishments and the tone of the writing prompted some U.S. intelligence experts to suspect that the unit's successes, albeit considerable, were magnified here. Suspicions increase when Dekel relates how Shai and Hagana deliberately spread tales, some of which were originally figments of British imagination, of their accomplishments in order to reinforce the Britons' high opinions of them. One can nevertheless get a good idea of how a dedicated, loyal, and determined group, within an environment secured by the loyalty of that segment of the population supporting them, was able to conduct a clandestine war against odds and win. This book permits us to understand some of the methods of operation of the Israeli services today.

Delmer, Sefton. BLACK BOOMERANG. New York: Viking Press, 1962. 298 pp., index [London: Secker and Warburg].

Delmer, a journalist and German expert, headed the British Political Warfare Executive's German black propaganda in World War II. This is his story of how and what black operations were run, with the greatest emphasis on the black radios that broadcast to Germany. Delmer created a first, according to Ewan Butler, when he revealed on a TV program that he had been responsible for these stations. That fact may have been a revelation to the British audience, but it as well as PWE's cooperation with OSS on black propaganda was divulged as early as 1947 in MacDonald's *Undercover Girl,* published in the United States. Of historical interest is Delmer's account of his employment of Otto John during the war. Delmer was later to be present at John's press conference in East Germany following his defection or flight. *Black Boomerang* gives one of the few opportunities to learn of black operations from an expert practitioner. It is difficult to accept as proven Delmer's claims of the effectiveness of certain of his operations; the book is weakest on answering the question of how the effectiveness of black propaganda, and especially black psychological warfare operations, can be ascertained. For a discussion of this point and a judgment on World War II operations see Cruickshank's *The Fourth Arm;* Constantine Fitzgibbon quotes the U.S. head of army psychological warfare as estimating in 1945 that black radios probably shortened the war by five minutes (see *Secret Intelligence in the Twentieth Century*). Peskett's *Strange Intelligence* contains a cameo shot of Delmer during the war.

Delmer, Sefton. THE COUNTERFEIT SPY. New York: Harper and Row, 1971. 252 pp., index [London: Hutchinson, 1973].

This was written to show what deception can do. Delmer drew a parallel between the situation of the Germans, starved for good information in 1944 before the Normandy invasion and thus vulnerable to deception, and more recent events. He saw Western intelligence services at the start of the 1970s as being in dire need of good intelligence on the Soviet Union and China and therefore equally good targets for deception. He must be regarded as one of the first to focus attention on deception and its practice in World War II. With the acknowledged help of such people as Colonel N. W. Wild, the head of the SHAEF deception unit, he gave us this story of deception revolving around a double agent code-named Garbo. Touched on are the XX Committee, the A Force, and deception successes using double agents. Montagu in *Beyond Top Secret Ultra* calls this as good an account of the Garbo network as could be written by someone who had not been in double agent work. Due to confusion on some identities (that of Tricycle) and minor errors (Philby was not in MI5 and Cicero was not an Abwehr operation), it is best to read this book after Masterman's *The Double-Cross System* and

Montagu's work, cited above. Masterman's book, which appeared at about the same time as this one, will sort out the double agents and their work on behalf of the Allies.

Deriabin, Peter, and Gibney, Frank. THE SECRET WORLD. Garden City, N.Y.: Doubleday, 1959. 324 pp., index [London: Arthur Barker].

The Secret World grew out of a series of articles in *Life* magazine in 1959. Deriabin was a former KGB staff officer who defected in Vienna in 1954 while on his first foreign assignment. Gibney was later to write the introduction and the commentary for *The Penkovsky Papers.* Early defectors such as Deriabin gave the West much of its foundation of knowledge of the KGB. Drawing from his own experience as a counterintelligence officer in the Kremlin guard and an SK (security) officer in Vienna, Deriabin contributes special insights into these roles of the KGB. His information on KGB training, tradition, methods of operation, and attitudes add considerably to the West's understanding of the Soviet intelligence and security system; the functioning of Soviet security and military CI during World War II (including Smersh) is also discussed. This account raises one significant matter without adequate follow-up. We are told that the Spetsburo or Special Bureau, in charge of acts of terror or violence, was "implicated in the 1941 killing of the GRU refugee Gen. Krivitsky." The reader might also appreciate more on the report that the former head of the Soviet illegals section impersonated a German Wehrmacht staff officer for a full year—surely one of the great intelligence adventures if it occurred as Deriabin describes it. On this and the Krivitsky matter, it seems that Deriabin's knowledge is second-hand and thus limited.

De Silva, Peer. SUB ROSA: THE CIA AND THE USES OF INTELLIGENCE. New York: Times Books, 1978. 295 pp., glossary, index.

De Silva was a West Point graduate who spent many years in senior positions in CIA. *Sub Rosa* is both his account of his own intelligence career and his view of the place and need of intelligence in U.S. society. Written at the height of the attacks on the intelligence community, it was meant to correct the picture painted of CIA by its critics and to defend CIA. The last third of the text deals with De Silva's Vietnam experience beginning in 1964; it is here his career reached its peak in its potential influence on great events. His views about the Vietnam War will probably be long debated, but much of what he recounts does not enlighten us about the intelligence effort and operations that provided the basis of his estimates and opinions. One reviewer (in the *Washington Post*) described De Silva as a West Point graduate who distrusted the military and a patriot who saw the grotesqueness of the efforts in Asia. What he has written also shows him to be a staunch supporter of CIA. The impression he gives of CIA work is that of a supervisor or station chief; but even here, De Silva was representative of a particular type of senior officer rather than of a generic model. Unwittingly, De Silva explains much of his understanding of his role as CIA chief in relating anecdotes such as his part in trying to get Rhee of South Korea to resign and hold new elections. There is one portion of his pre-CIA career the reader may wish he had elaborated on—his work as security officer for the Manhattan Project during World War II. According to Philip Stern's *The Oppenheimer Case* (New York: Harper, 1969), De Silva played an important role in this famous security case. In relative importance, what he might have said about Oppenheimer or anything concerning Soviet penetration of our nuclear program and U.S. counterintelligence leads on Soviet action would rank as high as his Vietnam experiences and certainly higher than the very personal "household" details he included.

Devore, Ronald M. SPIES AND ALL THAT: INTELLIGENCE AGENCIES AND OPERATIONS; A BIBLIOGRAPHY. Los

Angeles: California State Univ., Center for the Study of Armament and Disarmament, 1977. 63 pp., index.

This bibliography contains 556 items of which some two-thirds are categorized as books. The remainder are largely articles from newspapers or periodicals and some 70 government publications, mostly reports of the U.S. Senate and House. Only a handful of the entries are annotated. Devore's reasoning is that intelligence "conjures up extremes of ethical judgment and emotional feeling" and consequently he did not want to insert "subjective evaluation" in these notes. Whether one accepts his rationale or not, it is perhaps better that he did not comment further, judging from some of the books he recommends in his introduction. The inclusion of Accoce and Quet's, Copeland's and even Winterbotham's books on Ultra indicates that the author's knowledge is extensive rather than intensive. There is no biographic data to help the reader judge Devore's qualifications. The list also contains a number of titles only peripheral to the intelligence field. Still, the book will be useful to the student of intelligence.

De Vosjoli, P. L. Thyraud. LAMIA. Boston: Little, Brown, 1970. 334 pp., index.

De Vosjoli was the liaison officer of the French intelligence service in Washington. Here he has given us a rare work—a book in English by an insider dealing with French intelligence and security in the post–World War II period. *Lamia* is all the more welcome for this and for one perspective of the problems of French security and the influences that beset French intelligence. Leon Uris wrote a fictionalized version of the events described in *Lamia* under the title *Topaz.* Of De Vosjoli's intelligence activities, those he relates dealing with Cuba are of strategic consequence and historical significance. However, there is no support or confirmation for his claims that intelligence he acquired and passed to CIA played an important role in the Cuban missile crisis of 1962. Reliable published accounts of the last twenty years make no mention of any such intelligence contribution. As for those portions wherein De Vosjoli identifies certain individuals as Soviet agents, it should be noted that since the publication of the book, there have been no official revelations or actions that lend credence to his particular charges or substantiate them.

DIS SEE **Defense Intelligence School**

Donovan, James B. STRANGERS ON A BRIDGE: THE CASE OF COLONEL ABEL. New York: Atheneum, 1964. 425 pp., index [London: Secker and Warburg].

Donovan was the lawyer who defended Rudolph Abel and later negotiated his exchange to the Soviets for Gary Powers. During World War II he served in OSS as general counsel. This work is based on his original diary; though expanded, it is still in journal form. Letters to and from Abel, official transcripts of court proceedings, and cabled State Department reports on Donovan's East German exchange mission have been added. Much of what is written concerns the legal proceedings of the trial and matters relating to the exchange of prisoners. We do not find a professional analysis of the operation of Abel from the perspective of the intelligence officer; Donovan does, however, try to tell what Abel (real name William Fisher) was like. Wise and Ross in their writings judged Donovan to be a brilliant defender and the man who saved Abel's life. For the researcher interested in Abel the intelligence officer, illegal, and human being, Donovan's book, though helpful, comes nowhere near to filling the need. Actually, nothing has been published that reveals anything like all that must be known on the U.S. end of this illegal's career and other interesting facets of the case. See Powers's *Operation Overflight,* in which the pilot takes issue with some of Donovan's observations about him.

Dorwart, Jeffery M. THE OFFICE OF NAVAL INTELLIGENCE: THE BIRTH OF AMERICA'S FIRST INTELLIGENCE

AGENCY, 1865–1918. Annapolis, Md.: Naval Institute Press, 1979. 142 pp., bibliog., index.

According to the author, there had never been an attempt to examine thoroughly the origin, birth, and development of ONI. The operative word here is "thoroughly" since James R. Green tried his hand at it in a thesis in 1963. Dorwart calls this, based entirely on declassified material, the "first in-depth analysis of ONI's impact on American history between 1882 and 1918." He has done a fine job and set the pace for further research on the subject. Well organized, the book evaluates ONI's work, organization, methods, and outlook, particularly for the period 1882–1918, and is presented in a balanced and perceptive manner. Dorwart has an eye for the significant trend and for identifying the central issues of a particular period; he also has the ability to discern the importance or interest of a particular event. He pulls no punches in presenting his judgments on ONI's effectiveness (or ineffectiveness) or on the legality of some of its activities. His judgment at the end is particularly hard, but its all-inclusive nature on ONI's influence on U.S. intelligence as a whole will be questioned.

The book is loaded with anecdotal gems that amuse, enlighten, or both. Examples: President Cleveland's call for increased intelligence in his address to Congress; ONI's use of a foreigner to develop a reliable secret code in the 1880s, which it took great pains to keep confidential, fearing newspaper attacks; ONI's deception operations against Spain in the 1898 war; the ludicrous security in ONI in 1900; ONI's fear that Assistant Secretary Franklin D. Roosevelt was, in 1916, attempting to usurp naval intelligence work; the use of ONI agents at one period as salesmen for U.S. manufacturers in line with "dollar diplomacy." This work is far superior to Green's thesis, published as *The First Sixty Years of the Office of Naval Intelligence.* In describing President Cleveland's request to Congress, Dorwart would appear to have given a rather liberal interpretation of the president's actual words.

Downes, Donald. THE SCARLET THREAD: ADVENTURES IN WARTIME ESPIONAGE. London: Derek Vershoyle, 1953. 207 pp., no index [New York: British Book Centre].

Two things distinguish Downes's *The Scarlet Thread.* It is one of the first works by an intelligence officer (OSS in World War II) to express disenchantment with U.S. policy. It is also rare because it is the personal reminiscence of an American who admittedly served in British intelligence before Pearl Harbor. Among the locations at which he served while with OSS were Italy and North Africa. He was connected with the ill-fated team sent to Spain to collect intelligence, which *The Secret War Report of the OSS* characterized as the largest OSS blunder of the war. Downes writes with feeling of many of the intelligence and non-intelligence events in his career. He tells many stories of intelligence interest: of surreptitious entries to acquire the codes of Vichy France and of some neutrals: of the feuding of OSS and the FBI; of operations both successful and unsuccessful abroad. His description of the FBI's attitude toward and treatment of OSS assets turned over to them reads amazingly like the experiences of Dusko Popov and reveals J. Edgar Hoover's attitude toward spies, known only to a few when the book was published. Downes's account is partisan and cannot be relied on completely for accuracy. For example, he writes that Hoover and the FBI did everything possible to obstruct and embarrass British Intelligence in the United States before Pearl Harbor. This is a limited view and does not accurately describe the entire relationship between the two. For more views of Downes's work with OSS in Africa and Italy, see R. Harris Smith's *OSS* and Cave Brown's editorial comments in *The Secret War Report of the OSS.* There is a brief mention of Downes in Troy's *Donovan and the CIA.*

Duke, Florimond, with Charles M. Swaart. NAME, RANK AND SERIAL NUMBER. New York: Meredith Press, 1969. 154 pp., bibliog., index.

Mission Sparrow was composed of three OSS officers parachuted into Hungary in March 1944. It was headed by Duke, who had been chief of the OSS Balkan SI desk when selected for this assignment. This is Duke's story, published just after he died, of the mission's adventures in Hungary and in German captivity. Immediately obvious is the dearth of information on the preliminary staff planning, the rationale for the mission's dispatch, and any contingency plans for dealing with German countermoves to a Hungarian surrender, the reason for the mission. The author acknowledges the unresolved and unprobed treatment of these matters at the end of the book. It is his judgment that there remains a large element of doubt about what the mission might have accomplished; and he cautions that the whole story from the U.S. side is still classified. Duke was obviously constrained in telling what he knew. There was mention of Mission Sparrow and its purpose in the official OSS history. For German knowledge of Duke's contacts with the Hungarians, see Hoettl's *The Secret Front.* In Mure's *Practice to Deceive* there is the allegation that Dudley Clarke and the British deception unit A Force leaked to the Germans the peace approaches of the Hungarians in the hope the Germans would transfer troops to that country away from other fronts. Cave Brown's annotations in *The Secret War Report of the OSS* identify Duke and other members of his mission and speak of reasons for their dispatch beyond that of mere intelligence collection, the explanation given in the official text. Cave Brown also mentions rumors of the missions's betrayal by the Soviets.

Dukes, Sir Paul. THE STORY OF 'ST25': ADVENTURE AND ROMANCE IN THE SECRET INTELLIGENCE SERVICE IN RED RUSSIA. London: Cassell, 1938. 374 pp., index.

Dukes was the British SIS representative in the Soviet Union in 1918–1919 who operated under various disguises with the British code name ST-25. He was assigned there as the replacement for Captain Cromie, who had been killed, after relations with the Bolshevik government had been broken. This is a more complete personal narrative than the 1922 version, which was called *Red Dusk in the*

Morrow. It is the exciting and hair-raising story of Dukes's life of hide and seek in the USSR, of disguises and false documentation, of Soviet counterintelligence methods and close escapes, of illegal border crossings and internal controls by the Bolsheviks. According to Ronald Seth, Dukes was the only British intelligence officer to be knighted as a reward for the spying he had done. It is interesting to note that while Sir Robert Bruce Lockhart is still read and his name remembered, Dukes is almost forgotten, though both men were associated with British efforts in the USSR at that period. For another perspective on Dukes's work and as a complement to this book, one must read Agar's *Footprints in the Sea* since Agar was responsible for running couriers into the USSR for Dukes. Bernard Newman called Dukes's book "one of the most fascinating of the whole range of the literature of espionage." Dukes scrupulously had it read and approved by the chief of SIS, which may account for its vagueness about his prewar and wartime activities in the USSR. In pointing out this fact, Seth speculated that Dukes may well have been connected with SIS before 1918. Certainly, Dukes was a natural for the assignment to the Soviet Union in 1918; he was quick-witted, security conscious, and brave, with an instinct for danger. However, it is hard to accept his version that two weeks after his last meeting with the chief of SIS, he was ordered to leave for the USSR. His performance later was that of an experienced operative.

Dulles, Allen W. THE CRAFT OF INTELLIGENCE. New York: Harper and Row, 1963. 264 pp., bibliog., index [London: Weidenfeld and Nicolson].

The paperback edition (New York: New American Library [Signet], 1965) contained some additional information, particularly on certain cases that had surfaced in the press after the first edition. Dulles, the head of CIA for eight years, wrote this book to "tell what properly can be told about intelligence as a vital element." After touching briefly on a bit of intelligence history, the work describes and explores aspects of intelligence: requirements, collection, processing, analysis, and production. Dulles also touches on counterintelligence, deception, technical collection, and planning and has much on tradecraft. The book, which has been called a primer on intelligence, is a veritable storehouse on the philosophy of intelligence and on Dulles's general approach to it, which became part of the makeup of CIA under him; thus it provides the feel and sound of CIA of the Dulles era. Dulles also discusses the Communist intelligence services, the Communist subversive threat, specific cases, the role of intelligence in the United States and in any democratic society, problems of secrecy, and the selection of CIA personnel.

Beyond its importance as the intelligence philosophy of one of the famous figures of modern intelligence and of one of the principal services, this work is a realistic picture of intelligence, and it contains items of interest and significance. Dulles says that U.S. intelligence was on top of British, French, and Israeli plans on the Suez invasion of 1956 and on Sputnik; he viewed the acquisition of the 1956 Khrushchev speech as one of his major coups. There is the admission that in his years of CIA service, the problem of leaks of sensitive U.S. information (other than by hostile agents) was never reduced. We learn of Woodrow Wilson's concern with this same problem and of a 1915 memorandum by him on the means of safeguarding important diplomatic secrets. There is a discussion on deception and Soviet disinformation. There are discussions of technical collection, making Dulles, according to Blackstock and Schaf's bibliography, *Intelligence, Espionage, Counterespionage and Covert Operations,* one of the first officials of the intelligence community to expose details of collection by technical sensors. He mentions the methods of Soviet illegals and the problems they pose. Note his inclusion of Civil War stories in the historical section; by the time of his later *Great True Spy Stories,* he had learned not to trust many of these. His chapter on the evolution of U.S. intelligence lacks an important ingredient—the tradition of the use of presidential agents. Later information has made his account of Cicero and the Berlin Tunnel operations dated, as is the story of the Lisbon operation by OSS to acquire enemy codes. Dulles's treatment of the bomber and missile gap intelligence estimates will not satisfy everyone. Bowie of Harvard, also formerly of CIA, observed that Dulles was excited most by espionage and consequently did not treat analysis and the relationship of intelligence to policymaking fully.

Dulles used this work to answer and counter criticisms of CIA that had begun to increase after the U-2 and Bay of Pigs incidents, and his defense should be measured against later criticisms and the findings stemming from congressional and executive investigations. Powers, who wrote *The Man Who Kept the Secrets,* could be representative of those not satisfied in 1979 with some of the explanations. He judged the entire book as "an effort to obscure the importance of political action in intelligence" and said CIA was "never more meddlesome than during his [Dulles's] tenure as DCI."

Minor matters that are still debated or questioned include the incomplete account of why Colonel Wagner was unacceptable to the U.S. Army hierarchy in 1898, the labeling of Colonel Myasoedov as definitely an agent of the Germans, and the stated consequences of Colonel Redl's treason on the early battles in the east in World War I. Blackstock and Schaf, who were in U.S. military intelligence, referred to this book as an example of institutional bias found in intelligence literature.

Dulles, Allen W., ed. GREAT TRUE SPY STORIES. New York: Harper and Row, 1968. 393 pp., no index [London: Collins].

Dulles selected thirty-nine stories from books and articles, three-fourths of which cover World War II and the postwar period. He interpreted "spy story" broadly to encompass anything within what is called "secret intelligence operations." His aim was to draw on published materials to present clandestine intelligence as conducted "in the present historical era." Such operations he divided into eight categories, among which are defection, double agents, deception, and cryptology. He provided short introductory essays to each section but did not vouch for the accuracy of the stories he had included; of greater lasting value are his comments which one wishes were not so brief. He might have enlightened the reader on a number of matters, beyond his valuable remarks on the unreliability of Wennerstrom's claim of association with the Americans; the increasingly important role of illegals in Soviet penetration operations; his view of the Fields; his doubts about or difficulty in verifying many of the American Civil War stories of secret service (and his calling attention to Edwin C. Fischel's important articles on this matter). What he wrote of the Fields assumed greater significance following the allegations of Steven in *Operation Splinter Factor* that Dulles used them as a means of destroying certain popular leaders in Eastern Europe, allegations that were never considered serious by objective observers. Dulles was not able to say anything of Ultra and its overall role or its value in specific instances, such as its identification of the German agent Cicero along with the identification made by Dulles's agent George Wood. Though he could not vouch for everything in the stories he chose, Dulles might have made exceptions and commented on known flaws in certain of them, such as Alexander Foote's. The story of OSS's attempt to get Japanese codes in Portugal is unchallenged.

Dulles, Allen W. THE SECRET SURRENDER. New York: Harper and Row, 1966. 256 pp., bibliog., index [London: Weidenfeld and Nicolson, 1967].

Dulles capped his OSS service with Operation Sunrise, the negotiations for the surrender of the German and fascist forces in Italy in 1945. This is his first-hand account of the operation, based primarily on his own records and memory and those of his assistant as well as other reports and documents at their disposal. Their report to the Joint Chiefs of Staff served as a guide in writing this book. The German view came from interviews with those Germans involved in the talks. Dulles concentrated on providing a play-by-play record; there is little analysis of the overall meaning and significance of the operation. In the epilogue, the lessons learned are discussed, but these are confined to two: the importance of secret contact and secure communications and the problems of bringing a war to an end. Dulles does not reconcile the lesson of secret contact and measures with his revelation that word of the negotiations had reached the Japanese representatives in Switzerland. There is no appraisal of gains and the costs of political misunderstanding and distrust among the Allies stemming from the negotiations. The reviewer in the *New York Review of Books* claimed to discern in Dulles's manner of handling the negotiations and keeping his home office informed seeds of his future conduct as head of CIA. Bradley Smith and Elena Agarossi's *Operation Sunrise* attempted to analyze the political risks of negotiations with the Germans and the motives of the players and to evaluate the results, as well as to set out the sequence of events. But it is Dulles's book that unfolds the large and small events, explains the security arrangements, and gives the feel for personalities and their relationships that only a participant can provide.

E

Eisenberg, Dennis; Dan, Uri; and Landau, Eli. THE MOSSAD: ISRAEL'S SECRET INTELLIGENCE SERVICE; INSIDE STORIES. New York and London: Paddington Press Ltd., 1978. 267 pp., index.

Two of the authors, Landau and Dan, are Israeli journalists connected with *Ma'ariv,* Israel's largest newspaper. This fact should be noted not only because of their qualifications but also due to Israeli censorship of national security matters. Presumably, Israeli authorities allowed what is contained here—good and bad, right and wrong—to appear because it was written in English for publication outside Israel. Of the stories and incidents narrated, three (the Eichmann kidnapping, the Lotz affair, and the Eli Cohen case, the longest) have been the subjects of separate books (Harel's *The House on Garibaldi Street,* Lotz's *The Champagne Spy,* and Aldouby and Ballinger's *The Shattered Silence,* respectively). The story of the 1973 intelligence failure has been studied by many, including Chaim Herzog. The other incidents, such as the Cherbourg caper of the missile boats and the stealing of the Mirage plans for Israel by a Swiss, are retold with admiration. This tone could be accounted for if the authors' purpose is to defend the service and its overall record. They admit that Mossad's reputation has been tarnished by the Yom Kippur intelligence failure, the mistaken killing of an Arab in Norway, and other "flaps."

Despite the publisher's claim that every incident is true, such is not the case. In addition, the authors do not identify their sources. Errors are strewn about the text. Zwi Zamir did not replace Meir Amit as head of Mossad in 1968, but later. CIA did not warn Mossad that an Arab attack was imminent in 1973. Richard Helms did not attend Columbia, but Williams College. The authors may even have the agents used in an important Israeli operation wrong. For these and other reasons, this study is not useful for the historian or the professional who requires more meticulous attention to facts, sources, and evaluation. Such a reader demands the source of directly quoted conversations (for example, Cohen's alleged conversation with his Syrian captors) and for unexplained claims, such as that a Soviet DF had a role in Cohen's capture. *The Mossad* requires careful sifting to separate some very good inside information from the errors. Finally, one is left wondering why the authors were not able to sort out whether Mossad or another Israeli service was responsible for intelligence estimates or for a particular intelligence effort.

Eisenberg, Dennis; Landau, Eli; and Portugali, Menahem. OPERATION URANIUM SHIP. New York: New American Library/Signet, 1978. 196 pp., no index.

The authors claim this is "in essence the true story of how a cargo of uranium vanished on the high seas in 1968." Except for the fact of the diversion of two hundred tons of the uranium by the Israelis, however, this account is either unreliable or unsubstantiated. The authors have written more a script for a potential adventure movie than an accurate account: there's plenty of sex, gun battles, ship hijackings, illegal boardings, etc. A very crucial comment by a Euratom official in 1977 that goes counter to the substance of their version of events is given in a footnote with no comment by them. For a much more reliable account of this uranium diversion operation, see Davenport, Eddy, and Gillman's *The Plumbat Affair.*

El-Ad, Avri, with James Creech III. DECLINE OF HONOR. Chicago: Henry Regnery, 1976. 364 pp., index.

The Lavon affair in Israel and those responsible for it are still debated there. It was the result of a covert-action operation by the Israelis to worsen U.S. and British relations with Egypt in the 1950s by sabotaging their installations and making it appear that the Egyptians were responsible. Lavon, who was accused of giving orders for the operation, is alleged by El-Ad to have been the victim of a plot to destroy him. El-Ad was the principal agent of the Israeli sabotage in Egypt and thus has credentials to speak on the case. He claims his trial and imprisonment by Israel for ten years as an Egyptian agent were a plot to railroad him by Ben-Gurion and others. It is presumptuous for a non-Israeli to attempt to judge the truth of the various sides in the affair when the Israelis themselves are not certain they know it. El-Ad, though he has interesting things to say about the operation and about inefficiencies and feuding within the Israeli intelligence community, may not be an objective witness of all he relates because of his partisan and emotional involvement. Judgment must be deferred until more facts are forthcoming. For a later résumé and view of the Lavon affair and Israeli treatment of the author, see Steven's *The Spymasters of Israel.*

Elliff, John T. THE REFORM OF FBI INTELLIGENCE OPERATIONS. Princeton, N.J.: Princeton Univ. Press, 1979. 219 pp., bibliog., index.

The author developed this from the three-year study of the Police Foundation, for which he was the principal consultant. He also was leader of the Church committee's domestic intelligence task force for one year. The title is a bit broader than what actually concerns Elliff. Reform of FBI intelligence operations is analyzed from the legal point of view: how to eliminate legal abuses and violations of civil liberties in conducting such operations, not how to increase the operations' effectiveness. This distinction is particularly notable in Elliff's recommendation to split FBI foreign intelligence and counterintelligence operations from domestic security investigations. This step has long been advocated by persons concerned with intelligence and CI simply as a necessary way to upgrade their quality and the expertise of the FBI men involved. The study is thoughtful and basically sound, as the *Washington Post* reviewer called it, but there is debate on some of Elliff's recommendations as lacking realism, being too restrictive, or not being valid. His suggested restrictions on investigation of "sleepers," or foreign agents involved in domestic political and economic activities, including agents of influence, and his seeming acceptance of risks to sources and methods (he does not address this great concern of intelligence and security officers) are some of the points at issue. These are examples of what Elliff calls the traditional wide gap between officers involved in operations and those who frame laws from a distance. For the historian of CI, Elliff discusses (in a general way) the little-known case of a U.S. scholar engaged in espionage for the East Germans.

Engle, Anita. THE NILI SPIES. London: Hogarth Press, 1959. 238 pp., index.

Nili was the Jewish intelligence organization that operated in Palestine in 1917 on behalf of the British. The organizers, Aaron and Sarah Aaronson, were dedicated Zionists who hoped their services to General Allenby would further Jewish aspirations in the area as well as Aaron's own ambitions. Engle's book, written in an admiring, sympathetic tone, describes the political atmosphere of the Jewish community in Palestine within which Nili had to operate. The espionage organization and its work are only generally described. For all her praise of Nili's effectiveness, the author does not produce evidence of the organization's success. It may very well have deserved more British recognition for its sacrifices, but Engle fails to make a case on this point. Her admiration for the organization does not prevent her revealing some of Nili's poor security practices; it does affect her judgment as to the relative value of various intelligence efforts. Lawrence is dismissed as "just playing at war." Parenthetically, Engle states that Nili worked for Political Intelligence under Deedes of Allenby's staff, not under Meinertzhagen, who was director of military intelligence. Further research is needed to ascertain the exact contributions of the Aaronsons and their intelligence work, for which Sarah gave her life and Aaron later suffered ostracism by his own people as a "British agent." The couple is mentioned in Rowan's *The Story of Secret Service.*

Ennes, James M., Jr. ASSAULT ON THE "LIBERTY": THE TRUE STORY OF THE ISRAELI ATTACK ON AN AMERICAN INTELLIGENCE SHIP. New York: Random House, 1979. 288 pp., index.

A number of things connected with the Israeli attack on the USS *Liberty* in June 1967 are still considered unanswered or inadequately answered. Ennes served as an officer and cryptographic specialist aboard the ship and was wounded in the attack. He has brought up new facts about the attack, allegations of a U.S. Navy coverup of the truth, charges of deliberate Israeli intent to attack, and speculation about the Israeli decision. He is not clear as to the identities of those responsible for the "coverup" and admits that the *Liberty* story is still a puzzle: "for each question answered, another looms in its place." Ennes is also careful and general when dealing with the *Liberty*'s intelligence mission and its exact signals intelligence role; he covers nothing new here. Since he has nothing solid on the motive of the Israeli attack, he can only offer his own hypothesis. An article in the June 1978 issue of the *USNI Proceedings* cites Israeli jamming of U.S. Navy communications frequencies, as does Ennes, as the most telling evidence against the Israeli claim that they erred on the nationality of the target. Note the unconfirmed and hearsay story of the *Liberty*'s mysterious contact, believed by him to be a U.S. nuclear submarine. The same story appeared in Deacon's *The Silent War.* What the author relates of command, control, and communications weaknesses in the U.S. naval and naval intelligence organization is shocking. L. M. Bucher, in his review of this book, contended that the lessons of the *Liberty* were never made known to the planners of the USS *Pueblo* mission or to himself as commander.

Eppler, John. OPERATION CONDOR: ROMMEL'S SPY. London: Macdonald and Jane's, 1977. 243 pp., index.

Eppler, an Abwehr agent, was a member of the Kondor espionage and contacts mission to Egypt in 1942. The entire net was rounded up by the British after an inglorious performance. Eppler, born of German parents but raised in Egypt with an Egyptian stepfather, gives his version of his life as a German agent. His ability to recount verbatim many conversations so many years later will, not unjustifiably, be considered remarkable, especially in the context of a paucity of details about what exactly the mission accomplished. There are segments of interest, such as descriptions of Eppler's contacts with Anwar Sadat, the only first-hand accounts of such contacts by a German agent. Also intriguing are sections on the Grand Mufti of Jerusalem and General Rashid Ali of Iraq, both of whom conspired with the Germans. Eppler's tradecraft, or lack of it, is also instructive, though the author seems nowhere aware of the quality and security of his own performance in Egypt. The Kondor mission is treated by Mosley in *The Cat and the Mice* and also described in Sansom's *I Spied Spies.* Both must be referred to for a fuller story of the mission. Beyond these books, Lewin's *Ultra Goes to War* and Mure's *Master of Deception* must be consulted. They reveal that Operation Kondor was compromised: by Ultra and from the start, according to Lewin. Mure states British intelligence knew of the coming of the mission but is not certain at what point the British deception unit under Colonel Clarke entered the story. Mure still spoke of the Kondor story as "a tangled web indeed."

Eveland, Wilbur Crane. ROPES OF SAND: AMERICA'S FAILURE IN THE MIDDLE EAST. New York and London: W. W. Norton, 1980. 365 pp., index.

Despite the disagreement of some U.S. Middle East "hands" with the thrust of U.S. policy in the area since World War II, there have been relatively few published attacks. An attack by an intelligence officer is a noteworthy event. Eveland served as a military intelligence officer and attaché and later on special assignment with CIA in that part of the world. His work with CIA is the heart of his memoir and his argument. One would expect he would be writing from first-hand knowledge of all he relates, but this is not the case, a fact that weakens the impact of the book. Eveland is best when he divulges information on events in which he was directly or indirectly involved as a player or participant, such as some of the coup planning in the 1950s. As this is a subjective view, the full story does not always emerge. The sharp-eyed descriptions of some CIA, British, and other personalities with whom Eveland dealt or had contact in his time as a field representative for Allen Dulles are those of a man very familiar with his subjects. Where he writes without this relationship to events and where he speculates on behind-the-scenes factors and influences, he goes badly off target. One chapter typical of this tendency is aptly titled "On the Outside Looking In."

That Eveland was never a staff officer of CIA is clear from the many errors he makes about the titles and positions of CIA officials at the time of his association. His attitude toward his role is ambivalent: he accepted assignment to CIA and admits that he wanted to be "part of a new policy for the area." But he declares he never regarded himself as a covert operator. Similarly, he had no desire to learn the skills of a spy. Yet, he makes some smarting criticisms of CIA clandestine ways that show he understood nuances well enough to recognize poor methods of operation. His reliability on all facts is called into question by his statement that in 1960 there were coordinated CIA-Mossad operations in Athens to cover the Middle East and Africa and that CIA had turned over most of its intelligence responsibilities in the former area to Israel. The purpose for his writing is admittedly critical and polemical (he cites Kim Philby and John Marks, the first for urging him to write and the second for defining his book's scope). Even a sympathetic but not very knowledgeable review in the *Washington Post* wondered if Eveland's reservations and criticisms did not benefit from hindsight. CIA refused to review the book because, contrary to procedures, the author submitted it to the publisher before review.

Ewing, A. W. THE MAN OF ROOM 40: THE LIFE OF SIR ALFRED EWING. London: Hutchinson, 1939. 281 pp., bibliog., index.

Sir Alfred Ewing is remembered for his founding the World War I cryptanalytical bureau of British naval intelligence (Room 40). This author, his son, unfortunately was not able to discuss much of this contribution due to security restrictions. We do learn that Sir Alfred had wished to include a chapter on Room 40 in his own memoirs in 1933 but was refused permission by the Admiralty. In 1965, the University of Edinburgh revealed that the Admiralty tried to prosecute Sir Alfred after he made some disclosures about Room 40 in 1927. A. W. Ewing only tells us the Admiralty was upset that Sir Alfred had not cleared the speech, which had been promoted by Lord Balfour himself; as a minister, the latter had touched on Room 40 for the first time in a speech two years earlier. David Kahn's *The Codebreakers* has little to add on Sir Alfred, since it uses material from this book. Admiral William James, who later headed Room 40, confirms in *The Eyes of the Navy* that Sir Alfred had founded the organization that was to be a war winner. The story that it was formed by pure chance at the start of the war has never been contradicted; still, it is incredible there was no prior Admiralty thinking or preparations, considering that the War Office had been taught by the Boer War of the need for an expert staff of cryptanalysts (see Sir George Cockerill's *What Fools We Were*).

F

Farago, Ladislav. THE BROKEN SEAL: THE STORY OF "OPERATION MAGIC" AND THE PEARL HARBOR DISASTER. New York: Random House, 1967. 384 pp., notes, index [London: Arthur Barker].

Admiral Zacharias in *Secret Missions* described Farago's work in U.S. naval intelligence in World War II. It involved planning and research in pyschological warfare but was not related directly to cryptanalysis. This fact may partly explain the quality attributed to this work by experts. David Shulman in *An Annotated Bibliography of Cryptography* is very dissatisfied with it, saying it contains many errors. David Kahn in *The Codebreakers* and in a review of the book shares Shulman's opinion. They find unacceptable Farago's charge that H. O. Yardley, the great U.S. cryptologist, sold out to the Japanese in 1928. Walter Millis in his review in the *American Historical Review* found the book's jacket claims outrageous, Farago's picture of Yardley's contribution to the Washington Conference exaggerated, and the book as a whole lacking in credibility. In quality it comes nowhere near Roberta Wohlstetter's *Pearl Harbor, Warning and Decision;* the reader should check the many interesting revelations of the poor security of cipher systems, of their handling and distribution, and of their compromise with the work of other authorities because the indefatigable Farago picked up much good and accurate material along with the bad. Note in this regard his uncovering of the British possession of an Enigma machine by 1941 by capture of U-boats and raids; only the details of this story need checking because the central fact he gives is true. There is also a wealth of background on Japanese intelligence preparations for war. Experts have found the book unreliable as cryptological and intelligence history.

Farago, Ladislav. THE GAME OF THE FOXES: THE UNTOLD STORY OF GERMAN ESPIONAGE IN THE U.S. AND GREAT

BRITAIN DURING WORLD WAR II. 6th ed. New York: Bantam Books, 1978. 840 pp., index [New York: David McKay, 1971. London: Hodder and Stoughton, 1972].

Here is another example of a considerable effort resulting in a tome of uneven quality, controversial claims, and questionable conclusions. Farago's qualities were more those of a publicist than those of a scholar. The *RUSI* reviewer contested his claim that he was the first to study the microfilmed Abwehr records he used. Some reviewers thought this book well documented, yet there are only a handful of notes at the end of each chapter and hardly any citations of actual German documents. As for the documentation of matters from the non-German side, the *New York Times* reviewer observed that Farago did not sufficiently distinguish among sources, so good and bad evidence has been mixed. There are other discrepancies and errors, some hard to understand. Although Farago had access to Masterman's then unpublished report, *The Double-Cross System,* he still claimed that Lily Sergueiv was the most important single cog in the Normandy deception plan. Too, he did not associate what he called the Abwehr's most successful mission with the double agent Tate, who was run by the XX Committee.

The author had a penchant for the dramatic and for exaggeration: he made the United States appear to have been "swarming with German spies" in the middle of 1941. The FBI operation using William Sebold was described as the biggest deception of the war, and the FBI was pictured as the world's most formidable counterespionage force at one point in the war. The procurement of a German Enigma machine he attributed to a Polish-Swedish ring. He acknowledged that the British for most of the war controlled German espionage in Britain but said at the same time that the Abwehr sustained a "respectable coverage" of the British isles (and the United States) under difficult conditions. Then there are the minor errors.

On the other hand, there are better features, besides Farago's writing style and ability to distill facts. He presented the results of research into the so-called agent of Scapa Flow, Oertel. He also gave some good material on the intelligence defeats of the British in Holland before the Venlo incident (the kidnapping of two British intelligence officers). The additional background he exposed on the British ambassador to Ankara in the Cicero case may provide further clues to this case's security lapses. References to Bletchley Park and Enigma preceded official revelation of the secret (though his accounts of certain details and twists, such as the role of Trevor-Roper, must be read with caution or disbelief). Access to Masterman's report allowed him to make early use of its material on the British use of double agents for deception, although his use was sometimes incorrect. The book's principal fault is that it distorts the reality of German intelligence's effectiveness in its enthusiasm to tell an exciting string of anecdotes and gets some of the details wrong as well. A.J.P. Taylor thought its presentation sensational and said some of the British episodes contained "large quantities of undiluted nonsense."

Farago, Ladislav. THE TENTH FLEET. New York: Paperback Library, 1964. 319 pp., no index [New York: Ivan Obolensky, 1962].

The late Farago wrote this as an example of how brainpower can be harnessed for victory. It is the account of U.S. antisubmarine warfare in the Atlantic in World War II as conducted by the operational command unit called the Tenth Fleet. Established formally in 1943, the unit succeeded in bringing about the fusion of intelligence and operations to conduct ASW; to Farago this fusion was its outstanding feature. Persons familiar at first hand with the Tenth Fleet's history praised Farago's story as accurate and one of the most complete accounts that had been published at the time. Despite his failure to identify his sources, Farago obviously made good use of his wartime contacts and knowledge of U.S. naval intelligence to gain access to a wide range of material. In one area of crucial importance Farago is either equivocal or confusing. Written before Ultra became public knowledge, *The Tenth Fleet* deals with U.S. sources on German submarines and German suspicions that their codes were compromised or betrayed. At one point Farago categorically rejects the idea of allied cryptanalytic success ("I could find no evidence . . . of reading their mail"); at another he seems unsure ("it appeared he was reading encoded messages passing to U-Boats at sea"); elsewhere, "it is quite possible these uncanny deductions were facilitated by a new ability to read transmissions instead of merely intercepting them." Yet he also tells us that codebreakers gave a British admiral "Doenitz's decrypted signal ordering the departure of all U-Boats from convoy routes." Other intelligence sources, such as HF/DF, signal analysis, and radar, are adequately covered. Had Farago written this in the post-Ultra era, he might have produced a work comparable to Beesly's *Very Special Intelligence* dealing with the U.S. end of the Atlantic submarine war. Students of deception will be interested to learn that Admiral King forbade any black propaganda and that his philosophy was "I don't want any deception in the U.S. Navy."

Felix, Christopher (pseud.). THE SPY AND HIS MASTERS: A SHORT COURSE IN THE SECRET WAR. London: Secker and Warburg, 1963. 287 pp., no index [New York: Dutton. *A Short Course in the Secret War*].

An outstanding book on intelligence tradecraft and practice. It is the product of a former professional with a penetrating eye and a fine style of writing. The book is in two main sections. The first is composed of chapters explaining various aspects of secret intelligence operations ranging from counterespionage to agent–case officer relations. The types of operations Felix treats are in the human intelligence–collection category. This is the better section; it represents one of the first looks into the operational philosophies and practices of CIA by a former insider who cannot be classified as a disgruntled ex-employee. Felix lays out the strengths and weaknesses of U.S.

intelligence and CIA before both entered their times of troubles; though some views and opinions may be dated and some examples overtaken by new facts (e.g., the case of the reputed Scapa Flow sleeper), this segment is still highly recommended.

The second part recounts the author's experiences in Hungary in 1946–1947. His description of Communist security, takeover, and other techniques is especially important, furnishing lessons that should not be forgotten. Felix gives some tantalizing clues on a certain organizational jockeying for position in the U.S. intelligence set-up. He is actually referring to the Grombach intelligence collection group. Among the few who discuss this little-known phase in U.S. intelligence history are Lyman Kirkpatrick and Thomas Troy.

Felstead, Sidney Theodore. GERMAN SPIES AT BAY: BEING AN ACTUAL RECORD OF THE GERMAN ESPIONAGE IN GREAT BRITAIN DURING THE YEARS 1914–1918, COMPILED FROM OFFICIAL SOURCES. New York: Brentano's, 1920. 288 pp., no index [London: Hutchinson].

A devastating account of the failure of German intelligence against Britain in World War I. For anyone interested in counterintelligence and for lessons of how-not-to, this is a litany of incredibly inept German operations and of errors that led to the arrest, imprisonment, or execution of German agents. Published soon after the war, cleared by the War Office, and based on official records, it was one of the first works to reveal the extent of British successes against German espionage. These successes were to be repeated in the next war when the British made more use of the practice of using captured agents as double agents for deception. The work is a textbook on poor intelligence practices despite its occasional strange moralizing about the evils of espionage and lapses of style. There are also occasional slips or hyperboles, such as Mata Hari's being described as the most dangerous spy of all or the Japanese service's characterization as perhaps the world's best. We learn of the Germans' repeated use of poor agent material, badly conceived cover stories, documentation vulnerable to close scrutiny, of compromised accommodation addresses, and of the service's lack of compartmentation. There are entire sections on the counterintelligence aspects of postal censorship and of the use made of it by the British. The author was not aware at the time of the German agent Jules Silber in British postal censorship during that war, whose existence makes some of the German errors even harder to comprehend. Nor, of course, is there anything of the role of Room 40 in British CI successes.

Fielding, Xan. HIDE AND SEEK: THE STORY OF A WARTIME AGENT. London: Secker and Warburg, 1954. 255 pp., no index.

Fielding, an SOE officer, spent two years in Greece (twice infiltrated into Crete) and in August 1944 parachuted into France. This personal narrative he had originally intended to be "of wider scope, properly documented, and supported by contemporary evidence." But the necessary reports were not accessible in the War Office, not because of any security classification but rather because of lack of personnel to find and extract them from archives. Fielding provides some rare looks at SIS personnel sent into occupied Europe during the war and at friction within SIS teams; we have a glimpse of the frictions within SOE-Cairo and of office plotting within SOE there, which follows somewhat the pattern of SOE-Cairo's cabal to prevent the mission of Fitzroy Maclean to Yugoslavia (see Auty and Clogg's *British Policy Towards Wartime Resistance* as well as Davidson's *Special Operations Europe*). His version of his escape from the clutches of the Germans thanks to the bravery and presence of mind of Christine Granville is one record of how she managed it; another will be found in Seth's *The Art of Spying*. The author reveals that the Cretan resistance organization EOK was encouraged and created by SOE and himself; one of its purposes was to counter the attraction of the newly formed communist organization on the island.

Fisher, John. BURGESS AND MACLEAN: A NEW LOOK AT THE FOREIGN OFFICE SPIES. London: Robert Hale, 1977. 244 pp., bibliog., index.

Boyle's *The Climate of Treason,* with its revelations of new names and material, provides us with a measuring rod for Fisher's book, which was virtually contemporary. Fisher's fails the test not only in missing Anthony Blunt but in never speculating on the "fourth man" or on who may have been the Soviet talent scout and recruiter at Cambridge. He massages old facts and theories and devotes much attention to details that are not central to the case and its significance. He is more successful in chronicling the record "of human weakness, of evasions on the part of friends, relatives, officials and politicians—above all politicians." The manner in which these Soviet agents were tolerated and even accepted and their blatant weaknesses and behavior defended, rationalized, or ignored is well brought out. So is the way clues and even evidence were ignored or not passed to the proper authority and the way past official and personal conduct was rationalized once Guy Burgess and Donald Maclean were revealed as Soviet agents. Fisher discusses some important new counterespionage details that explain how Klaus Fuchs and Maclean were initially identified as possible Soviet agents. Pincher's *Their Trade Is Treachery* has facts and makes allegations that are not even hinted at in this book.

FitzGibbon, Constantine. SECRET INTELLIGENCE IN THE TWENTIETH CENTURY. London: Hart-Davis, MacGibbon, 1976. 335 pp., index [New York: Stein and Day].

The author served as an intelligence officer on the staff of General Bradley. His access to Ultra and his assignment to Bletchley Park in 1944 give him some first-hand knowledge of cryptologic matters. There is no record that he has had any experience in intelligence work since. Without indicating any access to privileged information, he has written a book with many errors of fact and judgment, and he often comments without providing the necessary supporting documentation. When sources are reliable, he says they are fragmentary. The contents do not befit the book's title. The author warns that few books on the subject are trustworthy but does not explain why or how his is. His version of the Cicero operation and his way of presenting Lucy as a British-U.S. channel of Ultra to the Soviets are a few examples of things wrong in this book. FitzGibbon would have done better to confine himself to matters about which he had some first-hand knowledge or that he had researched more thoroughly. He is not always clear about when he is speculating, though he claims he does so only when he is not sure. David Kahn's review in *Cryptologia* characterized the book as superficial, not very useful, without much new information, and wrong on a number of points.

Flicke, Wilhelm F. WAR SECRETS IN THE ETHER. 2 vols. Vol. I (parts 1 & 2): to World War II; Vol. II (Part 3): World War II. Laguna Hills, Calif.: Aegean Books, 1977. 305 pp., cryptanalysis appendix of publisher, index.

These two volumes, made available to researchers in 1953, were released by NSA. Kahn in *The Codebreakers* makes reference to the 1953 edition in dealing with the Axis. Flicke worked twenty-eight years in the German cryptographic services. The head of the German intercept service in 1934 commissioned Flicke to write a history of that service. The manuscript of the first volume was lost and had to be reconstructed, largely from memory. The second was written partly from memory and partly from notes. The work was completed in 1945.

This background and the circumstances under which the author had to write make more understandable the strengths and weaknesses of his product. Flicke had unique knowledge of the German service and consequently was a storehouse of first- and second-hand knowledge because of the time and continuity of his service. But there are enough instances of error or incomplete information to warn that not everything Flicke says is automatically authoritative and that memory and notes were not enough. For instance, he cannot be expected to have known the true reason why in 1942 Colonel Fellers, the U.S. Army attaché in Cairo, stopped transmitting messages the Germans had been able to read. CIA's study of the Rote Kapelle informs that what Flicke wrote on the subject was sometimes inaccurate, although Flicke himself did cryptanalytic work chiefly against Rote Drei targets. Part 3 was abridged somewhat by the publisher.

Foot, M.R.D. RESISTANCE: EUROPEAN RESISTANCE TO NAZISM 1940–45. New York: McGraw-Hill, 1977. 320 pp., bibliog., index [London: Eyre Methuen, 1978].

Foot aimed to analyze the whole field of wartime resistance to the Nazis, to explain what resistance could or could not do, and to assess whether the aims of resistance were achieved. Finally, he hoped to show where more research was needed. This book is less detailed and more superficial than his *SOE in France*, for which he had at his disposal original sources, albeit far from complete. Such is the penalty of trying to cover too much ground. Foot does not include German evaluations of European resistance when he comes to weighing its effect. On the other hand, because of his assiduous reading of the literature of SOE's history, he includes important facts, incidents, and anecdotes. A very useful bibliography can be found in the footnotes, particularly on SOE. Foot makes some telling points on resistance; one is that there was a moral imperative to resistance that justified it and made it inevitable—a point missed by some postwar critics of its costs and effectiveness. Errors are not major, but for the U.S. reader, there is an overreliance on R. Harris Smith's *OSS* as the authoritative history of that subject. For an analysis of resistance expressing doubts of its contribution versus costs, see Macksey's *The Partisans of Europe in the Second World War.*

Foot, M.R.D. SIX FACES OF COURAGE. London: Eyre Methuen, 1978. 123 pp., bibliog., notes, no index.

Foot has written about six heroes of the intelligence war in World War II. He sees these six as representative of the best. Of the six, two are women; his account of their bravery and abilities belies the opinion of those who consider women unfit for intelligence work, like the agent Richard Sorge. Those who doubt the ability of women in this field might change their opinions on reading the stories told here or seeing the statistics Foot provides. An unusually high proportion of resisters in World War II were women.

Six Faces of Courage is Foot's ode to the bravery of both men and women. His admiration for their qualities, including the integrity that he believes made their courage special, shines throughout. As a result, this is a moving book; however, it is also instructive. It identifies what helps make agents great in recounting the exploits and by reading into the character and motivation of these special people. R. V. Jones, who dedicated his own book partly to agents who collected intelligence, wrote the appropriate introduction.

Foot, M.R.D. SOE IN FRANCE: AN ACCOUNT OF THE WORK OF BRITISH SPECIAL OPERATIONS EXECUTIVE IN FRANCE 1940–1944. London: HMSO, 1966. 550 pp., bibliog., index.

The genesis of this official history is given in Patrick Howarth's *Undercover.* Briefly, it was a decision of the then British prime minister to proceed with such a work as a result of questions raised in Parliament about SOE activities in France. The task was entrusted to Foot, a historian and veteran of Combined Operations and the Special Air Service (SAS). The first version, the 1966 edition, was withdrawn and superseded by a 1968 impression with changes and additions; the 1966 version contained segments that should not have received security declassification. Foot traces the origins of SOE, security, training, and recruiting in the first section; the second concerns various operations of SOE in France, essentially those of the F Section. He makes no claim to be definitive and in fact outlines areas where material was scant, unsatisfactory, or lacking. Specifically, he cites lack of access to all SOE records; poor or incomplete SOE files and records; little access to knowledgeable Germans or to German records; no access to papers on major deception operations; little access to foreign records; no access to MI5, SIS, or escape and evasion records. Because the study was prepared in secrecy, Foot had severely limited access to former staff personnel and agents of SOE. Records of the RF Section of SOE were not available to him, and many files on particular operations and circuits, all training files, some important papers on the early development of SOE, and almost all messages exchanged with the field had disappeared. To these missing records, we must add the absence of any mention of the role of Ultra, which Foot in a later work on resistance said was an indispensable input into any complete history of the war. This is a formidable list of missing sources; yet some commentators still described *SOE in France* as a definitive study.

Despite Foot's care to make clear the limits of his research, the book was greeted with some controversy when it appeared. In France there was a feeling that it overstated the degree of British control of French resistance. Others felt that Foot ignored people who played important roles while making heroes of some less deserving. In *Britain and European Resistance,* David Stafford stated that *SOE in France* caused so much controversy that it was decided no further volumes should appear. The second edition, according to Foot, was pigeonholed. It would have been wiser, and more productive, to give Foot more time to complete the work and to tap a variety of sources and material. He himself had reservations about whether SOE papers were the best single source on the history of European resistance. As he wrote in 1977 in the foreword to *Resistance,* he learned from this experience in writing an official history "a lot about what to seek." This is, however, still an indispensable work on the subject. Dulles in the foreword to *Great True Spy Stories* also touched on the controversy this study caused in Britain.

Foot, M.R.D., and Langley, J. M. *MI 9:* THE BRITISH SECRET SERVICE THAT FOSTERED ESCAPE AND EVASION 1939–1945 AND ITS AMERICAN COUNTERPART. London: The Bodley Head, 1979. 330 pp., bibliog., index [Boston & Toronto: Little, Brown].

To study the literature of escape and evasion (E&E) as directed by Allied intelligence headquarters organizations and seen from this perspective, one should either begin with this book or end with it (until a newer and even more thorough work appears). It is the culmination of books by British officers connected with MI9—Airey Neave, Jim Langley, and Donald Darling—that progressively revealed more and more and improved our knowledge of the organization of British E&E and of the interservice frictions that existed. Langley and Foot, a historian and author on resistance, give the best and most detailed picture of the organizational and staff aspects of Allied E&E. MIS-X, the American counterpart of MI9, is treated, but it is the story of MI9 that gets the lion's share. The book has the added distinction of spelling out and describing in more detail some of the operational methods and techniques used. Among them were the use of POWs for the collection of intelligence, the use of code to communicate between POWs and the intelligence staff in London and elsewhere, and the operational support for escape planning provided to the POWs. The traumatic failure to free Allied prisoners in Italy during the Italian armistice, a failure in policy and operational planning, is dealt with frankly and extensively. According to a reviewer in the *Illustrated London News,* the staff muddle connected with this event and its consequences had never previously been investigated by historians. Foot and Langley regard their work only as a pioneer study showing future historians where to look. One reason for this attitude is that they did not have access to all British records on MI9 and admit that U.S. records "were cursorily skimmed." The *Illustrated London News* reviewer added that this book is a triumph of persistence, which uncovered records previously believed destroyed. The *RUSI* reviewer's praise for it as "excellent and long overdue" sums up the consensus. Langley's actual affiliation with MI6, incidentally, is revealed here, and the relationship of the deception organization A Force and MI9 is made clearer. Hutton's *Official Secret,* on escape devices, is a companion work. *MI9*'s U.S. edition has revisions and more on the U.S. role.

Foote, Alexander. HANDBOOK FOR SPIES. Garden City, N.Y.: Doubleday, 1949. 273 pp., no index [London: Museum Press, 1949. rev. ed., 1964].

Foote, an Englishman, served as a Soviet agent and wireless operator in Switzerland in World War II in what is known as the Rado-Lucy or the Rote Drei net. The revised 1964 edition was issued after his death, and according to its introduction, it includes some changes and some "annexes." The author of the annexes is not identified, but they are written as if it were Foote. Changes include: the identification of Lucy; deletions of some of Foote's account of life in the USSR after the war; and the addition of certain references to the postwar Canadian spy case that followed the defection of Igor Gouzenko. Despite its value as an early postwar look at the organization and functioning of a Soviet network, the book is marred by Foote's limited view of the net and by errors and distortions. The best authority for this subject, the CIA study *The Rote Kapelle,* states that the wireless traffic proves Foote's claims that Lucy material began to come to the Center in Moscow in early 1941 and that Lucy warned of the German attack on the Soviet Union are wrong. Also, Foote, who disliked Rado, minimized the latter's role and attacked his personal integrity on dubious grounds. Foote and Rado were *not* equals or nearly equals as Foote claimed, and each did not have his own network, code, and communications system; Foote is exaggerating his wartime importance. Evidence does not bear out his claim that he had subsources of his own. Beyond this, Foote was not even right as to the number of radios being used by the net.

David Dallin said Foote was not popular with the other Soviet agents and that Rado had no confidence in him, suspecting him to be a British agent. The CIA study includes the Soviets among those who suspected Foote of working for England and says that they accused him of betraying the Rote Drei net to the British. There is no evidence to support this suspicion. The above criticisms are not enumerated to discourage the study of Foote's description of a Soviet network and of Soviet recruitment, cover, network financing, communications, and overall methods of operation. Rather, the purpose is to alert the reader to its limitations as the authentic story (as one reviewer thought it). See Trepper's *The Great Game,* in which Foote is described as Rado's second in command.

Ford, Corey. DONOVAN OF OSS. Boston: Little, Brown, 1970. 346 pp., bibliog., index [London: Robert Hale, 1971].

Despite Donovan's prominence, the dimensions of his personality, and the innovative nature of his intelligence organization, Ford's biography was the first attempt in twenty-five years. The author relied in large part on Donovan's files, letters, and personal diary, most of which are made public here for the first time. The author did not claim that this was a complete history of OSS; however, he believed he was imparting essentially the whole story on Donovan. Critics felt that Ford's treatment did not accomplish that purpose. Too much of the book was devoted to describing at length particular OSS operations that were extraneous to the central purpose of the biography. Too, Ford's admiration for his subject dulled his critical capacities and led to an incomplete portrayal of the man, as did his reliance largely on Donovan's own records. His interviews, principally with persons considered members of the Donovan team, increased the dangers of not giving a full portrait of Donovan's life in intelligence. Donovan's role and contribution to national policy and to the foundation of U.S. intelligence are still subjects in search of the right authors. Troy's *Donovan and the CIA* is a new and auspicious start, setting new and higher standards of scholarship on Donovan.

Ford, Corey. A PECULIAR SERVICE. Boston and Toronto: Little, Brown, 1965. 328 pp., bibliog., index.

General William Donovan inspired Ford to write this book. Ford's interest in intelligence history probably was stimulated by his assignment on Donovan's staff in OSS. This is not a history of all U.S. intelligence in the American Revolution, as Donovan had suggested, but of portions of it. Covered are the cases of Nathan Hale, Major André, and Benedict Arnold and the work of the Culper ring in New York and Long Island; these incidents are supplemented by descriptions of other intelligence activities such as Washington's imaginative use of deception. Ford claims he brought together for the first time the "complete file" on the Culper ring. He was scrupulous in indicating where he used the device of filling in unknown events by recreating the most likely explanation of them. Where the facts are known, he created conversations to give an air of reality. These techniques did not offend Richard Morris of Columbia University, who in his introduction called the book "scrupulously documented and thoroughly researched." Ford was to be credited for tackling the question of who was the real head of U.S. intelligence during the revolution and for his careful dissection and disposal of earlier flights of fancy on the circumstances of the André capture. See also Pennypacker's *General Washington's Spies* and Van Doren's *Secret History of the American Revolution.*

Foster, Jane. AN UNAMERICAN LADY. London: Sidgwick & Jackson, 1980. 246 pp., index.

In 1957, Jane Foster Zlatovski and her husband were indicted by the U.S. as Soviet agents. Both had been named by Boris Morros, the FBI double agent, as working on behalf of Soviet intelligence; they refused to return to the United States to face charges. This is Jane's autobiography; it appeared subsequent to her death. Of particular interest is what she has to say about her experiences in OSS and the espionage charges against her, although on the first point there is not much of great import. She describes her efforts under the heading "The Happy Warrior" but concludes that her work in Morale Operations (covert psychological warfare) against the Japanese was of no consequence. She relates much about personal, social, and administrative matters but precious little about her operations. Her attempt to explain away charges that she was a foreign agent is where the main significance and weakness of the book lies. She claims she never was a Soviet agent. However, she admits that she lied under oath as to her Communist party membership and that she lied to OSS about her marital status (having married the fellow party member Zlatovski). Her dealings (including financial ones) with Soviet agents such as Morros, Soble, and the Sterns are pictured as innocent in intent and substance. As for the specifics of the indictment against her, she devotes only a little over one page to address them. Of the thirty-eight points of the charges, she answers only fifteen. For Morros's information on Jane and her husband, see his *My Ten Years as a Counterspy;* for other vignettes of her OSS days, see MacDonald's *Undercover Girl.* Carpozi's *Red Spies in the U.S.* contains segments on her personality and private life.

Fourcade, Marie-Madeleine. NOAH'S ARK: A MEMOIR OF STRUGGLE AND RESISTANCE. New York: E. P. Dutton, 1974. 371 pp., no index [London: Allen and Unwin, 1973].

An abridged version of the 1968 French edition, *Noah's Ark* is the memoir of the leader and principal agent of one of the great espionage networks of World War II. Officially called the Alliance but called by the Germans Noah's Ark, it was the only network to cover all of France and the only one of its kind headed by a woman. One of the first networks of any sort, it was organized by a man who was a conservative and the aide to Marshal Pétain. Praise of Fourcade and of her organization has been unstinting. David Schoenbrun wrote in the *New York Times* that Noah's Ark was the most effective spy ring in World War II. Foot in *Six Faces of Courage* selected Fourcade as one of six examples of the best of the heroes of resistance. R. V. Jones confirms the contributions of the Alliance and of Fourcade in the intelligence war against German V weapons. The SIS officer who dealt with the network says in the book's preface that the Alliance particularly well served the Allies with information on German sub bases and rocket sites, and Fourcade he describes as made up of the qualities of a great leader: courage, knowledge of one's profession, and an understanding of people.

This is the saga, poetic and moving in its presentation, of the network's life. Fourcade recalls vividly the problems, accomplishments, and anguish involved in such an effort. Techniques and the specifics of what was done are subordinate to the human side of the story and the human and emotional costs incurred. Some critics wished the author had given more detail on the type of information obtained. Besides intelligence on V weapons and submarine bases, the Alliance, we are told, gave warning of the departure of the German warships *Scharnhorst* and *Gneisenau.* Fourcade includes an example of a six weeks' "take" and backlog of intelligence. Fourcade mentions only briefly the fact that the network's being directly under SIS created friction in London with French intelligence. For those interested in rare items of intelligence history, there is the story of the British fascist who infiltrated SIS and subsequently the Alliance for the Germans. For those looking for another side of Sir Claude Dansey of SIS, there are Fourcade's memories of her dealings with him. Finally, there are the inevitable questions about the security of a network the size of Alliance, which Fourcade herself does not miss. In a 1955 discussion with Jean Overton Fuller, which the latter recounted in *The German Penetration of*

SOE, Fourcade spoke of the risks of large numbers and of new recruits to a clandestine network. Fuller had heard Fourcade's own security practice placed in doubt.

Fraser, Peter. THE INTELLIGENCE OF THE SECRETARIES OF STATE AND THEIR MONOPOLY OF LICENSED NEWS 1660–1688. Cambridge: Cambridge Univ. Press, 1956. 164 pp., bibliog., index.

The thesis of this essay is that the most important function of the secretaries of state under Charles II of England was the management of "intelligence." At that time intelligence was not only defined as extraordinary information about enemies abroad or plotters at home but also concerned the ordinary news of events, both domestic and foreign. This work represents the result of a scholarly investigation of official records and previous studies of intelligence-collection methods, their practitioners, and their means during the period in question. We learn of the methods of intercept and opening of official and private correspondence; the use of funds by the secretaries for the employment of agents (from grants specifically earmarked for intelligence collection); the use of accommodation addresses and various means of transmitting intelligence; and other examples of tradecraft. The text and the appendixes give good details about British intelligence activities of the time. One chapter in particular has modern overtones. It concerns an inquiry into an alleged intelligence failure by a parliamentary committee and its partisan political purposes. Reviews in the *Times Literary Supplement* and the *Guardian* of the book, which was completed under an Oxford scholarship, were favorable.

Freedman, Lawrence. U.S. INTELLIGENCE AND THE SOVIET STRATEGIC THREAT. London: Macmillan, 1977. 198 pp., bibliog., index [Boulder, Colo.: Westview Press, 1978].

Freedman was a research fellow with the Royal Institute of International Affairs when this was published. It is a revised version of a doctoral thesis; the revisions were due to the new availability of large amounts of material on the formation of U.S. intelligence estimates. The two main components—the U.S. intelligence process and the strategic missile threat—are preludes to the final chapter on how well the U.S. intelligence community performs its estimation work and the influence of these projections on U.S. policy. Freedman's sources were official U.S. documents (including some recently declassified), works of other writers, newspaper articles, and interviews. Some of his conclusions are shared by U.S. experts on national security and intelligence. He is weakest when he strays into areas of human collection and of personalities, as in his discussions of Richard Helms and of the value of Penkovsky's information. On the latter point, he seems to have relied partly on Lyman Kirkpatrick, the former official of CIA, whose judgment of Penkovsky's material he misread. The reader's attention is directed to segments of Chapter 4 where Freedman discusses instances of Soviet strategic deception designed to affect U.S. perceptions and estimates of Soviet strength. Recommended for its insights into U.S. estimates is the Consortium for the Study of Intelligence publication *Intelligence Requirements for the 1980's: Analysis and Estimates,* edited by Roy Godson. Harry Ransom believed that Freedman had made good use of much of the overt material available, illuminated the reality of the U.S. strategic intelligence process, and exploded the myth of "objective" intelligence that would solve all policy disputes. For a first-hand look at the workings of the Office of National Estimates (ONE) see Cline's *Secrets, Spies and Scholars.* Cline was a supporter of the view that Penkovsky's material was of great value. For a position closer to Freedman's on this matter, see Pincher's *Their Trade Is Treachery.*

Freese, Jacob. SECRETS OF THE LATE REBELLION. Philadelphia: Crombargar and Co., 1882. 348 pp., no index.

The author raises great expectations by telling us that this is "the inner or secret history" of the Civil War. Freese, who was a judge in Alexandria during the conflict, acquired his information because of his position. The secrets of which he writes, covering only about a third of the book, deal not with intelligence collection or covert political action but rather covert efforts of the Confederates to establish land supply lines to the South. After Gettysburg, the Union naval blockade made the running of supplies by sea extremely risky, and consequently the Confederates attempted to establish secret land supply and communications lines to Washington. Laid out are routes of these lines and names of lookouts, river crossers, safe-house keepers, and providers of transports. So are a number of operations. These the author says are revealed for the first time, as are the names of persons on the Union side who traded with the Confederates. Two items are of special intelligence interest: President Jefferson Davis's insistence that all agents, couriers, guides, etc., who aided the Confederacy should be paid in gold, and the then senator and later President Johnson's failure to report the presence of a Confederate agent in Washington, an old friend.

Friedman, William F., and Mendelsohn, Charles J. THE ZIMMERMANN TELEGRAM OF JANUARY 16, 1917 AND ITS CRYPTOGRAPHIC BACKGROUND. Laguna Hills, Calif.: Aegean Park Press, 1976. 33 pp., no index.

Research into the Zimmermann Telegram of World War I should include this short paper. It was completed in 1938 and finally declassified by the U.S. government in 1965. Tuchman knew of its existence but was unable to see it for her *The Zimmermann Telegram.* She had to modify her original account in a later edition issued after this study became available.

Mendelsohn was a cryptanalyst in Yardley's MI8 and his American Black Chamber. Friedman is the famous U.S. cryptologist associated with the breaking of the Japanese code. Their thesis that the British did not disclose which version of the Zimmermann Telegram they broke because there was a second code, No. 0075, involved in the telegram. Had they done so, they would have revealed they were intercepting and breaking U.S. diplomatic ciphers as well as German ones. David Kahn in *The Codebreakers* credits this work as a very thorough study based on examination of messages in State Department records and on Mendelsohn's studies of German diplomatic codes. In light of the recent (1980) disclosure that Alexander Szek in Belgium made German codes available to British Naval Intelligence in 1914 (hitherto denied), the authors' scepticism of the British version of the capture of the Wassmuss code in Persia as the basis for later successes may very well prove to be very perceptive. For more details on this book's classification in 1938, its declassification in 1953, and its reclassification, see Clark's *The Man Who Broke Purple.* C. J. Edmonds's article in the January 1960 *Royal Central Asian Journal* is another explanation of the source of the German code.

Frolik, Josef. THE FROLIK DEFECTION. London: Leo Cooper, 1975. 178 pp., index.

Frolik, a Czech intelligence officer, defected in 1968. He relates details of particular operations run in the West with which he was familiar, including recruitment or attempted recruitment of British members of Parliament and labor leaders. Due to British libel laws, this book does not give the names of the latter. Deacon in *The British Connection* gives the name of one of those fingered by Frolik; Pincher's *Inside Story* also reveals certain names. Pincher gives background information on how the names of British labor leaders who were targets of Czech intelligence were raised in Parliament and later in the British press. Readers will be interested in Pincher's claim that British intelligence and security authorities were not much impressed with Frolik's information against certain trade union figures. DIS's *Bibliography* found "unsettling" Frolik's comment on U.S. intelligence officers.

Frolik's memoirs are not exactly accurate on the actual details of his defection, partly for reasons of security, it seems. Experts do not recall his supposed meeting with

Richard Helms. Though attention has been directed to his revelations of Soviet recruitment attempts against British figures, his naming of Soviet agents in Prague during World War II and their suspected roles against the non-Communist resistance should not be missed.

Fryer, Mary Beacock. LOYALIST SPY: THE EXPERIENCES OF CAPTAIN JOHN WALDEN MEYERS DURING THE AMERICAN REVOLUTION. Brockville, Ont., Can.: Besancourt, 1974. 222 pp., bibliog., notes, no index.

Most works on British espionage on the North American continent during the American Revolution give the impression that all British efforts were out of New York City. This book gives us the chance to see that there was a larger organization. The glimpse we get of the secret service of the British Northern Department, with headquarters in Canada, is based largely on the papers of Frederich Haldimand, British military governor of Quebec from 1778 to the end of the war. The author, descendant of a Tory who settled in Canada, became interested in John Meyers while doing research on one of her own ancestors. Meyers, who was from New York State, served as a Loyalist spy. From Fryer's description, a good deal of this service was as courier for the British between Canada and New York City, although Meyers achieved fame at the time for his attempt to kidnap the American General Philip Schuyler. For a wider view of the Northern Department's Secret Service, Mathews's *Frontier Spies* must be consulted, since *Loyalist Spy* concentrates on one particular agent.

Fuller, Jean Overton. BORN FOR SACRIFICE: THE STORY OF NOOR INAYAT KHAN. London: Pan Books, 1957. 251 pp., no index [London: Gollancz, 1952. *Madeleine*.].

This is a biography of the author's friend Noor Inayat Khan, an SOE radio operator who was captured by the Germans and lost her life. According to Foot in *SOE in France,* the 1957 version added new material to the first edition but also included fresh mistakes of a trivial nature. No one questions that Noor Inayat Khan showed great courage in adversity and died without succumbing to German attempts to get her to talk; the debate is on whether SOE should have sent her to France in the first place. According to a fellow agent quoted by Foot, she was not the right type, had no sense of security, and never should have been sent. For the latest views of Fuller on the subject, see her *The German Penetration of SOE* (below).

Fuller, Jean Overton. THE GERMAN PENETRATION OF SOE: FRANCE 1941–1944. London: William Kimber, 1975. 192 pp., bibliog., index.

It is the thesis of the author that warnings were received in London about the arrests of agents but were discounted; it was incompetence rather than perfidy that caused SOE in London to continue operations under German control. This work is based on the author's study of the overall pattern of operating and what she called the chain reaction of arrests of agents that occurred. Among the agents whose arrests were reported to London but were not correctly interpreted there she lists Prosper. She also examines the fate of Prosper's network (among others), which went by his name. One reviewer thought this book exposed German successes in France against the British, which were not as widely known as were those in Holland in the North Pole operation. That reviewer was not quite correct, because much has been written of the successes and failures of SOE and other operations in France; it would be closer to fact to say that the French cases did not provide the concentrated drama of the Dutch fiasco. Criticisms of SOE's French operations in the late 1950s resulted in the British government's decision to select Foot to write *SOE in France.* Although the French troubles caused bitter feelings and political acrimony, the response never came close to equaling the furor over the Dutch case. Fuller's conclusion that incompetence rather than perfidy was responsible for the

French disasters precludes any new cause célèbre. Foot, on the other hand, concluded that "Prosper's downfall, tragic as its consequences were, was brought on in spite of their bravery by the agents' own incompetence and insecurity." Fuller alerts us to the possibility that this may not have been the full story and that errors in London need to be considered in any final accounting.

G

Gallagher, Thomas. ASSAULT IN NORWAY: SABOTAGING THE NAZI NUCLEAR BOMB. New York: Harcourt Brace Jovanovich, 1975. 230 pp., index [London: Macdonald and Jane's].

Gallagher recreated all the drama and excitement of what Foot in *Resistance* calls "the most important act of sabotage on record." The book recounts not only the destruction, by an SOE party of nine Norwegians, of the Norsk Hydro heavy-water plant in Norway but a later separate operation that deprived the Germans of a large stock of heavy water on its way to Germany. According to one British historian of resistance in World War II, these operations were significant for more than just their strategic value, which is well known. They prevented the Germans from doing experiments that could have convinced them of the feasibility of an atomic bomb, according to R. V. Jones, who called the first raid "an epic of daring, endurance and sabotage." These operations, we are told by Stafford in *Britain and European Resistance,* were a feather in the cap of SOE advocates of sabotage over resistance. Also, they helped SOE's position and greatly increased its credibility. Gallagher tells the story in popular style, emphasizing both the good planning and the bravery that went into the success. The extent of the author's research into official records, memoirs, and diaries is indicated in the preface, as are the names of those interviewed. Footnotes are absent; sources are indicated only in the text. Haukelid's *Attack on Telemark* is a first-hand account of the operations by one of their participants. Piekalkiewicz's *Secret Agents, Spies and Saboteurs* contains an interesting photo essay.

Galland, Joseph S. AN HISTORICAL AND ANALYTICAL BIBLIOGRAPHY OF THE LITERATURE OF CRYPTOLOGY. Evanston, Ill.: Northwestern Univ. Press, 1945. 209 pp., no index.

Clearly intended primarily for the cryptologist, this work contains "information concerning the technique and history of cryptography and its varied manifestations in the related fields." The annotations are technical and descriptive rather than evaluative. In many cases the author lets the titles speak for themselves, feeling that these give "an adequate idea of the contents and even the value of the works." Nontechnical works that he classifies as "of historical interest" are in the minority and as a rule are given little annotation and no evaluation. Considering that Galland enjoyed the advantage of having many people contributing to his commentaries (including such figures as William Friedman), it is a pity that evaluative comments were not provided for the nontechnical works. Kahn includes this book in *The Codebreakers* in the category of "more important sources." Shulman's *An Annotated Bibliography of Cryptography* fills the gap of the intervening years.

Garlinski, Jozef. HITLER'S LAST WEAPONS: THE UNDERGROUND WAR AGAINST THE V1 AND V2. London: Julian Friedmann, 1978. 238 pp., bibliog., index [New York: Times Books].

The author delved into the archives of many countries—among them France, the Netherlands, Denmark, and Poland in addition to Great Britain and Germany—to write this short history. He tries to present the subject from the points of view of the Allies, the Germans, and the resistance. The development of these weapons and the Allied efforts to discover their nature and halt their development and deployment are treated. It is with the contributions of the resistance, especially that of the Poles, that Garlinski is mainly concerned. This slant is almost inevitable since he is both a Pole and a veteran of Polish resistance. The book appeared at about the same time as R. V. Jones's *The Wizard War* and, in the opinion of one British reviewer, neatly complements it. It should assure that the vital contribution of European resistance to the struggle against these German weapons is never overlooked—especially not that of the Poles.

Garlinski, Jozef. INTERCEPT: THE ENIGMA WAR. London: J. M. Dent and Sons, 1980. 204 pp., bibliog., index [New York: Scribner, 1979].

Garlinski was assisted in writing this book by Colonel Tadeusz Lisicki, the commander of the Polish cryptanalysis unit in Britain in World War II. The best part of the book covers the cryptanalytical aspects of the attack on the German Enigma and the roles played by the Poles, the French, and the British. Whether this portion is complete cannot be known until there is full disclosure of records. Garlinski is not as successful when he tries to write of the role of Allied cryptanalysis in certain events and periods of the war. He admits that his picture is incomplete, that there probably are errors, and that at times he has to resort to hypotheses. Because all records were not available, the author relies too heavily on secondary sources and authors such as Winterbotham whose accounts have been challenged. Consequently, he is prone to repeat errors or speculations, such as that of Malcolm Muggeridge that Lucy in Switzerland was the channel the British used to pass intelligence from decrypts to the Soviets. This segment compares unfavorably with Lewin's *Ultra Goes to War,* which employs more authoritative sources. Garlinski, who has some much better histories of the war to his credit, might have been better advised to tackle this task later. He himself observes that the cryptographic victory, so deep a secret in archives until recently, was "still only partly disclosed." Bennett's *Ultra in the West* and Calvocoressi's *Top Secret Ultra* should also be consulted on the role of Ultra.

Garlinski, Jozef. POLAND, SOE AND THE ALLIES. London: George Allen and Unwin, 1969. 233 pp., index.

The author is a Pole who served in the Polish cavalry and then with the Polish Home Army as an officer. His book first appeared in Polish under the title *Politicians and Soldiers.* In it we find a good picture of Polish events and SOE relations to them with a primary focus on Polish personalities and activities in the covert war. All events are put into context (diplomatic, political, and economic). Sir Colin Gubbins of SOE says in the preface that the book describes in clear and objective terms the dilemma of the Poles. This "sad but inspiring" story is told well and with feeling. In explaining the exceptional status of the Polish Sixth (Intelligence) Bureau in London vis-à-vis SOE and the special treatment accorded the Poles, Garlinski reveals the confidence SOE had in them. He also calls attention to the work of Soviet agents and Soviet partisans, as well as that of Soviet forces, against Polish resistance organizations. Garlinski's research made use of much material that had not previously been tapped, material from both Allied and German sources.

Gayn, Mark, and Caldwell, John. AMERICAN AGENT. New York: Henry Holt and Co., 1947. 220 pp., no index.

This is said to be Caldwell's story of his OWI (Office of War Information) work in China in World War II. Gayn supplies the general background in each segment. The result is confusion. Caldwell, a member of an old American missionary family in China, distances himself from intelligence operations: he writes that he had instructions not to engage in espionage. However, he also divulges that he did assist U.S. intelligence personnel in China in giving them what aid he could or information that came his way. Gayn's remarks, along with the title, give the reader another picture. He speaks of Caldwell's involvement in the "Dark War" to gain the enemy's secrets and to sow doubts in the enemy's mind. More categorically, he says Caldwell under cover of his OWI position was to gather intelligence on Japanese troops and convoy movements and on Japanese-held territories in China; he was to help organize an underground escape and evasion organization; and he was to get Chinese pirates on the coast to spy for the United States. Caldwell tells us nothing of these secret duties. What little he says of the intelligence world is from the viewpoint of an observer, or a coopted official at the very most, and he imparts nothing of significance to the intelligence historian.

Gehlen, Reinhard. THE SERVICE: THE MEMOIRS OF GENERAL REINHARD GEHLEN. New York: World Publishing, 1972. 380 pp., glossary, no index [London: Collins. *The Gehlen Memoirs.* Canada: Nelson, Foster and Scott].

Most reviewers were justifiably disappointed in this book. Gehlen's account of his intelligence career and his judgments of his success cannot be accepted as the final word. He has the habit of taking credit for successes and discounting the possibility that he may have been wrong. Blackstock and Schaf in *Intelligence, Espionage, Counterespionage and Covert Operations* call this book unreliable and often deliberately misleading. A sensational revelation, the identification of Martin Bormann as a Soviet agent, is not supported by any evidence. The event that did much to burst the Gehlen myth, the uncovering of Heinz Felfe of the BND as a Soviet penetration, is not well treated. While there are some worthwhile observations on intelligence's role in policy formulation and national security, remarks that the FBI functioned perfectly and had Soviet intelligence under control in the United States show the author's tendency to make judgments without first-hand knowledge. George Bailey's description of Gehlen's book in the introduction as the most informative on intelligence he has read is excessive praise; it is typical of the effusive homage of Gehlen found in popular works. For a more balanced judgment of Gehlen as head of Foreign Armies East, see Kahn's *Hitler's Spies.* Höhne and Zolling's book on Gehlen, *The General was a Spy,* was the immediate cause for Gehlen's own memoirs.

George, Willis. SURREPTITIOUS ENTRY. New York and London: D. Appleton-Century, 1946. 214 pp., no index.

One of those fascinating, little-known books of intelligence history that does not deserve the neglect it has suffered. It is probably the earliest work after World War

II by a disgruntled U.S. intelligence operative. The author worked as an undercover agent for the U.S. Treasury Department and as an investigator for the Canadians and then served with OSS and ONI. While with the latter two organizations he was involved in some two hundred cases of surreptitious entry. It is in the recounting of some of these that the book's main interest lies. We are informed of techniques of safe opening, lock picking, clandestine photography, the opening of mail (flaps and seals), and the use of listening devices (bugging). The book is thus a good handbook on clandestine techniques of entry (including the opening of letters and sealed documents) and on surveillance. On the latter, there is not much in published literature other than this, Monat's *Spy in the U.S.*, and a few other books. George believed that his activities caused him to be tainted so that neither government nor private business would employ him after the war. George headed the OSS team that made entry into Amerasia's offices and compiled an inventory of the holdings. This operation was later revealed in a court case and used against the U.S. government, so it may be what George thinks tainted him.

Gilchrist, Andrew. BANGKOK TOP SECRET: BEING THE EXPERIENCES OF A BRITISH OFFICER IN THE SIAM COUNTRY SECTION OF FORCE 136. London: Hutchinson, 1970. 230 pp., no index.

This fills a number of needs in the history of intelligence and can serve for instruction on certain intelligence subjects. The author tells the story of the little-known SOE operations into Siam in World War II. The book is about Gilchrist's personal activities as a desk officer, with enough fill-in material to make the story comprehensible. It would be valuable for training because it recounts intelligence operations from the perspective of the headquarters desk officer. Operational, training, bureaucratic, political, and other factors and problems that need to be dealt with by the desk officer in the preparation, dispatching, and evaluation of operations are covered. One chapter on the problem of determining whether one's agents are under enemy control is instructive; so is that on the bureaucracy and structured thinking associated with psychological warfare. Gilchrist was blessed with a sense of humor and prior experience in Siam to enhance the story and to finger the ludicrous. He was later British ambassador to Iceland.

Giskes, Herman J. LONDON CALLING NORTH POLE. London: William Kimber, 1953. 208 pp., no index [New York: British Book Center].

Giskes's story of his successful counterespionage operation against SOE and Dutch military intelligence recounts what was probably the most successful German operation of its type in World War II. The German techniques of running a controlled network became models for teaching such CE operations after the war. The success of Giskes and the Abwehr was, as Foot wrote in *Resistance,* partly due to obtuseness in London. The tragic consequences for Dutch resistance and British resistance operations were great. The events had political ramifications after the war due to Dutch anger and suspicions of British motives, which were expressed in the media and Dutch parliament and even affected intelligence liaison relations. In 1953, according to De Silva in *Sub Rosa,* the Dutch expelled the MI6 representative after the British told the visiting Dutch delegation sent to examine the disasters that all Dutch resistance records had been destroyed in a fire. Until the British released information on their successes against German agents in Britain the North Pole operation was the symbol of German superiority in certain techniques. Worthy of note are: Giskes's indication of the endemic problem of the CI versus the police approach; his single reference to the use of the nets for strategic deception; the failure to "turn" a single set of the Dutch service BI; the denial that the agent King Kong betrayed the Arnhem operation in 1944; the account of CE work and operations elsewhere. Giskes's account of the means and imagination employed to win this intelligence victory still stands as the accurate and intriguing account from the German side. Dulles in *Great True Spy Stories* called it one of the most effective German counterespionage operations of all time because of its complexity, extent, duration, and cleverness in execution. See de Jong's article in the January 1980 *Encounter* and his conclusion that no treason or British duplicity caused the disaster.

Glen, Alexander. FOOTHOLDS AGAINST A WHIRLWIND. London: Hutchinson, 1975. 266 pp., index.

Glen, leader of the Oxford polar expedition of 1935, served in British naval intelligence during World War II. Despite Edward Crankshaw's praise of this book, there is little in it of interest to the student of intelligence. Glen has not told very much of his intelligence duties in Yugoslavia up to the German attack in 1941. Nor does he presume to deal with British and particularly SOE operations in the Balkans in 1940–1941 though he mentions the names of some SOE men in Yugoslavia at the time. His subsequent service in Yugoslavia in 1944 was to clear British mines in the Danube in support of the Russian advance. If he had any intelligence duties or activities beyond this, he does not mention them.

Godson, Roy, ed. INTELLIGENCE REQUIREMENTS FOR THE 1980's: ANALYSIS AND ESTIMATES. Washington, D.C.: National Strategy Information Center, 1980. 223 pp., no index.

The proceedings of a colloquium held by the Consortium for the Study of Intelligence in November–December 1979. The group's purpose is to study U.S. intelligence, to stimulate interest in it, and to look for ways of improving it. The particular purpose of this volume is said to be "to increase understanding of what makes for good analytical intelligence and to explore various approaches to improving the system that produces it." Eight papers, with discussion, are included. Some of the contributors later assumed positions as advisers to the Ronald Reagan camp and/or as members of the Reagan transition teams on intelligence—

Codevilla, Godson, Cline, Pforzheimer, Ikle, and Sullivan. For this reason alone, their papers and the comments they generated have more than an academic interest. Also noted are the following: Israeli organization for intelligence analysis receives a rare description and evaluation; the Soviet intelligence system, usually studied from the point of view of operational organization and collection techniques, is here considered in terms of its organization for analysis and estimates; three papers deal with the subjects of deception and surprise. There are insiders' opinions on U.S. national intelligence estimates of Soviet strategic forces and objectives and some frank views on the U.S. system of analyzing intelligence. The discussion sections are typically too short and too general. In addition to the Reagan team members, the participants included many prominent figures in the world of U.S. national security and intelligence, both active officials and members of a developing "intelligence lobby." The *RUSI* reviewer thought Ray Cline's comments and the comparisons of different national intelligence establishments were the better parts of the work while obsession with the Soviet threat, lower-quality items on deceptions, and faith in "evaluation" were the weaknesses.

Godson, Roy, ed. INTELLIGENCE REQUIREMENTS FOR THE 1980's: ELEMENTS OF INTELLIGENCE. Washington, D. C.: National Strategy Information Center, 1979. 125 pp., no index.

This is the proceedings of the first meeting, in April 1979, of the Consortium for the Study of Intelligence. With the papers being predominantly written by senior retired U.S. intelligence officials, the bulk of the contributions reflect the thoughts and views of the intelligence careerist with practical experience. The treatments of the basic needs and components of successful intelligence vary in quality. Some contain real nuggets and leads that should be developed further. The discussion sections after each paper are too brief, too general, and often too disjointed. Despite the knowledge and range of experience of some of the contributors, they evidently felt constrained in presenting their expertise in a public forum for the first time. The consortium's existence and purpose showed the shift within the United States away from consideration of the desirability, legality, or morality of intelligence activity to technical and historical examination of methods and effectiveness. It is symbolic of the change in attitude toward intelligence in the United States since the days of the Church Senate committee hearings on intelligence.

Golan, Aviezer. OPERATION SUSANNAH: AS TOLD BY MARCELLE NINIO, VICTOR LEVY, ROBERT DASSA AND PHILIP NATHANSON. New York: Harper and Row, 1978. 378 pp., index.

Operation Susannah was the Israeli intelligence effort to sabotage U.S. and British installations in Egypt, using members of a Jewish network there, in such a way that Egyptians would appear to be responsible. It resulted in the arrest of members of the net, the execution of two of them, and the suicide of an Israeli intelligence officer captured in Egypt. Most of this book is devoted to the prison experiences of the net's members; the first two chapters (about a hundred pages), however, do discuss the operation and the Israeli network—its creation, training, and capture. Many things about this version of the operation are unsatisfactory. The most eye-catching is the effort to deny that the operation was designed to disrupt Egyptian relations with the United States and Britain, with no proof advanced for this twist, which is contrary to expert opinion. The author gives little space to the resultant Lavon affair and to the question of who in Israel ordered the operation and its exact purpose if not as described. There is a faint hint that the book may have been partly designed to counter Avri El-Ad's version of events (see *Decline of Honor*), published in 1976. The author never refers to El-Ad by that name but by the Western one of Avraham Seidenberg or his operational name of Paul Frank, a practice that may be significant. Included are names of Israeli and British agents who the Operation Susannah prisoners claim were caught by the Egyptians in separate and unrelated operations. For the most recent treatment of the operation, see Steven's *The Spymasters of Israel.*

Goudsmit, Samuel A. ALSOS. New York: Henry Schuman, 1947. 254 pp., index [London: Sigma. *Alsos: The Failure in German Science*].

The Alsos mission was to determine how far the Germans had progressed in the building of an atomic bomb during World War II. It was organized on the recommendation of General Groves, head of the U.S. Manhattan Project; and Goudsmit was its scientific chief. This is his personal account. He has a special interest in examining why the Germans failed, and a good deal of space is devoted to this question. This preoccupation is understandable for a scientist who had been in Germany on a fellowship in the 1920s and had prewar personal and professional ties with many of Germany's top physicists. Goudsmit's general account of the mission's work should be supplemented by that of Pash, *The Alsos Mission,* which is much more operational and intelligence oriented than this. Pash believes another objective of the mission was to keep German scientists from falling into the hands of the Soviets: if it was, Goudsmit does not mention it. Related are anecdotes on the cover story of the mission and that of the Manhattan Project, which proved transparent to the "clan" of scientists. An early and interesting work on aspects of the scientific war.

Gouzenko, Igor. THE IRON CURTAIN. New York: Dutton, 1948. 279 pp., no index [Toronto: J.M. Dent, 1948. *This Was My Choice.* Montreal: Palm, 1968].

Gouzenko's defection from the Soviet embassy in Ottowa at the end of World War II was one of those intelligence events of strategic consequence. The GRU code clerk's disclosures of Soviet espionage against its allies has been called a watershed in U.S. attitudes toward the USSR. The revelations shocked the West and, according to one writer, caused concern in the U.S. military about the U.S. lead in nuclear technology. The case was an eye-opener on the methods, levels, and quality of Soviet agents, as well as their political and ideological motivations, and was the prelude to subsequent discoveries of other well-placed Soviet spies. Reading of Gouzenko's attempts at defection and Canadian reactions (including that of the government) reminds us how far the West has come in its understanding of Soviet intelligence, the value of defectors, and the need for procedures to handle them when they appear. Gouzenko's story must be supplemented by the reading of the Canadian Royal Commission's report of 1946, based to a great extent on Gouzenko's testimony and documentary evidence. John Sawatsky in his book on the RCMP Security Service, *Men in the Shadows,* provides a look at the RCMP's handling of the case and the later problems of Canadian authorities with Gouzenko's resettlement and demands.

Grant, Robert M. U-BOAT INTELLIGENCE, 1914–1918. London: Putnam, 1969. 192 pp., bibliog., no index.

According to a *RUSI* review, Grant, an ordained minister and professor of theology, wrote this attempt to show how the British Admiralty's intelligence division played its part in defeating the German submarines in World War I. It is difficult to understand how Grant felt he could accomplish this purpose by basing his study largely on *German* records captured in 1945. Grant's methodology was to rely on the search of statistical records and the compilation of a "bean count"; but here again, he does not explain how British naval intelligence's part could be fully and satisfactorily covered by this method. Nor does one have the feeling that the accumulated facts are properly put in perspective. The same *RUSI* review calls the work "scholarly, concise, accurate and sound" but allows that the value of the study is "methodological." A number of interesting anecdotes are found; had they set the pattern, the book would have made more interesting intelligence reading. Some of these, such as the story of the German attempt to deceive the Allies in an operation directed at the U.S. naval attaché in Copenhagen in June 1918, were previously known to only a few.

Green, James Robert. THE FIRST SIXTY YEARS OF THE OFFICE OF NAVAL INTELLIGENCE. Ann Arbor, Mich.: University Microfilms, 1971. 116 pp., bibliog., no index.

A 1963 Master's thesis by the author, formerly an instructor at the U.S. Naval Intelligence School. Based entirely on unclassified material, it can hardly do justice to its aim: to cover the history of an intelligence and security service between 1882 and 1943. Even so, Green has not exhausted overt sources or adequately conveyed the events he might have thoroughly covered. For example, his quick survey of naval intelligence collection in the Civil War includes the names of only two men assigned to Great Britain to collect information on Confederate ships being built there. There is no indication that Green consulted published works that provided considerable detail on U.S. collection efforts in Britain at that time. As indicated earlier, Green's work does not measure up to Dorwart's *The Office of Naval Intelligence,* which was published sixteen years later and had the advantage of access to declassified material. Green's judgments on the effectiveness of ONI in various periods are generally sound, an important mark in favor of his effort.

Grendel, Frédéric. BEAUMARCHAIS: THE MAN WHO WAS FIGARO. New York: Thomas Y. Crowell, 1977. 297 pp., bibliog., index.

Grendel's biography covers all facets of the life of a remarkable man who rose from humble origins to accomplish great things in the worlds of business, diplomacy, intrigue, and letters. His role as an agent of kings Louis XV and Louis XVI is not a major aspect of this work. Similarly, though Beaumarchais's important part in the

French covert involvement in the American Revolution is discussed, as is the important role he played in France's choosing to become openly involved against Britain, these are subsidiary elements of Grendel's story. A great admirer of his fellow Frenchman, the author accords Beaumarchais credit for French policy during the American Revolution in the face of the caution of the French king and his foreign minister, Vergennes. Since historically this is Beaumarchais's greatest accomplishment in the record of human affairs, the intelligence historian will wish Grendel had spent more space on it.

Gylden,Yves. THE CONTRIBUTION OF THE CRYPTOGRAPHIC BUREAUS IN THE WORLD WAR. Washington, D.C.: Government Printing Office, 1935. 87 pp., no index.

Gylden undertook this to show his Swedish compatriots "the extraordinary great part played by cryptography during the first World War" and thus to stimulate Swedish interest in creating a permanent cryptanalytical bureau. Considering the performance of the Swedes in the next few years in cryptanalysis, if this work did not convince them, something else did. Strictly speaking, Gylden has recounted the history of *military* cryptology, not the broader field the title implies. Much of what he writes is from the French, Austrian, and German experiences. Givierge and Ronge wrote about their respective services after the war and German cryptologic successes were largely on the Eastern front; from these Gylden draws heavily. There is nothing on British accomplishments in military cryptology. Gylden provided not only a work on the successes of cryptology but also a primer on cryptographic security. He stresses the errors in the use of codes and ciphers; the lack of security, training, and discipline among cryptographers, and the inertia associated with the employment of codes. William Friedman edited the book, made corrections, and added some valuable comments, both technical and nontechnical. One of these is that Gylden handled the subject in "a masterly manner"—high praise indeed. Kahn lists the work as one of the more important sources for *The Codebreakers* and bases one of his three chapters on World War I partly on it. In light of new evidence about Alexander Szek, however, Gylden may be wrong about the nonexistence of a man who procured a German code for the British. Note, too, the use of a compromised code by the Russians prior to the war to deceive those who were intercepting the traffic and decoding it. Shulman in *An Annotated Bibliography of Cryptography* commented that Gylden was an excellent cryptanalyst and this book was more accurate and thorough than Yardley's *The American Black Chamber.*

H

Hagen, Louis. THE SECRET WAR FOR EUROPE: A DOSSIER OF ESPIONAGE. New York: Stein and Day, 1969. 280 pp., index [London: Macdonald, 1968].

Experts on the subject as well as those slightly less expert have spoken highly of this book. Hagen has written a good, detailed account of certain espionage cases in West Germany since 1945. He has a knack for conveying the essence and feel of these humint collection cases. Conceptually, the author equates the clandestine struggle in Germany with that in Europe as a whole. Practically all cases are those of eastern European services against West Germany or against Allied targets in West Germany. There are good sections on Frenzel, Stashinsky, and Otto John. The weakest chapter, on the Gehlen organization, contains the bulk of the minor errors to be found; the reader should be wary in particular of some accounts of how certain agents were uncovered. The postscript chapter represents Hagen's view that a two-way flow of information supplied by intelligence services is necessary for a balance between East and West. In the context of the Communist victories recounted, it may be misread as a justification of that massive espionage.

Haldane, R. A. THE HIDDEN WAR. New York and London: St. Martin's Press, 1978. 190 pp., bibliog., index [London: Robert Hale].

During World War II Haldane served as the personal intelligence staff officer to the British director of intelligence, home security. It is a pity that with his intelligence background and the research he did, he did not come up with something better than this. His aim was to tell the story of secret communications in perspective against the background of events; he did not succeed. Perhaps one reason was, as he commented, that nobody is qualified to write about such a wide subject or to have full confidence in some sources. Another reason was that the full story of Ultra was not available to him. But Haldane was not discriminating in separating reliable sources from less reliable and unreliable; he was not good at separating the wheat from the chaff. Thus, he relied on Cookridge for SOE and on Richard Deacon and Alexander Foote for the full story of Lucy. He perpetuated the old canard about the German agent at Scapa Flow who supposedly aided in the sinking of the *Royal Oak.* His version on Cicero was nowhere complete, and neither was his treatment of the Rote Kapelle. Other errors or inadequacies dot the work. Questionable items include his assumption that Felfe was a Soviet agent during World War II. Where he used excellent sources, his accounts were good as in the chapter on the submarine war for which he relied on such authorities as Beesly. And there cannot be much debate about his conclusion that secret communications played an important part in winning World War II. What could be debated is how reliably Haldane documented his positions.

Haldane, R. A. THE HIDDEN WORLD. London: Robert Hale, 1976. 207 pp., bibliog., index [New York: St. Martin's Press].

During World War II, Haldane served as the personal intelligence staff officer to the British director of intelligence, home security. Any intelligent layman with a smattering of knowledge on the subject will immediately discern that this is a poor man's survey of the history of cryptography. The reader will note the errors in the text and will be put on guard by some of the comments on certain books in the author's bibliography. The severest criticism of *The Hidden World* was in David Kahn's review in *Cryptologia.* Kahn called it one of the worst books ever written on cryptology and used the words "inaccurate," "ill-produced," "ill-organized," and "of no value" in his unsparing characterization of it.

Hall, Charles Swain. BENJAMIN TALLMADGE: REVOLUTIONARY SOLDIER AND AMERICAN BUSINESSMAN. New York: Columbia Univ. Press, 1943. 284 pp., notes, index.

At the time he wrote this, Hall was with the FDR Library in Hyde Park, New York. More recently, he has been on the faculty of the U.S. Army War College. His versions of the role of Tallmadge in the New York network and of the Arnold-André case do not add any new material. Hall acknowledges his debt to Pennypacker for his material on the stage in Tallmadge's career when he was involved in intelligence and he considers Van Doren's *Secret History of the American Revolution* as the definitive work on Arnold's treason. One can question Hall's designation of Tallmadge as "the manager of Washington's Secret Service during the Revolutionary War." Experts see Tallmadge as the man who ran *one* of the American nets, the Culper ring in New York, and as having been designated by Washington *at one point* as chief of intelligence. In reality, Washington himself was the chief of American intelligence; Tallmadge was basically a high-level case officer running agents. He was not, as a result, a manager of the secret service during the whole war, as one is led to believe. Ford's *A Peculiar Service* has more details on Tallmadge and the Culper net and looks at the question of who was secret service chief.

Hall, Richard. THE SECRET STATE: AUSTRALIA'S SPY INDUSTRY. North Melbourne: Cassell Australia, 1978. 245 pp., index.

There is no doubt of this book's partisan nature. Hall frankly calls it "a polemical book about the twin cults of security and intelligence in Australia." A journalist once employed in the office of the leader of the Australian Labor party, he wrote what he believed to be the first sustained, critical analysis of the Australian security and intelligence agencies. Hall may be said to represent the lack of consensus on Australian intelligence and security that came into greater public view in the early 1970s. He saw his country as "out of the U.S.-U.K.-Soviet Union intelligence duel" and could see no value to communications intelligence in peacetime. Agee, Marchetti, and Copeland are the U.S. sources he relied on—one reason for the nature of his chapter on CIA and the errors that riddle it. Hall, writing a pioneer work on the ASIO and ASIS, has shown a lack of balance that inevitably colors his views and affects the way he uses facts. Obviously well-connected and in certain cases well-informed, he makes us understand how some Labor party adherents saw Australian security and intelligence organizations as partisan. It was not until 1977 that the Australian government first acknowledged the existence of ASIS and a signals intelligence service. Thwaites's *Truth Will Out* gives a view of the Petrov affair and its effect on the local political scene as well as an opinion of Hall's book from the side of Australian security.

Hall, W. Reginald, and Peaslee, Amos J. THREE WARS WITH GERMANY. Edited and illustrated by Joseph P. Sims. New York: G. P. Putnam's Sons, 1944. 297 pp., index.

Because of the importance of Admiral Hall, one would be led to think this book by him has something of significance on his work in British naval intelligence in World War I. Actually, it concerns the litigation of U.S. claimants against Germany for damages done in the United States in World War I. Hall is featured for his assistance in the case; there is little on his work in intelligence. This book will mainly interest those doing research on German sabotage in the United States during World War I and its aftermath. Landau's *The Enemy Within* is more detailed than this on the postwar investigations and litigation, though it was written before a final court decision was given. For historians concerned with Hall, who had been refused official permission to publish his biography begun in 1932, his affidavits included here are a poor substitute. A notable exception is the short section on German germ warfare plans and activities. This is a unique case of the involvement of an intelligence service in such operations and is worth further research.

Hamilton, Alexander. WINGS OF NIGHT: THE SECRET MISSIONS OF GROUP CAPTAIN CHARLES PICKARD. London: William Kimber, 1977. 195 pp., index.

The specialist in intelligence will not find many works devoted to those who had the job of infiltrating and exfiltrating personnel, including agents, into and from German-occupied Europe by landing aircraft on secret landing strips. An early, tentative work on the subject was Jerrard Tickell's *Moon Squadron* (New York: Doubleday, 1958; London: Allan Wingate, 1956). Among those exfiltrated by Pickard were General de Lattre de Tassigny and René Massigli. This book is good on some aspects of the air support provided intelligence operations in World War II. It is also a memorial to a man who, in addition to being involved in such operations as a pilot and squadron commander, had an incredible war record before being killed. He was in the Bruneval raid landing paratroopers and led the air raid on Amiens prison in February 1944 that succeeded in freeing some two hundred Frenchmen, many of the resistance, due to the precision of the bombing. For another view of Pickard's work and his personality, consult Gibb McCall's *Flight Most Secret* (London: William Kimber, 1981).

Hamilton-Hill, Donald. SOE ASSIGNMENT. London: William Kimber, 1973. 186 pp., no index.

A selection of anecdotes of this Scot's wartime experiences. Some will be of value and interest to those concerned with Balkan affairs during World War II. Some readers will find Hamilton-Hill's grasp of the strategic and diplomatic context of events he relates to be weak. Note the author was in the Auxiliary Units before joining SOE. These were designed to undertake resistance activities against the Germans in the event of a successful German invasion of Britain in 1940. Because of the many names of SOE members mentioned in the book, an index is sorely missed.

Hampshire, A. Cecil. ON HAZARDOUS SERVICE. London: William Kimber, 1974. 256 pp., bibliog., index.

Hampshire authored a number of books on naval warfare. This one touches aspects of that war that are not too well known and that have features of covertness or of special operations. The sad story of Q ships of World War II, judged completely ineffectual by most experts, is told. Tales of poor security practices in the British Navy and by shore staffs at British naval bases are not neglected. Perhaps the account of the blockade runners from Sweden is the most enthralling section. Ralph Barker's 1976 *The Blockade Busters* develops this particular story, which, in addition to being a testimony to imaginative and courageous special operations, exposes the absence of British planning to produce or stockpile a stategic item—high-quality ball bearings. The Swedish operation of 1941 was regarded as SOE's first major success.

Hampshire, A. Cecil. THE SECRET NAVIES. London: William Kimber, 1978. 259 pp., bibliog., index.

Covers three areas of British special naval operations in World War II. These are: the covert sea operations unit used by a number of intelligence services to transport agents, arms, supplies, escapees, evaders, and prominent figures into or out of occupied Europe; the unit under a cover name of RMBPD that was the frogman/kayak means of destroying ships in harbors; and the Intelligence Assault Unit or AU, targeted against important enemy documents and material. Hampshire recounts not only better-known operations, such as that of Colonel Hasler against shipping in Bordeaux, but little-known ones, such as the destruction of German warships in Leros, the finding of Italy's highest security codes in Capri, and the high priority given by SIS to the capture of enemy ciphers by AU. Though it reads a bit like a regimental history and should include more evaluations of the overall results of some of these operations, this work serves one good purpose in intelligence history: it sheds some light on these little-known units and their activities, though inevitably, according to a *RUSI* review, many areas and operations are not included. Most special units, we are informed, were controlled by nonnaval intelligence officers seconded to the Admiralty.

Handel, Michael I. PERCEPTION, DECEPTION AND SURPRISE: THE CASE OF THE YOM KIPPUR WAR. Jerusalem: Hebrew Univ. of Jerusalem, 1975. 64 pp., bibliog., no index.

A well-organized and lucidly written analysis. Handel, a lecturer on international relations in Israel, has studied the ideas of others who have investigated the problem intelligence services confront in discerning impending attack. These he develops, expands, and then applies to the events leading up to the Arab attack in 1973. The conclusion he arrives at and the paradoxes he lists are obviously the work of a man who has pondered the problem of surprise, but they are also from the perspective of an Israeli and a Westerner. They are presented as of universal application but how valid this characterization is cannot be decided. There will be differences with his view that the Israelis in 1973 were "probably not deceived but . . . deceived themselves." This theory is in line with the thrust of his analysis that self-deception rather than deception by one's adversary is the greater danger. Chaim Herzog, the former chief of Israeli Military Intelligence, in 1975 characterized Egyptian deception as "eminently successful, extremely well conceived and very well carried out." Readers will agree that Handel's work is insightful and stimulating and that it represents some of the high-quality thinking now devoted to deception analysis.

Harel, Isser. THE HOUSE ON GARIBALDI STREET: THE FIRST FULL ACCOUNT OF THE CAPTURE OF ADOLF EICHMANN TOLD BY THE FORMER HEAD OF ISRAEL'S SECRET SERVICE. New York: The Viking Press, 1975. 290 pp., index [London: André Deutsch].

Much is to be learned from this excellent account of the Israeli operation to kidnap Eichmann in Argentina in 1960. The story of the detailed planning and investigation, the preparations, and finally the execution of the operation is of instructional quality and has a realism seldom found in works of intelligence fiction. The arrangements for cover, documentation, transportation, safe-keeping facilities, security, and surveillance are described. So is the strong motivation of those who were involved, another reason for the operation's success. Harel admits his account, though faithful and factual, keeps some details secret, such as the names of Israelis and others involved and the exact identity of their particular services. Harel does not expand on what assistance the agents had in Argentina beyond that of the "fortuitous" assistants he mentions. Nor does he expand on cover and documentation arrangements. Because of international and legal implications, his attempt to shield the Israeli government from the operation is understandable but transparent. These are minor points that do not affect the basic value of this book. DIS's *Bibliography* makes the perceptive comment that Harel represents here the Israelis' concern to present their concept of the ethics of their intelligence activities, the concept of the men who created Israeli intelligence. Harel, who as intelligence chief actually led the operation, was later to be criticized by some for his unorthodox behavior and for the risk his personal involvement as chief entailed. For this and other details of the operation, see also Steven's *The Spymasters of Israel.*

Harris, William R. INTELLIGENCE AND NATIONAL SECURITY: A BIBLIOGRAPHY WITH SELECTED ANNOTATIONS. rev. ed. Cambridge, Mass.: Harvard Univ., Center for International Affairs, 1968. 930 pp.

This is divided into two sections. The first is Harris's ninety-two-page introductory essay. The remainder is the bibliography itself, broken up into twenty-seven categories. Included are titles of books, government studies and publications, articles, theses, and research monographs. Items are listed in as many categories as are applicable, sometimes on the basis of only one pertinent section. The research, therefore, is impressive. The initial bibliographic essay is striking for its candidness and its observations. Harris modestly explains that he lacks background or experience in intelligence and thus the expertise to evaluate any of the works. He also concedes that the work is unwieldly, is largely unplanned, and thus is of complex organization. He has excellent and telling comments to make on the general quality of works of nonfiction and the uncritical recommendations and comments of many reviewers, some of whom are not familiar with intelligence. There is a valuable discussion of deception, a specialty of his. The introduction allows us to understand the reasons for and to be more tolerant of the weaknesses in the bibliography. Among these: annotations are few and those that are to be found are brief; annotations are not always indicative of a thorough knowledge of the work commented on; some categories are inexplicably lacking obvious works (such as the important works on the FBI not to be found in the category of security and counterespionage); covert political action is not one of the categories. The impression left is that of an archival and technical effort on which much time and effort was expended and that serves as one of the guides to the growing literature on intelligence and national security. Harris makes it clear that he deliberately chose to leave more thorough annotation to subsequent bibliographers.

Hartcup, Guy. CAMOUFLAGE: A HISTORY OF CONCEALMENT AND DECEPTION IN WAR. Newton Abbot, Eng.: David and Charles, 1979. 150 pp., bibliog., notes, index.

Hartcup is one of the official British historians of World War II's combined operations and the war in the air. The vantage point here is British, as are the bulk of experiences recounted. Americans, Germans, and others get only brief mention. The author deals primarily with visual deception; other aspects of deception, such as false transmission of intelligence by radio, the planting of false operational orders, and other ruses de guerre, are in the main outside the province of this work. Naval deception is confined entirely to visual measures. The book does give a wider view of British camouflage (in the strict sense) than was provided by Barkas in *The Camouflage Story* or Maskelyne in *Magic—Top Secret* right after the war. It discusses the neglected contribution of operations research to camouflage. To his credit, Hartcup tries to evaluate results of methods and campaigns. At times he is wrong; for example, he is unaware of the fiasco of the decoy landing craft tanks (LCTs) before the Normandy invasion (described by Cruickshank in *Deception in World War II*). Seeing things from the British experience or perspective, he makes debatable judgments on Japanese susceptibility to deception. He gets full credit for the brief but unique account of the work of D Section in India, for a host of anecdotes, and for his general conclusions on the future of deception, including the visual variety. However, he is wrong when he laments the lack of available information on Soviet camouflage. There are numerous writings in Russian, particularly on Soviet methods used in World War II. See Reit's *Masquerade* for more on U.S. camouflage than is contained here.

Haswell, Jock. BRITISH MILITARY INTELLIGENCE. London: Weidenfeld and Nicolson, 1973. 262 pp., bibliog., index.

Major Haswell was selected by British army intelligence to write an official history of the Intelligence Corps. He arranged to publish this work unofficially after financial difficulties ended governmental support. Its original sponsorship and purpose explain why it reads like a unit history. The advantage of full access to all records of the Intelligence Corps not only gave him items of value but let him ascertain a constant factor in the history of British military intelligence: the prejudice against intelligence and intelligence officers within the British military service throughout most of the last two hundred years, a factor that explains the neglect of military intelligence in time of peace. Haswell thinks military or martial virtues are incompatible with qualities that make for a good intelligence officer; that view may be the reason for the unfavorable notice given the work by certain U.S. military intelligence figures. The *RUSI* review found that the author was right in drawing attention to the sad treatment of the corps after each war but also noted he did not cover all aspects of British military intelligence; only field intelligence in recent years was adequately dealt with. The review also observed that despite the author's access to official material, the book had numerous errors and omissions. For additional reading, see Parritt's *The Intelligencers,* which traces the development of British military intelligence up to 1914.

Haswell, Jock. THE INTELLIGENCE AND DECEPTION OF THE D-DAY LANDINGS. London: Batsford, 1979. 185 pp., bibliog., index [New York: Times Books. *D-Day: Intelligence and Deception*].

In this book, unlike his others, Haswell has attempted to tackle a specific event and subject in depth. Unfortunately, he contributes nothing of significance to our knowledge and understanding of deception in conjunction with the 1944 invasion of France. He is adept at formulating or reemphasizing some general concepts and maxims on deception previously identified by others. He provides no references and is prone to repeat old or make new errors. Examples: Cicero gets sole credit (along with the British deceptions using him) for German reinforcement of the Balkans; the old story of sacrificing Coventry to protect Ultra is repeated; Hitler's reasons for maintaining large forces in Norway are pictured as more simple than they were; the extent of Soviet support for Allied deception plans is presented as definitely known, when it still is not; Canaris is depicted as the master of disinformation. Then there are errors not directly associated with deception: the author's judgment of the accuracy of Gehlen's Soviet estimates; the view that Hitler lost the war because he ignored his intelligence staff; the reason given for the creation of SOE; the belief that French resistance suffered because of the lack of centralized control; the version of Allied knowledge from Ultra of Rommel's request to Hitler for panzers *prior* to the invasion (not supported by the findings of such researchers as Bennett; see *Ultra in the West*). Look to other writings for a better, more balanced, and more comprehensive picture of Allied deception associated with the invasion.

Haswell, Jock. SPIES AND SPYMASTERS: A CONCISE HISTORY OF INTELLIGENCE. London: Thames and Hudson, 1977. 176 pp., bibliog., index.

Haswell makes no great claims; he recognizes that a book of this sort could not be more than an introduction to this vast subject. In contrast to some illustrated works in the "coffee-table" category, this deserves to be recognized as a good introduction to the subject. Haswell has selected his vignettes well, included lessons and observations, and presented everything in a crisp, readable style. Errors or exaggerations are only occasional and not critical to the overall worth of the work.

Haukelid, Knut. ATTACK ON TELEMARK. New York: Ballantine, 1974. 160 pp., no index [London: Kimber, 1954. *Skis Against The Atom*].

Formerly titled *Skis Against the Atom,* this first was published in 1954 by Ryerson. Haukelid was one of the Norwegians who took part in the daring SOE operations that first damaged the German heavy-water production facility in Norway and later sank the stock being sent to Germany. His story covers more than these two operations, for he also dwells on his work in the Norwegian resistance before and after these attacks. Haukelid was described by Gallagher in *Assault in Norway,* which deals with these same operations, as a powerful man with a chest that looked bullet-proof, "a kind of [Henry] David Thoreau with brawn." This hero was also the twin brother of the actress Sigrid Gurie. Gallagher's account must be read to get a fuller awareness of the courage and daring of these raids, which have been praised by experts as among the most important acts of sabotage in history and indeed by one author (Foot in *Resistance*) as the most important on record. Haukelid's account is good but too modest and too terse; he even fails to inform the reader that he was awarded the British D.S.O. He gives only a flavor of his life "of extreme deprivation and hardship" (in Gallagher's words) between operations. General Gubbins's introduction lets us know that he, the head of SOE, considered Haukelid's account understated. See also the pictorial essay of these operations in Piekalkiewicz's *Secret Agents, Spies and Saboteurs.*

Heiman, Grover. AERIAL PHOTOGRAPHY: THE STORY OF AERIAL MAPPING AND RECONNAISSANCE. New York: Macmillan, 1972. 171 pp., bibliog., index.

Heiman, formerly a reconnaissance expert with the U.S. Air Force, traces the developments in cameras and planes from earliest days and ends by describing current radar and infrared photography as well as satellites that have been officially acknowledged by the United States as reconnaissance devices. The book, part of the Air Force Academy series, devotes greatest attention to aircraft and cameras and especially to U.S. developments, although some foreign contributions are briefly mentioned, such as the work of Sidney Cotton. The contributions of George Goddard are duly acknowledged. The emphasis on technical developments means that in a book of this size, the work of individuals and units involved in combat reconnaissance and PI is not expanded on as much as one would like; thus we have only a cursory account of the Cuban missile crisis in 1962. (For an expert account of this crisis, see Don Moser's "The U2, Cuba and the CIA" in the October 1977 edition of *American Heritage*.) Heiman's book is recommended by specialists in the fields of aerial photography and PI as a very good general account of the subjects.

Hill, George A. DREADED HOUR. London: Cassell, 1936. 272 pp., index.

Of Hill, Sidney Reilly said that "never could man wish for more gallant and devoted a collaborator"; Robert Bruce Lockhart called him "as brave and as bold as Reilly." Hill was raised in Russia, served as an intelligence officer on the Salonika and Western fronts in World War I, and ended up with a British aviation mission to Russia. In *Dreaded*

Hour, he takes up the story of his life where he left off in *Go Spy the Land* (below). However, he says virtually nothing about secret service activities in which he was involved during his three years in government service after the end of World War I. He disposes of his travels to many capitals of Europe, to the Mediterranean, and even to the Caucasus in a few sentences and with the remark "my work was fascinating, full of interest." The remainder of the book recounts his experiences in business not connected with intelligence. An interesting historical footnote to his career is that Hill served as head of the SOE mission in Moscow during a large part of World War II. See Dennis Wheatley's *Drink and Ink* (1979) for a glimpse of Hill's personal difficulties once his intelligence work ended.

Hill, George A. GO SPY THE LAND: BEING THE ADVENTURES OF I.K. 8 OF THE BRITISH SECRET SERVICE. London: Cassell, 1932. 276 pp., index.

The first of Hill's two books, this memoir of his experiences in Russia does not read as if it is the full or exact story he might have wished to tell. In his later *Dreaded Hour* (above), he confesses that his first work "presented many problems," but he does not elaborate on what they were. His version of how he came to undertake secret service work in Russia is difficult to acccept, as is his account of starting a *private* bureau of intelligence after the Communists took over Russia. These points aside, there is much of historical interest—such things as his assistance to Trotsky and advice to the Communists in setting up an intelligence and counterintelligence organization or his remarks about the early cryptanalytic capabilities of the Soviets. Hill served in Russia both in uniform and in hiding until the end of the war. He returned to Russia for short missions and as British political officer in Odessa in 1920. Note his respect for the Soviet secret service, and his belief that "the most brilliant counterespionage work" was needed to counter it.

Hilsman, Roger. STRATEGIC INTELLIGENCE AND NATIONAL DECISIONS. Glencoe, Ill.: Free Press, 1956. 183 pp., index.

This book's task was to identify doctrines that prevailed in intelligence agencies, examine them, and compare them with alternatives. The purpose was to discover what role U.S. agencies concerned with strategic intelligence are supposed to play in determining foreign policy. Hilsman served in OSS and CIA and later as head of the State Department's INR. Critics of the book were mostly laudatory. Harry Ransom in *The Intelligence Establishment* called it one of the three groundbreaking treatises on intelligence. DIS's bibliography, however, characterized it as provocative, difficult to read, and not regarded by all leading intelligence authorities as an incontrovertible treatment of the subject. Codevilla, in a 1979 paper given at a symposium on analysis and estimates, described Hilsman's work as perhaps the best book on the subject. At the same time, he felt it dealt more with the opinions of various figures in U.S. intelligence at the time rather than evaluating the kind of system that would best suit the United States. Blackstock and Schaf's bibliographic notation called it an excellent summary of U.S. strategic intelligence doctrine of the first postwar decade. It also said that Hilsman's views were later modified.

Sections of the book vary in quality and style. Part 2 is perhaps the best; it describes the attitudes of various categories of individuals, from decision makers to academics and critics of intelligence. Chapter 1 of the first section, "Background and Growth," is not wholly accurate. Part 3 is much more academic and theoretical than the rest of the book in evaluating doctrines and making recommendations.

Hinchley, Vernon. SPY MYSTERIES UNVEILED. New York: Dodd, Mead, 1963. 254 pp., no index [London: Harrap, 1963].

This purports to cover thirty years of espionage history through case histories and comment. Among the cases are those of Cicero and Burgess and Maclean and the death of General Sikorski. Hinchley claimed practical experience in espionage and counterespionage and believed he had the capacity to present new information, new angles, or "new reconstructions" based on a "fresh and factual viewpoint." He predicted that his book would create astonishment and incredibility. His prediction is fulfilled; only a few examples will suffice to show why. Burgess and Maclean, he says, were not spies but renegades. Blake was a British-controlled agent used to deceive the Soviets. Commander Crabb was possibly on a mission for U.S. intelligence when he made his ill-fated underwater try at inspecting a Soviet warship. General Sikorski was the victim of a German design. Hinchley either was egregiously wrong about or lacked credible sources for his "new angles" at the time he wrote. This judgment is still true from a much later perspective.

Hinsley, F. H., with E. E. Thomas, C.F.G. Ransom, and R. C. Knight, BRITISH INTELLIGENCE IN THE SECOND WORLD WAR: ITS INFLUENCE ON STRATEGY AND OPERATIONS. Vol. 1. London: HMSO, 1979. 577 pp., index.

This official history, ending with the German invasion of the USSR in June 1941, was eagerly awaited, especially in light of the British government's decision in the 1960s not to follow up Foot's history of SOE in France. Strictly speaking, as R. V. Jones pointed out in a review, this is not a history of intelligence. He is right, for it has the central concern of determining how intelligence was used and its value and justification. Its principal task is reconstructing the influence of intelligence on major decisions, operations, and the general course of the war. The authors have academic and scientific credentials. Hinsley worked at Bletchley Park in the naval section, as did Thomas, who continued in naval intelligence after the war. Knight was in wartime guided weapons research and development, while Ransom was previously a fellow at Oxford. They were given access to official records, but not unlimited use of those documents. Many records no longer existed; information on methods and persons were excluded from revelation because they were still covered by the Official Secrets Act; "domestic records" of some of the intelligence-collecting bodies similarly could not be cited as sources or directly quoted. The war in the Far East is not covered; it was primarily a concern of the United States, and British records alone could not adequately give an account. The authors make no pretentious claims about their work. They regard it as a compact, coordinated, but broad treatment and acknowledge that room exists for further research, even on matters about which they have given the fullest possible account.

Much of the work is of intelligence significance. The authors confirm the importance of the Czech agent A-54 in acquiring first-class political and military intelligence during the first two years of the war (see Moravec's *Master of Spies*); they support R. V. Jones and others and deny Winterbotham's version of official motives during the German air attack on Coventry; they confirm the success of German deception plans for Barbarossa in misleading British staffs in London (but not Bletchley Park) until almost ten days before the invasion of Russia; they explain the organization of British intelligence since the turn of the century; they provide the dates on which the British advised the United States of Bletchley Park's work on Axis ciphers and the United States exchanged to them information from Japanese diplomatic traffic; they show the complete failure of British sources to learn of the 1939 German-Soviet negotiations. These are only a few examples.

The book has not escaped criticism. One is that the authors' decision to keep the naming of individuals to a basic minimum deforms the intelligence process since, as Ronald Lewin complained in his review in *RUSI,* the human factor is inescapable, as is the effect of individual judgment. This decision leads to odd situations; for instance, Menzies as "C" is never once mentioned. Another criticism is that the book, though frank about some matters, remains silent on others. One will also note the method of citing secondary sources such as Barton Whaley as presumed authorities on particular matters. The relative space and attention given to subjects can also be questioned. There is, for instance, a lengthy account of the Dakar Operation Menace. Yet there is no delving into the question of whether British estimates of relative air strengths during the Munich crisis played a critical role in British decisions. Sir Maurice Oldfield, former head of SIS, was quoted in the *London Times* as saying the book was written "by a committee, about committees, for committees."

Hobman, D. L. CROMWELL'S MASTER SPY: A STUDY OF JOHN THURLOE. London: Chapman and Hall, 1961. 186 pp., no index.

Considering Thurloe's success and his place in the history of British intelligence and security (not to speak of intelligence history in general), it is incredible that this is the first extensive account of his career. Hobman based it almost entirely on the seven volumes of the Thurloe state papers, found after his death. She conveys the story of Thurloe's intelligence and security activities on behalf of Cromwell and his regime and describes his work as the organizer and brain of the widespread espionage system without which, some experts contend, Cromwell would not have survived. Thompson and Padover in *Secret Diplomacy* wrote that "the French Revolution had its Committee of Public Safety, the Soviets their GPU and Oliver Cromwell had his John Thurloe." Hobman is not consistent in her view on this latter point. She relates a number of intelligence operations that are precedents to similar modern techniques: foreign involvement in the attempted assassination of a head of government; an enticement operation along the lines of the latter-day Trust designed to lure émigrés into captivity; the betrayal of the intelligence service by a trusted employee (like Philby); the reluctance of a chief of a service to turn over all assets to his successor; the use of the Swedish diplomatic packet to send British dispatches (similar to the German use of Swedish communications in World War I); intelligence and other operations against émigrés; and attacks against British diplomatic representatives abroad. In recounting Thurloe's successes against the mails, Hobman neglects the cryptanalytical work of John Wallis, without which, according to Richard Rowan, the interception of mail and pouches would have been mere censorship. This omission may indicate the author was not interested in such technical details. For the historical record, she identifies Thurloe's secretary Samuel Morland as another man who betrayed him; only Cromwell's agent in The Hague, George Downing, was previously fingered by some writers. The book could have used an index.

Hoettl, Wilhelm. THE SECRET FRONT: THE STORY OF NAZI POLITICAL ESPIONAGE. New York: Praeger, 1954. 327 pp., index [London: Weidenfeld and Nicolson].

Hoettl's intention was to tell something of those activities of the German service, the SD, that he felt affected the course of events. These were primarily in covert action rather than in collection of intelligence. His purpose, he informs us, is *not* to unveil the technical workings of a secret service. Hoettl served for seven years in the SD as an expert on central, southern, and southeastern Europe. Among his foreign assignments were Zagreb, chief of the SD advisory section for Italy, and senior SD officer in Yugoslavia. No sources, notes, or documentary supports are presented. Hoettl tells of SD operations in Italy, Yugoslavia, Hungary, and Rumania. He gives his version of the Tukhachevsky affair (he wonders who was fooling whom in this tale of German and Soviet intrigue) and treats the reader to valuable character sketches of leading SD, SS, and Nazi figures he knew. We find the claim that at one point the Germans were reading Allen Dulles's traffic from Switzerland. Hoettl does not tell much about his own operations against the Allies. Whatever else he did does not equal in importance his role as the intermediary of the SD to the OSS in peace feelers in the later stages of the war. He provides special insights into SD motives for contacts with the Allies. Though Hoettl speaks from first-hand knowledge or with an insider's awareness of many events (and thus must be treated seriously as a source), the reader must still be on the lookout for sporadic unsound judgments, such as his opinion that the Abwehr had attained heights of proficiency or his suspicions about the Venlo kidnapping. One British reviewer commented that he often fails to distinguish between first-hand information and conjecture based on the unverified observations of others. The book was first published in Austria under the pseudonym Walter Hagen. For Hoettl's role in the SD, see Dulles's *The Secret Surrender* and Bradley Smith and Elena Agarossi's *Operation Sunrise.* Sweet-Escott's *Baker Street Irregular* speaks of a number of inaccuracies in this book.

Höhne, Heinz, and Zolling, Hermann. THE GENERAL WAS A SPY: THE TRUTH ABOUT GENERAL GEHLEN AND HIS SPY RING. New York: Coward, McCann and Geoghegan, 1972. 347 pp., bibliog., index [London: Secker and Warburg. *Network: The Truth About General Gehlen and His Spy Ring*].

Based on *Der Spiegel's* series on Gehlen, which stung Gehlen into writing a defense of his work, this was first published in Germany. The coauthor Zolling died while work was being completed on the English edition. Hugh Trevor-Roper in his introduction, which reveals little liking or sympathy for Gehlen, calls it a fine combination of historical scholarship and journalistic investigation. The reader will find it objective and accurate in some of its broad conclusions and judgments of Gehlen's work and not so reliable on others and on a number of details. The authors' story of Gehlen's defeat by the Soviets after the war and the fate of many of his agents in East Germany is widely supported. That his organization was penetrated and neutralized in certain important aspects is also fact. There is doubt that Gehlen's successes in the USSR during the war were as portrayed by the authors. One is advised to refer to Kahn's *Hitler's Spies* for a more thorough look at this question. Experts also reject as foolish the notion of an alliance between Gehlen's service and the state party. The authors' portrayal of the Americans' view of Gehlen's importance when they captured him is off the mark. The errors of detail are almost inevitable in a book that relies on a number of unverified sources. For instance, most of the sources for Chapter 7 come from "private ownership." These sources are responsible for some incredible items, such as the story that Richard Helms refused to tell President Johnson that the information about the Israelis' plan to attack the Arabs in 1967 came from Gehlen and the story that someone in the U.S. government gave Gehlen a gift to buy a house. This book does not show any major improvements on the 1954 *Der Spiegel* coverage. See also Gehlen's memoirs, *The Service.*

Holmes, W. J. DOUBLE-EDGED SECRETS: U.S. NAVAL INTELLIGENCE OPERATIONS IN THE PACIFIC DURING WORLD WAR II. Annapolis, Md.: Naval Institute Press, 1979. 218 pp., index [Cambridge: Patrick Stephens].

The title came from the author's comment on the dilemma of balancing security and the use of sensitive intelligence in wartime operations in the Pacific. Secrecy, he wrote, was "a double-edged weapon" sometimes "inflicting deeper wounds on its wielder than upon its opponents." Holmes served in Hawaii in World War II in a number of intelligence staff positions at headquarters. He was in a position to experience at first hand much of the intelligence war, particularly since he was one of the select few with access to decrypted Japanese traffic and to other communications intelligence. Holmes is an invaluable contributor to our knowledge of naval intelligence organization, personnel, operations, and problems in fighting the Pacific war. The author personally observed and experienced many of the above and was affected by many of the organizational and personnel changes he recounts, especially as chief of the estimates section, which supported U.S. fleet intelligence by coordinating Ultra with other intelligence information. He is the first person to write with this advantage. Ronald Lewin in a *RUSI* review rightfully calls the book a pioneer work in the United States and describes it as having all the authenticity and authority of Patrick Beesly's account of the Admiralty's Operational Intelligence Center. Francis Raven in his write-up in the April 1980 *Cryptologia* said that Holmes wrote a great book, authoritative on the subject of U.S. naval intelligence operations against the Japanese, especially comint support. On the part of the book devoted to comint, however, Raven says that Holmes is frequently confused and sometimes wrong. Readers are referred to this article for further specifics on technical faults. Many will second *Military Review*'s hope that this book will serve as a pathfinder for other studies of the U.S. use of Ultra-derived intelligence. See, among many interesting items, those on the neglected Joseph Rochefort and Ultra traffic on the *Indianapolis* sinking.

Houghton, Harry F. OPERATION PORTLAND: THE AUTOBIOGRAPHY OF A SPY. London: Rupert Hart-Davis, 1972. 164 pp., no index.

Houghton was convicted as a Soviet spy in what is referred to as the Portland naval secrets case. His version of the affair is utterly unsatisfactory. Though he claims he repents for what he did, he is at the same time resentful and even cocky. Above all, he is less than frank. He makes it appear he was recruited in England and that his motives were chivalrous in that he was forced into espionage to protect his old girlfriend. Many of his other stories are similarly unreliable or products of self-deception and a vivid imagination. The last third of the book is his plaint about his trial and imprisonment. One word describes the whole work—unreliable; reading Bulloch and Miller's *Spy Ring* or West's *The New Meaning of Treason* will show why. West calls Houghton perhaps the most unattractive of all the British traitors she analyzed in her book.

Household, Geoffrey. AGAINST THE WIND. London: Michael Joseph, 1958. 238 pp., no index [Boston: Little, Brown].

Household was a writer of some reputation even before the war. He had also been in banking and other businesses in places such as Spain, South America, and Rumania, making him a natural for some sort of intelligence or security work when World War II began. He entered British Field Security and served in Greece, Egypt, Lebanon, Syria, Palestine, and Iraq; he was a member of the British team that was to sabotage in 1940 the Rumanian oil fields at Ploesti. We are dealing here primarily with a novelist who offers mere glimpses of his war experiences; consequently, one does not learn as much as one would like of the intelligence and security side. His Rumanian experience in 1940 is the one episode of potential strategic significance; the account of it is a rare discussion of the operation by a participant. However, his suspicion that the operation was betrayed to the Rumanians by officials of a British oil company in London have never been substantiated.

Howarth, Patrick. UNDERCOVER: THE MEN AND WOMEN OF SPECIAL OPERATIONS EXECUTIVE. London and Boston: Routledge and Kegan Paul, 1980. 234 pp., bibliog., index.

Service in SOE and access to individuals who also were veterans of the organization or familiar with its history (like M.R.D. Foot) gave Howarth enviable advantages when he wrote this. Much of the ground he covers has been dealt with in previous books; but he adds an extra dimension and insight into the organization, the persons staffing it, and personal relationships. We learn more of the relations between Hambro and the Earl of Selborne, for example. We are also reminded of little-known incidents such as the recruitment by the Soviets of a captain in SOE who was arrested for passing classified information. Howarth's bibliography is one of the most complete on SOE, though one can take issue with his opinion of the relative merits of some works.

The *Economist* gave this book a good review, and one

knowledgeable American described it as a nicely done condensation of a number of works on SOE; but there are shortcomings nevertheless. Howarth does not explain satisfactorily how it was that James Klugmann was able to have an important position with SOE-Cairo when it was SOE-London's policy to exclude communists from its ranks. (For more on Klugmann, see Pincher's *Their Trade Is Treachery.*) He has not elaborated on the SOE-Cairo intrigues against Fitzroy Maclean, which are mentioned elsewhere. There are only some four pages on Holland but nothing on the British figures in London who directed SOE operations into that country during the disastrous stage. Peter Calvocoressi called the book an ode not so much to an organization but to its people. This may account for the feeling that Howarth unintentionally painted too glowing a portrait of the organization in his anxiety to pay tribute to individual members and operatives. M.R.D. Foot in a 1981 *Journal of Strategic Studies* review thought this work would contribute to reconsideration of SOE as a strategic tool.

Howe, John. A JOURNAL KEPT BY MR. JOHN HOWE, WHILE HE WAS EMPLOYED AS A BRITISH SPY IN THE REVOLUTIONARY WAR. Concord, N.H.: Luther Roby, 1827. 44 pp., no index.

In *Turncoats, Traitors and Heroes,* Bakeless called John Howe (from whose manuscript he quoted) British General Gage's favorite secret agent. This journal is believed to be the only published personal memoir of a Revolutionary War agent that survived. In it, Howe described his work as a British agent first in that war and then in the War of 1812 as a U.S. agent. The confusion on exactly who Howe was and whom he served as a deserter and agent remained, even after Bakeless's account, until the publication in 1977 of Frank E. McKone's *General Sullivan: New Hampshire Patriot* (New York: Vantage). McKone believed there was a substantial case that Howe was one of the many aliases of John Hall, a private with eighteen years of service in the British army who rose to captain in the revolution and served England well in four wars. *General Sullivan* must be consulted for a fuller version of Hall's work as a British agent, including his role as a link in the defection of Benedict Arnold. McKone commented that Howe's manuscript, which was "neither widely read or understood," was rewarding reading only if truth could be separated from fiction. Finally, since this work was a transcription, there was no certainty that the original manuscript was not longer.

Hoy, Hugh Cleland. 40 O.B., OR HOW THE WAR WAS WON. London: Hutchinson, 1932. 280 pp., index.

In light of present knowledge of Room 40's accomplishments, this is a disappointing work. However, it must be seen from the perspective of the time in which it was written. It is an early disclosure of Admiral Hall's activities in British naval intelligence in World War I. Hoy was private secretary to Admiral Hall, and according to the publisher his book is the first to reveal to the general public the work of Room 40 in winning the war. But Admiral William James in *The Eyes of the Navy* informs us that Hoy had never been in Room 40, though his book throws further light on Hall's influence on world affairs. Actually, Lord Balfour and Sir Alfred Ewing had let out the general secret before this. Hoy wrote this book constrained by the Official Secrets Act and by personal obligation, he reminds us, not to write about certain things. He does treat such matters as the Zimmermann note, the case of Sir Roger Casement, the neutralizing of Trebitsch Lincoln, and the capture of Carl Lody. Hall's genius comes through, and one is left regretting the loss of a record of his entire intelligence work when the British government refused Hall permission to publish his memoirs of the war.

Huminik, John. DOUBLE AGENT. New York: New American Library, 1967. 173 pp., index. [London: Robert Hale, 1968].

This is the drawn-out story of a metallurgical specialist who operated as an FBI agent against the Soviets. Huminik claims he was a double agent for six years, but the actual time of his service depends on how one defines "double agent." Much of what he tells of meetings with the Soviets (more than sixty-five in all) concerns developmental work by them. It was only toward the latter stages that he received payment and was asked to acquire classified information. There is thus much on Soviet techniques for developing a prospective agent in the private sector and the inducements offered. The case illustrates the problem faced by a CI service in running a double agent, even one who is not high-level or particularly sensitive (which Huminik was not, although he tends to overdramatize his own significance). The point was eventually reached at which a decision had to be made whether to provide any information of value to the Soviets so the case could continue. According to the author, the FBI staff directing him was amazed the operation continued as long as it did when only "junk" was passed to the Soviets; one consequently is left wondering about the Soviet purpose. FBI exposure was one of a series in 1966. See Sullivan's *The Bureau,* in which the FBI's Hoover is shown refusing to use this case for deception.

Hunt, David. A DON AT WAR. London: William Kimber, 1966. 282 pp., index.

Even though Hunt served in British military intelligence in the Mediterranean, including service with General Alexander's staff from 1942 to 1945, intelligence is not central to this memoir. The scholar and later diplomat is interested in the bigger picture, and intelligence and intelligence operations intrude only insofar as they affect the main decisions and movement of the war. After the war, Hunt worked on one of the volumes of the British official history of the war.

Hunt formed a low opinion of the value of agents but a high one of deception operations as a campaign- and war-winning technique. He writes of eight instances of deception used by the British and/or the Allies in the Mediterranean, though he does not provide any in-depth description or analysis of them. Nor does he dwell on the role of communications intelligence, except for giving instances of poor British or German security; talking about deciphering the traffic of Colonel Fellers, the U.S. Army attaché in Cairo; and telling the story of the British capture of the German communications intelligence unit in July 1942. Hunt was in no position to discuss Ultra's contribution, if he was privy to it, due to constraints at the time of writing. He is not correct in saying that the Greeks were surprised by the Italian attack in 1940 and that the Germans were not aware of Italian intentions to switch sides in 1943. On the latter point, see Irving's *Breach of Security.*

Hutchinson, James. THAT DRUG DANGER. Montrose, Scotland: Standard Press, 1977. 188 pp., index.

RF was the section of SOE that worked with the Free French in running operations into France during World War II. Hutchinson was in command of RF for one year beginning in August 1942. In 1944, he parachuted into France himself after having undergone facial surgery as a security measure since his identity was known to the Germans. Comparatively little has been written by persons with positions like the author's in SOE's RF Section on the British view of their liaison and working relationship with the French. One would have hoped for more details and inside information on the principal events in which the author played a role and the people he knew—the Moulin missions, Yeo-Thomas, relations with the BCRA, character sketches of persons connected with the latter organization, etc. Unhappily, Hutchinson chose to devote only some twenty pages to that important assignment, in contrast to some seventy-five pages assigned to describe his Jedburgh mission, including peparations for it. In the historical sense, this was a reversal of the order of importance of his impact on the larger picture. The RF Section was at the cutting edge of British–Free French relations during the war, and Hutchinson could have increased our knowledge of much that happened during his stewardship of RF. See Foot's *SOE in France* for cameos of Hutchinson.

Hutton, Clayton. OFFICIAL SECRET: THE REMARKABLE STORY OF ESCAPE AIDS—THEIR INVENTION, PRODUCTION AND THE SEQUEL. New York: Crown, 1961. 213 pp., no index [London: M. Parrish, 1960].

Hutton was in British intelligence in World War II in charge of the production of escape aids. Though he does not mention his exact unit, it was MI9, since he names Brigadier Crockatt as his superior. A journalist and public relations man connected with films before the war, he worked to create an effective system of aids for escapers and evaders—maps, compasses, clothing, shoes, etc. He was described as the brains of this effort by some, while others saw him as "eccentric."

This book should be basic reading in escape and evasion training. It describes how imaginative aids and equipment were developed, produced, and made available to servicemen prior to capture and gotten into the prisoner-of-war camps despite close enemy scrutiny. The equally imaginative disguises, used in conveying these aids to POWs were the other reason for success. Foot and Langley in *MI 9* wrote that Hutton's enthusiasm was as unlimited as his ingenuity and that he had a capacity for getting into trouble with civilian officials. His impatience with the bureaucracy, so well brought out in this book, continued after the war. The last two chapters are devoted to his legal problems stemming from his 1950 effort to publish a fictionalized version of his experiences. Hutton may have been flamboyant and unconventional, but he was also careful not to reveal everything. How communications were maintained between British intelligence in London and British POWs is not explained. It was revealed by Foot and Langley in their excellent work, published in 1979, which contains a number of references to Hutton.

Hutton, J. Bernard. WOMEN IN ESPIONAGE. New York: Macmillan, 1972. 188 pp., index [London: W. H. Allen, 1971. *Women Spies*].

Hutton, a pseudonym, is described on the jacket as a former Czech official. Blackstock and Schaf state that he was once the editor for Czech and Soviet Communist newspapers. Anyone with a modicum of knowledge of the subject will quickly determine that this book is unreliable. What is not definitely known to be either wrong or right has no documentation to back it up, and what is within acceptable limits of accuracy can probably be found better treated elsewhere, with the exception of the pages on the Rinaldi case. Oddly enough, this latter Soviet espionage operation, spanning a number of countries and uncovered in 1967, has never been fully treated up to now. Rinaldi's book in Italian is considered an ex parte apologia.

Hyde, H. Montgomery. THE ATOM BOMB SPIES. London: Hamish Hamilton, 1980. 223 pp., bibliog., notes, index [New York: Ballantine, 1981].

According to Hyde, this was undertaken at the suggestion of his old boss at the British Security Coordination (BSC), Sir William Stephenson. From this statement and the wording of the acknowledgment, one is led to believe that there will be much on Stephenson's role. This is not the case. Hyde began this as a book on Gouzenko and went on to write about the atom spies in Britain and the United States. Stephenson appears mainly in the early period when, according to the author, his presence in Ottowa in 1945 "largely contributed to saving Gouzenko" because Stephenson urged the Canadians to take in Gouzenko and to protect him. Everything Hyde relates of Stephenson's role was contained in his 1963 book *Room 3603*. About one-third of this book deals with the Rosenbergs, and Hyde concludes that no final judgment can be made until the FBI releases all documents. Since the FBI never released anything on the matter, Hyde regards the claim by Martin in *Wilderness of Mirrors* that the Rosenbergs were identified in Soviet traffic deciphered by the United States as lacking a credible source. However, he does not provide any source for his story that Fuchs was identified as a Soviet agent in broken traffic. As for Pontecorvo, Hyde relies too much on an anonymously written Italian magazine article without explaining why we should regard it as so accurate or authoritative an account. Those fascinated with the fine art of the calculated leak will learn that it was Sir William Stephenson who gave Drew Pearson the story of Gouzenko that led to the first Canadian arrests.

Hyde, H. Montgomery. CYNTHIA. New York: Farrar, Straus and Giroux, 1965. 240 pp., no index [London: Hamish Hamilton. *Cynthia: The Spy Who Changed the Course of the War*].

When he wrote of the British agent Cynthia, an American, in *Room 3603* (below), Hyde did not identify her. He did so in this book. The grandiloquent subtitle of the British edition obviously claims too much for her accomplishments. Amy Thorpe, the agent, did not live to see the debate about this book and the legal problems it caused. Barton Whaley called it a sensationalized and scantily researched biography. He pointed out, as did David Kahn, that Hyde was wrong in insisting that the naval victory at Matapan was due to the acquisition of an Italian cipher by Cynthia. The Italian naval attaché in Washington had not received the Italian cipher used at this battle. This fact was brought out in a suit against Hyde by heirs of the Italian from whom Cynthia allegedly acquired the cipher. According to Ronald Lewin, these legal actions have raised doubts about her achievements as a spy. Hyde acknowledges that most of the material for this biography was supplied by Amy Thorpe or members of her family or friends, although he also made use of his recollections of her and his notes. The verdict on Thorpe and her work for British Security Coordination is still out, and further research is needed to provide support for William Stephenson's tribute to her (according to Hyde) that Cynthia was "the war's greatest unsung heroine."

Hyde, H. Montgomery. ROOM 3603: THE STORY OF THE BRITISH INTELLIGENCE CENTER IN NEW YORK DURING WORLD WAR II. New York: Farrar, Straus and Co., 1963. 257 pp., bibliog., index [London: Hamish Hamilton, 1962. *The Quiet Canadian*].

The work of Sir William Stephenson and the British Security Coordination (BSC), the British intelligence organization for the Western Hemisphere that he headed in World War II, is one of the fascinating intelligence stories of that war. Hyde was on Stephenson's staff and had the additional advantage of access to Stephenson and his files after the war. For these reasons, he has produced what amounts to the best book so far on BSC and Stephenson. At the time of its publication in England, questions were raised in the British Parliament as to whether Hyde had violated the Official Secrets Act. Charles Ellis, Stephenson's deputy, in the foreword to Stevenson's *A Man Called Intrepid* on the same subject, explains that Hyde's book was a "partial leak" about the BSC and confirms that it had the approval and concurrence of British intelligence officials as a counter to the threat posed to British and U.S. intelligence cooperation by Kim Philby's defection to the Soviet Union.

Hyde has not only revealed much about the BSC's security and counterintelligence work and cooperation with the United States in these fields even before Pearl Harbor and the aid given to create OSS; he has been frank about certain special operations that fell under one category of their instructions—to mobilize U.S. public opinion in favor of aid to the Allies. Stephenson created a covert propaganda organization in the United States that Hyde called "one of the most powerful weapons Stephenson had." It is wise to assume there is more than what we are told here. In a U.S. television program on the BSC in the late 1970s, in which Hyde was interviewed, the conclusion was drawn that many BSC activities had yet to see the light of day, especially those designed to induce the United States to enter the war and to discredit opponents of the Allies.

Hyde admits such activity before Pearl Harbor when he writes, "Stephenson's organizations spread covert propaganda designed to strengthen the interventionist groups throughout the country and discredit the isolationists." He brings to light British cryptanalytical successes long before Ultra was revealed: the breaking of German agent, military, and submarine ciphers. For further details and corrections of what he writes the following should be consulted: the author's *Cynthia* for the identity of that agent and an expanded account of her work: Johns's *Within Two Cloaks* for clarification of BSC's place in the British intelligence structure; Kahn's *The Codebreakers* on the reason for the operation to acquire Vichy France's ciphers; Montagu's *Beyond Top Secret Ultra* for the correct version of the timing and purpose of Montagu's trip to the U.S.; and Ogilvy's *Blood, Brains and Beer.* See also Sweet-Escott's *Baker Street Irregular* for SOE's liaison under BSC in Washington and Pincher's *Their Trade Is Treachery* for allegations about Ellis as a Soviet agent.

I

Ind, Allison. ALLIED INTELLIGENCE BUREAU: OUR SECRET WEAPON IN THE WAR AGAINST JAPAN. New York: David McKay, 1958. 287 pp., index [London: Weidenfeld and Nicolson. ***Spy Ring Pacific: The Story of the Allied Intelligence Bureau in South East Asia*****].**

The Allied Intelligence Bureau (AIB) was, as Ind reminds us, a combined Allied intelligence organization and only one of several intelligence organizations under the control of General MacArthur in the Pacific in World War II. In it were represented the United States, Great Britain, Australia, and Holland. The AIB's intelligence-collection operations and organizations are described, including the very effective Coastwatchers under the Australians. We are told of some of the special operations against Japanese targets, both successful and unsuccessful. Ind's story is of great value because so little has been written about the AIB, and Ind, as deputy chief, was in a good position to tell it. He recounts unique or interesting events or operations that took place, such as that Japanese cipher systems were retrieved from beached Japanese ships and crashed aircraft or that AIB recruited Moslems as agents for use in the Far East with the approval of King Saud of Saudi Arabia. These agents were to stir up religious wars in the interest of the Allies; most were killed. There is no mention of the reading of Japanese codes; consequently, Ind has overdrawn the relative importance of AIB's contributions to victory. Corson in *The Armies of Ignorance* calls to our attention that General Charles Willoughby in his book on MacArthur quotes the latter as saying, "The history of AIB is a secret, little publicized but highly important chapter in the story of the Southwest Pacific." Both MacArthur and Ind may have been right in their estimates of the AIB's effectiveness, but we still need a more up-to-date treatment. Knowledgeable commentators have singled out Ind's sections on operations into the Philippines as particularly good.

Irving, David, ed. BREACH OF SECURITY: THE GERMAN INTELLIGENCE FILE ON EVENTS LEADING TO THE SECOND WORLD WAR. London: William Kimber, 1968. 190 pp., notes, index.

This British work uses as its basis a remaining example of the work of the German Air Ministry's monitoring and intercept service, the Forschungsamt or Research Office. It was one of a number of German services involved in cryptologic matters before and during World War II, was attached to the minister's office, and had no relationship with the Luftwaffe's own intercept and cryptologic unit. It broke traffic, tapped telephones, and opened letters. This work analyzes the report in question, with a preface by Donald Watt on what he knows of the German code-breaking services and efforts. The book is badly organized, making it difficult to ascertain what was in the original source and what are the credited remarks. Happily, there is much to excite one's interest and curiosity. We find such things as the information that the British received from Polish Intelligence in 1939 German cryptographic machines and keys used for military and diplomatic ciphers; that the British were known to have exchanged a set of such machines with the United States in return for one of the four U.S. machines capable of decoding the Japanese Purple cipher. This book was written, the reader should remember, six years before Winterbotham's *The Ultra Secret* and five years before Bertrand's *Enigma.* The statement that the French had an agent in the Research Office who helped them reconstruct the German cipher machine can only refer to the Asche that Bertrand later wrote about. We learn which ciphers the Research Office had succeeded in breaking, including those of U.S. diplomatic traffic, up to March 1941 and how the Germans learned of the Allied plans to mine Norwegian waters in 1940. Barton Whaley called this the best single study on German cryptanalytical work, which is excessive praise but gives an idea of some of the nuggets to be found. See also Flicke's *War Secrets in the Ether*. Watt, in a 1975 article in *RUSI*, advised that the only example in this book of the breaking of a British cipher turned out on examination to be a deliberate British plant.

J

James, Coy Hilton. SILAS DEANE—PATRIOT OR TRAITOR? East Lansing: Michigan State Univ. Press, 1975. 121 pp., notes, index.

The late James's conclusion that Deane was not in the pay of the British while he was serving as a commissioner in France during the American Revolution is supported by most scholars. There has never been solid evidence to the contrary, though correspondence between Lord North and King George III provides some indications, not proof, that Deane might have been recruited. This correspondence and other surviving documentation make it clear James did not provide a balanced account of all of Deane's activities in France. And there is no denying by James or anyone else that Deane, whatever the reasons, was imprudent in his correspondence, using expressions critical of his country and France and generally sounding defeatist. The British intercepted Deane's correspondence and had it published by Rivington in New York in their psychological warfare campaign against the colonies. James also informs us that when Deane was in financial straits on his return to France after his recall, he was lent money by French Foreign Minister Vergennes and that Deane made apologies for Benedict Arnold's desertion, both before and after the war ended. On the basis of existing, hard evidence, James is closer to the truth in *not* accusing William Carmichael of being a British agent or "the first mole in U.S. history," to quote one U.S. historian inclined to this view.

James, M. E. Clifton. I WAS MONTY'S DOUBLE. London and New York: Rider, 1954. 192 pp., no index.

James's narrative concerns the role he played in the deception operation in which he doubled as General Montgomery just prior to the invasion of France in 1944. Up to the appearance of Bennett's *Ultra in the West* in 1979, it had been assumed that the effort to deceive the Germans had gone unnoticed. Bennett discovered the last German intelligence by Foreign Armies West prior to the invasion, which concluded that, based on reports of Montgomery's presence in Algiers, there was a strong possibility of an Allied invasion of southern France and the Balkans. Bennett wondered whether the operation using James as a decoy might have been the cause of this German misreading of Allied intentions. James may have been right even though he narrated his story in an overdramatized and exaggerated manner. We know from Cave Brown's *Bodyguard of Lies* that James's version does not include details on his trying conduct, which endangered the operation. Captain Harry C. Butcher in his book *My Three Years with Eisenhower* (New York: Simon and Schuster, 1946) also touched on James's behavior; James plaintively commented that Butcher did him "a rather bad turn." James had neither the knowledge nor the access to write the full history of this operation, which was only one small segment of the overall deception plan called Bodyguard, not central to it as James presented it. Nevertheless, Bennett's findings and the fact that the scheme was a rare example of a human decoy operation in support of a strategic deception plan lend the book special interest. Note that Dudley Clarke and Dennis Wheatley, both of whom were later to be revealed as important figures in British deception, were mentioned by James as connected with the operation.

James, William. THE EYES OF THE NAVY: A BIOGRAPHICAL STUDY OF ADMIRAL SIR REGINALD HALL. London: Methuen, 1955. 207 pp., index [New York: St. Martin's Press, 1956. *The Code Breakers of Room 40*].

Since Admiral Hall was refused official permission to write his war memoirs, James's effort will have to do as second best. James was well placed to undertake the task. He was a close colleague of Hall and in charge of Room 40 from 1917 to 1918, where as service head he interpreted deciphered messages. After the war, he was deputy director of intelligence. Hinsley, in his first volume on the history of British intelligence in World War II, called James one of the two senior British officers of the interwar period with an understanding of the importance of intelligence. In addition, James had access to Hall's papers and the advantage of having taken part in passing for publication writings on the war when at the Admiralty. He had no access to "unreleased official papers."

Many of Hall's famous activities and operations are treated. Above all, James tells of Room 40 and how Hall dominated it and used the intelligence from it. James claimed his version on the Zimmermann note is the first full one. Among the bombardment of intriguing stories are many examples of deception practiced by Hall; "There was nothing Hall enjoyed more than planning ruses to deceive the Germans." James's explanations for Hall's difficulties with his own service and other components of the British government and with his retirement should be supplemented by reading Hinsley's book.

Though James has written an important book on one of the outstanding figures of intelligence, not all has been revealed. James allows for this fact when he writes in his foreword that Hall's autobiography would have been "a book of historical importance." Revelations by other authors put in doubt James's story of the captured Wassmuss code book as the true source of the crucial cryptanalytical breakthrough on diplomatic traffic, while Friedman and Mendelsohn's research raises questions as to whether James's cryptanalytical account of the Zimmermann note is the full one (see *The Zimmermann Telegram*). See C. J. Edmonds's article in the January 1960 *Royal Central Asian Journal* for that author's position that James's version of the Wassmuss ciphers is not correct. See too McLachlan's *Room 39* for the Admiralty's refusal to allow James to include names and tributes to Room 40 personnel, alluded to by James. Friederich Katz's *The Secret War in Mexico* (Chicago and London: Univ. of Chicago Press, 1981) also analyzes the breaking of the Zimmermann telegram. So does Kahn's *The Codebreakers*.

Johns, Philip. WITHIN TWO CLOAKS: MISSIONS WITH SIS AND SOE. London: William Kimber, 1979. 210 pp., index.

In World War II Johns held important positions in both SIS and SOE: he was head of SIS stations in Portugal and Brazil and headed the Dutch/Belgian section of SOE. In addition, he served with SIS in Belgium until the evacuation of 1940. This is the personal narrative of a man who obviously likes people and likes to reminisce as much about his travels, personal and social life, and acquaintances as he does about intelligence activities. He does tell us about some SIS personnel and SIS stations in operation, such as that in Lisbon. He imparts a feel for the organization and atmosphere of SIS headquarters under Menzies and is frank in his view on the value and effectiveness of the SIS operations with which he was familiar. Though he is candid about SOE's performance in Holland prior to his stewardship, he adds nothing to what we know of those disasters, and there is a broad-brush treatment of his SOE career. This, he explains, is due to his not having a wartime diary or notes. There is nothing said of the North African invasion and of any operations, especially deception, in support of it from Lisbon. John's picture of SIS-Lisbon will come as a surprise in view of what has been previously written about it. He criticizes Stevenson's *A Man Called Intrepid* for the erroneous impression it gives of the relationship between SIS and Sir William Stephenson's British Security Coordination (BSC) in New York, and the relative importance of each organization. The *Economist* reviewer thought it the best short account of resistance in the Low Countries in English.

Johnson, Brian. THE SECRET WAR. New York: Methuen, 1978. 349 pp., notes, no index [London: BBC Publications].

Based on a BBC television series of the same name, this book is an account of aspects of the scientific, technical, and cryptologic war. Covered are the war of beams, radar, German V weapons, the Battle of the Atlantic, and Enigma; there is also a chapter entitled "Misfortunes of War." The volume is illustrated with scores of excellent photographs, some published for the first time in a book in English. R. V. Jones's *The Wizard War* is a necessary companion as far as beams, radar, and the V weapons are concerned. The contention that "up to the moment the first V1 landed, the British knew little about this weapon" should be compared with Jones's account. The segment on the Battle of the Atlantic concentrates on the scientific war and does not touch on Ultra. The Enigma portion, if it does not give us the first pictures of Colossus and the Geheimschrieber machines, at least publishes among the first pictures of them and provides details on the latter machine that are not to be found again until later (see Lewin's *Ultra Goes to War* and Calvocoressi's *Top Secret Ultra*). For those who feel R. V. Jones's work is too personalized an account of certain aspects of the scientific war, *The Secret War* will present a wider perspective.

Johnson, Haynes. THE BAY OF PIGS: THE LEADERS' STORY OF BRIGADE 2506. New York: Norton, 1964. 355 pp., bibliog., notes, index [London: Hutchinson, 1965].

Johnson wished "to tell faithfully and with complete candor the history of the Bay of Pigs." Along with other Cuban exiles, the four commanders of the brigade—Manuel Artime, José Perez, San Roman Eineido Oliva, and Enrique Ruiz-Williams—told their portion of the story to Johnson, who underlined their contribution by listing them as collaborating authors. Wyden, in his 1979 *Bay of Pigs,* listed Johnson's study as one of his sources and called it "a masterful, encyclopedic reconstruction of the exile Cubans' involvement," but he noted that few nonexile sources were available at the time it was written. Perhaps as a consequence, Johnson devoted much less attention to the story of the operation from inside the U.S. government and especially CIA. Allen Dulles in *The Craft of Intelligence* criticized the book as based largely on the accounts of the four Cubans and containing what he termed a new crop of myths. Conversely, Kirkpatrick in *The Real CIA* called it an excellent piece of work. This difference among CIA officials reflects the split in that organization on the operation—Kirkpatrick as CIA's inspector general ran the agency's internal investigation of it. See Powers's *The Man Who Kept The Secrets* about the inspector general's report and the reaction in CIA. Johnson put more faith in the reliability and objectivity of the Castro government's published versions than experience with such regimes would seem to justify when he calls such sources the most significant for the book.

Johnson, Stowers. AGENTS EXTRAORDINARY. London: Robert Hale, 1975. 192 pp., no index.

A history of the ill-fated SOE mission to Macedonia and to the Bulgarian partisans that ended in the death of its two leaders. One, Frank Thompson, was executed in 1944 by the Bulgarian government. He was sympathetic to communism and, according to Foot's *Resistance,* was a promising poet and "a strong romantic radical libertarian." The author relies on interviews for that portion of the mission's life that took place after the record ceased when communications were broken. Johnson inserts two chapters that deal with subjects very remotely connected with the mission. One covers the alleged role of Kim Philby in destroying the Bulgarian Communist leader Kostov. The other purports to tell the story of attempts of British intelligence to penetrate the Bulgarian Communist party before and during World War II. Both chapters lack credible sources. For more about Thompson's mission and SOE-Cairo headquarters' knowledge of Bulgarian control of his radio operator, see Sweet-Escott's *Baker Street Irregular*. See also Barker's *British Policy in South-East Europe* for one explanation for the mission.

Jones, R. V. THE WIZARD WAR: BRITISH SCIENTIFIC INTELLIGENCE 1939–1945. New York: Coward, McCann and Geoghegan, 1978. 533 pp., glossary, notes, index [London: Hamish Hamilton. *Most Secret War*].

This is not only one of the great works on scientific intelligence in World War II but one of the great personal memoirs in intelligence literature, superbly told. Jones's contributions to the Allies' victory were enormous and strategic. One U.S. expert (Sayre Stevens, formerly CIA's deputy director for science and technology) believed Jones deserved recognition as the developer of scientific intelligence. In fact, Stevens dubbed him the patron saint of technical intelligence. As scientific adviser to the secret service (MI6) and head of scientific intelligence on Britain's air staff, Jones played a crucial role in the scientific and technological struggle involving radar, navigational beams, electronic warfare, and V weapons. One reads with fascination how he absorbed, analyzed, and interpreted intelligence and used it to advocate policy; one also observes with admiration the working of a fine brain, a sharp intuition, and a natural flair for intelligence and deception. The *USNI Proceedings* reviewer wrote that Jones had a unique grasp "of what might be called the metaphysics of the intelligence process."

Most of the elements of modern intelligence collection and analysis are covered in the work: elint, communications intelligence (the role of Ultra), prisoner interrogation, agent reporting, aerial photography, and captured material. The book is dedicated to the agents, pilots, and other men who risked their lives to collect the intelligence needed. Jones stands in marked contrast to figures in military intelligence like General Strong and Sir David Hunt (see their books) who downgrade agents' importance. It is not clear what organizational lessons this book teaches for today. Some do not think that Jones's argument for small organizations with close participation of the director in analysis is persuasive in light of the realities of present-day scientific intelligence demands. Jones's writings have been criticized by some not for what he said but for the way he said it—those objections have centered around the feeling that he displayed a penchant for self-advertisement and personal recognition. It may have been this feeling in the British establishment that deprived Jones of honors after the war. For another look and perspective on aspects of the scientific war covered here, see Brian Johnson's *The Secret War.*

K

Kahn, David. THE CODEBREAKERS: THE STORY OF SECRET WRITING. London: Weidenfeld and Nicolson, 1967. 965 pp., bibliog., notes, index [New York: Macmillan].

Kahn observed that cryptanalysis was the most important form of secret intelligence but never had a chronicler. He regarded his work as a serious study of cryptology seeking to cover its entire history, with two goals: to tell how the various methods of making and breaking codes and ciphers developed, and how these methods have affected men. The consensus among both specialists and students (technical and nontechnical) is that Kahn certainly succeeded to a large degree. No one before him ever came near to doing what he did. More than half of the study deals with the twentieth century. Shulman in *An Annotated Bibliograpy of Cryptography* called this the best work of its type ever written, thorough in its treatment. Another writer called it the first in-depth history of cryptology, containing enormous quantities of information on the technology and development of cryptographic systems (Weber, *United States Diplomatic Codes*).

Kahn's scholarship is prodigious, as is his knowledge of the subject. They are more characteristic of the professional cryptologist and scholar than of the amateur cryptologist and journalist that Kahn is. The notes and bibliography are themselves formidable and a gold mine of source material, including as they do some evaluations of reliability. Shulman observed that what faults there were are far outweighed by the strengths.

The main strength of the work, according to some experts, is that segment that covers cryptology up to World War II. The biggest and most obvious omission in it is the absence of full discussion of Allied successes against German cryptography, of Bletchley Park, and of the role of this communications intelligence in the 1945 victory. Kahn, it is said, knew something of these matters but was not able to expand this knowledge to deal with them since they were still highly classified. His refusal to attempt to do so on the basis of what he had is a testimony both to his good judgment and to his discretion. But he warns us at the start that his study is not exhaustive because secrecy still covered much of World War II cryptology. There may also be reservations with some of his assessments and judgments. Not everyone accepts unreservedly that Friedman alone made the U.S. preeminent in his field. A major landmark and contribution to cryptologic and intelligence history.

Kahn, David. HITLER'S SPIES: GERMAN MILITARY INTELLIGENCE IN WORLD WAR II. New York: Macmillan, 1978. 552 pp., bibliog., notes, index [London: Hodder and Stoughton].

Kahn here again displayed many of the talents shown by his pioneering *The Codebreakers:* a great capacity for research, encyclopedic treatment and description, and an ability to present facts and opinions in a readable manner. Originally a dissertation for his doctorate at Oxford, the book is probably the most complete work on the subject to date. Kahn's purpose was to describe and examine the effectiveness of German intelligence, its personnel, operations, and organization. What he writes is really on a broader subject than military intelligence: the German information-gathering mechanism was concerned with more than military intelligence.

Kahn does not have quite the feel, the expertise, and the background for this subject that he shared in *The Codebreakers*. He is excellent at reducing confusion (if that is possible) on German organizations for intelligence and security. His evaluation of Gehlen's wartime work is one of the few in-depth looks at this matter, which has been obscured or distorted by some biographers, as well as by Gehlen himself. He covers a variety of intelligence-collection systems and discusses at length their evaluative organizations and efforts. New or little-known topics called to our attention include German prewar photo reconnaissance over a number of countries, including the Soviet Union and England, and the Klatt operation on which the Germans relied for important information of the Soviet front. The author is also one of the few to discuss the early Abwehr. There can be no better summary of the overall dismal record of failures that German intelligence left.

Yet, one must also set out the book's shortcomings. A work that selects the agent Cicero as "the most successful spy of the war" will justifiably raise eyebrows and create doubts about its author's overall ability to judge. Similarly, Kahn states that Baron Schluga was the most successful German agent of World War I; he needs to provide more convincing evidence than he does for such a claim. The sheer volume of information he culled probably prevented him from discriminating and spending time digging further into the overall effect of a particular collection effort. A very good example of this is the Klatt operation out of Sofia. There are significant omissions as well as less significant ones. Kahn does not tell us of the Abwehr's access in 1938 to the NKVD defector in the Far East, General Lyushkov, and what was learned from him. There is nothing on the Kondor operation in Egypt, a minor matter but mentioned here as proof that one cannot use the adjective "comprehensive" in describing the book. The two major shortcomings have to do with Kahn's understanding of intelligence and counterintelligence (CI) and his explanations for poor German intelligence. Kahn omits CI because of his narrow understanding of the function. Good CI may have ended German reliance on such operations as Klatt and on many double agents before Normandy and may have reduced German vulnerability to deception and raised warning signals about the security of German ciphers. Kahn thus cannot deal with the subject of German intelligence and "vigorously eliminate" all discussion of counterintelligence. In short, one of the important reasons for German intelligence defeats was the very absence of good CI, which he does not list. Surprisingly, too, in his reasons for the poor German performances in intelligence, he does not include the vital one, the Allied success against German ciphers and especially against German intelligence traffic. This was as much a basic factor as the five reasons he lists and an odd one for a cryptologist to omit.

Karalekas, Anne. HISTORY OF THE CENTRAL INTELLIGENCE AGENCY. Laguna Hills, Calif.: Aegean Park Press, 1977. 106 pp., no index.

This is the unclassified history prepared in April 1976 for the U.S. Senate Select Committee to Study Government Operations with Respect to Intelligence Activities, better known as the Church committee. Karalekas was a staff member involved in the investigation of CIA. Deletions were made in the original text, and the discussion of covert operations was reduced to general descriptions. The work is a well-researched study that reflects the author's training as a scholar, her knowledge of U.S. history and government, and her grasp of intelligence work. They allowed her to put intelligence in proper context. One British writer believed the book was the best history of CIA ever written. Good as it is, however, it is not flawless, particularly where judgments are made. The enormity of the task of writing a history of an intelligence service is in itself daunting. Add to this the time required to sort out conflicting views, and one can see there will be a tendency to accept prevailing opinions and judgments. An example of this tendency is some of her comments on the CI staff. Another is her repetition of the idea that Covert Operations was the best path of advancement for a CIA officer. Those familiar with the agency know that this is not entirely true and that in the mystique and by the standards of the professionals in the Clandestine Services, the foreign intelligence operative and foreign intelligence–collection operations were considered the elite. DIS's *Bibliography* called the book the best public text available on CIA's history but somewhat biased and uneven in some areas.

Katona, Edith Zukermanova, with Patrick Macnaghten. CODE-NAME MARIANNE: AN AUTOBIOGRAPHY. London: Collins and Harvill, 1976. 210 pp., no index [New York: McKay].

The author was a Czech who served as an agent of the naval section of the French intelligence service between the years 1938 and 1942. This is her story of her intelligence activities against the Italians. These can be described as of little consequence and as what are called "low-level" in the trade. Katona was a romantic about the intelligence business, and if her value as an agent had been equal to her passion for the work, this book would have been closer to the glowing description of it by the publisher.

Kaufman, Louis; Fitzgerald, Barbara; and Sewell, Tom. MOE BERG: ATHLETE, SCHOLAR, SPY. Boston: Little, Brown, 1974. 265 pp., index.

The story of that amazing combination of scholar and professional athlete who served in OSS from 1943 to 1945. The authors have given a journalistic account of Berg's wartime work, with sources indicated only in the text. According to them, Berg went into Yugoslavia in 1943 to evaluate the situation there, dropped into Norway, and entered a German-held factory in Florence disguised as a German officer. His greatest intelligence contribution, again according to the authors, was in uncovering German scientific secrets in general and atom research and planning in particular. It is difficult at this point to judge how accurate or complete this story of Berg's work in intelligence really is. Some of the story is based on material released to Berg's relatives by the U.S. government under FOIA. There are quoted tributes, albeit general in nature, from General Groves of the Manhattan Project and Whitney Shepardson, head of OSS's SI. There is, however, no mention of Berg in Pash, Goudsmit, the OSS history, or in any major work on OSS. Exactly what role Berg played and what intelligence contributions he made have yet to be determined.

Kaznacheev, Aleksandr. INSIDE A SOVIET EMBASSY: EXPERIENCES OF A RUSSIAN DIPLOMAT IN BURMA. Philadelphia: Lippincott, 1962. 250 pp., no index [London: Robert Hale, 1963].

Burma was this Soviet junior officer's first assignment. When he defected to the United States in 1959, he had served there for two years as an "associated member" of Soviet intelligence or what is known in the West as a coopted officer (one who assists but is not a career staff intelligence officer). Kaznacheev's book is a valuable look inside the organization and workings of a Soviet embassy and its satellite missions. Especially interesting are descriptions of the organization of Soviet intelligence in foreign missions and the role Soviet intelligence plays in foreign policy as compared to those of other Soviet agencies. Most valuable because it is so rare is his first-hand account of Soviet disinformation and covert psychological warfare operations involving forgeries, plants, and political warfare. This book should be on any list of works on Soviet deception. The author was coopted full-time by Soviet intelligence and was able to observe these things from a working level. As a translator, he was able to get some idea of the extent of Soviet penetration in Burma for the collection of intelligence. Dulles in *The Craft of Intelligence* was of the opinion Kaznacheev's book did a great deal to debunk the picture of Soviet skill and U.S. incompetence.

Kent, Sherman. STRATEGIC INTELLIGENCE FOR AMERICAN WORLD POLICY. Hamden, Conn.: Archon Books, 1965. 220 pp., no index [Princeton, N.J.: Princeton Univ. Press, 1949, 1966].

This is one of those works that had both a wide and a profound influence on the development of U.S. intelligence after World War II. DIS's bibliography calls it a foresighted early work on the theory and ideal operation of national intelligence production whose principles were established in practice. Blackstock and Schaf called it one of the early basic texts on postwar strategic intelligence doctrine. Harry Ransom selected it as the classic primer on strategic intelligence and one of the three groundbreaking treatises on intelligence. Angelo Codevilla in a paper on analyses and estimates (see Godson, *Intelligence Requirements for the 1980's*) put Kent's work in the special place of the first and most prominent of books that focus on how the organization of intelligence might affect its functions and the quality of its product. The 1960s editions have a new preface by Kent in which his outlook on the relative importance of research and analysis is reconfirmed. New collection developments not contemplated when the work was originally written are discussed, as are new means of handling and analyzing data. Kent, however, does not comment on his 1949 view that "CIA should stay out of primary substantive work" and serve as a coordinator rather than competitor. Changes in the last thirty years, including the organization of national estimates within CIA, which Kent headed, have made this book somewhat outdated but certainly not obsolete. Recommended for another look at the theoretical treatment of the subject is Pettee's earlier *The Future of American Secret Intelligence.* For a look at the functioning and quality of the U.S. strategic estimative process on the Soviet strategic threat, see Freedman's *U.S. Intelligence and the Soviet Strategic Threat.* Cline's *Secrets, Spies and Scholars* contains some first-hand comments on Kent, his views, and his difficulties in finding a publisher. Cline referred to Kent's work as a reflection on the author's experiences in OSS and one that became a rational model for a generation of intelligence collectors and analysts.

Kerr, Walter. THE SECRET OF STALINGRAD. Garden City, N.Y.: Doubleday, 1978. 248 pp., bibliog., index [London: Macdonald and Jane's, 1979].

The importance of this study is that it is a very rare example, if the analysis and facts are correct, of Soviet deception on a "grand strategy" level. Its thesis is that the Soviets deceived not only the Germans but their own allies as well. With the Allies, the deception was in connection with Soviet demands for an Allied second front in World War II and urgent calls for Allied material help. Kerr refers to the alleged concealment from the Allies in 1942 of the existence of troops in a strategic reserve that constituted the key to the Soviet victory at Stalingrad. Kerr was a war correspondent in the USSR and spent ten years in research. Crucial to his argument is his discovery of a map in the Soviet armed forces museum in Moscow that showed this reserve and that Kerr believes is authentic. He also uses interviews with Soviet officials. The dearth of reliable information from the Soviets is another factor he does not neglect to take into account. This cannot be considered the final work on the facts and Soviet motives. But it is an example of careful investigation of what material the author had to work with; there are grounds for suspicion of the Soviets in that the Soviets have only owned up to their use of "newly activated" tank and mechanized units as elements of strategic surprise at Stalingrad. What the book does is open up new avenues of research that, if the deception is confirmed, could provide insights into the channels and means used by the Soviets.

Khokhlov, Nicolai. IN THE NAME OF CONSCIENCE. New York: McKay, 1959. 365 pp., no index [London: R. Muller, 1960].

Illegal operations and those involving assassination and sabotage are among the most sensitive of the KGB's techniques. The latter two, called "wet affairs" in the KGB, have been in its arsenal from the earliest days of the Soviet regime. The special bureau responsible for these acts of violence had different names, and by the time the author joined it, it was known as Department 13 of the KGB. This is his story of his life and work as an agent dating back to 1941. We are told of the planning, preparation, and special practices involved in Soviet illegal operations and, on top of that, given the testimony of a Soviet intelligence officer involved in "wet affairs," the first of a series of postwar defectors from that section. This is above all the story of a man's struggle with his conscience and of the mental journey that led to his defection. The intelligence specialist might wish that Khokhlov had dwelt at least as much on matters of professional interest as he did on his personal dilemma and thought processes, but organization and practices take a back seat. His discussion of Soviet technical devices to which he was exposed is an example of the type of material Khokhlov might have included in greater amounts. Contrary to the usual practice, Khokhlov published this without any official help or encouragement. In fact, his criticism of U.S. intelligence, which he felt had failed to live up to certain commitments, are known to have displeased Allen Dulles. Khokhlov includes a description of the assassination attempt against him by the Soviets. For more on the history of Department 13, see Barron's *KGB*.

Kim, Young Hum, ed. THE CENTRAL INTELLIGENCE AGENCY: PROBLEMS OF SECRECY IN A DEMOCRACY. Lexington, Mass.: D. C. Heath, 1968. 108 pp., bibliog., no index.

The articles, essays, and reports in this collection range in date from 1947 (that of Allen Dulles) to 1967. The pieces vary in quality. The book's subtitle does not exactly fit the issues debated: not only the place of secrecy in a democracy but also the place of covert operations in our system. On one side in the debate, the essay of Christopher Felix stands out for its depth and the elegance of its style. Cottam, on the other side, makes some telling points in his piece. One is that by the time plans for Cuba came under discussion, CIA's past successes should have argued not for the exploitation of nonattributability but against it. It is interesting to compare Dulles's stricture in 1947 that an intelligence service should not be flamboyant with Blackstock's accusation that CIA inspired publicity for its own covert operations. Note that in contrast to some collections published in the acrimonious 1970s, this work allows for a balanced participation of points of view.

Kimche, Jon. SPYING FOR PEACE: GENERAL GUISAN AND SWISS NEUTRALITY. London: Weidenfeld and Nicolson, 1961. 162 pp., index [New York: Roy].

Kimche was born in Switzerland and was a correspondent of the *London Evening Standard* during World War II. His reason for writing this was his belief that the story of the Swiss and of General Guisan, the chief of their armed forces, had too long been ignored. He purports to tell how the general and Swiss intelligence ensured Swiss neutrality by their ability to compete with the services of the warring powers and by using their intelligence to warn of possible attack. The style is journalistic and there are no source references or attributions for what he divulges as "inside information" and for some fascinating facts. There is no citing of German documents to support his claim that it was Guisan's policy that caused the Germans to respect Swiss neutrality and existence. Many reviewers criticized the work for its many errors but above all for the author's failure to support his many sensational statements with evidence. That failure is especially lamentable because Switzerland was one of the great intelligence battlefields and Swiss intelligence's role was crucial in a variety of ways. We cannot, unfortunately, accept Kimche's story of that war and much else with confidence.

Kirkpatrick, Lyman B., Jr. CAPTAINS WITHOUT EYES: INTELLIGENCE FAILURES IN WORLD WAR II. New York: Macmillan, 1969. 281 pp., bibliog., index [London: Rupert Hart-Davis].

Kirkpatrick headed the OSS intelligence detachment with the U.S. Twelfth Army Group. The detachment was involved in liaison and coordination of intelligence. It was also in special operations. He is thus in a good position to discuss the role intelligence played in one of the five major events or battles he examines here—the Battle of the Bulge. Others dealt with are Pearl Harbor, the German invasion of the USSR, Dieppe, and Arnhem. His section on Pearl Harbor contributes nothing of any significance. As for the other intelligence failures or failures to heed intelligence, his treatment of Arnhem and the Bulge is made out of date by new information. The reader is referred to Lewin's *Ultra Goes to War* on Arnhem, Bennett's *Ultra in the West* on both Arnhem and the Bulge, and Koch's *G-2: Intelligence for Patton* also on the Bulge for more up-to-date information of what intelligence and analyses were or were not available prior to these battles. Kirkpatrick was in error in believing, as did others, that the agent Lucy provided warning of the German attack on the Soviet Union. He does not conclude that Barbarossa, the German plan to invade the USSR, was a deception success on the part of the Germans, contrary to the later thesis of Whaley (*Barbarossa*). Wohlstetter's *Pearl Harbor, Warning and Decision*) is regarded as the best on that subject.

Kirkpatrick, Lyman B., Jr. THE REAL CIA. New York: Macmillan, 1968. 301 pp., index [London: Collier-Macmillan].

If anyone could have written an inside story of the real CIA up to 1965, it was Kirkpatrick. He was in a number of positions with a level of access that few CIA men could match—inspector general for eight years, member of three groups involved in organizational studies, and executive director/comptroller, not to speak of earlier positions of operational authority. He wrote this as his legacy "to the people of the free world on the role of intelligence in a free society." The method employed is to include autobiographical material, which makes the book also a story of his career in intelligence, a device later employed by Cline in *Secrets, Spies and Scholars.*

Kirkpatrick was selective; since the appearance of this book, we have learned of many matters that were not touched on here. He made it clear from the start that he would tell what he could without revealing secrets or giving any information to his country's enemies. Consequently, he did not say much about the report of his inspection staff on the Bay of Pigs operation, although some things can be deduced from his remarks, nor did he provide any insights about personal and professional differences in the

CIA hierarchy of which he was both an observer and a participant. Nor did he reveal his strong feelings about certain types of operations—he was silent about particular CIA operations except for Cuba. For the facts about these subjects and others one must turn to Powers's *The Man Who Kept the Secrets* and to congressional reports of the 1970s that dealt with investigation of CIA, or to other sources. The reader should not lose sight of the things of historical value included: a rare first-hand picture of the work of an OSS detachment with a U.S. army in World War II; a look at the Polish intelligence school in Scotland during the war training agents to work against both the Germans and the Soviets; close-ups of certain CIA directors; the story of the creation by General Strong of G-2 of a collection system in 1942 separate from OSS and outside the normal government channels; glimpses of CIA cooperation and problems with Batista in Cuba and of CIA's resistance to the attacks by Senator Joseph McCarthy; some details of the early organizational and bureaucratic history of CIA. There is some dated material (such as that on the German attack in the Ardennes) but other still up to date, as on the case of the National Redoubt and its influence on strategy at the end of World War II or the problem of secrecy and the role of intelligence in a democracy. Blackstock and Schaf in their bibliography were of the opinion this book was one of those by retired officials whose "memoirs tend to read like institutional advertising."

Kirkpatrick, Lyman B., Jr. THE U.S. INTELLIGENCE COMMUNITY: FOREIGN POLICY AND DOMESTIC ACTIVITIES. New York: Hill and Wang, 1973. 212 pp., bibliog., index.

Kirkpatrick describes the function of the intelligence community and the role of intelligence in policy formulation prior to 1965, the date of his retirement from CIA. Though this work is dated, it is one of the few dealing with the subject by a knowledgeable author. Blackstock and Schaf found its evaluation of the role of intelligence in policymaking good. But they found disappointing the author's views on the role of intelligence in society and on what controls Congress should have. Likewise disappointing to them was his treatment of the domestic activities of various intelligence organizations.

Kirkpatrick, Lyman B., Jr., and Sargent, Howland H. SOVIET POLITICAL WARFARE TECHNIQUES: ESPIONAGE AND PROPAGANDA IN THE 1970s. New York: National Strategy Information Center, 1972. 80 pp., bibliog., no index.

The two essays in this short work deal with espionage and propaganda separately. Kirkpatrick's on Soviet espionage is a general survey of Russian and Soviet intelligence since the seventeeth century and contains selected operations as examples. According to DIS's *Bibliography,* the author intended to expand this essay into a book on Soviet foreign policy and espionage. Kirkpatrick has done well in measuring the true proportions of the Soviet system of intelligence and security and its pervasiveness. The subject is put in proper perspective with a frankness that was not universally welcomed in the anti–national security atmosphere at that time. Aside from the repetition of the minor error that the Swiss net in 1941 gave warning of the German intent to attack Russia, there is a more significant lapse. Kirkpatrick concentrates on Soviet state security and by doing so gives the impression that operations such as those of Sorge and Lucy and the Rote Kapelle were of that service rather than of military intelligence. As a consequence, there is the tendency to give only passing attention to the latter service.

Sargent, who was assistant secretary of state for public affairs and then president of the Radio Liberty Committee, concentrates on overt Soviet propaganda in his essay and describes its role as a Soviet offensive weapon. For those interested in Soviet covert propaganda modus operandi, there is no development of this parallel aspect of Soviet propaganda and political warfare.

Klass, Phillip J. SECRET SENTRIES IN SPACE. New York: Random House, 1971. 221 pp., index.

As the senior avionics editor of *Aviation Week and Space Technology,* Klass is quite knowledgeable on his subject. The book's jacket calls this the first report on the secret satellites of the United States and the USSR. It is a well-written history of the development of various generations of reconnaissance satellites of the two countries, with greater knowledge displayed of the U.S. side. Klass also presents his views of their value to international stability as a result of the intelligence they provide. Because of this value, he wishes to bring them to the public's attention and calls for removal of some security wraps. This was subsequently done by the U.S. president who officially admitted such reconnaissance capabilities. The work has been favorably commented on by many reviewers, and one in the *USNI Proceedings* called it "the most definitive book available on U.S. photographic satellite systems." Blackstock and Schaf described it as a remarkable exposé of the development of these programs and the reasons for them. Klass indeed shows his grasp and vast store of knowledge, including an awareness of some matters still classified. Note that he foresaw the danger of satellite killers and recognized them as well within the state of the art. A very good introduction and nontechnical explanation of satellite reconnaissance, though specific details may not always be precise.

Knorr, Klaus Eugen. FOREIGN INTELLIGENCE AND THE SOCIAL SCIENCES. Princeton Center of International Studies Research Monograph, no. 17. Princeton, N.J.: Princeton Univ. Press, 1964. 55 pp., bibliog., no index.

Knorr was director of the Princeton Center of International Studies at the time he wrote this. He examined the relationship, similarities, and differences between intelligence and the social sciences. The portion of intelligence he was concerned with was what he called the predictive function. He did not consider intelligence sources and techniques of collection or, generally, problems of intelligence organization and the management of intelligence production. Knorr found that social sciences have provided intelligence with certain tools that allow both fields to identify, seek, validate, process, and interpret data. He concluded that social sciences had made a vast contribution to intelligence production and that modern intelligence was unthinkable without social science inputs. His recommendations included federal support for research in the social sciences from which intelligence will profit and the development of a theory of intelligence (and possibly a doctrine). Knorr has continued his study of the interrelationship of the academic and intelligence worlds and recently was involved in research of material that the intelligence community had selected for release.

Koch, Oscar W., with Robert G. Hays. G-2: INTELLIGENCE FOR PATTON. Philadelphia: Whitmore Publishing and Army Times Publishing, 1971. 167 pp., no index.

General Koch served with General Patton in the invasion of North Africa. He then became his G-2 for the remainder of the war. He describes the organization and functioning of Patton's intelligence staff and intelligence support for Patton's operations. In this short book, most matters get a broad-brush treatment; but a number of anecdotes and examples of intelligence at work are found to whet the appetite. Koch touches on the security of the operation for invading Africa (Torch); the use of Patton as part of the deception plan for the invasion of Normandy; the correct intelligence estimate of the Italian army's intelligence chief on Sicily that this island was the target for Husky (the Allied Sicilian invasion plan); the labeling of the National Redoubt as a myth by his staff, the only one to do so. Writing before the declassification of Ultra, Koch cannot treat the role communications intelligence played in his intelligence work and in the operational decisions of Patton. There are hints, however, as in his version of what happened at Avranches. Any future study of the role of intelligence before the Battle of the Bulge will have to include his staff's estimates of German capabilities before the battle. Accounts by U.S. Army intelligence officers at Koch's level of responsibility in World War II are rare. Robert Allen in *Lucky Forward* (New York: Vanguard Press, 1977), about the Third Army, called Koch brilliant, scholarly, self-effacing, and "the greatest G-2 in the U.S. Army," whose merits went unrewarded.

Kofos, Evangelos. GREECE AND THE EASTERN CRISIS, 1875–1878. Salonika, Greece: Institute for Balkan Studies, 1975. 260 pp., bibliog., index.

The author completed this for his doctorate at the University of London. In 1976 he was a foreign affairs adviser to the Greek prime minister. Because he had access to records of the Greek Foreign Office, Kofos was able to reveal new information, particularly about Greek clandestine activities in territories with a Greek population but under Ottoman rule and about the covert support given by the Greek authorities to their compatriots in such areas. These territories were later to become a part of modern Greece; in the meanwhile, covert support continued as one means of projecting Greek interests. A scholarly, balanced work.

Koop, Theodore F. WEAPON OF SILENCE. Chicago: Univ. of Chicago Press, 1946. 291 pp., index.

Koop was special assistant to Byron Price, the director of the U.S. Office of Censorship in World War II. That organization, comprising ten thousand censors, had the authority to examine mail, newspapers, cables, magazines, films, and radio broadcasts. Its records were classified until 1971. Koop's book came twenty-five years earlier and has the distinction of being the first personal account of censorship's contribution to U.S. security, intelligence, and economic and psychological warfare efforts. It recounts the success of voluntary censorship in preserving such secrets as the development of the atomic bomb, Magic, the state of plans for the invasion of France, and the proximity fuse. Technical workings of various forms of civilian censorship are explained, and a bit on the related problems of military censorship is provided. Koop later became deputy director under Price, and the book glows with praise of the latter and the organization; it is slightly biased, for nowhere are any faults of Price or his agency mentioned. That he and it might not have been infallible is indicated by Kahn's findings reported in *Hitler's Spies:* the German networks in Mexico and the United States sent at least five hundred microdots of information to their controls in Germany. A book on such a vast effort written so shortly after the event cannot do it justice. Censorship, for example, may have been the principal source for running the blockade, as he says: but Ultra has to be considered in any final judgment.

Krivitsky, Walter G. IN STALIN'S SECRET SERVICE. New York: Harper and Bros., 1939. 273 pp., no index [London: Hamish Hamilton. *I Was Stalin's Agent*].

The subtitle is "An Expose of Russia's Secret Policies by the Former Chief of the Soviet Intelligence in Western Europe." New facts, alternative views, and the perspective of time have shown that this memoir by a famous Soviet military intelligence defector is of mixed quality. Some of what Krivitsky wrote has been confirmed, some questioned, some challenged. In retrospect, his chapter on the Soviet trials of the 1930s and his version of the role of both the Germans and Stalin in the Tukhachevsky affair stand up well. As for his account of his own intelligence activity, it is relatively brief. He mentions only two major Soviet military operations in which he was involved, and his version of one has been contested by one of his detractors. We know now that what he reveals here of Comintern and intelligence-organization espionage and covert action in the United States and the West is not all he knew. Flora Lewis states that in his stream of revealed secrets there are many half-truths and many omissions. Elisabeth Poretsky, the widow of Ignace Reiss, Krivitsky's old friend and colleague in Soviet intelligence, is the most specific and passionate attacker of Krivitsky and of his revelations. In her story of her husband and his friends, *Our Own People,* she levels many charges and criticisms against him and his book. According to her, he had only the rank of captain; Soviet intelligence never had a centralized control post for Europe, as he claimed; he took credit for operations with which he had nothing to do; and he claimed knowledge of operations to which he was not privy. It is true that Krivitsky was not a general and was not chief of intelligence for Western Europe. He does not even give his true service (the NKVD) at the time of defection. He never gives the full story of what he knew, and he makes errors of fact. For this, blame must be put on some of the private Americans who advised him on what he should say; Krivitsky realized too late that he had followed bad guidance. Researchers should keep in mind that the main thrust of the book is correct even though details may not be. Martin's *Wilderness of Mirrors* contains material on Krivitsky's purported revelations of Soviet espionage that is not mentioned in this book.

L

Lampe, David. THE LAST DITCH. New York: Putnam's Sons, 1968. 240 pp., index [London: Cassell].

The Auxiliary Units were organized by the British to carry out guerrilla warfare in the event that the Germans invaded and occupied Britain in 1940. They became one model for the creation of resistance on the Continent, and it was here that Gubbins, later of SOE fame, gained experience as the man in charge of creating this British underground army. *The Last Ditch* was a try to write of the Auxiliary Units as a main topic; up to then they had been mentioned only briefly in such works as Peter Fleming's *Operation Sea Lion* (New York: Simon and Schuster, 1957). The organization, training, and planning for what are called stay-behind organizations (for intelligence gathering, resistance, psychological warfare, sabotage, etc., in enemy-occupied areas) are not to be found in intelligence literature as the main subject of a work, so Lampe's book is unique in this regard. Fleming himself was the first commander of the first auxiliary unit; in his review of Lampe's work in *Book World* he found Lampe's opinion of the military capabilities of the Auxiliary Units much higher than any held at the time. He was of the view that "accuracy was not [Lampe's] strong point" and said that in the areas familiar to him (Fleming), Lampe's treatments "seldom contain more than a grain of truth and often less." Lampe had previously written on the Danish resistance movement.

Landau, Henry. ALL'S FAIR: THE STORY OF THE BRITISH SECRET SERVICE BEHIND THE GERMAN LINES. New York: Putnam's Sons, 1934. 321 pp., index.

_______. SECRETS OF THE WHITE LADY. New York: Putnam's Sons, 1935. 308 pp., index.

______. SPREADING THE SPY NET: THE STORY OF A BRITISH SPY DIRECTOR. London: Jarrolds, 1938. 280 pp., index.

Landau served for some two-and-a-half years as head of the Military Division of the British Secret Service in Holland, from 1916 to the armistice. His was one of four sections, the other three being concerned with naval, counterespionage, and press matters. He ran networks in occupied France and Belgium, of which the one named White Lady was the largest and considered the most successful. These were largely involved in reporting German troop movements. Each of the three works listed here covers much the same ground, but all three must be read to get the full story the author wishes to relate, for each has some information not found in the others. They are the personal chronicle of a field intelligence officer, not that of the headquarters intelligence staff officer. The author's admiration for the agents in the nets shines through. The work of these nets adumbrated some experiences in World War II, as did the German counterespionage methods. German counterintelligence organizations and their divisions and weaknesses were repeated in the next world war. There is little on Landau's postwar intelligence associations since he admits that he was unable to tell more than he does. There may be some bias in the author's claims for the effectiveness of his networks versus that of others, but this is not what sets off warning signals. More surprisingly, he calls Elsbeth Schragmüller the director of the German secret service in Belgium. His chapter on the Admiralty's Room 40 citing three cases of captured or stolen German codes has a number of errors. He states he was assigned to investigate the case of Alexander Szek, the man whose relatives said was a British agent who stole the German codes and then disappeared; yet he calls him Sol, not Szek. What Landau has to say of Szek is of renewed and current importance in view of the reopening of the matter in 1981 by Roskill's *Admiral of the Fleet Earl Beatty* (New York: Atheneum, 1981) in which Admiral

Oliver is quoted as confirming everything previously denied about Szek's work as a British agent. See Rowan's *The Story of Secret Service* in which Landau admits taking liberties with certain material and in which Rowan shows that in one case Landau's account does not agree with that of another author.

Landau, Henry. THE ENEMY WITHIN: THE INSIDE STORY OF GERMAN SABOTAGE IN AMERICA. New York: Putnam's Sons, 1937. 310 pp., index.

After wartime intelligence service in Holland (see above), Landau acted for a period as an investigator of claims by Americans against the German government for damages done in the United States by acts of sabotage prior to that country's entry into World War I. This book, written before the final court decision, is in two parts. The first is a brief history of German sabotage and intelligence activities both before and after the U.S. entry into the war. The second concerns the investigation of the claims and the litigations and is of interest only when it relates details of German intelligence. Its intelligence facts are already divulged in previous literature, with one possible exception. *Military Review* in 1979 pointed out that Landau's book was the only printed source till then that treated the Jahnke affair. It felt this book had been generally neglected by historians of U.S. intelligence, perhaps because it contains errors and is undocumented. (Kurt Jahnke was the chief of German Naval Intelligence for North America in 1917 with headquarters in Mexico City. He planned to incite troubles in the United States and on its Mexican border to pin down U.S. troops.) Jahnke's work, however, is mentioned briefly in William James's *The Eyes of the Navy.* The chapter on Room 40 is the same as the one previously included in Landau's *Spreading the Spy Net,* but this time he gives the name of the British agent as Alexander Szek, not Sol as he mistakenly did before (see above). In contrast to his other three books, here he is not writing of intelligence matters from knowledge derived from actually participating in the events or being reasonably close to them. Nevertheless, he offers as one of his conclusions that the United States needed a counterespionage service. An item of interest is Landau's allegation that Admiral Hall, ex-chief of British Naval Intelligence, had in 1925 ten thousand decoded German messages in the basement of his home. For more current research on Jahnke's activities in World War I, see Friederich Katz's *The Secret War in Mexico* (1981). For his career in German intelligence in World War II, consult Schellenberg's *The Labyrinth.*

Langelaan, George. KNIGHTS OF THE FLOATING SILK. London: Hutchinson, 1959. 320 pp., no index [Garden City, N.Y.: Doubleday. *The Masks of War*].

The author, an Englishman, spent most of his life in France. His story of his wartime work is divided into two main sections. One has to do with his mission to France in World War II and the training and preparation for it. What is particularly unconventional about this part is that he underwent facial surgery, a move that was rare but duplicated by the head of SOE's RF Section, Colonel Hutchinson (see *That Drug Danger*). Otherwise, there is not much in this mission to hold the researcher's interest. The title fits only this portion. The remainder of the war was spent in assignments in British Field Security, in liaison with the Americans, and in an intelligence assignment attached to the Anglo-American Psychological Warfare Branch. Though Foot in *SOE in France* called the book well written, others may find its organization confusing. Several chapters concerning counterespionage work and British security are chronologically hard to fit, as are the author's particular affiliations. There are some episodes describing the pursuit of investigative leads and suspected agents seen from the field or working level that are of value because so little has been written of the security work in the war from this vantage point. The U.S. edition deleted several of the chapters on such episodes, probably as a result of the publisher's judgment of the lack of appeal of such mundane matters.

Langley, James M. FIGHT ANOTHER DAY. London: Collins, 1974. 254 pp., no index.

Langley was introduced in the specialized literature of escape and evasion (E&E) in Neave's *The Escape Room* as the head of a section of Britain's MI9 known as IS9 (d). The record was set straight not in this book but in one by Foot and Langley entitled *MI 9: The British Secret Service. . . .* It was there that we learned that Langley was only nominally on MI9's staff and was commanded and paid by MI6 until 1944. His job was to encourage the establishment of E&E nets in northwest Europe and to serve as the "point of junction" between MI6 and MI9. Knowing this makes what he has to reveal in this book about relations between the two all the more interesting and reliable. This is only one of the subjects where Langley has added knowledge beyond that supplied by Neave; others are the political and bureaucratic infighting, Dansey's hard-nosed approach to MI9's problems, and bureaucratic errors and operational mistakes. Langley discusses his own mistakes in hiring such agents as the infamous Dutch King Kong and the British Paul Cole, both of whom became double agents of the Germans and caused great harm to Allied E&E operations. The book also relates his experiences as co-commander of the Allied POW rescue unit. Consider this book a way station to the more thorough treatment to be found in *MI 9: The British Secret Service,* published five years later.

Lasby, Clarence G. PROJECT PAPERCLIP: GERMAN SCIENTISTS AND THE COLD WAR. New York: Atheneum, 1971. 297 pp., bibliog., notes, index.

Based on an extensive study of U.S. government documents supplemented by interviews with knowledgeable individuals, this book traces the evolution of U.S. thinking and policy and describes the efforts to identify, locate, and utilize German scientists and technicians at the last stages of the war and after it. It is also the story of the search for German scientific installations and secrets and of the tug-of-war in the government on how best to make use of what was acquired. Lasby clarifies the reasons for changes in U.S. policy and the effect certain Soviet actions had, including the shock of U.S. officials on learning of Soviet espionage from Gouzenko after his defection in Canada. We also learn the Soviets began to deport thousands of German scientists to the Soviet Union one month after President Truman approved a new U.S. policy ending U.S. indecision on whether to exploit these scientists for military and civilian purposes. Though one review called this a definitive study, that is not the opinion of others, despite a general consensus as to its high quality. One reviewer found the closing chapter on accomplishments to be weak and to rely too much on sweeping estimates of the U.S. military. What is more to the point is that this is largely a treatment of the overt side of the story. The covert or intelligence side needs to be researched to produce a fuller picture of the total effort and to fill in what Lasby tells of the general work of various organizations involved.

Lawrence, T. E. SEVEN PILLARS OF WISDOM: A TRIUMPH. London: Jonathan Cape, 1935. 689 pp., indexes [Garden City, N.Y.: Doubleday].

Any bibliography of intelligence should include Lawrence's famous opus for more than one reason. First, it influenced and inspired a generation about irregular warfare. Lawrence's influence is still felt, as one writer put it in 1977, through a large school of followers in what had become a fashionable field. Second, it was considered a "masterly textbook on the tactics and strategy of irregular warfare," to quote Robert Graves. Barton Whaley called it a succinct but fully rounded theory of the guerrilla. Third, it was judged to be a literary masterpiece, a status rather unusual for a book of this type, though some thought it tortuous. Fourth, Lawrence was connected with British intelligence before World War I, placing him in a category of knowledge and experience above that of the wartime intelligence officer. The debate about the accuracy and even the truthfulness of Lawrence's account continues unresolved, and no significant new evidence has been uncovered on these crucial points of disagreement. An interesting bit of information on Lawrence appeared in a 1981 interview in the *London Times* with Sir Maurice Oldfield, the recently deceased head of Britain's SIS. Oldfield spoke of once having found a file on Lawrence in the old Arab Bureau in Cairo that later disappeared. He called Lawrence's book one of his favorites of "spy" literature. Presumably, then, he found nothing in Lawrence's file and learned nothing from his SIS position that adversely affected his opinion of the book.

Lawson, John Cuthbert. TALES OF AEGEAN INTRIGUE. New York: Dutton, 1921. 258 pp., no index.

For those aware of the potential problem of intelligence officers' making decisions on their own and affecting policy, this is a fascinating case study of a true-life example of this tendency and its dangers. Lawson was in Crete in 1916–1917 with British naval intelligence. There he conducted intelligence and counterintelligence activities, successful and some unsuccessful, which he describes in this book. One involved a clandestine entry into the Austrian consulate to get copies of its correspondence with Vienna and Athens. But it is Lawson's candid account of how he undertook a series of political, psychological, and military measures without official sanction and guidance that is more instructive and sobering. To what extent his freewheeling was a product of the man's personality, his contempt for superiors (especially civilian and Foreign Office), or the lack of close guidance and control might only be determined by a full biography. Sir Basil Thomson cites Lawson as an example of the interference of secret services in Greece in that war (see *The Allied Secret Service in Greece*). Mackenzie discussed him in his *Greek Memories.* Though Mackenzie saw him as a man who could use his wits and called his exposure of a particular forgery a "creditable piece of work," Mackenzie also regarded "his assumption of omniscience [as] often ludicrous"; Lawson, continued Mackenzie, was good as long as he was describing his personal activities, but his exaggerated notion of his own influence made his account of no value except as a guide to local events. Whether Mackenzie meant to include Lawson's picture of the lack of coordination among the British intelligence services in Greece as an example of his "assumption of omniscience" is doubtful, judging from Mackenzie's own experience and memoirs.

Leasor, James. GREEN BEACH. New York: William Morrow, 1975. 237 pp., bibliog., no index [London: Heinemann].

Leasor wrote a journalist's account of the portion of the Dieppe raid in 1942 concerned with the attempt to dismantle a German radar station. It centers on the adventure of Jack Nissenthal, the sergeant in the RAF who was selected as the radar expert to supervise the work. Leasor made use of some official records and interviewed a number of persons on the mission, including Nissenthal himself. There are some good anecdotes, but the book is not as good on the radar war and background as, say, Millar's book on the Bruneval raid; there is no specific documentation and too much on personal and human-interest matters. The latter material appears not only at the expense of more background; the intelligence picture of both sides and specifics about authoritative sources on crucial intelligence items also were not developed as they might have been. Leasor's dramatic story of the orders to kill Nissenthal if capture were imminent is clarified by R. V. Jones in *The Wizard War:* the order was applicable to Jones if he had gone on the raid and somehow was transferred to Nissenthal. The *New York Times* review also cautioned that some statements on the high-level planning were open to challenge.

Le Caron, Henri. TWENTY-FIVE YEARS IN THE SECRET SERVICE: THE RECOLLECTIONS OF A SPY. London: William Heinemann, 1892. 305 pp., index.

Le Caron (real name Thomas Miller Beach), an English-born immigrant to the United States, served as a British agent against the Fenians for some twenty years. This is his story of his life as an agent after the American Civil War, when he held various positions in Irish revolutionary organizations in the United States. His first agent success was to provide intelligence on Irish plans to invade Canada from the United States, which led to the invasion's ignominious defeat. A good portion of the book is devoted to the convoluted politics and divisions of the Irish movement; the remainder is the author's version of his work as a penetration, in which he displays some of the problems associated with the high-spending, temperamental agent and his handling. One notices, too, that there is a strange discrepancy in what he says of his secure handling. He credits his handler in London for protecting his identity as an agent, yet tells that, after the Irish invasion of Canada, he met with a number of British officials there and "my identity was known to some of the officers"; there he also met the physician of a visiting prince. Incidentally, Gilbert McMicken, the Canadian official he was in contact with, was in charge of the Canadian Frontier Police, the first secret service in Canada (see Sawatsky's *Men in the Shadows*). LeCaron's reputation has subsequently been questioned, and his full role in events such as those involving Parnell remains obscure; Winston Churchill in *Great Contemporaries* described him as "a strange figure . . . in the deep-hidden employ of the British Government." Rowan in *The Story of Secret Service* used adjectives like "notorious" to describe him and calls him a hireling. For a summary of Le Caron's work as an agent and the role he may have played in the Parnell case, see Deacon's *A History of the British Secret Service.*

Lester, Richard I. CONFEDERATE FINANCE AND PURCHASING IN GREAT BRITAIN. Charlottesville: Univ. Press of Virginia, 1975. 199 pp., index.

In books about the intelligence war during the American Civil War, writers usually confine themselves to that connected with the military campaigns in the United States and restrict themselves to events in that country. Lester has broadened this picture with his study of Confederate attempts to purchase ships and arms in Great Britain and the Union's intelligence effort to identify these efforts. He describes Confederate uses of cover and go-betweens to purchase or lease ships and the methods that side employed to evade Union surveillance and British laws of neutrality. Confederate techniques of ownership transfers, frequent name changes, and partial ownership are well presented. So is the Union effort to uncover them. Lester shows the Union had created a well-organized and -developed system of espionage and surveillance against the Confederates as well as revealing a bit on preclusive buying as an aspect of its economic warfare. The story of how the secret report of the Confederate secretary of the navy on a complicated plan to get two rams out of Britain fell into the hands of the U.S. minister indicates the level of success of Union espionage and the difficulties encountered by the South. Lester does not prove, however, that the federal organization in Britain was as successful in identifying and preventing the shipment of arms and ammunition to the Confederacy. In contrast to the numerous examples involving ships, his chapter on ordnance purchases does not cite one instance of Union espionage in this regard or of diplomatic representation to the British government designed to block such Confederate purchases. This is an obvious area for further research.

Leverkuehn, Paul. GERMAN MILITARY INTELLIGENCE. London: Weidenfeld and Nicolson, 1954. 209 pp., no index [New York: Praeger].

A reserve officer, Leverkuehn served with the Abwehr in Iran and then (1941–1944) in Turkey. He was chief of the Abwehr station in Istanbul and also responsible for Near East operations. He was suspected by Hitler at one time of contacts with the British, according to Brissaud's *The Nazi Secret Service.* Leverkuehn describes some of his experiences and his service's organization and functions along with giving brief stories of some of its work in espionage and counterespionage. The result is a highly selective account, even allowing for Leverkuehn's caveat that it was not his intent to write a complete history but to select the most typical or important episodes. There is much that he has left out or missed, and his loyalty to his old service and its ex-chief Admiral Canaris is undiminished. One must go to other writings to learn of the Abwehr's stunning defeats at the hands of the Allied services or of Canaris's activities within the service and the regime. Whaley alleged that Leverkuehn's account was carefully censored by its British editor-translators, (see *Codeword Barbarossa*). This, if correct, may account for Leverkuehn's not including significant Abwehr activities that he warns us at the beginning of the book are not to be found in the service's files. The Klatt operation in Sofia is, however, given a short treatment. Leverkuehn's views on Canaris are also discussed in Colvin's *Chief of Intelligence.*

Lewin, Ronald. ULTRA GOES TO WAR: THE FIRST ACCOUNT OF WORLD WAR II'S GREATEST SECRET BASED ON OFFICIAL DOCUMENTS. New York: McGraw-Hill, 1978. 363 pp., bibliog., index [London: Hutchinson].

Michael Howard called this perhaps the most important book on World War II since Chester Wilmot's *The Struggle for Europe* (London: Collins, 1952). Lewin uses actual Ultra intercepts to show how such intelligence was used in combat and in decisions in the conduct of the war and reinforces this research with interviews with many individuals who were privy to Ultra during that period. The view is largely British, and the areas are Europe, Africa, the Mediterranean, and the Atlantic Ocean. He also covers the story of how the cryptanalytical success was achieved and how Ultra was processed and distributed. There is no question that the praise heaped on the book is largely deserved. Drew Middleton in the *New York Times* said that any important future history of the war must consult it. At the same time, some critics recognized that it was not the full story of Ultra and (as Howard put it) was only the beginning of the reexamination of the history of the war in the light of Ultra's revelation. The *USNI Proceedings* reviewer, while calling it the first scholarly attempt to deal with the subject, found that a relatively small amount of Ultra material was available to Lewin when he began to research the book. Lewin himself informs us that the full Ultra traffic sent to Fighter Command of the RAF had yet to be released and that what had been released generally covered "only very limited areas of the world-wide landscape." Subsequent publications have improved on aspects of Lewin's work or corrected certain errors. Calvocoressi in *Top Secret Ultra* makes us aware of how much material of Bletchley Park is *not* in the records of the British Public Record Office. He also gives evidence that Ultra intelligence on the German preparations for the Ardennes offensive in 1944 was not lacking. Bennett in *Ultra in the West* supports Calvocoressi. He believes Lewin was mistaken in saying that for Ultra, the law of diminishing returns began in September 1944 and in the German return to telephone and teleprinter links after Falaise. His version of the cryptanalytical breakthrough against Enigma, good as it is, has technical errors and cannot be regarded as definitive; his evaluation of Bertrand's role is premature. To say that the Purple machine was directly derived from the Enigma is not accurate. U.S. experts, while recognizing the work's strong features and its appreciation of the contributions of the intercept services and of security to success, thought its limited account of the Pacific war was not accurate in some respects. For more on Ultra aspects in the naval war, consult Beesly's *Very Special Intelligence.*

Lewis, David. SEXPIONAGE: THE EXPLOITATION OF SEX BY SOVIET INTELLIGENCE. New York: Harcourt Brace Jovanovich, 1976. 158 pp., bibliog., index.

The use of sex to lure and entrap potential agents is known to be a technique of Soviet and bloc intelligence services. Barron's *KGB* contains a chapter on it that dwells too long on particular cases and only scratches the surface of what has been learned of this operational technique as practiced by the Soviets. *Sexpionage* nowhere comes close to treating the subject either adequately or accurately. Lewis, a British writer, has produced what can only be described as a potpourri of fact, rumor, and speculation. Though he recognized the problems of finding accurate information and reliable sources on the subject, he has proceeded without assuring us that he solved them. The story of the purported sex school run by the Soviets has no reliable attribution or documentary support. Where he lacks material, he weaves in operations that were not sex blackmail cases at all. Lewis would have been better advised to have written a book on Soviet bloc operations using sex and thus could have included other known cases and reduced his resorting to rumor. The treatment of the case involving Leonore Sutterlin and the Soviet illegal Runge could have served as a model for a better work.

Lewis, Flora. RED PAWN: THE STORY OF NOEL FIELD. Garden City, N.Y.: Doubleday, 1965. 266 pp., bibliog., index [London: Arthur Barker. *The Man Who Disappeared: The Strange History of Noel Field*].

Although she had no ready access to classified information and was refused any facts on the case but what she considered obvious, Lewis (the wife of Sidney Gruson) wrote a fine study of her subject. As one reviewer commented, she tracked down thousands of leads and unearthed an impressive amount of information. Above all, she put Field and his activities for the Soviets and OSS in proper perspective and at the right level of importance. She placed him in the category of a minor figure who played a negligible role and whose fame and notoriety stemmed from two events. The first was Stalin's purge of Titoism in which Field was used to destroy individuals by charging them with ties with U.S. intelligence via the conveniently placed Field. The second resulted when his name was brought to light during the U.S. concern about exposing Soviet and communist infiltration of the government after Word War II. Lewis's summing up of Field is excellent, though one could add terms such as "spotter," "agent of influence," or "support agent" to describe the roles Field is shown to have played. There are some minor errors to be found on the supposed death of Rado and the work of Alexander Foote and in the description of Ludwick as head of Soviet intelligence for Western Europe. We now know that Ludwick's name was Ignace Reiss. Reiss's widow, Elisabeth Poretsky, incidentally, does not mention Field in her memoirs, though Field worked for her husband; she does identify Field's mother as a communist courier, confirming Lewis's story. A reviewer felt that Field was a stupid idealist who was put on an undeserved pedestal by the author and that what aid OSS gave the communists during the war is overstressed. Lewis's book is a good account of an example of the interwar phenomenon, some intellectuals' fatal attraction to and involvement with the Soviet cause and ultimately with Soviet intelligence. For Allen Dulles's comments on Noel Field, see his *Great True Spy Stories.*

Library of Congress, Congressional Research Service. SOVIET INTELLIGENCE AND SECURITY SERVICES: A SELECTED BIBLIOGRAPHY OF SOVIET PUBLICATIONS, WITH SOME ADDITIONAL TITLES FROM OTHER SOURCES. 2 vols. Washington, D.C.: Government Printing Office. Vol. 1 (1964–1970): 1972. 273 pp., index. Vol. 2 (1971–1972): 1975. 329 pp., index.

These volumes contain some thirty-five hundred items, listed alphabetically. There is a descriptive synopsis of each but except for an occasional adjective, there is no evaluation of individual pieces. There is an overall evaluation of these works and a caveat to be found in Volume 1's introduction and Volume 2's preface. The compilers call attention to the "dramatic reversal" of the Soviet position regarding Soviet espionage abroad beginning in 1964. Other general comments are that discrepancies can be found among the data, that information on some matters available in the West is frequently at variance with the Soviet version, and that the material is really useful to the student and specialist who know how to use it. Other caveats concern Soviet propaganda and disinformation motives in allowing such works as these to appear. Though this compilation is described as a cross section of such writing, there is a noticeable preponderance of works in Baltic languages or published in these areas. The explanation seems to be the availability of such material in contrast to other material.

Lindsey, Robert. THE FALCON AND THE SNOWMAN: A TRUE STORY OF FRIENDSHIP AND ESPIONAGE. New York: Simon and Schuster, 1979. 358 pp., no index [London: Jonathan Cape, 1980].

Books rushed into print shortly after an event are usually of indifferent quality, especially when they deal with classified matters. This is an exception, and an especially surprising one since it is the first on the case. The author covered the trials of Christopher Boyce and Andrew Daulton Lee as correspondent for the *New York Times.* He captured much in his research and writing: the drug world; the poor security practices existing in intelligence agency–private contractor working arrangements; poor personnel selection and monitoring standards and practices; inadequate or poor monitoring of sensitive installations for vulnerabilities and violations; Soviet tradecraft and handling of "walk-ins," persons who volunteer themselves as agents; the broad sweep of the espionage case. It is, as the *Washington Post* reviewer put it, an uncommonly thoughtful and perceptive book. Not surprisingly, there are errors and some aspects that cause criticism. Knowledgeable persons call his estimate of the damage done possibly exaggerated, even though it was considerable. There is a tendency toward broad, flat statements, such as, "By the early 1970s, no KGB agent had ever penetrated the U.S. operations." The plethora of direct quotes and of descriptive detail lacks any source notes whatsoever. The overreliance on the families and attorneys of the defendants and on the defendants themselves means that Lindsey's account reflects their story and point of view more heavily than it should.

Listowel, Judith, Countess of. CRUSADER IN THE SECRET WAR. London: Christopher Johnson, 1952. 287 pp., no index.

The hero and subject of this book is not named Peter Nart, as the author says, but Jan Kowalewski. A member of the Polish General Staff, Colonel Kowalewski organized the Polish cryptologic service in 1918 and headed it until the end of the Polish-Russian War in 1922. He is the Pole referred to by Yardley in *The American Black Chamber* who went to Japan and assisted the Japanese in improving their cryptanalytical work. According to Kahn's *The Codebreakers,* he also helped them improve their codes. Although Listowel does mention this part of his life, she is more interested in his work as a Polish representative in Lisbon and his contacts during World War II with Hungarian, Rumanian, and Italian officials. These contacts take up the bulk of her story so that even Kowalewski's responsibility for providing contact with the Polish underground is not discussed as fully as one would like. The long, verbatim accounts of his conversations with Axis representatives make a poor substitute for descriptions of his cryptologic and underground adventures, especially because there is no evidence that the contacts were anything but peripheral to other, similar efforts or that they led to anything of any significance. Kowalewski's contact work in Lisbon is also mentioned in Colvin's *Chief of Intelligence,* but there the emphasis is on reported secret German contacts with him.

Lockhart, Robert Bruce. COMES THE RECKONING. London: Putnam, 1947. 374 pp., index.

Lockhart, who gained his fame in Russia after World War I and authored the best-seller *Memoirs of a British Agent,* was the director general of Political Warfare Executive (PWE) for four years during World War II. PWE was involved in both overt and covert operations. The overt were mainly concerned with British propaganda activities against enemy and enemy-occupied areas, and were in cooperation with the U.S. Office of War Information (OWI); PWE worked with OSS on secret and black operations. Lockhart devotes most of the book to political commentaries and discussing his contacts; consequently, even the overt side of PWE does not get his full attention. Except for passing references to black or secret work of PWE, he tells nothing of this side of the work. It was later revealed in such books as Delmer's and Cruickshank's works and Owen's *Battle of Wits.* Lockhart is not very forthcoming on other subjects such as relations between PWE and SOE. He does inform us that PWE carried out deception operations prior to the Allied landings in North Africa and Sicily and participated in deception plans to tie down Germans in the west in 1942. As for the Overlord operation, Lockhart relates that PWE had the main burden for the propaganda campaign for D-Day but does not mention any PWE role in the deception scheme. PWE's role in collecting information and other activities and where it operated are not made quite clear. Lockhart speaks only of "every form of overt and covert attack" and of political warfare demanding "a highly specialized intelligence service of its own." Foot in *SOE in France* mentions that a PWE agent was parachuted into France. Cruickshank in *The Fourth Arm* said that PWE was not allowed to send agents into the field—this was SOE's job. Be it noted that at the same time Lockhart was being very circumspect about black activities such as black radios, the secret was being revealed by MacDonald (see her *Undercover Girl* and Delmer's *Black Boomerang*). See also Cruickshank on PWE's collection activities and the use of its leaflets to reinforce deception after the Normandy invasion.

Lockhart, Robin Bruce. ACE OF SPIES. London: Hodder and Stoughton, 1967. 187 pp., index [New York: Stein and Day, 1968].

The caveats that are inserted by the author make it clear this book must be read with circumspection. He warns that he had to contend with the Official Secrets Act and that records of the SIS were few and not easily acquired; he also makes no apologies for a "certain lack of completeness in this biography." This biography of the British agent Sidney Reilly adds very little to what was already known and does not help to prove or disprove the many speculations in what has been said about him and about his disappearance. It is a popular account that lacks documentary support and seems to have been pieced together from available fragments of fact and pieces of speculation. Lockhart handles the Soviet Trust operation only adequately; as for his contention that Reilly was involved in the famous Zinoviev Letter, what evidence he had for this he allowed had come partly from the Soviet Union and was purportedly confessed by Reilly to the Soviets. The son of Sir Robert Bruce Lockhart, the famous contemporary of Reilly who also worked in Russia, this author might have been better advised to be cautious in some of his judgments, considering what hard evidence he possessed or was willing to identify. Readers will be surprised that he included stories about Reilly that can only be described as tall. Even combined with Pepita Reilly's *Britain's Master Spy,* this book leaves many questions about Reilly unanswered.

Lonsdale, Gordon. SPY: TWENTY YEARS IN SOVIET SECRET SERVICE. New York: Hawthorn, 1965. 220 pp., no index [London: Neville Spearman].

Konon Molodiy, who used the name of Lonsdale, was the Soviet illegal caught in the British roundup of the

Portland spy ring in the early 1960s. This is a very unreliable work, without redeeming qualities. It is bursting with anti-Western propaganda notable for the absence of any finesse whatsoever. Even the publisher (British) is compelled at the end of the book to add an afterthought that calls attention to the Soviet censorship of the work, its glaring omissions, and its propaganda. The last is described as "clumsy, awkward and without subtlety." According to Eleanor Philby, in her *The Spy I Loved* (London: Hamish Hamilton, 1968), the Lonsdale memoirs were compiled by Kim Philby, and the Soviets offered to withdraw them from the English market in exchange for the release of the two Krogers, who had been involved with Lonsdale. Lonsdale had been released from a British prison in exchange for Greville Wynne.

Lord, John. DUTY, HONOR, EMPIRE: THE LIFE AND TIMES OF COLONEL RICHARD MEINERTZHAGEN. New York: Random House, 1970. 395 pp., bibliog., index.

Meinertzhagen served as an intelligence officer with British forces in Africa and the Middle East prior to and during World War I. His fame in intelligence history is centered around the Meinertzhagen satchel ploy he employed in the Palestine campaign of Allenby to deceive the Germans and Turks as to the direction of the main British attack. Meinertzhagen is also remembered for his conversion to the Zionist cause. Lord, the author, could have developed Meinertzhagen's intelligence work more fully. As an example, the work of the Nili spies is covered in a little more than one page, and the exact value of the intelligence they provided is not made clear. There is some confusion even in this short account, for he says they were employed by Meinertzhagen, not by Political Intelligence under Deedes, as Engle says in *The Nili Spies.* Meinertzhagen's work is mentioned by Lawrence in *Seven Pillars of Wisdom.* Haswell in *British Military Intelligence* pointed out that the only authoritative source on his activities is Meinertzhagen himself; the *RUSI* reviewer commented that much of what Lord tells us has been covered by Meinertzhagen's diaries and that the biographer failed to search out supporting evidence for some of Meinertzhagen's claims other than an occasional confidential report quoted. Haswell even raised the matter of the satchel story as requiring further confirmations since some of those who used it after the war (such as Lloyd George and Cyril Falls) were well acquainted with Meinertzhagen.

Lord, Walter. LONELY VIGIL: COASTWATCHERS OF THE SOLOMONS. New York: Viking Press, 1977. 297 pp., index [Canada: Penguin].

A popular history of the Coastwatchers, the organization that had intelligence collectors on Pacific islands reporting on Japanese movements. More specifically, this is the story of the men in the Solomon Islands during the crucial fighting in 1942 and 1943 who were only one of the Coastwatchers groups providing intelligence on enemy naval, air, troop, and supply movements. Lord also describes their work in rescuing Allied air and navy personnel and assisting in their evasion of capture. The book is more for the historian of the war than for those interested in its intelligence features, for the author devotes much detail to things not of particular interest to the latter. Beyond this, Lord neglects matters of interest to the intelligence expert—such as preparations, training of personnel, and command and control arrangements. And whereas he went to great pains to interview many on the Allied side, there is relatively little from the other end to give an idea of how much the Japanese knew of the Coastwatchers and what they tried to do to neutralize them by various methods, including the use of direction finding. Eric Feldt's *Coastwatchers* (Oxford: Oxford Univ. Press, 1947) is regarded as a basic work on the subject. See also Ind's *Allied Intelligence Bureau.*

Lotz, Wolfgang. THE CHAMPAGNE SPY: ISRAEL'S MASTER SPY TELLS HIS STORY. New York: St. Martin's Press, 1972. 240 pp., no index [London: Vallentine, Mitchell].

Lotz was the Israeli illegal who posed as a wealthy German in Egypt until caught. He was sentenced and then released. This is his story, published, according to his version, despite his differences with the Israeli service on whether it should be allowed (see *A Handbook for Spies,* below). Fuller, more varied pictures of Lotz have appeared and should be compared to his version. For instance, Dan and Ben-Porat's *The Secret War* gives a version of how Lotz handled the matter of his Israeli identity at the time of his trial that is at variance with Lotz's account. Eisenberg, Dan, and Landau in *The Mossad* give a portrait of Lotz both as a person and as an agent that includes his strong and his weak points. Steven's *The Spymasters of Israel* discusses his varying abilities as an intelligence collector. This is nevertheless a rare work—the story of a post–World War II non-Soviet illegal operation written by the illegal himself. One should also read Lotz's *A Handbook for Spies* for a more complete insight into the man and his experiences in Egypt.

Lotz, Wolfgang. A HANDBOOK FOR SPIES. New York: Harper and Row, 1980. 146 pp., no index.

In the preface, Lotz, the Israeli agent who operated in Egypt (see *The Champagne Spy,* above), advises he wrote this in response to the requests for advice of those who were thinking of making a career in espionage. On the final page, however, he tells us that it was written because he had invested his money badly. Whatever his motive, *A Handbook for Spies* not only reflects his experiences and his outlook stemming from his work in Egypt but reveals much about Lotz himself. He cames through strong and clear as a man of many parts: unconventional, impatient with routine and the bureaucracy, lover of the good life, a bit egotistical, proud, and, in the words of his army record, "a man of action with a flair for the unusual and the unconservative." And though he does not dwell on this, Lotz is also very obviously a man of courage. Some of his observations on the agent and espionage are universally pertinent, while others seem to fit his particular experiences and circumstances. This book, as is indicated in the comments on *The Champagne Spy* (above), must be read for further insights into Lotz's Egyptian experience and its aftermath, characterized by strained relations between Lotz and the Israeli service. Within it, too, are veins of valuable lessons on the problems and challenges of handling agents of a special caliber.

Lovell, Stanley P. OF SPIES AND STRATEGEMS. Englewood Cliffs, N.J.: Prentice-Hall, 1963. 191 pp., no index.

Lovell was for over three years director of research and development for OSS. His organization was involved in the creation of special items to be used for intelligence, sabotage, or subversion—items from counterfeit funds to explosives. He calls this but a part of OSS history—the part that came into his purview. It is a chatty book that brings out information on some technical accomplishments and contains cameo shots of certain personalities, among them General Donovan. In cases where Lovell was not directly involved and when he recounts how the new items were used, he is not as good. As an example, he claims that his visit to London in connection with an intelligence item on Peenemünde led to the attack on this important target, an exaggeration of the effect of his role in the decision-making process. There are a number of small errors, such as the name he gives SOE. Lovell's book received further attention with the appearance of John Marks's *The Search for the "Manchurian Candidate,"* wherein Lovell's brief references to OSS research in truth drugs and interest in hypnotism are spotlighted as the first tip-offs of such research by the U.S. government. Lovell, incidentally, had been asked by General Donovan not to write a book until twenty years had passed from the day of the request. Despite any shortcomings, this is valuable in that it deals with a category of intelligence support (technical) not ordinarily used as the main topic of a work.

Lucas, Norman. SPYCATCHER: A BIOGRAPHY OF DETECTIVE-SUPERINTENDANT GEORGE GORDON SMITH. London and New York: W. H. Allen, 1973. 179 pp., no index.

Smith was with the British Special Branch until his retirement in 1963; he began his career in counterintelligence in the early 1940s as a liaison officer with MI5. Lucas was a friend of his, which may partly account for his dubbing Smith the "No. One Spycatcher" of Scotland Yard. Though Smith was involved in some way with the Vassall, Fuchs, Portland, and other cases, the author has not proved that Smith's role and that of the Special Branch were more central and crucial to the discovery and identification of the agents involved than those of others. Lucas plays down the role of MI5 in cases such as that of Fuchs; here the author fails to give due recognition to William Skardon and to describe Skardon's work adequately. In his account, Lucas has given a particular perspective that is biased toward his friend at the expense of other CI organizations and factors. He served as a witness in the hearings of the tribunal created by the British home secretary to look into the Vassall case. See Martin's *Wilderness of Mirrors,* Bulloch and Miller's *Spy Ring,* and West's *The New Meaning of Treason.* The latter provides a brief summary of the Romer Commission's findings on the work of Special Branch and MI5 and admits that neither organization discovered the Portland spy ring.

Lüdecke, Winfried. BEHIND THE SCENES OF ESPIONAGE: TALES OF SECRET SERVICE. London: Harrap, 1929. 250 pp., no index [Philadelphia: Lippincott. *The Secrets of Espionage: Tales of Secret Service*].

The contents first appeared as a series of articles in German and Swiss newspapers. Lüdecke was a Swiss journalist, and what he wrote would have been forgotten except for the resurrection of his claims on the authorship of the Zinoviev Letter. In 1968, Chester, Fay, and Young in *The Zinoviev Letter* quoted Lüdecke as the source for their fingering of Sidney Reilly as the person who transmitted the Zinoviev Letter to the right hands for its appearance. Reilly's widow had vigorously denied this, calling Lüdecke's section on Reilly in this book "abounding in inaccuracies." Robin Bruce Lockhart, however, wrote in 1967 that he had received evidence from the USSR that Reilly had confessed to the OGPU that he had been responsible for the letter (see *Ace of Spies*). One's faith in Lüdecke's reliability is diminished by the quality of much else he writes here. This collection of espionage stories contains eyebrow raisers, such as his calling Mata Hari "one of the subtlest and cleverest secret agents thrown up by the late war"; it devotes only one line to the agent Alfred Redl while allocating much space to obscure agents; and there are numerous errors throughout.

M

McChristian, Joseph A. THE ROLE OF MILITARY INTELLIGENCE 1965–1967. Washington, D.C.: U.S. Department of the Army, 1974. 173 pp., index.

General McChristian was J-2, Military Assistance Command, Vietnam (MACV), for the period he examines. The monograph is principally concerned with and of greatest value on the organization of military intelligence. We are provided with details and charts of the organization and functions of various components. At the same time, the author's philosophy on unity of intelligence command, cooperation with the Vietnamese allies, and the size of the required intelligence effort inevitably come through. The official sponsorship and unclassified status of the study limited the author in ways that are obvious to those familiar with the subject. The DIS *Bibliography of Intelligence Literature* believed that since the work was unclassified, much of what the author might have wished to say had had to be omitted. Blackstock and Schaf in their bibliography regarded McChristian's book as a valuable and useful account of the buildup period of combat intelligence in Vietnam pending an official history of the Vietnam War. One finds omissions of various types and of varying degrees of importance. Discussion of classified units and classified efforts are omitted to keep the monograph unclassified; working relations with CIA in Vietnam are barely touched upon; the difficult worlds of counterintelligence and counterespionage require histories in themselves. Additionally, there are some evaluations of the efficacy of the intelligence effort in Vietnam that should be examined more fully with the perspective of time. McChristian later became chief of U.S. Army Intelligence.

MacCloskey, Monro. SECRET AIR MISSIONS. New York: Richards Rosen, 1966. 159 pp., no index.

The author organized, trained, and commanded the squadron of the U.S. Fifteenth Air Force responsible for dropping agents and supplies into Italy, southern France, and the Balkans in World War II. He flew fifty missions himself. This, he says, is the story of how his unit was formed, equipped, and trained and flew missions; there are also stories of some of the missions themselves. It is a cross between a unit history and a collection of letters to home. Since hundreds of agents were transported and thousands of sorties to drop supplies to the underground were flown, there might have been more on missions, such as the hazardous Lagoon Green effort in northern Italy or the dropping of British agents to eliminate a particular German commander. MacCloskey explains the omissions: it was not easy after twenty years to relate certain stories because of the special record keeping required for highly classified operations. Another reason is obvious: it is written from the vantage point of the air support officer rather than of the intelligence officer or agent. Still, air support of intelligence operations has not often been described at this operational level and especially not by the crews themselves. For another look at air support, see Hamilton's *Wings of Night* and Gibb McCall's *Flight Most Secret* (1981).

McCoy, Alfred W. THE POLITICS OF HEROIN IN SOUTHEAST ASIA. New York: Harper and Row, 1972. 464 pp., index.

This was advertised as an exposé of CIA involvement in the drug traffic. The author was a graduate student at the time, and the book appeared when CIA was under attack at home. It purported to show that CIA tolerated the production and traffic of drugs when it assumed the role of the French in Indochina. The *New York Times* review did not consider this an exposé of CIA involvement but rather an "unraveling of the complexities of the Southeast Asian opium and heroin trade." Blackstock and Schaf's bibliography called it a "carefully documented but controversial book." One may disagree that it was carefully documented because the practice of using unidentified sources or questionable source attributions was so frequently employed. Marchetti and Marks in *The CIA and The Cult of Intelligence* also alleged that CIA overlooked the drug trade of its ally, the Meo tribe of Laos, until such traffic was perceived as a major U.S. problem. The best way to judge this work's accuracy concerning CIA's alleged misfeasance and tacit acceptance of the heroin trade is to compare it to the results of later congressional investigations of the CIA. The Church committee's final report quoted CIA's inspector general's report of no evidence of CIA involvement. It concluded with its own finding of no participation by CIA air proprietaries in illicit drug traffic. A later report of the Senate permanent intelligence committee was still classified as of 1981.

MacDonald, Elizabeth P. UNDERCOVER GIRL. New York: Macmillan, 1947. 305 pp., no index.

MacDonald's book is not widely known despite a number of distinctive features and firsts. To begin with, she was probably the first female operative with OSS to have written of her experiences with the organization. Second, she revealed the work of black radios during the war, the existence of a British effort with which OSS cooperated, and the identity of the British chief of black radios. This was done years before the latter broke silence himself. Third, *Undercover Girl* was one of the earliest works on OSS Morale Operations (MO) and MO work in China and from India. Fourth, it was published at a time of transition in security procedures concerning publication of wartime experiences by OSS personnel. Fifth, it first made public the names of a number of OSS personnel. The book did give an idea of MO, but that was secondary to what she revealed of the organization and personalities of OSS in Washington, China, and Southeast Asia (General Donovan's comments in the preface on the value of what she wrote of psychological warfare notwithstanding). Her trained journalist's eye caught a number of humorous incidents and the subtleties of OSS personalities. There were passages on Jane Foster who was with her for a time and later attained notoriety (see Foster's *An Unamerican Lady*). Note some early reactions to male attitudes toward women in substantive war duties that adumbrated later feminist positions. For one prevalent view in OSS that MO was one of General Donovan's wildest follies, see Cline's *Secrets, Spies and Scholars.*

McGarvey, Patrick J. CIA: THE MYTH AND THE MADNESS. New York: Saturday Review Press, 1972. 240 pp., no index.

The title and contents of this book do not quite match. McGarvey spent three years in CIA and another three in DIA as a civilian. He also spent eight in uniform working on cryptologic matters. While with CIA, he was with the deputy director for intelligence (DDI), or analytical side, and never served in the clandestine service. Beyond the fact that he spent only a minority of his fourteen-year career with CIA, he himself stated that the crisis in U.S. intelligence involved not only CIA but also nine other governmental departments and agencies. He categorically assures the reader that this is a compilation of his personal experiences in intelligence and not an exposé of CIA. He also admits that he could not pose as an expert on the organization of U.S. intelligence. His placing of the President's Foreign Intelligence Advisory Board (PFIAB) over the National Security Council (NSC) and putting Science and Technology under basic intelligence are good proofs of this and show a careless and unreliable work. There is a mixture of autobiographical, descriptive, and critical portions, with observations and criticisms flowing confusingly back and forth between CIA and the remainder of the intelligence community. Among the criticisms are the foolish practices and shortcomings he observed from his level and his belief that CIA is "an insufferable bureaucratic morass" whose reality belies the myth of efficient intrigue. His proposals include functional reforms and steps to gain greater control over the intelligence community. The work was reviewed prior to publication by CIA, which led to certain changes and deletions. DIS's *Bibliography* thought it biased, containing frequent errors of fact and lacking realistic solutions. Thomas Ross's review called it "bad writing, bad taste, bad logic."

Mackenzie, Compton. AEGEAN MEMORIES. London: Chatto and Windus, 1940. 410 pp., index.

The distinguished novelist served in British intelligence in World War I. His prosecution for his third volume of his war memoirs, *Greek Memories,* had an effect on this, the fourth, according to the author. It caused him to change *Aegean Memories* from what he had planned; a certain amount of interesting espionage material was omitted. All the same, he does not spare us facts and details on the infighting within the British government and its intelligence organizations and the jockeying for intelligence supremacy in Greece in World War I. He has some extreme examples of lack of coordination, misdirection in intelligence work, rivalries, and even insubordination. As if this were not enough, he gives further insights into rivalries with Allied secret services (above all, the French) and rivalries among French secret services.

With typical frankness, the author recounts his work as director of the Aegean intelligence service until his recall to London. His reputation as a rather difficult and hard-to-control chief of intelligence is supported by many extracts from this work alone. He meets with a political leader without permission; he tries to use his influence with the Greeks to oppose the appointment to Greece of a British general; he destroys certain of his intelligence records when recalled to London. Mackenzie gives his own justifications for his activities in Greece; his disgust with what he called "this competitive wrangling" among secret services is a sentiment shared by officers faced with similar scenarios elsewhere and at other times. There are additional shots of the head of SIS, "C" (Mansfield Cumming), who first appeared in *Greek Memories.* And for the historical record, we have the case of the British ambassador's advancing funds to an intelligence officer to conduct espionage and an incident in Egypt that was a precursor of the Cicero-type operation of World War II. This volume and the others on his Greek experiences must be supplemented by Lawson's *Tales of Aegean Intrigue* and Thomson's *The Allied Secret Service in Greece* despite reservations on some of the contents of these two.

Mackenzie, Compton. FIRST ATHENIAN MEMORIES. London: Cassell, 1931. 394 pp., index.

This is the second volume of Mackenzie's war memoirs; it covers the first period of his intelligence activities in Athens, 1915 to the start of 1916, when he was the chief of the counterespionage section. Mackenzie became disenchanted with intelligence and its effectiveness, and he serves as a role model for other and later critics of intelligence work. Here he gives his description and judgment of British intelligence organizations and operations as he found them: disorganized, confused, uncoordinated, and marked by conflicts. Some of the descriptions of intelligence practices are hilarious; these are to be found not only in the chapter "Absurdities of Secret Service" but throughout the book. This all leads him to the conclusion that "nearly all intelligence work in war is a waste of time, money and energy." The volume deals only with the period of his counterespionage work in Athens against the Germans, which at times was so open that it caused him to be attacked politically in Greece. Mackenzie explains there was method in what he did—distracting the enemy's attention from his real, productive CE work. To some, this a case study of a foreign intelligence service under the exigencies of war and survival operating in a neutral, weak, and divided country. Bywater and Ferraby in *Strange Intelligence* thought Mackenzie's sweeping condemnation of all secret service was based on inadequate knowledge. Hunt in *A Don at War* believed Mackenzie's works were among those that gave the Germans the wrong impression of agent operations and of the British secret service.

Mackenzie, Compton. GREEK MEMORIES. London: Chatto and Windus, 1939. 448 pp., index.

Mackenzie was prosecuted in 1933 under the Official Secrets Act of Britain for publishing this book, the third volume of his war memoirs. He was found guilty and fined, and the edition was withdrawn. This later edition, the author assures us, was not censored. Nor were any secrets omitted. In this volume, Mackenzie moves into the action phase of his career, and one can understand the horror of British authorities at the time of its appearance. He frankly recounts the operations of his organization not only against the Germans in Greece (outside the Salonika area) but also against those in Greece who were considered enemies of the Entente. We are informed of his involvement in the nudging of British policy in Greece; the use of economic warfare and control methods; the pursuit of German intelligence officers and operatives to the point of arrest; the operations against the Greek royalists. He tells of relations with the French and especially the French intelligence services in Greece, whom he regarded as competitors as well as allies. There are glimpses, too, of "C" of the British service (Mansfield Cumming). This is the story of an intelligence officer of great vigor and talent who helped create an organization within a foreign, sovereign state that acted as a security service. It is also a case of a "high profile" of an intelligence officer. Bywater and Ferraby in *Strange Intelligence* wrote that the Allies' conflicting policies and the ill-controlled activities of their secret agents resulted in a situation in Greece that was "both Gilbertian and tragic."

Macksey, Kenneth John. THE PARTISANS OF EUROPE IN THE SECOND WORLD WAR. New York: Stein and Day, 1975. 258 pp., bibliog., index [London: Hart-Davis MacGibbon. *The Partisans of Europe in World War II*].

It is the thesis of the author that guerrilla warfare in World War II was marginal in its contribution to victory and costly for the results attained. Macksey contends that the efficacy of guerrillas and partisans in that war is a myth that has been perpetuated and that this myth needs to be exploded as was that of the effects of Allied strategic bombing. Macksey doubted that partisans made a contribution equivalent to that of uniformed organizations such as the British Special Air Service (SAS); he submits that it was only when the Germans were losing that guerrilla warfare began to have some effect, and even then it could not stop German counterattacks, which continued almost to the end. Macksey is a former regular soldier who has become a noted military historian and writer on tank warfare. His conclusions in this book have not gone unchallenged. The *Times Literary Supplement* review thought his viewpoint reflected the preference of regulars of his former profession for small raiding parties and was critical of the author's failure to provide footnotes and his lapses into journalese. For a view different from Macksey's, see Foot's *Resistance.*

McLachlan, Donald. ROOM 39: A STUDY IN NAVAL INTELLIGENCE. New York: Atheneum, 1968. 379 pp., notes, index [London: Weidenfeld and Nicolson].

Room 39 ranks as one of the best books on intelligence and perhaps the best book on naval intelligence ever written. A study on a separate subject sponsored by CIA (done in conjunction with Mathtech) included the opinion that this was an extraordinary book and perhaps the best single study of intelligence—its organization, collection, uses, and misuses. *RUSI*'s review found it a fascinating book that revealed many erstwhile secrets. It thought the account of Winn and the Admiralty's U-boat tracking room of particular interest. McLachlan served on the staff of the director of naval intelligence from 1940 to 1945 and thus was well placed to study his subject—how British naval intelligence worked. He made use of the personal memories of many, including Admiral Godfrey and his successor at NID. The product is perhaps one of the best books on intelligence ever written. The book would have been even more complete had the author been free to include what he knew of Ultra in the naval intelligence war. Due to security constraints, McLachlan could only allude to Bletchley Park as "Station X" and write elliptically about the communications intelligence success. Lewin in *Ultra Goes to War* gives an example of an incident in this book in which McLachlan was forced to use the cover story of an agent's report from Norway to disguise information derived from Ultra (the PQ17 Convoy disaster). Perhaps for this reason McLachlan only briefly mentions the existence of the Intelligence Assault Unit under the NID that was targeted against enemy cryptologic material (see Hampshire's *The Secret Navies*). Reading this is an enriching experience, and the list of pertinent, interesting, and significant items it contains is very long. To mention a few at random: a view of Admiral Godfrey and his relations with Churchill; an explanation of Godfrey's attitude toward women in intelligence; mention of Naval Section 17Z; the treatment of various sources of the intelligence, especially OIC, the Operational Intelligence Center. Montagu's *Beyond Top Secret Ultra* and Beesly's *Very Special Intelligence* provide further information that was not or could not be included here.

Maclean, Fitzroy. TAKE NINE SPIES. New York: Atheneum, 1978. 337 pp., bibliog., no index [London: Weidenfeld and Nicolson].

Maclean's distinguished career in diplomacy and in various assignments in World War II did not include intelligence work. Consequently, the author of this and the earlier *Eastern Approaches* (1950) makes no claim to any special knowledge or insight into the subject of espionage. He has taken nine spies and studied what evidence there was to estimate their personalities and motives. Of the nine he examines (Mata Hari, Azef, Redl, Sorge, Cicero, Lonsdale, Philby, Penkowsky, and "William Martin"), six are Russians or Russian spies. This is good reading and good for training courses on the character and motivation of spies, despite the fact that Maclean offers no particular new insights into most of the cases. It is instructive for its many examples of agent handling, professional and amateurish, good and bad. One will find facts not generally known about the Cicero case, its discovery and exploitation. Cicero was uncovered by various means, one of which is not mentioned—by Allen Dulles in Switzerland. The case Maclean makes for strategic consequences of Redl's espionage at the start of World War I is not accepted by everyone. Rowan's *The Story of Secret Service* claims the Austrians revised their war plans after Redl was uncovered. There is no mention of the incident in which a real body containing valid documents was washed ashore a few months before Montagu's "William Martin" deception prior to the Sicily invasion. Schellenberg's claim that he approved of Sorge's assignment as a journalist to Tokyo is not mentioned. And we now know more about Philby and his Cambridge friends than appears here. These omissions or debatable points are mentioned not to detract from what Maclean produced but to reinforce one's inclination to read further on these cases once *Take Nine Spies* is completed. An index would have been of great help. A rare look into the defection of General Lyushkov of the NKVD in 1938 is included.

Marchetti, Victor, and Marks, John D. THE CIA AND THE CULT OF INTELLIGENCE. New York: Knopf, 1974. 398 pp., index [London: Jonathan Cape].

One of the most important books on intelligence to appear since the end of World War II due to its legal, political, and imitative consequences. The authors held respectable positions in intelligence—Marchetti was executive assistant to the deputy director of central intelligence, and Marks was the staff assistant to the State Department's director of intelligence and research. Their disenchantment with U.S. intelligence policies and practices, which resulted in this book, also resulted in lengthy legal procedures and maneuvers, described in the introduction from the point of view of the American Civil Liberties Union. CIA's version of its legal position and rationale for proceeding against the book are in Colby's *Honorable Men;* Thomas Powers's *The Man Who Kept the Secrets* gives another account of CIA actions and reasons for concern. Powers includes items he says were deleted from Marchetti and Marks's book, deletions upheld by the court.

Colby's book contains a very important revelation that must be kept in mind in reading this book. CIA policy, as laid down by him as director, was that there was to be no objection to any opinions of the authors in the book and that mistakes were similarly not to be objected to since what was not true could not be considered classified. The form in which the work finally appeared, with blank sections to show where deletions had been enforced, might lead the reader to assume that everything else in the book is correct. There is the additional hazard, where fact and opinion are mixed, of the reader's not identifying the latter as such. DIS's *Bibliography* makes a comment perhaps representative of the national security establishment's evaluation of the book: that it is an uneven work whose polemics tend to throw out of balance any of the authoritative material it contains. Nevertheless, the amount of accurate material that is divulged is enormous and transcends covert-action activities which trouble the authors most. A new edition appeared in 1980 containing some twenty-five passages previously deleted but now permitted as a result of a freedom of information decision. The appendix contains the 1968 off-the-record remarks on covert action given by Richard Bissell, the former chief of CIA's Clandestine Services and U-2 program.

Marks, John. THE SEARCH FOR THE "MANCHURIAN CANDIDATE": THE CIA AND MIND CONTROL. New York: Times Books, 1979. 214 pp., notes, index [London: Allen Lane].

Marks used as the basis of this investigative study 16,000 documents released to him by CIA under the Freedom of Information Act. Even at that, this can only be considered an interim study since at a late point in the research, CIA uncovered 130 boxes of material stretching into the 1970s and related to a second-generation CIA program. The author used personal interviews to supplement his documentary research and acknowledged that he was assisted by a team of researchers. He recognized the results as far from the whole story, even allowing for the appearance of the new material. Only a few insiders, he believed, could write the full story of CIA's twenty-five-year research into human behavior and mind control. Marks's modest claims for the study were matched by a restraint in presenting what he had learned. He allowed the facts to speak for themselves with only an occasional sally into judgment for emphasis or summary. Both the author and the Church committee, which looked into the matter, found no evidence that the research was cleared with higher U.S. government authority. See Lovell's *Of Spies and Strategems* on the OSS work on truth drugs and hypnotism that provided the lead into such U.S. government research.

Marshall, Bruce. THE WHITE RABBIT. London: Evans, 1952. 256 pp., index [Boston: Houghton Mifflin].

The heroic and gruesome story of F.F.E. Yeo-Thomas's career in the RF Section of SOE during World War II. The gruesome part covers his imprisonment, terrible ordeal in a German concentration camp, and escape and comprises some sixty percent of the book. Yeo-Thomas was captured on his second mission to France to rescue the resistance leader Brossolette. He was betrayed and became one of the few SOE men to survive German captivity. There are early snippets on SOE's F and RF sections and on the strained relations between F and the French BCRA. Howarth in *Undercover* considered Yeo-Thomas's intervention with Churchill, described by Marshall, as of critical importance. It resulted, he said, in the transformation of support to the resistance in France "from the theoretical to the practical." Without meaning to detract from Yeo-Thomas's bravery and his amazing capacity to endure hardship, one can question the professional wisdom of sending a man from SOE headquarters, the head of the planning section and privy to many operations in France, on such a mission. Sweet-Escott in *Baker Street Irregular* provides an explanation for the permission given to Yeo-Thomas to go to France and informs of the formal SOE policy on staff officers' going into enemy-occupied territory adopted in 1944. Marshall, the author, was also in intelligence during that war, partly with RF Section.

Martelli, George. AGENT EXTRAORDINARY: THE STORY OF MICHEL HOLLARD. London: Collins, 1960. 286 pp., no index [New York: Doubleday. *The Man Who Saved London: The Story of Michel Hollard*].

Hollard was a genuine but not too well-known hero of World War II. Martelli has admiringly written his story, using reconstructed dialogue. Hollard organized on his own the network named Agir that eventually comprised up to one hundred persons collecting intelligence throughout France. He acted as principal agent and courier within France and to Switzerland, where he made forty-eight crossings to pass information to the British. Hollard's net was the first to find a V1 site, located many others and produced the first complete plan of such a site. After some three years he was betrayed. Under captivity he underwent incredible horrors; he had managed, however, to arrange for his net to function without him. R. V. Jones in *The Wizard War* writes of Hollard's accomplishments against the V1, as does Garlinski in *Hitler's Last Weapons.* Garlinski is of the opinion that calling Hollard "the man who saved London" was exaggerated, since many contributed in various ways to defeat the German V weapons. In addition to being a story of "incredible courage" (General Horrocks), the book gives certain lessons in operations. Hollard's net survived for a long period because it dispensed with many systems of communication and contact that create vulnerabilities to detection. Perhaps for reasons of discretion,

Martelli does not have very much to say about the arrangement Hollard made in 1941 with his relative, General Guisan, the Swiss commander in chief, that allowed him entry into Switzerland in exchange for Hollard's cooperation with Swiss military intelligence.

Martin, David C. WILDERNESS OF MIRRORS. New York: Harper and Row, 1980. 228 pp., index.

Martin, the son of a CIA analyst, was with *Newsweek* when he wrote this. He attempts to delve into the counterespionage (CE) and counterintelligence (CI) war between CIA and the Soviet services and uses the careers of William Harvey and James Angleton of CIA as literary vehicles to do so. His sources, in order of importance, are retired intelligence officers, documents gotten under FOIA, and the public record. He concludes that the war has gone against CIA: what the KGB has not done, CIA has done itself.

This is a penetrating look into some issues and challenges faced by CIA, and the cognoscenti recognize it as based on information stemming from the bowels of that agency. John Maury, a former senior officer, wrote in the *Armed Forces Journal* that despite its shortcomings it was an "exciting collection of largely true spy stories." Like Powers's *The Man Who Kept the Secrets,* it brings to light much information and benefits from access to special sources. The amount of facts and opinions on the role of individual CIA officers involved in CI and CE and that of Soviet defectors is unprecedented. One need only look at the index to see how much information Martin has accumulated. Edward Epstein, however, in his review in the *New York Times,* believed Martin's sources boil down to one critic of Angleton, a former insider.

Despite its many merits, the work has a number of flaws, both major and minor. Though Martin gives many details, they do not necessarily add up to the full picture or the correct one in specific instances. Martin himself recognizes in his foreword the difficulty of working with the compartmentalized knowledge of his sources and the fragmented information available. The rivalry between Harvey and Angleton, around which the author spins his story, did not exist, nor was there enmity between the two men. Accurate as Martin is on aspects of the Nosenko issue, experts say it is hyperbole to conclude that the case paralyzed CIA's counterespionage work and that the impression that the issue debilitated the entire organization is erroneous. It is bold to try to sum up long careers and the totality of the two men's philosophical and operational underpinnings as well as their effectiveness on the basis of one or two cases. Similarly, it is tenuous analysis to attempt to decipher motives, which he does in Angleton's supposed atonement for not spotting Philby. To picture Harvey, senior as he was, as a man of transcending importance within CIA is to distort reality. CIA veterans also reject Martin's portrayal of CIA as a world of men with virtually no redeeming qualities. Examples of minor errors: the Americans did not learn the art of CI from Philby; Colby was not station chief in Rome in the 1950s; Blake was not responsible for the discovery of the German North Pole deception operation in Holland; Hood had decided to retire long before the *New York Times'* exposé against CIA; Angleton did not visit Ezra Pound. Epstein, in his critical review, points out that Martin used no references or footnotes; he also alleges that Martin quotes almost verbatim from other works. He notes Martin gives the impression he interviewed certain individuals whom he quotes. Martin's reply to Epstein's criticisms in the July 6, 1980, *New York Times* explains the reason for the absence of footnotes.

Mashbir, Sidney Forrester. I WAS AN AMERICAN SPY. New York: Vantage Press, 1953. 368 pp., index.

Mashbir had the distinction of being one of the first officers selected by the U.S. Army to study the Japanese language after World War I. In Japan he acquired the language, which later led to his leading the Allied Translator and Interpreter Section (ATIS) on MacArthur's intelligence staff. ATIS handled captured documents and the interrogation of prisoners as an allied, interservice group. He also did some propaganda broadcasting in Japanese. Admiral Zacharias in *Secret Missions* praised Mashbir, a contemporary, and his plan for intelligence collection against the Japanese in time of war, which was never implemented. The contents of this autobiography are much less dramatic than the title implies. Written at a time of turmoil in the United States on the question of responsibility for postwar international developments, the book contains much in the category of personal and political testimony. Barton Whaley called it the superpatriotic memoirs of an eccentric and a U.S. intelligence pioneer. Its value lies in the fact that it is one of the few books on U.S. intelligence against Japan covering the post–World War I era. The reader will note Mashbir's account of the tapping of telephone lines in Mexico as well as rumors about massive Japanese infiltration of the United States via that country during World War I. For a discussion of Mashbir's claim that he and Zacharias prepared the first draft and implementing directives for the later CIA, see Troy's *Donovan and the CIA.*

Maskelyne, Jasper. MAGIC—TOP SECRET. London and New York: Stanley Paul, 1949. 188 pp., index.

The author served in Britain, the Middle East, Italy, and India in World War II and was involved in camouflage and illusion efforts, some of which he describes. He warns that the full story will probably never be told; certainly there is a generalized, rather skimpy account of what he was involved in even though he does speak of some of the camouflage methods used, illusory tricks employed, and escape and evasion devices and concealment means. He says nothing of any relevance about the organizational setup of his unit or its relationship to the operational, intelligence, or deception staffs in the Middle East and elsewhere. Dudley Clarke, the founder and chief of the deception organization in the Middle East (A Force), is referred to only as a person "interested in my battle-illusions." One must forgive Maskelyne's enthusiasm when he claims that as a result of the camouflage work done in the Middle East, the whole system of Arab and other espionage in North Africa was discredited in the eyes of Rommel and his commanders. Interestingly, he never mentions his work on escape and evasion devices in Britain, which is described in Foot and Langley's *MI 9.* See that book and Mure's *Master of Deception* for conflicting accounts of Maskelyne's real and cover assignments in the Middle East.

Massing, Hede. THIS DECEPTION. New York: Duell, Sloan and Pearce, 1951. 335 pp., no index.

Massing, the former wife of Gerhard Eisler, was recruited into Soviet intelligence in the 1930s and functioned as an agent spotter and recruiter, courier, and general support agent until 1938. These memoirs of her life as a communist and Soviet agent open up another view of the world of European and American idealists of the time who served, in one way or another, Soviet purposes and Soviet organizations. This is her version of her relationship with Alger Hiss, the Noel Fields, Sorge, Laurence Duggan, and Walter Krivitsky, plus others who achieved fame or notoriety at a later date. Her defection followed the killing of Ignace Reiss (Ludwick), whose widow convinced her to contact U.S. authorities after the war. Her testimony at the second Hiss trial was the new evidence for the U.S. case. See Lewis's *Red Pawn* for that author's version of Massing's performance at the trial; note also Massing's admission that she had a bad memory. Two reviews of the book expressed the view that Massing's motives for her actions were not clear from her account, nor was the reason she continued to work for the Soviets while claiming she was disillusioned with them. For a fuller picture of the period of freewheeling Soviet espionage in the United States and of Western Europeans like Ludwick as central figures in the Soviet apparat, see Poretsky's *Our Own People,* Krivitsky's *In Stalin's Secret Service,* and Bentley's *Out of Bondage* in addition to Lewis. The opinion of some U.S. security observers is that Massing was a prolific and accurate source on Soviet espionage and probably among the best defectors in that regard. There is still some debate about whether her public disclosures were complete.

Masson, Madeleine. CHRISTINE: A SEARCH FOR CHRISTINE GRANVILLE. London: Hamish Hamilton, 1975. 248 pp., bibliog., index.

The biography of the Polish heroine of World War II who operated as an SOE agent in Hungary, Poland, and France. She was the first woman dropped into France from Algiers. The author devotes much space to her life to the neglect of her operational work. Except for her short experience in Vercours in 1944, the rest of her operational work in Hungary and Poland is only sketched in, and we are left with little about her accomplishments in escape and evasion or other lines of endeavor. While she was Francis Cammaerts's courier and assistant, she saved his life and that of Xan Fielding. The latter in his book *Hide and Seek* felt the British did poorly by her after the war. Cammaerts describes this book as a fair and balanced picture. The author does convey some good insights into Polish attraction to and capacity for clandestine work. Consult Fielding's book for his account of how Granville saved his life.

Masterman, John C. THE DOUBLE-CROSS SYSTEM IN THE WAR OF 1939 TO 1945. New Haven, Conn. & London: Yale Univ. Press, 1972. 198 pp., index.

Masterman was head of the XX or Double Cross Committee throughout the war as a member of M15. This report he completed shortly after the end of the war. Except for a few cuts and verbal changes, the author says, it is in its original form. Declassified on the insistence of the author, it is one of the great works of intelligence literature, an outstanding one in the area of deception, and perhaps the greatest work yet written on double agents. It is a textbook on the acquisition, handling, control, and exploitation of such agents. Never has their systematic employment been revealed by a government to such an extent and with so much frankness. Many details Masterman provides have become well known to students of intelligence and deception operations, and the lessons, theory, and practice he spells out had become inbedded in varying degrees in postwar thinking and operations even before the work appeared. This happened despite Masterman's warnings that no fixed principles or invariable rules could be derived from this history and that in the future advantages comparable to those enjoyed against the Germans were unlikely to occur.

Principally dealt with is the deceptive use of double agents rather than their employment for counterespionage and positive intelligence. Masterman was reluctant to judge the XX Committee's work in deception, but John Bevan, the controller of LCS, the deception body in London, went on record that the Germans were deceived largely by such agents. Dennis Wheatley, also in LCS, said in *RUSI* that only this book gave an entirely truthful account of the part played by MI5 in deception. The book, however, contains a few errors (although surprisingly few for a report so early after the events) and has one major omission. Masterman seems in error on the inspiration for Operation Mincemeat. His conclusions were premature on the probable success of certain deception plans and operations: Dakar in 1942, the 1943 invasion deception for Norway, the 1943 deception operations designed to make the Germans fear an invasion of Western Europe. The principal omission is of any mention of the crucial role of Ultra. Masterman can only make veiled references to "secret sources" that gave final confirmation of their control of the whole German network and that the agents were believed.

Major criticism of the work has come from Mure in *Master of Deception*. Mure objects to what he considers the impression that deception rested solely on MI5 and its double agents, is critical of XX Committee's handling of its double agents, and contests Masterman's remark that Torch, the invasion of North Africa, was a triumph of security rather than of deception. Masterman clearly stated that "the home of successful deception was in the Middle East" where Mure served and which Mure felt was neglected by Masterman and others of the London-based group, as was the work of Dudley Clarke, Mure's superior. Masterman's book contains the first word of the Pearl Harbor questionnaire given to the agent Tricycle and whose significance was missed or not emphasized by U.S. and British intelligence. See also Montagu's *Beyond Top Secret Ultra* for the only other first-hand account of the XX Committee's work. DIS's *Bibliography* calls this a classic and a veritable treatise on counterintelligence and deception. Masterman's reasons for his fight to publish this report are given in greater detail in his *On the Chariot Wheel* (below).

Masterman, John C. ON THE CHARIOT WHEEL. London: Oxford Univ. Press, 1975. 378 pp., index.

The autobiography of the late Sir John contains only a few chapters of special interest to the student of intelligence. These pertain to World War II; MI5; the publication of his report on double agents, *The Double-Cross System* (above); and his visit to the United States on a fellowship at Yale and as a means to publicizing the book, whose success surprised him. He outlines his long effort to publish that famous book and his reasons. Mure in *Master of Deception* joined Colonel Noel Wild, the former head of SHAEF's deception organization, in criticizing Masterman for publishing *The Double-Cross System.* This autobiography adds very little in an intelligence sense. Among the few new items is the tale of Duff Cooper's attempts to abolish the XX Committee and the disclosure that the latter group did not begin its real deception until it was sure that all German agents were under its control. Masterman's views on the value of positive intelligence are admittedly based on his special experiences during World War II and consequently debatable. For intimations that Masterman was connected with MI5 before the war, see Dennis Wheatley's *Drink and Ink* (1979).

Mathews, Hazel C. FRONTIER SPIES: THE BRITISH SECRET SERVICE, NORTHERN DEPARTMENT DURING THE REVOLUTIONARY WAR. Fort Myers, Fla.: Ace Press, 1971. 202 pp., bibliog., notes, index.

The author published this study herself, having become intrigued by the activities of loyalist spies and by the Smyth brothers during the American Revolution. The fascination resulted from her research of the manuscripts of the British military governor of Quebec during that war, General Haldimand. She expanded her study to write of the organization and operations of the British Northern Department's secret service. Many of the loyalists employed by it located in Canada at the end of the war. Mathews made good use of the Haldimand papers and of other sources to write what is a rare history about this portion of British intelligence on the North American continent during the period in question. Here we have the world of clandestine operations and organizations: couriers, dead drops, secret writing, cover, double agents, book ciphers, concealment devices. We learn of secret negotiations, attempts to capture and neutralize important opponents, lapses in security, provocation operations, lines of command and jurisdiction, and the creation of information-gathering networks. This is far and away a more satisfactory treatment of the Northern Department than Fryer's *Loyalist Spy*. H. M. Jackson's *Justus Sherwood*, privately printed, was not available to the author of this bibliography for comparison.

Maugeri, Franco. FROM THE ASHES OF DISGRACE. New York: Reynal and Hitchcock, 1948. 366 pp., index.

Admiral Maugeri served in the Servizio Informazione Segreto (SIS), the Italian naval intelligence service; he was its head from 1941 until the Italian surrender. He headed an intelligence organization operating against the Germans after the Italian armistice until the capture of Rome (which he considered to be the underground continuation of the SIS). The memoir deals with various facets of his career during the war, but disclosures of an intelligence interest are not many. Communication intelligence he mentions as one of the successes of his service, and Kahn's section on Italian naval cryptanalysis in *The Codebreakers* is based almost entirely on Maugeri. The exact extent of Italian success is not explained here; the author merely informs us in a general way that the SIS B Section broke many enemy naval codes. There are a few instances of counterespionage successes against the Americans and the French and one tale of a planned communications deception operation against the British. He tells how Italian naval intelligence was organized and mentions that it failed to learn of the Allied landing in North Africa but says nothing of Sicily and whether the deception of Operation Mincemeat was an indirect factor in Italian estimates. Most of Maugeri's attention to intelligence is devoted to the underground intelligence network he headed, which OSS history credits with the first successful maritime exfiltration by OSS from Italy—that of an important Italian expert on torpedoes. Because so little on Italian intelligence in World War II has been translated into English, Maugeri's book is all the more to be prized, even though it is patently an incomplete account of the SIS. Note his revelation that the Tenth MAS under Prince Borghese, whose frogmen won the admiration of its enemies by its attacks on allied warships, was concerned primarily with CE after the fall of Mussolini.

Meyer, Cord. FACING REALITY: FROM WORLD FEDERALISM TO THE CIA. New York: Harper and Row, 1980. 411 pp., notes, index.

Meyer's career spanned the World Federalist Movement and CIA where he rose to be deputy chief of the Clandestine Services. This is an attempt to tell enough of the story of his life for an understanding of his career—a blending of autobiographical and historical events. It also is to set the record straight on a number of historical events coming at the time of a shift in U.S. attitudes toward national security and intelligence, and it reflects the opinions and world view of many CIA officers who served with the author. There are two distinct sections. The first is largely autobiographical and deals with Meyer's personal life, career, and involvement in events. The second, which concerns mostly the Soviet threat and reality, puts the role of U.S. intelligence in its proper context and explains its raison d'être.

Some things about which Meyer writes are first revelations or add to our knowledge of particular events. His account of his secret suspension, ordeal, and trials during the McCarthy period evokes the temper of the times; there is the most authoritative and balanced summary of Radio Free Europe's role in the Hungarian revolution of 1956; there is the critique of CIA Director Colby's stewardship and handling of such matters as the Family Jewels (CIA secrets) and the dismissal of James Angleton as head of CIA's counterintelligence. His discussion of Watergate and its effects on CIA supplements what Colby and Walters had written previously in *Honorable Men* and *Silent Missions,* respectively, from the viewpoint of the top of the agency. The chapter on Chile should be read carefully for its account of events. Even an unsympathetic review in the *Washington Post* allowed that his defense of CIA's role there is convincing "up to a point." There is a good treatment of Operation Chaos, the CIA attempt to identify foreign connections of the antiwar movement in the U.S. The chapter on the Soviet strategic threat contains a view Meyer gained from special access to intelligence while working on strategic warning arrangements in the U.S. intelligence community. However, the *Foreign Affairs* reviewer called the part on the Soviet menace "a long and uninspired editorial." Meyer also deals with the Soviet system of intelligence analysis and estimates, something very infrequently covered in the literature of Soviet intelligence, which usually concentrates on the operational and collection stages.

Certain parts call for correction, disagreement, or further elaboration. It is obvious that the author could not tell all he and CIA know about the organization, manning, and activities of a Soviet embassy. One can argue that it was not President Carter who broke the tradition of appointing a nonpolitical director of central intelligence. A spate of cases of CIA ex-staff and retired and contract personnel involved with the Soviets counsels for caution in judgments about past security. For the fuller story of how his book was submitted to CIA for security review, see his column in the *Washington Star* of 20 March 1980 on the matter and the 1980 edition of Marchetti and Marks's *The CIA and the Cult of Intelligence.* Meyer anticipates criticisms of selective response to issues by stating that he wrote only on matters already revealed elsewhere. Smith's *OSS* contains a profile of Meyer and quotes the 1966 *Esquire* article on his earlier problems stemming from loyalty allegations. The National Intelligence Study Center gave Meyer's book its 1981 award as the outstanding book on the subject of U.S. intelligence in 1980.

Meyer, Karl E., and Szulc, Tad. THE CUBAN INVASION: THE CHRONICLE OF A DISASTER. New York: Praeger, 1962. 156 pp., index.

The authors were familiar with Cuban and Latin American affairs when they tackled the story of the 1961 Bay of Pigs operation designed to overthrow Castro. Though written shortly after the event, this was well done and stands up in its essentials almost two decades later. Meyer and Szulc were aware that all the facts were not known at the time they wrote. All the same, they tried to recreate the mood, the compulsions, and the factors that went into the operation, relying to some extent on "confidential interviews" with Americans and Cubans. The thesis presented was that it was the intelligence bureaucracy and the bureaucracy in general that were the institutional villains, rather than individuals. Wyden in the 1979 *Bay of Pigs* called this book not only the first on the subject but fascinating, detailed, and shrewd in its interpretation of Cuban politics. His other judgment—that it was "astonishingly short on facts" for a volume by trained reporters—is true, although "astonishingly" seems strong in view of its publication date. Wyden's book must be read for a more comprehensive treatment as well as for an explanation of Szulc's knowledge, as a *New York Times* reporter, of the operation before it took place. See also Johnson's *The Bay of Pigs.* Writing in 1964, Johnson thought the Meyer and Szulc treatment had excellent political analysis and understanding of the Cuban problem and was unusually good in its overall grasp but exaggerated Manuel Rey's importance and thus suffered from heavy reliance on Rey's viewpoint.

Miles, Milton. A DIFFERENT KIND OF WAR: THE LITTLE-KNOWN STORY OF THE COMBINED GUERRILLA FORCES CREATED IN CHINA BY THE U.S. NAVY AND THE CHINESE DURING WORLD WAR II. Garden City, N.Y.: Doubleday, 1967. 607 pp., index.

Admiral Miles coheaded the Sino-American Cooperative Organization (SACO), the joint Chinese-American organization designed to create intelligence, coast watching, meteorological intelligence, sabotage, communications intelligence, and guerrilla warfare capabilities against the Japanese. Published after Miles's death, this book was based on his original manuscript but prepared by Daniel Hawthorne. Miles was assigned to China by the U.S. Navy with only a very broad and general directive to guide him: to prepare the China coast for a future U.S. Navy landing and do what he could in the meanwhile to help the navy "heckle the Japanese." He saw it as his duty and proper role to cooperate with an ally without reservation or guile. This conviction was a fundamental cause for his disagreements with other segments of the U.S. presence in China, apart from organizational jockeying for position of primacy in intelligence in the area, profound differences over the merits of the Chinese Nationalist government and its intelligence chief, and personality clashes.

What Miles has to say is partisan, and his conclusions in many instances are controversial. His claims of the strategic efficacy of certain of the SACO operations, especially in human collection, have been questioned, and his belief that SACO might have shortened the war in China if it had not been interfered with would be hard to prove. The book's main value lies in its accounts of such matters as the organization and development of his Navy Group China, the history of jurisdictional battles of U.S. intelligence components there and of the rivalries that prevailed, the problems of liaison and joint efforts with an ally, and the difficulties of fusing clandestine intelligence and conventional military outlooks and organizations in China. See Smith's *OSS* or Caldwell's *A Secret War.* For an opinion running counter to Miles's on the intelligence picture in China see Holmes's view from the navy's headquarters in Hawaii (*Double-Edged Secrets*). Stratton's *SACO—The Rice Paddy Navy* is another look at SACO by one of its veterans. Volume 2 of the U.S. War Department's *The War Report of the OSS* gives a good précis of the OSS's side of the story and its evaluation of SACO's accomplishments.

Millar, George. THE BRUNEVAL RAID: FLASHPOINT OF THE RADAR WAR. Garden City, N.Y.: Doubleday, 1974. 210 pp., bibliog., notes, index [London: The Bodley Head].

An account of the 1942 raid by the British to capture a German Würzburg radar situated on the French coast. Millar, who served as an agent in France, based his book on British documents on the raid and interviews, of R. V. Jones among others. This book is surprisingly good on the outlines of the radar war; Churchill and Cherwell's reservation on radar before the war is explained. Millar is not exaggerating, it seems, in saying that to all intents and purposes the Germans knew nothing of Britain's radar before the war—Johnson's *The Secret War* tells of German attempts in the spring of 1939 to determine if the British had an operational radar network comparable to their own. The work done by the Photographic Reconnaissance Unit, by French resistance forces, and by British scientific intelligence is also discussed in Jones's *The Wizard War* and in *The Secret War.*

Minott, Rodney G. THE FORTRESS THAT NEVER WAS: THE MYTH OF HITLER'S BAVARIAN STRONGHOLD. New York: Holt, Rinehart and Winston, 1964. 199 pp., bibliog., notes, index [London: Longmans, Green, 1965].

This story of the German National Redoubt was written by a U.S. historian who became fascinated by why so many "highly-intelligent and hard headed soldiers" could have erred in believing the threat of a last stand by the Germans. The book was based on declassified U.S. Army material; the author also advises that he was cleared to read classified records on the matter. The result is fairly good as an initial try, but the research is incomplete, so his conclusions must be regarded as tentative. Minott was aware that all the strange details about the National Redoubt may not have come to light at the time; he was right, for he did not have Ultra to assist him. According to Bennett in *Ultra in the West,* Ultra lent no support to rumors or to aerial photos and gave a fair picture of the actual situation.

Minott's case is weakened by the lack of the necessary supporting evidence for his theory that the error on the Redoubt was one of U.S. self-deception reinforced by German deception. There is little on German deception measures or on the positions of the various Allied intelligence organizations. Only a few pages at the end of the book are devoted to the latter, and consequently the account is general. The tidbits he has on Soviet warnings of the Redoubt raise the fascinating possibility of Soviet disinformation designed to influence the direction of Allied attacks to the south, but Minott does not pursue that idea. See also Strong's *Intelligence at the Top.* Forrest Pogue in his biography *George C. Marshall: Organizer of Victory* (New York: Viking, 1973) called Minott's work a provocative study of the National Redoubt question. Persico's *Piercing the Reich* should also be consulted.

Minshall, Merlin. GUILT-EDGED. London: Bachman and Turner, 1975. 317 pp., index.

Len Deighton in the foreword describes the author as an entertaining raconteur, a writer of verve and exuberance, and a man who loves life. He served in British naval intelligence in World War II. Among the experiences he describes are his failed mission on behalf of SOE to block the Danube River, his service in Yugoslavia as head of the British naval mission to Tito, and his service in London handling the direction finding (DF) of German naval radio transmissions. Minshall is in the best tradition of the establishment eccentric who defied orders and superiors, quarreled with people in authority (Godfrey of naval intelligence disliked him), and found organizations such as the Foreign Office and the regular navy insufferable. His version of the failure of the Danube operation is uncritical of his own behavior and thus suspect. There are errors of historical fact that show he is not well versed on details of intelligence history: Buchan is named as head of British intelligence in World War I; the SDECE is called the French service prior to World War II; he states that David Kahn wrote about Ultra in his first book. What he has to say of his sexual encounters and conquests and of his killings of Gestapo men on trains reads like a James Bond novel and perhaps explains his friendship with Ian Fleming. See some operational and security gems such as the use of art student cover for crew members from the navy assigned to the Danube operation and his selection for the assignment despite his reputation in Rumania as a spy and a person involved in subversion even before the war, or his revealing that the head of the Bucharest secret police in 1940 was in the pay of the British.

Mitchell, Harvey. THE UNDERGROUND WAR AGAINST REVOLUTIONARY FRANCE: THE MISSIONS OF WILLIAM WICKHAM, 1794–1800. Oxford: Clarendon Press, 1965. 260 pp., bibliog., index.

The object is declared by the author to be "to show that the counterrevolution in France could never have posed the danger it did had it not been for the objective of the British government." Mitchell felt that Britain's involvement with the French royalists had been largely neglected by historians and that Wickham, a principal agent of the secret war, was more important than he had been pictured by British historians (although not by French historians, who linked his name with every conspiracy). An excellent study of political warfare and subversion that can be read with profit because of the modern parallels to be drawn. All the problems and techniques used in later times to deal with émigrés are found in it. Then there are the covert and clandestine methods of double agents, electoral subsidies and operations, newspaper subsidies, support of front organizations, intelligence collection, counterintelligence, and counterespionage. The conflicts and intrigues among émigrés that Mitchell recounts have an eternal ring to them, as do some of the security problems that are described. Mitchell has drawn on Wickham's published correspondence in particular and on archives and secondary sources to give us this scholarly work. It contains a good bibliography, and its appendix on British secret service expenditures for the years 1795–1800 adds to it material not usually found in such studies. Especially revealing is the fact that Wickham was aware that Montgaillard, the man who conceived the ill-fated attempt to buy the Republican General Pichegru, "had relations with" the French Directoire. The *American Historical Review* critic thought this book was best on British policy and execution and weak on French actions and responses. The *Times Literary Supplement* review considered it the definitive account of Wickham's mission, although it disagreed with the picture of Wickham as a colorless and unimaginative person, albeit overoptimistic.

Molden, Fritz. EXPLODING STAR: A YOUNG AUSTRIAN AGAINST HITLER. London: Weidenfeld and Nicolson, 1978. 272 pp., index [New York: Morrow, 1979].

According to the author, he had to rely on his memory and on documentary evidence since he had little in the way of notes or a diary. Molden as a young man joined the Austrian resistance to Hitler, deserted from the German army, and became involved in helping organize Austrian resistance, making numerous crossings into Austria to set up intelligence and resistance nets. In the process he became involved with the Swiss, French, and U.S. intelligence services. He explains his purpose and that of the organization he belonged to as one of working with, not for, the Allies; the political and social connections he had stemming from his family and his father's position in the *Neue Freie Presse* facilitated his entrée into and work in Austrian resistance circles. There are interesting segments on his intelligence agreement with the Swiss, his contacts with the French, and his dealings with the Soviets. For students of cryptology, Molden advises he turned over the Abwehr Milan code to the Swiss. Molden was one of three Austrians to get the U.S. Medal of Freedom, and his story easily explains why. This book must be read with Persico's *Piercing the Reich.* The latter provides insights not contained in Molden's account, such as the incident of OSS X-2 suspicions that Molden was a German agent and the attitude of U.S. intelligence in its relationship with him. Molden later married Allen Dulles's daughter but they subsequently were divorced. He became a publisher in postwar Vienna.

Monat, Pawel, with John Dille. SPY IN THE U.S. New York: Harper and Row, 1961. 208 pp., no index [London: Frederick Muller, 1964].

Monat's story first appeared in *Life,* and Dille was the magazine's military affairs editor. Monat was a colonel in Polish intelligence (Z-2) and an armed forces attaché to the United States in 1955–1958. Technically, Z-2 was the intelligence branch of the Polish armed forces. After his return to Poland, he defected to the United States in Vienna in 1959.

The story is devoted mainly to Monat's intelligence activities in the United States. He discusses the organization and security of a Polish embassy; the use of illegals; the technique of what is known as "false flag" recruitment (the recruiter pretending to be of another nation); illegal purchases, under cover, of prohibited items; the use of blackmail, including sexual, to compel a person to work for a foreign service. There are good segments on methods of countersurveillance and on the choice of rendezvous points and dead letter or dead drops. Monat also goes into arrangements for the clandestine contacting of agents and the passage of intelligence. Dille's recreated conversations may or may not be accurate in every detail, and Monat was not entirely frank about his family situation and the reasons for his defection. Blackstock and Schaf opined in their bibliography that caution was in order when using this book, which they describe as a cold war sensation. Whether Monat was involved in all the activities he writes of or not, the technical descriptions he gives of the tradecraft involved are of a professional level.

Montagu, Ewen. BEYOND TOP SECRET ULTRA. New York: Coward, McCann and Geoghegan, 1978. 182 pp., index [London: P. Davies, 1977].

An outstanding memoir of intelligence in World War II and a rare reminiscence in that Montagu is the only British officer involved in naval deception in that war to write about it. He was in addition the only member of the XX Committee, which directed British double agents, who was actually running such agents for his particular service (the navy). Montagu wrote this as the story of "his war," not of Ultra or British naval intelligence where he served. He recounts how his access to Ultra and work on the XX Committee made him privy to the highest secrets and allowed him to conduct deception operations, mostly connected with naval matters.

There are many items and anecdotes to delight or

enlighten the intelligence buff: Montagu's experiences with J. Edgar Hoover in the Popov (Tricycle) operation; SIS distrust of SOE security and thus its care in what Ultra it passed the latter; various naval deceptions, both ad hoc and long range, including failures; the identification of German attempts at deception from broken Abwehr traffic; a feel of what it was like to have Ultra as a daily intelligence source; the use of Ultra and its importance in the double agent effort. The section on double agents is partly from his report at the end of the war, which was incorporated in Masterman's report and ultimately in *The Double-Cross System.* Brief sections on the London Controlling Section (LCS) give us a first-hand view of this organization's work, general though that view may be. The short chapter on Mincemeat is disappointing in that it contributes nothing new. Some questionable items intrude themselves: on German belief that Dakar was the target of Torch; the perpetuation of the story that OSS mounted an operation (in Portugal) to steal the Japanese code; the claim that high-level German messages, as VE Day approached, dealt with hopes of a last redoubt in southern Germany. (See Bennett's *Ultra in the West* on this last item.) A reviewer in *RUSI* did not believe Montagu got as much naval Ultra as he implies and felt that the book's story has largely been told elsewhere, with only some gaps filled. The reviewer later changed his mind. David Kahn's review in *Cryptologia,* on the other hand, found the book contained a wealth of material and new insights into the use of Ultra.

Montagu, Ewen. THE MAN WHO NEVER WAS. Philadelphia: J. B. Lippincott, 1954. 160 pp., no index [London: Evans, 1953].

The story of the best-known deception operation in World War II. The best-selling book and the movie on which it was based (with some license) have made this operation one of the most famous deception ploys in history. In *Beyond Top Secret Ultra* (above), Montagu gives the latest version of how official permission was granted to tell this story. The 1954 book is an account of the inspiration, planning, preparation, and execution of the operation code-named Mincemeat, which most experts believe played a crucial role in deceiving the Germans prior to the Allied landings in Sicily in 1943. Here we observe the selling of a plan, the attention given to detail, the knowledge of the enemy's psychology and thinking, the careful anticipation of a sequence of events, and the security consciousness.

Montagu, for all that, has not told everything or given all details about the use of a body carrying faked letters and documents to mislead the enemy, for security reasons or for reasons of discretion. One of these details was the availability of Ultra, which played a pivotal role in the whole scheme. He also failed to mention an incident involving the real loss of a courier, whose body was washed ashore in Spain just prior to the invasion of North Africa. See Colvin's *The Unknown Courier,* Darling's *Sunday at Large,* and Butler's *Mason-Mac* for information about this incident, which, when it was brought to the planners' attention at the start of Mincemeat's preparations, resulted in a cessation of action to determine whether the plan's concept was unrealistic in view of the real, recent, and similar incident. Cruickshank in *Deception in World War II* places Mincemeat in perspective and explains its place in the overall deception plan for Sicily worked out by A Force. German dissenters about Mincemeat's effect on German dispositions included General Warlimont and Gert Buchheit of the Abwehr who still represent the minority opinion many years after the event. See also Mure's *Practice to Deceive* for views of the British Mediterranean deception group on the operation and Wheatley's *The Deception Planners* for his version of who inspired the idea. In *The Unknown Courier* Colvin also comments on what he regarded as planning and documentation weaknesses of the operation.

Moore, Dan Tyler, and Waller, Martha. CLOAK AND CIPHER. London: George G. Harrap, 1965. 227 pp., no index [Indianapolis: Bobbs-Merrill, 1962].

Best described as an introduction to cryptography and cryptanalysis. The authors outline basic cryptographic methods and systems used over time and efforts and means employed to break them. They include secret writing and other forms of concealment, presumably embraced by the "cloak" in the title. Moore was in OSS, where he served at one point as liaison with the U.S. Navy Cryptographic Bureau. He and Waller have given not merely explanations of certain systems but historical examples and anecdotes that illustrate uses, misuses, successes, and failures of cryptology. Many of these make good reading, and the reader is not taxed by the recitation of long stories. The book is, however, pre-Ultra and thus suffers this important omission. It also lacks enough information on the latest developments ushered in by the computer and its applications to cryptology. There are minor errors, such as calling the Abwehr "naval intelligence" and Colonel Nicolai the head of German intelligence in World War II.

Moravec, Frantisek. MASTER OF SPIES: THE MEMOIRS OF GENERAL FRANTISEK MORAVEC. London: The Bodley Head, 1975. 240 pp., no index [Garden City, N.Y.: Doubleday].

General Moravec's, one of the important memoirs of intelligence, has not had the recognition it deserves. He was head of Czechoslovak military intelligence from 1937 to 1945. His daughter arranged to have this book, based on his notes, published after his death. There are no known reasons for doubting the authenticity of these notes. Moravec's high qualities as an intelligence officer are apparent as one reads this book. He recounts stories of his work with agents, especially A-54, and the acquisition of advance warnings of Hitler's plans for the invasions of Czechoslovakia, Poland, and Western Europe in 1940 and the USSR in 1941; there are sections on his role and planning for the assassination of Heydrich (whose killing was of no value to the Allied cause, according to Robert Bruce Lockhart) and prewar liaison with the French and Soviet intelligence services. For those interested in counterintelligence, there are good portions on the Czech destruction of a Hungarian espionage network and on German penetrations in Czechoslovakia, while his description of President

Beneš's dealings with the Soviets during the war opens some interesting avenues for analysis and research. The recruitment of the Hungarian colonel who continued to work for the Allies as Hungary's chief of intelligence until his death in 1942 is only one example of Moravec's talents in intelligence and counterintelligence.

John Masterman in the preface judged Moravec's account to be essentially true but felt Moravec's reports on major events may have been a little less accurate and decisive than Moravec believed. This view seemed reasonable until the publication of Hinsley's *British Intelligence in the Second World War* in 1979. From it we learn that Moravec's agent Paul Thümmel (A-54) was of vital importance to British intelligence until 1941. It was A-54, the history informs us, that provided the Czechs and SIS advance notice of Germany's plans in the Sudetenland in 1937 and Czechoslovakia in 1938–1939 and of the attack on Poland. A-54 continued to provide first-class political and military intelligence for the first two years of the war. This testifies to the importance of these memoirs to intelligence history. There is nothing on Moravec's work after he fled Czechoslovakia in the wake of the Communist takeover in 1948. The *Economist* review quoted Masterman as stating that Moravec created "probably the most successful spy service of the war years." Piekalkiewicz's *Secret Agents, Spies and Saboteurs* contains a chapter on Agent A-54 that has details on the operation provided by Czech subordinates of Moravec.

Morros, Boris, as told to Charles Samuels. MY TEN YEARS AS A COUNTERSPY. New York: Viking Press, 1959. 248 pp., no index [London: Werner Laurie].

Morros, the Hollywood producer, played the role of double agent of the FBI between 1947 and 1957. He tells here of his recruitment by the Soviets to perform services largely in the capacity of a support agent—providing cover, finances, or courier and other assistance to Soviet operations. Soviet agents he fingered included the Sobles, the Sterns, and the Zlatovskis (Jane Foster), all of whom were indicted for espionage. The picture of Soviet tradecraft used is sometimes surprising for its unprofessionalism—note the Soviet officer's meetings with Morros the agent at Luchow's after he warned Morros not to attend parties where Soviets were present, or instructions to meet on a street in Washington where movie distribution offices were located when Morros was in the industry himself.

At the start of the book it is stated that the full results of the work of Morros as a counterspy would not be revealed for years. Whatever was undisclosed, it was in addition to other gaps or omissions in the story. First, Morros's version of how he became an FBI counterspy is less complicated than and not as complete as was actually the case. Second, the extent of the intelligence work attributable to the Sobles is not made clear. Third, there is virtually no description of FBI methods of operating in running him as a double agent. For Jane Foster Zlatovski's version of her relationship with Morros and her severe opinion of him, see her *An Unamerican Lady,* published in 1980. Consult Carpozi's *Red Spies in the U.S.* for his explanation of why Morros was motivated to cooperate with the FBI.

Mosley, Leonard. THE CAT AND THE MICE. New York: Harper and Bros., 1958. 182 pp., bibliog., index [London: Arthur Barker].

The first of the postwar books dealing with the German Operation Kondor, this is incomplete, as could be expected. The author was aware of the capture of the Kondor agent Eppler when as a war correspondent in Cairo in 1942 he assisted the British in a ploy to hide the arrest from the Germans. Mosley stated he had to eliminate some details and suppress or change some names for security reasons. He is most in error when he calls this operation "the most daring act of espionage of the war." Only the route and the long trek used to get Eppler and his radio operator Monkaster to Cairo were daring; the rest of the performance of the two was appalling from professional and security points of view.

Historically, the case stands out for two reasons. Anwar Sadat, the future president of Egypt, makes an appearance in it; and Eppler and his radio operator survived the war despite their reported noncooperation with their captors. Meanwhile, we have learned that British intelligence in Egypt (SIME), knew of the coming of the Kondor mission early and had it under surveillance while it was on its way, thanks to Ultra. The British use of the captured code and radio set for deception is described by Mosley; for more on the deception and the operation as a whole see Sansom's *I Spied Spies,* Lewin's *Ultra Goes to War,* and Mure's *Master of Deception.* Eppler's account, *Operation Condor,* should be read after these are studied. Cave Brown has drawn heavily from Mosley for his section on the case in *Bodyguard of Lies.*

Moss, W. Stanley. ILL MET BY MOONLIGHT. New York: Macmillan, 1950. 190 pp., no index [London: Harrap].

In April 1944, SOE carried out the dramatic kidnapping of the German divisional commander on Crete, General Kreipe. Moss, with fellow SOE officer Patrick Leigh-Fermor, was responsible for this successful operation. The two were members of a group in Cairo that achieved fame in SOE—the Tara group, which boasted Billy Maclean, David Smiley, and Xan Fielding. This is based on Moss's diary, with explanatory notes. The British War Office forbade publication in 1945; this version is some sixty pages shorter than the original. Moss claims the bulk of the story remained unaltered. Not explained is the rationale of SOE for the operation in the first place. Note that Cairo was not aware that the original target, the hated General Muller, had left the island before the date of the operation. Aside from SOE reasons, details of the planning for the operation in Cairo would have added considerable professional interest to this story of boldness and daring. There is also no explanation for the planned operation to repeat this success two months later, which was aborted due to betrayal by the communist-dominated resistance organization on Crete. Note the familiarity of the techniques used to take General Kreipe, which have been adopted and adapted by terrorist groups in more recent times. Hunt in *A Don at War* questioned the benefits derived from this operation. His view was shared by Sweet-Escott, an SOE staff officer, who recounts the happy reaction of Kreipe's staff to the news of his disappearance in *Baker Street Irregular.* Moss later served in Siam. An essay on the operation containing some good photographs is found in Piekalkiewicz's *Secret Agents, Spies and Saboteurs.*

Moyzisch, L. C. OPERATION CICERO. New York: Coward-McCann, 1950. 209 pp., no index [London: Wingate, 1952].

Cicero was the Germans' code name for their agent who was the valet of the British ambassador to Turkey in 1943. Moyzisch was the SD officer who ran the case, which lasted some six months. Writing early after the war, he was hasty in declaring that he was the only person who knew all the facts of the case. Neither he nor Von Papen, the German ambassador who added a postscript, was in a position to tell anything but the German side of the story. German disbelief that the Cicero material was genuine is well brought out, and one needs to read Schellenberg's memoirs *The Labyrinth* to get additional flavor of the German indecision and dilemma in whether to believe Cicero's intelligence. Many works and disclosures since Moyzisch's account enlighten us on aspects unknown to the Germans. The most important were that Cicero was identified by various means in the course of the operation and used as an unwitting deception channel. Dulles tells in *The Secret Surrender* how he learned of Cicero. Hugh Trevor-Roper wrote that Cicero at one point was used to deceive the Germans. Mure in *Practice to Deceive* tells of his learning in the Middle East of the Allied use of Cicero for deception. It is also known that the agent's identity was betrayed by Ultra.

British trust of servants who turned out to be spies has a tradition. Compton Mackenzie in *Greek Memories* tells of the theft of British plans in Alexandria in World War I by the servant of a British general. And the British ambassador whom Cicero served had previously employed a valet in another post who was dismissed as a suspected agent. Two of the matters not fully clarified to this day are Cicero's ties in Turkey and his status in the embassy which allowed him the access he had. We also have no full inventory of the deceptive material passed to the Germans. The case dramatizes how overall lack of good intelligence and fear of an adversary's cunning combine to create a dilemma for an intelligence service and policymakers. For one of the earlier discussions and analyses of the deception probabilities in the Cicero case, see Cave Brown's *Bodyguard of Lies.* See also Kahn's *Hitler's Spies* for a discussion of the value and German use of Cicero's material and for that author's disagreement with Schellenberg on German cryptanalytic gains from it. For Trevor-Roper's statements on British deception via Cicero, see Peis's *The Mirror of Deception* and Maclean's *Take Nine Spies.*

Muggeridge, Malcolm, THE INFERNAL GROVE. Chronicles of Wasted Time, no. 2. New York: William Morrow, 1974. 272 pp., index [London: Collins, 1973].

World War I produced its literary critics of secret service such as Compton Mackenzie; World War II brought forth Muggeridge among others. This second volume of his memoirs is a delightful, iconoclastic account of his experiences, including lengthy accounts of his work as an intelligence officer of SIS in Mozambique and intelligence liaison with the French in North Africa and Europe. Superbly written, his book is a collection of memorable phrases and bon mots about intelligence that are good for the intelligence officer's perspective and sense of humor. Two chapters in particular are recommended ("On Secret Service" and "The Victor's Camp") for what Muggeridge has to say about Bletchley Park material and its use in operations and for his anecdotes about Kim Philby and his experiences as a chief of station in Africa. He had, in the past, been a staunch defender of Philby against suspicions of his loyalty. The reader should keep in mind that this was published the same year as Winterbotham's *The Ultra Secret* and divulges some of the secrets of the Allied communications intelligence success. Muggeridge had done so earlier (1967) when he speculated in an article that the British used Lucy in Switzerland as the channel to disguise and pass the Soviets intelligence derived from deciphered German traffic. This "ferocious critic" of the wartime SIS, to use an expression from one review, had one of his operations, run jointly with OSS, described in the latter's history (see Cave Brown's *The Secret War Report of the OSS*). Other items to catch the eye in Muggeridge's account include Philby's insistence that all Bletchley Park material should go to the Soviets, the British reading of Gaullist traffic, glimpses of the Tyler Kent trial, and the myth of security involving Bletchley Park material, with the French in Algiers supposedly not aware of this source.

Mure, David. MASTER OF DECEPTION: TANGLED WEBS IN LONDON AND THE MIDDLE EAST. London: William Kimber, 1980. 268 pp., bibliog., notes, index.

The title can be misleading. This is not really about Dudley Clarke, the head of A Force under whom the author served and the man he describes in *Practice to Deceive* (below) as the genius of British and Allied deception in World War II. What he has to say of Clarke appears mainly in the first part. His purpose is to destroy the impression he believes was created by Sir John Masterman and others about the architects of the deception successes. Constructive contributions in his earlier book on the role of Clarke and his unit now extend to polemics against the Londoners and civilians in deception work. Mure contrasts the London "private armies" with the symmetry of those under Clarke; he believes Masterman perpetuates errors on proper methods of running deception operations; he, like Colonel Wild, head of the SHAEF deception group, attacks the impression he feels Masterman gives and the organization in London until Wild assumed control. In pressing his attack, Mure divulges more names, insights, and facts on deception, though the U.S. role is neglected. The role of the London Controlling Section is made clearer, as is its jurisdiction and command at various stages. Questions he raises on double agents, their primary functions, and their handling bear looking into. To his credit, he provides space to Ewen Montagu and Colonel J. A. Robertson of the XX Committee to reply to some of the issues raised.

On the negative side, there are questionable facts and opinions. Mure allows he had no access to official records and in the absence of an official history of deception "can retain the fun of deduction." Few will agree that Eden was a "slavish admirer" of Stalin; the classifying of Montagu as a professional naval man will surprise everyone, including Montagu. Mure weakens his argument on the professional versus civilian question by insisting on "officers from those good regiments." His discussion of the Tricycle (Popov) double agent case and the Pearl Harbor intelligence requirement given him are not particularly good, and he repeats his earlier speculation that Germans opposed to Hitler deliberately accepted British deceptions. He abandons speculation when he flatly says the success of the XX system in England was "made possible by the anti-Hitler elements within the Abwehr." One will find in reading Masterman that he called the Middle East the home of deception and credits the success of the XX system to the "professionals of MI-5." Michael Howard in his review felt it should have been possible to give Clarke and his organization the credit they deserved without damning virtually all others concerned with deception, thought that Mure lacked real knowledge of what had happened in London, and regarded the book as the surfacing of old secret service rivalries. Howard, Mure informs us, was selected to write the official history of deception, succeeding the late Peter Fleming.

Mure, David. PRACTICE TO DECEIVE. London: William Kimber, 1977. 263 pp., bibliog., index.

Mure served in the Middle East as a deception officer under Brigadier Dudley Clarke. Among his duties was that of chairman of the Middle East equivalent of the XX Committee, designated the Thirty Committee. From Baghdad and Beirut he was involved in deception operations and ran double agents; most of the events he relates, he contends, were those in which he had a direct part. He relies more on recollection than on records, claiming a photographic memory that allows him to recall messages thirty years later. Mure does not always succeed in making it clear what is from direct involvement and first-hand knowledge, what is not, and what is opinion. A great service he has performed is to accord to Dudley Clarke the recognition he deserves for his creative and effective work in deception. The book helps balance the picture of Allied deception in World War II; earlier London-oriented writers tended to obscure the work done in the Mediterranean and the Middle East. There is also an unequivocal tribute to the role of Ultra in successful deception. Those who believe Mure goes too far in favor of the Middle East should consult Cruickshank's *Deception in World War II,* which supports some of his claims. The *Economist,* in an otherwise favorable review, says he had a "startlingly inaccurate passage on Hungary." Mure himself subsequently recognized that he was wrong in writing that Colonel Fellers, the U.S. attaché in Cairo, was used to pass deceptive material when it was learned that the Germans had broken his cipher. His theory that Admiral Canaris of the Abwehr may have deliberately assisted in putting over British deceptions is, without more compelling support, merely another speculation about that figure. Of profound significance is Mure's claim that Dudley Clarke leaked the approaches of the Hungarians, Rumanians, and Bulgarians for a negotiated peace as part of a plan to force the Germans to send troops there; but it is an instance in which he fails to indicate his source or sources. Cave Brown makes the same point in *Bodyguard of Lies* in connection with the Hungarian and Rumanian peace feelers but does not specifically attribute it to Clarke. Other startling items to be found are the casual manner of Mure's selection into A Force (Clarke's unit) and his admission that he is "by nature a congenital liar and romancer." Sir Maurice Oldfield, the former head of SIS, was quoted in the *London Times* as considering this book one of his four favorites on intelligence.

Myagkov, Aleksei. INSIDE THE KGB: AN EXPOSE BY AN OFFICER OF THE THIRD DIRECTORATE. New Rochelle, N.Y.: Arlington House, 1976. 131 pp., no index [Richmond, Surrey, Eng.: Foreign Affairs Publishing].

Myagkov was stationed in Germany with the KGB when he defected to the British in 1974. According to DIS's *Bibliography,* he was in 1977 the West's only defector from the KGB's Third Directorate. This is the directorate responsible for counterintelligence and security in the Soviet armed forces, and not much has previously appeared on it. For example, Barron's *KGB* devotes only two pages to it. Myagkov has drawn a picture of the KGB that he is familiar with; his knowledge and perspective are largely bound by his association with this one department where operations are concerned. The story of Soviet operations from East Germany into West Germany against all Western targets, massive though they are known to be, sounds exaggerated. Some readers may feel he devotes too much of a small book to the sins and foibles of the Soviet political and army hierarchies. What he has to say of his KGB training is more in keeping with the interests of the specialist in intelligence. The *RUSI* reviewer thought this an important book if it were genuine. DIS's *Bibliography* assures us that it is based on solid documentation, much of it material Captain Myagkov brought out with him. Better prose and editing, more documents like those in the appendixes, and a greater focus on the Third Directorate would have helped.

N

Neave, Airey. THE ESCAPE ROOM. Garden City, N.Y.: Doubleday, 1970. 319 pp., no index [London: Hodder and Stoughton, 1969. *Saturday at MI 9*].

Neave, after escaping from a German prison, joined MI9 where for a time he headed Room 900, the escape and evasion (E&E) section for Western Europe. Neave could not use classified documents in writing this and thus relied on his memory and on conversations with those who were involved in E&E with him. The author wanted it to be his "own account of the men and women of the Resistance" involved in the effort. He was the first of MI9's staff to write of this organization's direction of the escape system and of the underground E&E nets it set up in Europe. For this reason alone, the "outstanding" grade given it by Foot and Langley in their more comprehensive history *MI 9* was a bit excessive. This later history and those of Donald Darling and Langley himself fill in many details that Neave, lacking access to official records and for other reasons, was not able to include.

Neligan, David. THE SPY IN THE CASTLE. London: MacGibbon and Kee, 1968. 183 pp., index.

Neligan was a member of the Dublin police's G Division, the anti-Fenian section, after World War I. This tells how he served the Fenian cause, first in G Division and then as a double agent while working for the SIS as an agent in the field. It is a gripping story that captures the tension, danger, duplicity, and violence of the post–World War I time of troubles in Ireland. It is also an account of the intelligence and counterintelligence war that was to play a vital role in its outcome. This was a no-holds-barred war of extermination that some think became the precursor of such clandestine and covert wars of the present in many parts of the world. Neligan, in describing his role as an agent of the Irish Michael Collins, cites instances of odd and insecure clandestine practices by both the British and the Irish that can only be classified as unprofessional. He claims that he, among others, was involved in providing the intelligence to the Fenians that resulted in the location and the massacre of the British Cairo Gang in November 1920. There were other Fenian penetrations of the British; Foot in *Six Faces of Courage* tells of Michael Collins's female agent in British headquarters in Dublin in 1919 who passed him copies of the secret British reports she typed.

Newman, Bernard. SPY AND COUNTERSPY: STORY OF THE BRITISH SECRET SERVICE. London: Robert Hale, 1970. 244 pp., bibliog., index.

Published posthumously; edited and with additional sections by I. O. Evans. We cannot know what the book would have been like had Newman lived to complete it; as it is, it is not worth reading. A good judgment is contained, unintentionally or not, in a note at the start by Basil Lidell Hart. Hart states he was unable to comment on espionage; however, he always felt Newman should have pursued his studies and writings in military tactics and strategy. This compilation of Newman's notes based largely on secondary sources is a work of poor quality containing many questionable judgments and errors (markedly in the coverage of twentieth-century espionage). Newman obviously did not do his homework. Thus, his chapter on German agents in World War II shows no hint of knowledge or suspicion of Allied control and manipulation. The chapter on the American Revolution shows what little research and study of this period he had undertaken. Newman was aware of the problems of writing on espionage when he confessed that "espionage is not easy to write about. . . . information is sparse and some authors have been tempted to give their imaginations free rein."

Nicolai, Walther. THE GERMAN SECRET SERVICE. London: Stanley Paul, 1924. 299 pp., no index [London: Harrap, 1929].

Colonel Nicolai was head of German military intelligence in World War I; his responsibilities also extended to counterintelligence. These memoirs, poorly translated by George Renwick, contain an extra chapter by the latter on Colonel Alfred Redl, the Russian spy in the intelligence department of the Austro-Hungarian general staff. From the perspective of over half a century, it is a big disappointment. Nicolai had the mentality of a German staff officer and used this book as a means of perpetuating the "stab in the back" myth of German defeat. It is a book of generalities, obsessed with the inferiority in intelligence (political and economic) that has plagued the Germans. Nicolai spends much time on counterintelligence aspects of German military intelligence, telling us little of his service's espionage and nothing of German political action, subversion, and sabotage in that war. The style is often oblique, making certain passages hard to understand, and errors of fact and questionable judgments fill the book. When Nicolai avers that when the war came, the German secret service did not have the time and means to extend its organization into England, he cannot mean all of German intelligence, even naval intelligence. We know the attempt had been made prior to 1914 and destroyed by the British when war was declared. Giskes in *London Calling North Pole* wrote that Nicolai did not tell all and that "he carried silence beyond the grave concerning his mysterious assistants and their fateful activities." Nicolai does give us a feel for the attitude of the German military toward intelligence, for the importance of communications intelligence in the German victories on the eastern front, and for the consequences to his service of being burdened with propaganda within Germany and the German army. Strong's *Men of Intelligence* contains a useful section on Nicolai and that author's summation of his intelligence role.

Norman, Bruce. SECRET WARFARE: THE BATTLE OF CODES AND CIPHERS. Newton Abbot, Eng.: David and Charles, 1973. 175 pp., bibliog., index.

Norman aimed to share some of the excitement and fascination of "the strange world of secret intelligence."

A number of fairly well-known cases and events in history are recounted, with the bulk taking place from World War I to the present. Each is more or less a précis of the subject, with little new contributed despite an impressive list of interviews. Someone with less of a tendency to popularize would have made better use of interviews with such important sources as Georges Painvin and Admiral James, to name two. Norman's enthusiasm for the subject of codes and ciphers was not matched by an equal depth of treatment. There are also errors (as in the discussion of Lucy) or missing facts on cases dealt with. Perhaps the most significant fault is the tendency to credit cryptology as the crucial element in a number of events when that judgment is unwarranted. An example is his attributing to SOE's coded messages to the French resistance the credit for saving the Normandy invasion of 1944 because the resistance prevented German panzer divisions in southwest France from reaching the battle area.

O

Ogilvy, David. BLOOD, BRAINS AND BEER: AN AUTOBIOGRAPHY. New York: Atheneum, 1978. 176 pp., index [London: Hamish Hamilton].

In his book on the British Security Coordination under Sir William Stephenson, H. Montgomery Hyde described Ogilvy as "the most remarkable of the younger men to join Stephenson's BSC." Despite this impressive introduction, Ogilvy has very little to say of his wartime intelligence work. According to him, that work was related to economic warfare; his position was that of responsibility for such operations in Latin America, where firms that dealt with the Germans were identified and neutralized. Hyde's *Room 3603* speaks of his work in poll taking for the BSC; Ogilvy does not tell of this work. The author's great admiration for Stephenson is proclaimed. He puts him in the same class of the greats in British intelligence as Hall, Walsingham, Wiseman, and André [sic]. The wit displayed in this autobiography would have enlivened any wartime intelligence stories Ogilvy must know but fails to include.

Orlov, Alexander. HANDBOOK OF INTELLIGENCE AND GUERRILLA WARFARE. Ann Arbor: Univ. of Michigan Press, 1963. 187 pp., no index.

Sherman Kent in the preface to the 1966 edition of his *Strategic Intelligence for American World Policy* called Orlov's book remarkable and one that should be read. DIS's *Bibliography* used the term "authoritative." Orlov defected from the NKVD while serving in Spain during the civil war. He had been a lecturer on intelligence and counterintelligence at the Central Military School in Moscow. This is a recreation of the approved textbook he wrote for use in Soviet intelligence training. He brought the work up to date by using examples from the period when he was with Soviet intelligence and also others of a later date. It is primarily on how illegals operate—how Soviet intelligence creates, organizes, and runs illegal networks that operate parallel to and supplement the legal residentura and replace the latter when diplomatic relations are broken. It is a valuable, needed, and rare insight into an intelligence practice of which the Soviets have been masters and on which they have traditionally relied. Technical collection is not discussed, and the discussion of guerrilla warfare is based on experience in Spain and is only a fraction of the total work. In addition to the value of its material on operating methods of illegals, the book is important for its emphasis on Soviet reliance on espionage as a means of acquiring needed information, compared to the Western preference for and emphasis on open sources.

Bailey in *The Conspirators* gives Orlov's true name as Aleksandr Nikolsky; Bailey says that Nikolsky seems to have acquired an unsavory reputation in Spain, causing the two top men of Soviet intelligence there to ask for his recall, and that Nikolsky was responsible for the murder of Spanish Trotskyites. Bailey points out that Orlov defected at the time of the great purges in his service. Krivitsky also wrote that resentment against Orlov and his service led to a demand by the chief of Soviet military intelligence in Spain that he be recalled. Orlov always denied the accusations made against him by Krivitsky. Brook-Shepherd's *The Storm Petrels* only scratches the surface in its treatment of Orlov.

Owen, David. BATTLE OF WITS: A HISTORY OF PSYCHOLOGY AND DECEPTION IN MODERN WARFARE. London: Leo Cooper, 1978. 200 pp., index.

Using secondary sources, Owen attempts to treat psychological factors in military history "as a single coherent narrative" for the first time. The deception segments are the better part and are better treated. Owen understands deception and has a sensitive grasp of it. There are many excellent examples of deception in both world wars, especially by the British; the book is written primarily from their angle. Three chapters on Fortitude and the Normandy invasion rate good marks but do contain some errors. His appreciation of the importance of deception in military history extends to the present. Unhappily, he fails to provide any examples of Soviet deception—prewar, wartime, or postwar. His segments on psychological warfare add little and sometimes intrude on the more significant discussions of deception. The chapter on the radio war is based on Delmer's *Black Boomerang,* with no effort at independent evaluation made of its effect. He does not provide a single reference, and there is no bibliography, but it is apparent he repeats well-known errors. He accepts Winterbotham for much on Enigma, retells that author's Coventry story, spotlights Maskelyne at the expense of greater figures under Dudley Clarke, and even implies acceptance of Clifton James's claims before anyone knew there was a chance they might be right. The *RUSI* review cited his perpetuation of the error that the 80 Wing was able to bend German navigation beams and considered the book's value seriously limited by its lack of references.

P

Page, Bruce; Leitch, David; and Knightley, Philip. THE PHILBY CONSPIRACY. New York: Doubleday, 1968. 300 pp., no index [London: André Deutsch. *Philby: The Spy Who Betrayed a Generation*].

The authors were members of the *London Sunday Times* Insight Team. This was the product of several hundred interviews, but none with Eastern European sources. There is no claim that this is the whole story on Philby. John Le Carré in the introduction called it "brilliant but necessarily incomplete." According to Pincher in *Inside Story,* the British Foreign Office tried to stop its publication and added that its publication focused fresh attention on the whole Burgess-Maclean-Philby affair and on weaknesses in and rivalries among British services. Trevor-Roper in *The Philby Affair* found it had the virtues and faults of instant history or high-quality journalism but lacked dimension and reflective depth and persisted in some questionable assertions. With the exposure of Anthony Blunt's role as the "fourth man" and other revelations in and on the heels of Boyle's *The Climate of Treason* we have more reliable facts on these cases, but, as Le Carré guessed in 1968, we must still regard our knowledge as incomplete. This book, despite any shortcomings, is still an incredible, vivid story of the official ineptitude and personal attitudes that allowed these Soviet agents to gain and exploit for so long their diplomatic and intelligence positions. For an early leak on Enigma and Allied success in deciphering German traffic, see pages 162 and 163. Consult Pincher's *Their Trade is Treachery* for the names of other persons allegedly recruited at Cambridge as Soviet agents.

Paine, Lauran. THE TECHNOLOGY OF ESPIONAGE. London: Robert Hale, 1978. 184 pp., bibliog., index.

Paine traces the history of some major scientific and technological developments from World War II to the present and writes of the enormous strides made in the application of such discoveries to intelligence operations and to intelligence collection. Spy satellites, the U-2, electronic espionage, audio operations (microbugs), and other topics are discussed. A general survey on these developments, the book is useful as an introduction to the world of technological espionage. Paine includes some facts revealed for the first time. He puts the whole subject in proper perspective by clearly recognizing and acknowledging that technological collection does not in itself reveal intentions and that in certain instances intentions are more important than sensors. A number of errors or questionable conclusions should warn the reader that the author has not fully mastered his subject; these are in addition to an occasional tendency to exaggerate.

Parritt, B.A.H. THE INTELLIGENCERS: THE STORY OF BRITISH MILITARY INTELLIGENCE UP TO 1914. Ashford, Kent, Eng.: Intelligence Center, 1971. 232 pp., bibliog., no index.

Parritt was a member of the British Intelligence Corps. This is the first half of a planned two-volume history. The central theme is contained in the very first sentence: the "British army has never liked or wanted professional intelligence officers." Parritt then proceeds with facts and anecdotes to show that this was so and to trace the development of military intelligence up to the start of World War I. Despite the service's attitude, it is interesting to learn, four field marshals had served in intelligence, two of them actually as spies. The author connects the development of military intelligence with some particular conflicts with other intelligence activities, but he does not with others. Parritt is unrestrained when judging individuals and their performances; the inspector of the intelligence corps indicates in the preface that there are points of disagreement on certain persons. Some will protest the imbalance of coverage. Less than six pages are devoted to that most interesting war of intelligence, the American Revolution, and all are on the André affair. It is, on the whole, an honest portrayal of military shortsightedness luckily balanced by improvisation at a time of need and the critical innovations of pioneers. This should be read in conjunction with Haswell's *British Military Intelligence.*

Pash, Boris T. THE ALSOS MISSION. New York: Award House, 1969. 256 pp., no index.

Pash was military leader of the World War II Alsos mission, the top-secret unit whose purpose was to determine what work the Germans had undertaken in atomic weapons and research and to acquire intelligence on their overall scientific progress, facilities, and personnel. The mission also had the aim of locating and capturing German scientists to prevent their falling into Russian hands. Lasby in *Project Paperclip* praised Alsos for its excellent planning and the courage and zeal of Pash. This is a first-hand, authoritative account that reveals the work of the mission and the personality of Pash himself. He is good on how intelligence leads were acquired and pursued to get further intelligence for the successful accomplishment of objectives. Many administrative and logistical details of the mission are imparted that are not of interest to the intelligence specialist other than those involved in providing support, and there are direct quotes that may not be exact after a quarter of a century. Goudsmit, the scientific head of the unit—whose book *Alsos* must be read as a complement to Pash's account— said, "Pash never failed us." The Alsos mission has been praised as a model of military-civilian cooperation. Lasby's book is required for a fuller understanding of the evolution of U.S. policy on German scientists. Pash was earlier involved as a security officer in the investigation of Soviet attempts to steal U.S. atomic secrets, a fact he mentions, and he is cited in works about these cases.

Pearson, Anthony. CONSPIRACY OF SILENCE. New York: Quartet Books, 1978. 178 pp., no index.

An expansion into book form of articles that Pearson, a British journalist, wrote for the magazine *Penthouse*. It purports to give the background of the Six-Day War of 1967 and of the Israeli attack on the USS *Liberty.* Much in this book is unreliable, and Pearson's inability to produce respectable evidence further weakens his case. His source for the part on the war and the *Liberty* is stated to have been a British major, now dead. Charges that there was a U.S.-Israeli conspiracy to start the war, that CIA's chief of counterintelligence passed nuclear secrets to the Israelis without the knowledge of his government, or that the Israelis betrayed an agreed master plan are examples of material without evidence or support. Added to these are incredible statements that CIA agreed to let the Israelis do the intelligence collecting in the Middle East (which cropped up again in Eveland's *Ropes of Sand*) or that CIA covertly assisted Biafra. Note too that the story of the alleged Polaris submarine's presence and contact with the *Liberty* also appears in Deacon's *The Silent War.* Pearson's frank admissions about the low ebb in his career at the time he undertook to write on the subject should also be noted.

Peers, William R., and Brelis, Dean. BEHIND THE BURMA ROAD: THE STORY OF AMERICA'S MOST SUCCESSFUL GUERRILLA FORCE. Boston: Little, Brown, 1963. 232 pp., index [London: R. Hale, 1964].

Peers, then a colonel, commanded OSS Detachment 101, which conducted unconventional warfare operations behind Japanese lines in Burma. He is one of the few senior OSS operational commanders to have published his wartime experiences. The story he tells is mainly the broad picture of the OSS effort in Burma and the largely paramilitary and guerrilla support provided to Allied military operations. Intelligence collection, escape and evasion, and sabotage operations are mentioned, but only briefly in a general way. Peers's perspective is that of the commander and career officer whose job is to support military operations. The strategic and tactical picture of both military and paramilitary operations is more thoroughly treated than details of organization and of intelligence and counterintelligence work; consequently, the merits of the book for the researcher will be found in the former. There are, all the same, some interesting individual items of historical and professional interest: the use of opium as a necessary means of payment in the area; General Donovan's visit to an OSS team behind Japanese lines; a similar trip behind enemy lines of the U.S. general commanding the India-Burma theater; the loss of as many Anglo-Burmese agents as personnel of all other nationalities; the encoding and decoding of up to ten thousand messages per month by hand using three cryptographic systems. The appendix contains a list of all military personnel, regardless of nationality, associated with 101 operations. Peers later rose to be a general and was the author of the investigation report of the My Lai killings in Vietnam. Coauthor Brelis served in 101 and became a writer and foreign correspondent after the war. Consult the U.S. War Department's *War Report of the OSS.*

Peis, Günter. THE MIRROR OF DECEPTION: HOW BRITAIN TURNED THE NAZI SPY MACHINE AGAINST ITSELF. London: Weidenfeld and Nicolson, 1977. 181 pp., bibliog., index.

Peis traces the history of German agents in World War II who ended up under Allied control and used for deception. He had planned to write in 1959 the story of the German agent 3725 or, as the British called him, Tate, as the "greatest spy ever to work for the Germans." He discovered that the circumstances were not as he thought and that he had a lead into the British deception scheme in which Tate (who Montagu said in *Beyond Top Secret Ultra* was the most valuable wireless agent) was a central figure. The result is this rather disjointed story of Tate and deception operations such as Mutt and Jeff, Celery, and others that are also treated in Masterman's *The Double-Cross System.* The real value of Peis's work is its view of these operations from the vantage point of the Germans and its position as another starting point for examining the claims of effectiveness that have been put forward from the Allied side: General Warlimont's dissenting view of Mincemeat's effect before Sicily; the findings on Celery, or the claims of a former Abwehr officer that his service had come to the conclusion (by the end of 1943) that Tate was under control. See Masterman's work on British fears that Tate might have been compromised at the same time. The problem is the uncertainty of the recollections of persons Peis interviewed. Peis himself injected some incorrect beliefs, e.g., that the Dieppe raid or the North Pole disasters were parts of British deception plans as was the loss of the Allied plans just prior to the North African invasion (see Colvin's *The Unknown Courier* and Darling's *Sunday at Large* on the true state of affairs). And there is the tendency at times to exaggerate—a good example is his tying the U.S. "Europe first" strategy to the capture of German saboteurs in 1942.

Penkovsky, Oleg. THE PENKOVSKY PAPERS. Garden City, N.Y.: Doubleday, 1965. 411 pp., no index [London: Collins, 1966].

In 1976, the final report of the Church committee of the U.S. Senate investigating intelligence activities officially confirmed that *The Penkovsky Papers* were prepared by CIA personnel who used actual materials made available by this important U.S. and British penetration into the USSR's military intelligence, armed forces, and ruling hierarchy. This report ended over ten years of debate about the authenticity of the papers (for one early doubt of the original version of the papers' "odyssey and authorship," see Blackstock's *Agents of Deceit*). Victor Zorza, the Soviet expert, was one of the critics of the papers' true authorship, as was John Le Carré. Wise and Ross in *The Espionage Establishment* imparted the telling comments and views of the U.S. Department of State that "the genuineness of the material was placed in doubt by the way the book was created along with damage to one of the greatest intelligence coups in years." Pincher in *Inside Story* claims British defense and intelligence authorities had opposed publication of the book and had wanted no association with it. The reasons given by the Senate report for its appearance were "operational," presumably having to do with the propaganda war.

Penkovsky provided material of great intelligence significance that in some instances is still of analytical value to Western intelligence and in others is of pertinence to current intelligence questions. Consequently, intelligence scholars would benefit from a new effort—one that would put the valid and verified Penkovsky material contained in these papers in its original form and context, rather than leaving them neglected because of their official sponsorship and the original means used to publish them. Similarly, the introduction and commentary of Frank Gibney, despite his assurances of the papers' authenticity, contain some very knowledgeable and perceptive comments. See Wynne's *Contact on Gorky Street* for the memoirs of the British intelligence agent who handled Penkovsky. De Silva in *Sub Rosa* explains the reason for the rebuff of Penkovsky when he first approached the U.S. embassy in Moscow. For varying views of the value of Penkovsky's intelligence, compare Cline's *Secrets, Spies and Scholars* with certain observations outlined in Pincher's *Their Trade Is Treachery.*

Pennypacker, Morton. GENERAL WASHINGTON'S SPIES ON LONG ISLAND AND IN NEW YORK. Brooklyn, N.Y.: Long Island Historical Society, 1939. 288 pp., index.

Pennypacker in 1930 wrote *The Two Spies, Nathan Hale and Robert Townsend.* This book he considered the second edition of that work, with new material. Pennypacker first identified Robert Townsend as the principal agent in New York and definitively identified Abraham Woodhull, another member of the network, as the agent known as Culper Senior. Townsend was one of Washington's outstanding agents who insisted on his identity's being tightly held, an insistence that partly accounted for his success and survival.

Pennypacker's work was based on correspondence that survived between Washington and Major Benjamin Tallmadge, the man who ran the New York network known as the Culper ring. It covers the use of codes and code names, secret writing, secret couriers and signaling, and the other paraphernalia of clandestine operations. Washington's belief in the vital importance of good intelligence, his reliance on the Culper net's information, and his flair for and use of deception based on reliable intelligence are well brought out and illustrated. Note that Washington used a form of the Meinertzhagen satchel ploy to cause the British to turn from an objective. And perhaps there is a moral to the story of the American Quaker who made gold available to Washington to be used only for the secret service. Carl Van Doren in *Secret History of the American Revolution* states Pennypacker's book contains much useful material but unsupported conjecture as well. Though he does not identify the latter, Van Doren appears to have considered the way Major André and Benedict Arnold are linked by Pennypacker's account as speculation. Corey Ford's 1965 *A Peculiar Service* provides more information on the Culper ring and complements this important study of a portion of the American Revolution's intelligence history.

Perrault, Gilles. THE RED ORCHESTRA. New York: Simon and Schuster, 1969. 510 pp., bibliog., no index [London: Arthur Barker, 1968].

Rote Kapelle was the name the Germans gave to the network of Soviet espionage and subversion they discovered after their attack on the Soviet Union in 1941. This study first appeared in French in 1967 and became a best seller. Perrault (real name Jacques Peyroles) does not fully and precisely identify where he, a journalist, got his information. Among the sources identified are Gestapo and Abwehr reports and records of German military courts. He is not precise about his interviews or about "certain other documents" he claims access to.

Detailed though it is, the work is sometimes inaccurate. Perrault's description of the extent of the network and of the Swiss segment's independent role needs to be compared to that in CIA's *The Rote Kapelle.* The CIA's work indicates that much of Perrault's information concerning the secret writing specialist and radio operator Danilov is incorrect, e.g., that on when he was arrested and when he arrived in Belgium. Another inconsistency pointed out is that the German officer Henry Piepe's version of his investigation of the Rote Kapelle does not agree fully with that of Perrault. The principal flaw, however, according to U.S. experts, is Perrault's slanting of the story from the point of view of Leopold Trepper.

Perrault, Gilles. THE SECRETS OF D-DAY. Boston: Little, Brown, 1965. 241 pp., bibliog., index [London: Arthur Barker].

The author received the Prix de la Resistance for this work, which was first published in French in 1964. Perrault based this on a study of German records, on interviews with German intelligence officers and members of the French resistance, and to a lesser extent on interviews with U.S. and British officers. He claimed that no previous work had dealt with the totality of intelligence operations that preceded and prepared for D-Day, the invasion of France by the Allies in 1944. He produced a work of mixed quality. Perrault was able to identify and discuss certain elements of the overall deception plan, such as the communications and signal intelligence deceptions, the use of camouflage, the Patton ploy and James's impersonation of General Montgomery, and the air reconnaissance and bombing patterns used by the Allies to disguise their true objective.

The book has the virtue of trying to provide an overview of Allied deception and security efforts and operations connected with the invasion plan. Perrault deserves credit for digging up much information on deception methods employed. However, errors and gaps in the full story abound, since the author had no access to Allied records and relied less on Allied sources than on others. To date, there is no evidence to support his claim that Allied deception plans called for the deliberate sacrifice of French resistance groups, a strategy he called "undoubtedly the ultimate secret of Fortitude" (the overall deception plan). He is groping when he calls the North Pole disasters in Holland (the German penetration of SOE nets) part of the British deception plan. The use of double agents to deceive the Germans is touched on, but Perrault has no real information on the size of that effort and on the identities of the important agents and handling officers involved. Ultra is not included; a number of minor errors intrude. For the punctilious, the lack of documentation for facts and opinions is another mark against the book.

Persico, Joseph E. PIERCING THE REICH: THE PENETRATION OF NAZI GERMANY BY AMERICAN SECRET AGENTS DURING WORLD WAR II. New York: Viking Press, 1979. 337 pp., bibliog., index [London: Michael Joseph].

Inspired by the "brief and tantalizing account" in the declassified OSS history, Persico set out to explore the subject further. The result is the product of interviews with a long and impressive list of former OSS personnel and a handful of French and English experts and information from what he terms declassified CIA documents. More accurately, these are OSS documents declassified by CIA. The author has written an interesting and well-researched study that shows how well tersely written official histories can be fleshed out. He opens to further research a segment of the intelligence history of World War II previously little known or written on. Some reviewers praised it; Tom Braden, himself an OSS veteran, called it "the best book ever written on American espionage during World War II," and David Scherman called it "brilliantly researched" in the *Washington Post.* There have been dissenting voices. Drew Middleton in the *New York Times* questioned the high marks for effectiveness given by Persico to the operations in question.

Persico's claims that U.S. agents "reaped an abundant harvest of intelligence" are not proven adequately except for such cases as those of George Wood (Fritz Kolbe) or Gisevius. Similarly, his conclusion that by the end of German operations the United States had an espionage apparatus to rival any nation's may be biased, since he interviewed mostly OSS veterans and possesses no particular credentials to support such a broad judgment. That he may have exaggerated the success of all these operations into the Third Reich is shown by the intelligence on the German National Redoubt. Despite a heavy intelligence effort in this area, which accounted for half the agents lost inside Nazi Germany, the U.S. was wrong on this strategic question of ultimate Nazi intentions.

The lack of identification of sources for facts and statements is a weakness of the book that could easily have been avoided. Gibb McCall in *Flight Most Secret* (London: William Kimber, 1981) questioned Persico's figures on British operations into Germany, while Molden's *Exploding Star* gives another view of British policy on intelligence operations into the Reich, among other things. Note particularly that Persico's treatment of the OSS career and operational work of William J. Casey, the future head of CIA, was the most extensive in any book up to that time. See also the section on overseas targets in the U.S. War Department's *War Report of the OSS* on these OSS operations. The National Intelligence Study Center awarded Persico its book prize for 1978.

Peskett, S. John. STRANGE INTELLIGENCE: FROM DUNKIRK TO NUREMBERG. London: Robert Hale, 1981. 200 pp., index.

Peskett served in the RAF throughout World War II as an air staff intelligence officer. He performed a variety of duties, including examination of captured or shot-down enemy aircraft for technical intelligence, prisoner interrogation, work at Hut 3 of Bletchley Park as an expert on Luftwaffe organization and the nomenclature of German aircraft parts, and propaganda broadcasts by the RAF to the Luftwaffe. The author states he was encouraged to write this book by the air history branch of the British Ministry of Defense. From a strictly parochial and intelligence point of view, the book adds very little to our knowledge of science and technology work in the RAF. It is a light account largely of his travels and nonintelligence experiences during and shortly after the war. Only snippets or very general accounts of his intelligence work are found. The only distinguishing features are that this is perhaps the only work by an air science and technology officer published and that Peskett identifies a few additional figures connected with Hut 3.

Petrov, Vladimir, and Petrov, Evdokia. EMPIRE OF FEAR. London: André Deutsch, 1956. 344 pp., index [New York: Praeger].

In April 1954, the Petrovs, both members of the Soviet MVD, defected to the Australians. Vladimir had been with that organization and its predecessors since 1933, had attained the rank of colonel of Soviet State Security, and was the resident in Australia (the chief of the MVD station). Evdokia, his wife, was a code clerk. The story they tell lies outside the scope of the Royal Commission's inquiries into their revelations, which should be read in conjunction with any further study of their lives and their work in intelligence (see the Australian *Report of the Royal Commission on Espionage, 1955*). The important facts of Soviet intelligence activities in Australia that Vladimir Petrov revealed will be found in the commission's report but are not covered in this book. The Petrovs relate the story of their lives and their careers, as Soviet state security officers and as code clerks. We learn of the workings of Soviet diplomatic and intelligence installations abroad and of security, foreign intelligence, and code work performed. There is a chapter on Burgess and Maclean; it was Petrov's revelations about these two Soviet agents that precipitated a British white paper on their cases, for Petrov made public what he knew of these spies and of their escape to Moscow.

Petrov could have been more forthcoming on the internal organization and functions of a Soviet legal residentura (a Soviet intelligence station abroad) than he was. Evdokia's knowledge of Soviet cryptographic systems, though it is not elaborated upon here, would presumably have been of considerable interest to opposition services due to these systems' intrinsic importance. In the appendix, Petrov points out inaccuracies in Bialoguski's *The Case of Colonel Petrov.* The Royal Commission's report will give a better feel for the political controversy created by Petrov's disclosures, which cast reflections on certain members of the Australian Labor party. So too will Thwaites's *Truth Will Out,* which gives Australian security's view of the Petrovs' defection as well as revealing that *Empire of Fear* was ghost written by Thwaites.

Petrow, Richard. THE BITTER YEARS: THE INVASION AND OCCUPATION OF DENMARK AND NORWAY APRIL 1940–MAY 1945. New York: William Morrow, 1974. 379 pp., bibliog., index.

The intelligence portions of this fall into two categories: the availability and uses of intelligence by various parties prior to the German invasion, and the organizations for intelligence and resistance and their relationships to London during the occupation. Petrow included a number of items on the former subject that help us understand the state of intelligence in 1940, but he cannot be said to have exhausted the research possibilities, since the subject is not the focus of his attention. One has only to read Beesly's *Very Special Intelligence* or Hinsley's *British Intelligence in the Second World War* to see that Petrow was nowhere near being in full possession of the intelligence facts of this period when he wrote this. For the occupation, Petrow researched the period and managed to enlighten on aspects not well known. Among these were disagreements between SOE and the Norwegian Milorg resistance organization on what strategy to pursue as well as friction between SOE and the Norwegian government in exile. There is a chapter on the raid on the heavy-water installation of Norsk Hydro, but this operation has been covered in full by others, such as Gallagher in *Assault in Norway.* As for Denmark, the story of the foresight of the Danish military in creating a shadow intelligence organization to function when the Germans abolished the Danish army is one of the more important intelligence aspects he narrates. He has managed to put the timing of real resistance in both nations in its true time frame and to destroy certain myths that came into being after the war. He missed giving credit to the Norwegians for the intelligence they provided that assisted the X-craft attack on the *Tirpitz* and does not mention the intermediary role of the Norwegians in Stockholm in passing the Swedish intelligence on the *Bismarck*'s departure that led to the ship's destruction. An enormous amount of research went into this book (the acknowledgments and bibliography attest to this), but the intelligence aspects competed for his attention with the nonintelligence; also, lack of knowledge of Ultra and lack of access to full SOE records make this an incomplete, if good, version of the intelligence story. See Thomas's *The Giant Killers* for more specifics on Danish resistance operations and individuals.

Pettee, George S. THE FUTURE OF AMERICAN SECRET INTELLIGENCE. Washington, D.C.: Infantry Journal Press, 1946. 118 pp., index.

During World War II, Pettee was with the intelligence unit of the Foreign Economic Administration as an analyst; he was also in OWI. When this was written, he was on the faculty of Amherst. Kent in *Strategic Intelligence for American World Policy* labeled it a trailbreaker in the literature of strategic intelligence. Pettee was first to write of the experience gained in the late war in producing strategic intelligence, the shortcomings, and the need for U.S. strategic intelligence in the postwar world. He discussed means and steps to be taken to create the necessary intelligence capability. Pettee's perspicacity went far: he recognized intelligence as a special field requiring great competence, the accumulated knowledge of various disciplines and fields, and better governmental organization and saw the need for a central intelligence authority. The revolution in collection capabilities was also identified, as was the need for the proper organization and ways of handling and analyzing the information. Hilsman in *Strategic Intelligence and National Decisions* classified the book as one of the three studies on intelligence that had attempted a serious analysis of the subject; Ransom in *The Intelligence Establishment* called it one of the three groundbreaking treatises on intelligence. Even though it is dated, it is a book of historical value for the role it played in formulating ideas and ultimately the organization of U.S. intelligence in the postwar era.

Philby, Kim. MY SILENT WAR. New York: Grove Press, 1968. 262 pp., no index [London: MacGibbon and Key].

Hugh Trevor-Roper relates that the Soviets offered to withdraw Philby's book on his experience in British intelligence from the English market in return for the Soviet agents, the Krogers (Cohens). Earlier, they offered to withdraw Lonsdale's memoirs, *Spy,* for the same exchange. Philby had become associated with the propaganda agency Novosti's Tenth Section, staffed by KGB men, according to Barron's *KGB;* his activities there, including his compilation of the Lonsdale memoirs, indicate his involvement in Soviet propaganda activities since his flight. They justify Trevor-Roper's description of *My Silent War* as a work of careful and skillful propaganda. It is not, as some would like to believe, mendacious but highly selective, with the purpose of causing mischief. Trevor-Roper was generally accurate both in saying it was designed to embarrass the West and in believing the historical narrative was accurate and the factual account reliable as far as it went. Philby, however, was not entirely honest—Hyde in *The Atom Bomb Spies* indicated that Philby concealed the way Klaus Fuchs, the Soviet atom spy, was actually discovered. That Philby's memory is not infallible even when he uses it to serve his purpose was shown by his 1971 attempt to identify three prominent Lebanese as British spies, which caused Tass to pay judgments in legal suits that followed (see Barron); thus there may be other errors of fact in this book that British reviewers have not pointed out.

One important revelation made by Philby that seems to have been missed by many at the time was the secret of Allied cryptographic successes in World War II, with hints of Ultra. He informs that Abwehr traffic was being broken and read and tells of its importance to SIS's victory over the German service. The account of the Wood material's being forwarded by Allen Dulles from Switzerland and of its being verified by decrypted German diplomatic traffic points to broad cryptologic successes by the Allies; it must be remembered that this account was written in 1968 by a man who could speak from first-hand knowledge.

Philby included some rich details of SIS procedures and on SIS personnel and relationships. According to Pincher's *Inside Story,* this book, despite its obvious propaganda purposes, has too much detail that rings true about the ineffective features of the British intelligence and security services and about their rivalries to be dismissed. For more on Philby's career in British intelligence, his work as a Soviet agent for three decades, and this book, see Trevor-Roper's *The Philby Affair* and Boyle's *The Climate of Treason.* Muggeridge, who served with Philby during World War II, has a few sketches of him in *The Infernal Grove.*

Phillips, David Atlee. THE NIGHT WATCH. New York: Atheneum, 1977. 295 pp., index [London: Robert Hale, 1978].

Twenty-five years in CIA, Phillips attained the position of division chief before retiring in 1975. Almost all his career was in Latin America; he represents an example of the expertise, geographic and functional, that CIA developed. To speak and write in defense of U.S. intelligence, he retired and founded an association of ex-intelligence officers. *The Night Watch* can be said to be a number of things. It is the memoirs of a happy intelligence warrior who enjoyed his craft and took pride in his personal advancement. Second, it is a collection of anecdotes, mostly about CIA, and close-up shots of senior CIA personnel, from directors to directors of operations to officers like Richard Welch and E. Howard Hunt whose names became known for various reasons. Third, it is a careful recounting of major events and operations with which Phillips was somehow involved. A true professional, he tells his story without revealing the "good secrets," to use William Colby's term. Fourth, he gives a flavor of the work he did and of its demands, a sense of the moods and rationales at the time of events, and some retrospective judgments (the Guatemalan, Chilean, and Bay of Pigs operations). Fifth, there are his reactions and replies to attacks against CIA and his profession.

Admiration for Phillips's writing skill was more general than agreement on how much he had said and how thoroughly he had covered his subjects. Phillips's book appeared at the height of attacks on CIA, when only mea culpas would satisfy the extreme critics of intelligence. A close look will show that mixed with the generalities and careful presentation of his story, there are some primary-source nuggets for the intelligence researcher in some areas: the Bay of Pigs operation; the handling of intelligence of Lee Harvey Oswald in Mexico City; the events in 1965–1966 in the Dominican Republic; the operation to prevent Allende from assuming office; some CIA personalities. Howard Hunt in the *National Review* took strong exception to some items about himself.

Piekalkiewicz, Janusz. SECRET AGENTS, SPIES AND SABOTEURS: FAMOUS UNDERCOVER MISSIONS OF WORLD WAR II. New York: William Morrow, 1973. 523 pp., index [Newton Abbot, Eng.: David and Charles].

A best seller when it appeared in Germany in 1969, this illustrated book was developed from a series of documentary films the author produced for German television.

It covers twenty-seven exploits the author and the publisher classify as "undercover," although one (the bombing of the German dams in 1943 by the RAF) is not. The remainder involves samples of intelligence collection, special operations, deception, resistance, and partisan warfare. Piekalkiewicz put together condensed essays on each exploit combining research material, interviews with participants, and a selection of photographs and documents that prove his talent for and experience in effective visual presentation. It is possibly the best book of its type in English, though the expert will find some things that could have been improved. The expert, however, will also recognize that it contains a very valuable essay on the important German agent of the Czechs, A-54 (Paul Thümmel), years before Moravec's account of him in *Master of Spies;* that it has excellent photos and a good essay of the attack on the heavy-water plant Norsk Hydro; that the author was aware in 1969 that all German agents in Britain in 1944 were controlled by the British; and that many photos appear for probably the first time. The essays about which major reservations will be felt are the one dealing with the death of General Sikorski, where the author toys with the conspiracy theory, and that on Operation North Pole, where the view is put forward that the whole thing was a British deception. Other errors are more minor. Gehlen did not command fighting troops in the east; there were not as many Soviet radio transmitters in the Rote Kapelle networks as Piekalkiewicz says; the Rado net in Switzerland did not transmit to Moscow the date of the German invasion of Russia; Von Papen was not assassinated while serving as German ambassador in Turkey; President Roosevelt had no son by the name of Peter.

Pilat, Oliver. THE ATOM SPIES. New York: G. P. Putnam's Sons, 1952. 302 pp., index [London: W. H. Allen].

DIS's *Bibliography* called this the "best account of the Soviet atomic espionage rings operating in the U.S. during the 1940s and the 1950s." Seen from the perspective of over a quarter-century, the book stands up amazingly well, particularly considering its relatively early appearance after the events covered. It is penetrating in its analysis of motives and actions of the main figures and captures the mood of the time. There are facts that Pilat missed; we know of others, such as the Cohens, who were involved with the Rosenbergs. The circumstances of Fuchs's discovery are better known today. Also, recent research on released FBI documents has raised questions about the exact role of Ethel Rosenberg. Pilat frequently fails to indicate in his narrative the source of his information. For example, in five instances in which he describes Ethel's role as an active recruiter of her brother and as the one who copied his intelligence reports, the precise sources of this information are not named. A principal criticism is that the author is not consistent in his estimate of Julius Rosenberg's work as an agent. At one point, he judges him a flop as a spy. Elsewhere he talks of Rosenberg's having channeled a vast amount of military information to the Soviets, including the trigger of an atomic bomb, and says that the network to which he belonged was "too successful for domestic comfort and safety." Pilat was a journalist with the *New York Post.*

Pincher, Chapman. INSIDE STORY: A DOCUMENTARY OF THE PURSUIT OF POWER. London: Sidgwick and Jackson, 1978. 393 pp., index.

Pincher is well known in Britain as a reporter specializing in defense, national security, and intelligence matters. The *New York Times* reviewer described him as a person who sees himself as the guardian of British intelligence. Pincher became better known in the United States and elsewhere in 1981 as the writer of the story alleging that the former head of MI5, Sir Roger Hollis, was a suspected Soviet agent. This is a collection of reminiscences and stories based on his "inside knowledge" of British politics and defense and intelligence matters. The first two hundred pages deal primarily with intelligence and security subjects, and Pincher ranges widely about these. The core of this segment concerns Soviet intelligence activities. There is, however, a short chapter on purported U.S. intelligence operations in Britain. For those interested in this specialty, there are three chapters that touch on deception and disinformation. Pincher has a wide knowledge of the British intelligence and security services and the power structure to which they relate and reveals in a number of instances that he had access to closely held information. But as the chapter on CIA shows, he is prone to scoop up incorrect information on important issues and events. The *New York Times* reviewer spoke of Pincher's tendency to use anonymous sources and gossip but seemed unwilling or unable to judge the accuracy of the book's intelligence portions. Pincher is frank about his relations with British security, and here one finds a unique case of a British journalist's writing of his contacts and consultations with MI5. He also contributes a rare look into another aspect of security: the deliberate leak of sensitive information to the press. His *Their Trade Is Treachery* (below) contains certain charges going beyond allegations here, one of which first appeared in the later paperback edition of this book.

Pincher, Chapman. THEIR TRADE IS TREACHERY. London: Sidgwick and Jackson, 1981. 236 pp., index.

Pincher aimed to give details of the penetration of Whitehall, including the security and intelligence services, by the Soviets. What he revealed created a sensation in Britain and elsewhere. The most serious was the story of how Sir Roger Hollis, ex-chief of MI5, having fallen under suspicion that he was a Soviet agent, was the subject of an official inquiry. There is an avalanche of information about known agents such as Blunt, about others unequivocally named as Soviet penetrations of the British services for the first time, and about those of whom there were grave suspicions. Obviously Pincher, a journalist, had access to sources with highly privileged information on British intelligence and counterintelligence matters, as his sections on Hollis and Tom Driberg show. He is also first in relating little-known details of Blunt's knowledge of the Klatt case, of Soviet radio operators in Britain, of Blunt's recruitments and exposure, and of Soviet attempts at blackmail of certain accredited ambassadors in Moscow. The identities of his sources are, needless to say, never given. How accurate he is on the identities of new agents must await further authoritative disclosures. The reader will spot a number of errors: Pincher is not aware that Rado was not executed by the Soviets; he says Klugmann was with SIS, not SOE; he is wrong about U.S. reconnaissance capabilities at a particular time; he puts Krivitsky in the wrong position; he says Penkovsky forewarned that missiles were to be put in Cuba, which was not the case. He identifies the Soviet agent codenamed Elli as Sir Roger Hollis of MI5; yet Elli had been identified in 1946 as another person. The occasional sorties into higher statecraft and strategy are questionable—an example is the impression that a Russian army under Vlassov was already in being in 1942. Nevertheless, this is important in the literature of counterintelligence and espionage both for opening up for further study cases that some had assumed were exhausted of anything of importance and for containing a wealth of information.

Pinto, Oreste. SPY-CATCHER. London: Werner Laurie, 1952. 170 pp., index [New York: Harper and Bros.].

General Eisenhower supposedly called Pinto "the greatest living expert on security," while another description attached to him was that he was the world's greatest spy catcher. This is a short handbook on military counterintelligence, with interrogation and interrogation techniques as the centerpieces. Between April 1952 and August 1953 it had six printings. Major U.S. and British reviews lauded it as superior, factual, and objective. Since then Pinto's reputation has suffered; among the reasons was what he wrote about the Dutch resistance leader Christiaan Lindemans, known as King Kong. Pinto claimed he helped expose Lindemans as the German agent who betrayed the Allied airborne landing at Arnhem (Operation Market Garden). He even went so far as to call the King Kong case the most important spy case in the history of espionage. Until 1981, the evidence was that Pinto's version of King Kong's knowledge of Market Garden was wrong. According to Giskes in *London Calling North Pole,* King Kong did not betray Arnhem because he was not in a position to do so. In *A Bridge Too Far* (New York: Simon and Schuster, 1974), the author Cornelius Ryan quoted the German General Student to the effect that no one in the German High Command knew of the planned operation. However, Louis de Jong in a 1981 article in *Encounter* reopened the debate. He believed King Kong betrayed the Arnhem operation but did not verify Pinto's account of how Pinto discovered Lindemans to be a German agent. Pinto made another categoric pronouncement that is controversial by today's standards. He believed women were useless as spies or spy catchers. When one thinks of great agents of the war like Marie Fourcade, Lela Karagianni, Christine Granville, Andrée Borrel, and Andrée de Jongh, one must presume that Pinto was not aware of their work. Foot and Langley in *MI 9* mention Pinto as chief of the advance Dutch headquarters who sent Langley a warning about King Kong but offered no proof; they also outline why King Kong could not have betrayed the operation. Pincher's *Inside Story* tells of Pinto's attempts to find the Soviet agents Burgess and Maclean on behalf of a British newspaper and his first conclusion that they were not behind the Iron Curtain. This also detracted from Pinto's reputation, though Pincher had considered him "rather small time" to begin with.

Pohl-Wannenmacher, Helga. RED SPY AT NIGHT: A TRUE STORY OF ESPIONAGE AND SEDUCTION BEHIND THE IRON CURTAIN. London: Leo Cooper, 1978. 176 pp., no index.

The author, a German born in Poland, became a prisoner in Russia and ended up as a captain in the KGB. She defected to the West in West Berlin in 1956 with her son by a Soviet colonel. This purports to be her story, including some six years with the KGB. There are "Perils of Pauline"–like episodes and other features that give it an improbable tone and quality. She says she underwent imprisonment in the Soviet Union, near death from freezing, a marriage to a Soviet doctor who was a bigamist, another marriage to a Soviet colonel, and then recruitment into the KGB. Among her claims is that she was forced to undertake a mission to kill someone in Paris but warned the prospective KGB victim; for this she was not punished but protected. Important names, too, are dropped. She claims to have met Soviet leaders like Serov and Shvernik and the sons of Stalin and Beria. There are odd errors; she refers to the KGB by that name as of 1949 when it was so called only beginning in 1954; she speaks of the NWS when she seems to be referring to the NTS. And her description of CIA methods of operating sounds very implausible. No expert authority is known to have expressed any views of the book.

Popov, Dusko. SPY COUNTERSPY. New York: Grosset and Dunlap, 1974. 339 pp., no index [London: Weidenfeld and Nicolson].

Popov, code-named Tricycle, was a British double agent against the Germans in World War II. Masterman in *The Double-Cross System* first publicized his work and described him as one of the chief figures in the entire double agent system controlled by the XX Committee. With the appearance of Masterman's work, Popov no longer felt constrained in telling his own story, which is an elaboration of what Masterman had to say of him—his contribution to the deception of the Germans and his acquisition of German intelligence requirements and counterintelligence data on them. Among the many incidents and anecdotes associated with him is the famous Pearl Harbor questionnaire given him by the Germans prior to his 1941 visit to the United States. Masterman includes the story in an appendix and acknowledges that his group might have stressed the significance of this occurrence to the Americans. Popov's account fills in *his* details of J. Edgar Hoover's handling of the matter. The chapters on his treatment in the United States could only have been written by someone with intimate experience of Hoover's attitudes. Popov's treatment is reminiscent of Compton Mackenzie's story in *Greek Memories* of the horrified reaction of British authorities in Egypt in World War I to a double agent sent there for deception purposes. The book's main strength is the lessons it gives about case officer–agent relationships. Popov's is a rare first-hand account of double agent operations and deception of the XX Committee from the agent's vantage point. The author's theatrical and sybaritic qualities shine through; Michael Howard in his review in the *Times Literary Supplement* of another book said Popov was one of the great double agents of the war but his autobiography contained "an entertaining quantity of straightforward fiction," which Howard did not pinpoint. Mure in *Master of Deception* discusses the case at length and criticizes London's handling of the Pearl Harbor questionnaire and its general handling of the case, which he believes jeopardized the Overlord deception plan. See also Montagu's *Beyond Top Secret Ultra* for another first-hand view and for comparisons of the versions of the Washington phase. Attention is also called to Popov's claim that there are secrets that he does not reveal. There is, incidentally, no proof that Popov ever met personally with Hoover.

Poretsky, Elisabeth K. OUR OWN PEOPLE: A MEMOIR OF 'IGNACE REISS' AND HIS FRIENDS. Ann Arbor: Univ. of Michigan Press, 1970. 278 pp., index [London: Oxford Univ. Press, 1969].

An important work that contributes to our knowledge of the formative years of Soviet intelligence. In the 1920s and 1930s the Soviet services recruited an international band of intelligence operatives of which Poles, Letts, and Germans were most common. Elisabeth was the widow of one of the important figures of this group, Ignace

Poretsky, known as Ludwick or Ignace Reiss. He was an early revolutionary who worked successively for the Comintern, Soviet army intelligence, and the NKVD; for his services he received the highest Soviet decoration. He broke with the Soviets in 1937 and was murdered shortly thereafter. His widow describes the composition of the Soviet services of the early days, their early development, and their competition. There is a parade of figures who later achieved fame as intelligence operatives or agents: Sorge, the Rados, Krivitsky, and Eisler, to name some. It is her story not only of her husband and herself but of six contemporaries from the same town in Austrian Galicia who became revolutionaries and intelligence agents of the Soviets and who under Stalin all ended up being liquidated or dying under suspicious circumstances. Her descriptions of Moscow in 1936 during the purges and of the purges' effect on those in Soviet intelligence (not to speak of all of Soviet society) are chilling to read. Bitter at Walter Krivitsky because she felt he let her husband down when the latter broke with the Soviets, she has numerous corrections of his version of events and claims contained in *In Stalin's Secret Service.* Massing in *This Deception* credits her with being the one who brought Massing in touch with U.S. authorities after World War II. See also Dallin's *Soviet Espionage* for his comments on the way Ignace handled his break with the Soviets.

Powe, Marc B., and Wilson, Edward E. THE EVOLUTION OF AMERICAN MILITARY INTELLIGENCE. Fort Huachuca, Ariz.: U.S. Army Intelligence Center and School, 1973. 127 pp., bibliog., index.

The authors were instructors at the U.S. Army Intelligence Center and School; the book was designed to be used in the officers' advanced course. Treatment of the subject is both chronological and analytical. The work attempts to evaluate the effectiveness of U.S. military intelligence from the American Revolution up to Vietnam, after a brief look at the history of military intelligence in general. Vietnam is excluded from evaluation since it was too recent; the treatment of military intelligence coverage of that war is confined to a survey of some of the organizational aspects and methods of operating utilized. DIS's *Bibliography* described this study as well researched and valuable for unit instruction; it is a good piece of work, providing a broad-brush treatment, which serves as a general introduction to the subject. The authors do not regard it as a complete record and point out that it was drawn from unclassified sources. Inexplicably, they list five classified studies in their bibliography and refer to two of them in footnotes. There are some tantalizing hints on antisubversion work of military intelligence during the 1930s contained in a reference to a section of a secret study completed in 1961 by Bruce W. Bidwell. Corson's *The Armies of Ignorance* should also be consulted on the early history of U.S. military intelligence under Van Deman and Churchill.

Powers, Francis Gary, with Curt Gentry. OPERATION OVERFLIGHT: THE U-2 SPY PILOT TELLS HIS STORY FOR THE FIRST TIME. New York: Holt, Rinehart and Winston, 1970. 375 pp., no index [London: Hodder and Stoughton].

This is the late Gary Powers's account of his career as a U-2 pilot; his ill-fated flight over the Soviet Union; his capture, interrogation, trial, and imprisonment; and his experiences after his release. A number of items of particular interest stand out: the special U-2 missions flown over the Mediterranean area and the Middle East; collection priorities; his claim not to have been briefed on what to do if forced down in Russia; the relatively short version of his interrogations by the Russians; the failure of CIA to train pilots on how to handle interrogations. As for the broad program of the U-2s, Powers himself stated, "U-2 pilots were denied a broad overview. We caught only glimpses." For some interesting behind-the-scenes views of the Prettyman board, which studied Powers's performance and of disagreements with its findings, see Thomas Powers's *The*

Man Who Kept the Secrets (below). Wise and Ross's *The U-2 Affair* is one of the books devoted to Powers's mission and capture; the authors concluded that Powers was an ordinary man sent on an extraordinary mission.

Powers, Thomas. THE MAN WHO KEPT THE SECRETS: RICHARD HELMS AND THE CIA. New York: Knopf, 1979. 310 pp., bibliog., notes, index [London: Weidenfeld and Nicolson, 1980].

In 1980, the National Intelligence Study Center, which includes many names of former senior U.S. intelligence officers in its membership, presented Powers, a 1971 Pulitzer Prize winner, one of its book awards. The citation called this book "the most comprehensive book of its kind" and one that "will improve understanding of many aspects of the role of intelligence in the U.S. government." At the same time, it did indicate it had "some errors of fact and flaws in interpretation." The book also received a number of favorable reviews in the United States. The *New York Times Book Review* editors selected it as one of the best books of 1979. Intelligence professionals like Walter Pforzheimer note that such reviews were by individuals who were not in the position to know enough of CIA and Helms to make such judgments and who were certainly not professionally competent; consequently, the impression given that this is the flawless book on CIA is an exaggeration. Rather, the experts regard it as the most comprehensive book on the subject, as did the committee that gave it the 1980 award.

Powers made effective use mostly of interviews he had with more than forty former CIA people. He developed a commendable feel and grasp for the matters under investigation; one is particularly advised to read the notes. These often contain more revealing, comprehensive, and perceptive comments or explanations than the main text. Powers, admittedly hostile to CIA at the start, concludes that CIA, much to his surprise, operates under the control of the executive and is not freewheeling. He has captured much of CIA personalities and relationships; he has some good operational comments and reveals some operations or focuses on known ones, such as the WIN deception operation fiasco. There is good writing with some memorable bon mots, such as "War corrupts and secret war corrupts secretly." There are some harsh judgments of CIA's ability to predict a major attack. No earlier book on CIA by an outsider captures so many of its inner moods and secrets. On the other hand, there are errors of fact and flaws in interpretation, not to speak of important omissions or dated facts or judgments. We know now that CIA has been penetrated. The term "mole" was never a vernacular term in use by CIA; Ulmer did not serve in Greece "at the height of the civil war"; the description of the staff composition of CIA divisions is not quite accurate. It is as presumptuous to conclude that William Harvey "provides a good example of the sort of damage a long career in intelligence can do to a man's life" as it would be to presume anything similar of any other profession. There is no foundation for the story of a CIA officer and Lumumba's body, as far as anyone knows. His version of ABC correspondent Sam Jaffe's problems is incomplete or incorrect, in light of later press stories alleging Jaffe's ties with Soviet intelligence. Colonel Kilbourne Johnson was never the DDP; Carmel Offie left CIA before Dulles's appearance and was not removed as a security risk by the latter. Pforzheimer describes Powers's account of the first Marchetti case as badly garbled and calls his references to the deletion of the 168 passages as "the 1972 case" incorrect. His version of the U.S. contact with General Gehlen via OSS and Frank Wisner is wrong. The expression of some views, such as "the history of OSS . . . is marked by a preoccupation with Communism almost as intense as its commitment to victory against Germany," shows a lapse in his judgment and feel. He really is in no position to state that the Soviet agent Burgess was a spy of no importance. Experts regard his speculation on the Polish defector Joseph Swiatlo in connection with Steven's *Op-*

eration Splinter Factor and its thesis as quite wrong. Those familiar with the charges of the CIA analyst Sam Adams (regarding the North Vietnamese order of battle) point to possible errors or lack of perspective in the Powers account.

As for Helms, the book is actually not a biography but rather uses his career, as Powers puts it, as "an ideal pathway through the secret history of thirty years." His attempt to write of the man as a means of writing about the agency runs the risk of oversimplification and tends to jump to generalizations and conclusions. Powers himself stated of Helms that it was "hard for an outsider to judge" Helms's performance. It would appear that the same would apply to the man, whose "inherent decency," in Pforzheimer's words, was missed by the author, in the opinion of those who knew Helms best. Powers does not mention the spontaneous outpouring of respect and affection by CIA personnel on the day Helms departed from his office, an emotion-packed incident. Nevertheless Powers has written a book on CIA that can be classified as outstanding, especially for an intelligence outsider. See Pforzheimer's review in the spring 1980 issue of *The Washington Quarterly*.

Pratt, Fletcher. SECRET AND URGENT: THE STORY OF CODES AND CIPHERS. Indianapolis: Bobbs-Merrill, 1939. 249 pp., notes, index [London: Robert Hale].

David Kahn cites this as the work that got him interested in cryptology. He points out that it was the only book-length effort at a history of cryptology before his own *The Codebreakers*. Pratt attempted to trace the development of what he called "secret writing" in an episodic manner and by giving attention mainly to cases of successful decipherment. He realized that there were gaps in his account since the most interesting successes of that sort were probably kept secret, and he concluded that generalizations about cryptography on any but a hypothetical basis were impossible. The work is now dated, and a number of facts of the World War I era given were actually not as he pictured them. Oddly enough, he made only slight reference to Yardley on the last page without any further comment on his work. Kahn, in his preface to *The Codebreakers*, judged Pratt's work as one of special pleading that every event in history turned on cryptography and said this fault was accompanied by others. He cited errors, omissions, wrong generalizations, missing evidence, and an "unfortunate predilection for inverting facts" as weakening this as a history of cryptology.

Price, Alfred. INSTRUMENTS OF DARKNESS. London: William Kimber, 1967. 250 pp., index [1978 edition published in Britain by MacDonald and Jane's].

Price was a serving officer with the RAF Bomber Command when he wrote this. He had access to historical records and papers such as those of Lord Cherwell and to British scientists like R. V. Jones. In addition, he interviewed former RAF and GAF (German Air Force) personnel. However, he cites no authority for his material, and he does not include a bibliography. This is the story of the British electronic warfare (EW) effort; the Americans, either as scientists or as fighting allies, do not intrude. The work might be considered a predecessor to R. V. Jones's account of the same subject in *The Wizard War.* Price was in no position to discuss Ultra as an important factor and cannot match Jones's first-hand knowledge and access. Price's treatment of the RAF's 100 Group (the organization created to undertake EW missions of jamming, meaconing, intrusion, spoofing, and deception) is less full than Streetly's in *Confound and Destroy.* There is a good chapter on EW deception connected with the Overlord operation to invade France in 1944. Price's work still stands as one of the best on the subject. The increased importance of EW in scientific intelligence and scientific warfare makes its history a necessary subject for intelligence historians, and *Instruments of Darkness* is a basic work on its first large-scale, strategic employment in World War II. Clayton's *The Enemy is Listening* gives a view from the RAF's intercept service.

R

Rado, Sandor. CODENAME DORA. London: Abelard, 1977. 298 pp., no index.

Rado was a principal agent of Soviet military intelligence who operated in Switzerland until the disruption of his network during World War II. His name is associated with the Lucy ring, the Rote Kapelle, and the Swiss end of the Soviet military intelligence organization, the Rote Drei. He disappeared and was presumed liquidated by Stalin after the war. Dallin in *Soviet Espionage* quotes a former agent of the net who criticized Rado as one who would lose his nerve at critical moments and lacking the makings of a good spy. This was probably Foote, who in his *Handbook for Spies* described Rado as a scared, broken, and hunted man who went into hiding with his wife after the breakup of his network by the Swiss. Dallin also gives some details of Rado's lifestyle and poor security practices such as his affair with an agent; this must refer to his radio operator "Rosie," who Foote says was the means the Germans used to penetrate the network. Rado's account of his work as head of the Soviet network in Switzerland is full of holes and marked by its propagandistic qualities. Rado, in disgrace with his service after the war and writing this from a Communist country, could not be expected to be candid. His attacks on previous works on the subject of the Swiss net, however, regardless of their ideological and propagandistic motives, help correct the impression given by some of them that the "war was won in Switzerland" by the network. For a more reliable evaluation of Rado's work and that of his group, see CIA's *The Rote Kapelle.*

Ransom, Harry Howe. THE INTELLIGENCE ESTABLISHMENT. Cambridge, Mass: Harvard Univ. Press, 1970. 273 pp., bibliog., notes, index.

In 1958 appeared the author's *Central Intelligence and National Security* based on material Ransom had prepared for a Harvard seminar. *The Intelligence Establishment* is a revised, updated, and enlarged version of the original.

Ransom made it clear he did not pretend to write a complete or inside story of the U.S. central intelligence system; his purpose was to describe and analyze the U.S. intelligence community, which he felt was needed but required tight control by policymakers and attention by students of government and politics. The book is mostly concerned with CIA; the FBI gets very little attention. Ransom was a pioneer in academia's study of U.S. intelligence, and his writings were among those of serious academics raising the question of the role of intelligence in a constitutional society and the problems associated with its growth and control. He likewise perceived the relative neglect of intelligence by U.S. scholars and teaching institutions. Though Ransom had no experience in intelligence work or access to classified information (except, apparently, to one classified Air Force study he quotes from in his notes), he displays a good grasp of intelligence techniques, organization, and functions. The presentation is fair and unemotional; what views he expresses on organization, control, cover, and secrecy are set forth calmly. Much of the descriptive detail is now dated, and Ransom displays little knowledge or interest in counterintelligence. These faults and the errors to be found should not deflect attention from the central questions he raises of intelligence's role in a democratic society. It is interesting to note that while Blackstock and Schaf's bibliography, *Intelligence, Espionage, Counterespionage and Covert Operations,* called it "the best single work on the subject," DIS's *Bibliography* found it "less accurate and credible" than the 1958 version and said that it contained (unspecified) mistakes in its treatment of clandestine and technological operations.

Reilly, Pepita. BRITAIN'S MASTER SPY: THE ADVENTURES OF SIDNEY REILLY. New York: Harper and Bros. 1933. 288 pp., index [London: Mathews and Marrot, 1931. *The Adventures of Sidney Reilly, Britain's Master Spy*].

Pepita Reilly, the third wife of Sidney Reilly, was assisted in this work by an unnamed journalist. The first third is presented as Sidney's narrative of his role in the so-called Lockhart Conspiracy, his attempt to overthrow the Bolsheviks shortly after they took power. Pepita states that considerations of public policy compelled her to suppress certain facts in his story. The remainder is her narrative and is mainly devoted to her attempts to discover whether Sidney was alive and what had happened to him. Here we have another view of the work of the Trust, the Bolshevik operation intended to attract and destroy opponents of the regime by masquerading as an attempt to overthrow it. A striking passage in Sidney's account is his conviction that the Cheka could only be countered by an organization as secret, mysterious, ferocious, and inhuman as itself. The German experience in later years under the Nazis suggests this theory would have been a failure in practice. According to Chester, Fay, and Young in *The Zinoviev Letter,* Mrs. Reilly was often chronologically inexplicit, and the "political transaction" she was not at liberty to divulge was suggestive of the Zinoviev affair. Robin Bruce Lockhart, who wrote *Ace of Spies,* the biography of Sidney, is quoted in Deacon's *A History of the British Secret Service* as believing that Sidney was responsible for the Zinoviev Letter. For other information on the Lockhart Conspiracy and a slightly different version of how Reilly made contact with the Letts who were to overthrow Lenin and his followers, see Hill's *Go Spy the Land.* Pepita's book was withdrawn by the publisher after legal action for damages by Reilly's legal wife. Reilly's life and fate remained as elusive after publication as they were prior to it.

Reit, Seymour. MASQUERADE: THE AMAZING CAMOUFLAGE DECEPTIONS OF WORLD WAR II. New York: Hawthorn Books, 1978. 224 pp., notes, index [London: Robert Hale, 1979].

The subtitle of *Masquerade* is technically misleading: camouflage is only one form of or means used in deception. Reit, involved in camouflage and photo intelligence in World War II, discusses other means used to deceive the adversary in that war: double agents, electronic and radio deception, planting of information (the Mincemeat operation prior to the invasion of Sicily), impersonation, and concealment. The author is best when writing of matters strictly defined as camouflage or concealment. Although the publisher claims that many of the episodes are presented for the first time, only a few of them actually are new. Among the chapters with newer material are those dealing with early attitudes in the United States and Britain toward camouflage and measures taken during the Battle of Britain that resulted in decoy targets drawing off German bombers. Much of what the author writes is a recounting of well-known (to the student of the subject) incidents of deception, cover, and concealment in the war. This is best described as a popular account, one that is only an introduction to the measures and means designed to deceive an adversary (which the Russians encompass in their word *maskirovka*) and their application in World War II. A companion work that stresses visual deception as practiced by the British in the war is Hartcup's *Camouflage.*

Richardson, Cordell. URANIUM TRAIL EAST. London: Bachman and Turner, 1977. 142 pp., index.

This purports to be the factual story of Paul Sautter, an English civilian scientist, and of his involvement in the search for uranium supplies in Europe, especially in Germany, at the end of World War II. According to the author, a scientist and a graduate of Cambridge, it was based partly on Sautter's diary and writings and partly on the disclosures of Sautter to Richardson, whom Sautter considered a close friend and to whom he confided. The purpose of the hunt for uranium stocks was dual: to get them to the United States and at the same time to keep them out of Soviet hands. Sautter's organization is not exactly identified, and the author admits that some names were altered. Understandably, this evasiveness makes confirmation of Richardson's story all the more difficult. We know there were a number of special Allied scientific and technical intelligence groups on the hunt, Alsos, the T-Forces under SHAEF, CIOS, TIIC, and the 30 Assault Unit among them. Apart from that, Richardson's account is so riveted on sex, with virtually every episode including a description of some sexual encounter, that the intelligence and scientific denial purposes of Sautter's story become subordinate aspects or plots. The effect is to deprive the book of any semblance of seriousness and to force one to conclude that in the absence of any confirmation to show the author's account of Sautter's scientific search is accurate and reliable, this book should be ignored. There is no mention of Sautter in Pash's *The Alsos Mission* or in Goudsmit's *Alsos.*

Rintelen, Franz von Kleist. THE DARK INVADER: WARTIME REMINISCENCES OF A GERMAN NAVAL INTELLIGENCE OFFICER. London: Lovat, Dickson, 1933. 288 pp., no index [New York: Macmillan].

Admiral William James in *The Eyes of the Navy* wrote that one cannot separate fact from fiction in Rintelen's book because he embroidered his story with statements that were untrue. James provided two examples: mention of Rintelen's supposed meeting with the British naval attaché in the United States which never transpired, and the remark that an article appeared in the British press on the Zimmermann Telegram, again incorrect. With time, however, scholars have been able to separate much of the fiction from fact in Rintelen's account of his four-month sabotage mission to the United States in 1915 and contacts with General Victoriano Huerta of Mexico. We know from works such as Tuchman's *The Zimmermann Telegram* that his account of his dealings with Huerta is both incomplete and slanted, just as we know from Voska and Irwin's *Spy and Counterspy* of the counterintelligence work against him. Tuchman says that Rintelen's account of his meeting with Huerta makes him appear "a replica of Baron Munchausen." The outlines of his sabotage effort are known as well as his tradecraft, which he unwittingly pictures as amateurish at times. So too is the bad blood between him and Von Papen that colors his views of the latter. James says that it was from *The Dark Invader* that the public learned for the first time "a lot about Hall's activities." Revelations include an early and inexact account of the transmission, interception, and breaking of the Zimmermann Telegram. James also reminds us that Rintelen disclosed that the Germans were deciphering U.S. diplomatic traffic to Berlin while the two countries were at peace.

Robbins, Christopher. AIR AMERICA. New York: Putnam's Sons, 1979. 312 pp., bibliog., index [London: Macmillan. *The Invisible Air Force: The Story of the CIA's Secret Airlines*].

"Air America" as used by Robbins as the generic name for all CIA air activities under the web of "dozens of CIA air lines." The book is based on talks with many pilots connected with CIA's air activities and with the "bureaucrats" of CIA air support and on other writings, many of which were authored by critics of that agency (e.g., those by Marks, Prouty, McCoy, and Wise and Ross). There are errors, both large and small. One of the most significant is the author's emphatic insistence that CIA operations in Laos were hidden from Congress. He fails to note CIA sometimes contracted for services with private carriers and thus had the same absence of full control as any contracting party. His account of the full ramifications of the CIA airline CAT should be checked against the Church committee's report. One must presume that the absence of access to official records likewise resulted in a number of minor errors. Robbins respected the pilots involved and dedicated the book to them but does not like the "bureaucrats," who he says were dishonest with him. In the chapter on drug transportation, he confuses the reader. He writes a full chapter on how dope allegedly was or may have been transported by "Air America" planes, then quotes the findings of the Church committee exonerating CIA air proprietaries of this suspicion of illicit drug traffic; but he still ends the chapter with the opinion that CIA has a "Jekyll and Hyde attitude" toward narcotics without explaining how this follows. For serious students of intelligence, the book has the additional drawback of being written in a style appropriate for a series in an adventure magazine, with much detail on individual missions and on the lifestyles of pilots and their families. See Marchetti and Marks (*The CIA and the Cult of Intelligence*) on air proprietaries and air support of CIA.

Roosevelt, Kermit. COUNTERCOUP: THE STRUGGLE FOR THE CONTROL OF IRAN. New York: McGraw-Hill, 1979. 210 pp., index.

Roosevelt, a veteran of OSS, was the head of Operation Ajax, the combined Anglo-American intelligence plan to overthrow Premier Mossadegh of Iran in 1953. This is his story of the operation from its inception to its execution and his analysis of its meaning and use as a model for future similar efforts. His conclusions on the latter point, correct as was later shown, are those he says he reached at the time; he provides no up-to-date postmortem of the events. Roosevelt is frank on a number of events and has not hesitated to show warts, identified as such. An instance is his story of the superficial study of the Iran operation given it by top U.S. leaders before it was approved (which some experts question). Roosevelt was confronted with the problem of how to account for the British role; he initially resolved it by naming the British-owned Anglo-Iranian Oil Company (AIOC) as the instigator of the coup idea and partner of CIA. This solution proved as unacceptable to AIOC's successor British Petroleum as it was transparent; as a result, the first printing was withdrawn and corrected, with British intelligence properly substituted for AIOC in the new edition. A resume of these events can be found in Ambrose's *Ike's Spies*.

There have been many versions of the Iranian coup published over the years, and Roosevelt's first-hand account was expected to be as authoritative as any that one would be likely to get in the immediate future. This does not appear to be the case. Like many subjective accounts long after the fact, it presents statements that can be questioned. Some pertinent details are missing; the author does, after all, write without benefit of records and years after the events. Attention should be paid to some of the tradecraft employed and to the relatively high U.S. profile. There are few good tenets in these points worthy of adoption. Cottam believed luck and the excesses of the Communists were the extraordinary elements in the success of the coup. He missed, however, Roosevelt's willingness to take risks and to persevere as crucial factors in the outcome. Consequently, this book is necessary for an understanding of the covert and clandestine history of Ajax. Only Roosevelt could provide the intimate feel for this factor. But its shortcomings lessen its usefulness as a fully reliable reference.

Rositzke, Harry. THE CIA'S SECRET OPERATIONS: ESPIONAGE, COUNTERESPIONAGE AND COVERT ACTION. Pleasantville, N.Y.: Reader's Digest Press, 1977. 273 pp., index.

An OSS veteran, Rositzke served twenty-five years in CIA in a variety of assignments as senior officer. Three of these composed the bulk of his CIA career—Soviet operations, India, and operations against communist parties. He goes to great pains to emphasize that this is not a history of CIA's operations but is meant to redress the balance of the record on CIA. Without access to official records after retirement in 1970, he had to rely on recall. To protect sources and method, he alters the location of many operations, conceals identities, and leaves dates vague. The focus is on his major professional interest: secret operations against the Soviet Union, its intelligence services, and key communist parties. There is virtually nothing on his experiences in India; however, he does inform us that each of the wars between India and Pakistan was forecast by agents. There are segments on various types of operations of CIA against the Soviets and their allies. Much of what he writes of techniques has been said before, but he has blended in examples, some of which are new. Thus, he is perhaps the first expert Western official to verify the compromise of the Berlin Tunnel by the Soviet agent George Blake; he may be one of the first to discuss the WIN disaster in Poland. His descriptions of cross-border operations are rare for their intimate knowledge and because of his intelligence rank. His experience of secret operations and reflection give him a special perspective. He unequivocally calls the Soviet services "the most competent and aggressive secret service in the world." He bases this judgment on the Soviet operational record but does not discuss Soviet analytical or estimative performance. There are also questionable facts and opinions. Rositzke cannot be certain that Philby was the KGB's most productive postwar agent in the West; he is perhaps too categoric on the timing of Blake's recruitment; there are gaps in his knowledge of the Abel case. Research indicates that Truman himself wrote the 1963 article criticizing CIA. Rositzke's treatment of certain matters, like the Iran coup, shows that he is less familiar with them. His recommendations for the future include warnings against politicizing the intelligence function, appointing a counterintelligence ombudsman, and concentrating exclusively on strategic intelligence targets and the frank pronouncement that the heart of the U.S. intelligence problem is the large size of the intelligence bureaucracy. The selective picture he provides of CIA and its secret operations is as candid.

Roskill, Stephen W. THE SECRET CAPTURE. London: Collins, 1959. 156 pp., index.

The story of the capture by the British of the German submarine U-110 in May 1941 is handled by this skillful naval historian on two levels. One is the tactics of the battle in which the U-110 was captured, which are thoroughly described. The other is the intelligence meaning of the capture. Here Roskill is more indirect as to the exact nature of the haul and how the intelligence war was affected. He speaks of the capture as coming at a critical time in the war and says that it was "perhaps the most important and far-reaching success achieved by our anti-submarine forces during the whole course of the last war"; however, he does not explain the cryptanalytic importance of the capture and its relationship to Enigma. He was writing long before the release of the secret of Ultra and its role in the war; the book was first cleared by the Admiralty. Since Roskill could not be more specific at the time on the cryptologic aspects, *The Secret Capture* cannot be called the full story of the U-110 affair, as McLachlan said in *Room 39.* It does contain, on the other hand, one of the earliest hints in print of the Allied cryptanalytic successes. The contribution the material aboard the U-110 made to the breaking of German naval ciphers is discussed in a number of later and sometimes conflicting accounts. Among these are Lewin's *Ultra Goes to War,* Beesly's *Very Special Intelligence,* Calvocoressi's *Top Secret Ultra,* and Hinsley's *British Intelligence in the Second World War.* Note that Roskill mentions the capture of three Italian submarines during the war and the valuable intelligence, documents, and equipment obtained from them, again without elaboration.

Rowan, Richard Wilmer. THE STORY OF SECRET SERVICE. New York: Literary Guild of America, 1937. 670 pp., notes, no index [London: Miles, 1938. New York: Hawthorn, 1967. ***Secret Service: Thirty-Three Centuries of Espionage.*** **London: Kimber, 1969].**

A great work of scholarship, probably the best history of the subject in English at the time of its appearance, and one that should still be used as a lead-in for the study of intelligence history. Allen Dulles in the foreword to the 1967 edition said it was "the best single account of intelligence down to the time he wrote it in 1937 and it remains so today."

Despite the book's value, the style and Rowan's tendency to moralize may be trying at times. A number of faults can now be detected more clearly and errors identified. About a third of the work was devoted to World War I, and the selection of cases and allocation of attention to this war were not the best. As an example, pages are devoted to a German espionage school of no real or historical consequence while the famous British Admiral Hall is mentioned only once. The American Revolution receives only as much space as Mata Hari. Rowan is uncritical of many American Civil War spy stories, and there are now questions about the truth of the earlier accounts of the escapades of the Chevalier d'Eon, to whom he devotes a chapter. There is a strange duality in his attitude toward spies for a scholar of the subject that is exemplified best in his description of Thomas Beach (Henri le Caron). There is a tendency to exaggerate the impact or effect of an agent, such as the German Wassmuss in Persia in World War I, and to make premature judgments ("T. E. Lawrence's fame is as secure as it is well deserved"). He misses the significance of the Soviet intelligence and security apparatus up to that time, the Cheka of Dzerzhinsky getting only 2 paragraphs in 670 pages of text. Minor errors of fact are expected in a work of this scope and size. Compared to the monumental results achieved, however, all the foregoing flaws are small.

Rowan delved into the literature of espionage and into works of history to retell many of the important events of secret service. He points out that the Bolshevik Trust operation of the 1920s had its predecessor over a hundred years earlier in France when the French service used the ploy against the French royalists and the British. We learn of the Mongol use of agents to spread false information, Napoleon's use of deception, the identity of Captain Mansfield Cumming as "C" of the British secret service; we are reminded of the work of John Thurloe and not allowed to forget the name of Dr. John Wallis, the great cryptanalyst. There are some select quotes, such as "Cardinal Richelieu never permitted his fidelity to the church to retard his genius for being a Frenchman." Rowan identifies James Rivington, the famous New York bookseller and Tory, as one of General Washington's spies. Although an index is sorely missed in this 1937 edition, there are valuable notes on each chapter that often contain facts and perceptive observations not in the main text. The 1967 edition was updated by Robert G. Deindorfer after Rowan's death in 1964. This edition eliminated a few chapters of the original, combined some segments (such as chapters on World War I censors), revised others, and added sixteen more to cover World War II and the postwar period. The reader is advised to stick to the 1937 edition, for the later one adds little of value, contains errors, and makes a questionable choice of material. It comes nowhere near to giving the flavor or being truly illustrative of the later war, although some cases (e.g., those of Sorge and Christine Granville and the story of Magic) are fairly well presented.

S

Sansom, A. W. I SPIED SPIES. London: George Harrap, 1965. 271 pp., no index.

Sansom was head of British Field Security in Cairo in World War II. After it, he stayed on in Cairo as security officer of the British embassy when Donald Maclean served there (one spy he did not catch). The cases he is best in describing are those in which he had a direct investigative role: the Eppler (Kondor) case and Anwar Sadat's connection with it, the murder of Lord Moyne, the revolt of Greek troops in Egypt in 1944 and its suppression. Sansom reveals the use of the captured Kondor code for deception of the Germans. The many stories of security problems would make the book good as a training manual for such officers (not excluding problems of poor security of senior personnel); his work against Kondor is instructive for counterintelligence purposes up to a point. Sansom spells out the operational mistakes and the unprofessionalism of the German agents but makes no mention of intelligence available to the British that the Kondor mission was on its way (see Lewin's and Mure's comments in the notations for Eppler's *Operation Condor*). His other stories of the intelligence war in the Middle East, though interesting, are not authoritative accounts of someone privy to the innermost secrets of that struggle. His segments on Donald Maclean are from personal knowledge, and Maclean's activities outside the embassy are vividly described.

Sawatsky, John. MEN IN THE SHADOWS: THE RCMP SECURITY SERVICE. Garden City, N.Y.: Doubleday, 1980. 295 pp., index [Toronto: Doubleday Canada].

Sawatsky, a reporter with a Canadian newspaper, filled a void in the literature of intelligence and security by writing this. As he points out, very little had been written about the Royal Canadian Mounted Police's Security Service, and not a single book published was devoted exclusively to its work and problems. He provides a look at its history, the manner in which it related to the RCMP as a whole, and the way it functions. The internal conceptual, bureaucratic, and operational tugs-of-war are explained and described; the struggle of the security service to free itself from the paramilitary and police framework and mentality of the RCMP is a major part of its organizational history. We learn of the service's attempt to meet post–World War II challenges, particularly those stemming from the threat of Soviet espionage. Additional insights are provided into the manner in which Canadian authorities handled the Gouzenko case; later and more current problems of handling the defector are also to be found.

Sawatsky claims the RCMP's single contribution to this work was an interview with the RCMP historian, who provided material on historical background. He was denied access to official documents and as a result resorted to personal sources in the Canadian intelligence community. He was quite successful in this. The book contains considerable information from informed sources, and in one instance Sawatsky did not use sensitive information he uncovered. A number of features require caution from the reader. The author himself calls to our attention the "inadequacies of journalism," and occasionally he inserts his views and biases. An example is his virtually equating illegal acts by a security or intelligence service with U.S. services. His attributing to CIA a number of instances of pressure or influence on the security service are either wrong or unsubstantiated. Sawatsky might have allocated more space to some matters and less to others. Only a short paragraph is devoted to the tantalizing case of Gerda Musinger, for instance, while a full chapter discusses RCMP unionization. Conversely, segments like the one on the "watchers" are of adequate length and well done. The report of the Canadian McDonald Commission, which investigated wrongdoings of the service, was released too late for purposes of comparison (*Commission of Inquiry Concerning Certain Activities of the Royal Canadian Mounted Police* [Ottawa: Canadian Govt. Publishing Center, August 1981]).

Schellenberg, Walter. THE LABYRINTH: MEMOIRS OF WALTER SCHELLENBERG. New York: Harper and Bros., 1956. 423 pp., index [London: André Deutsch. *The Schellenberg Memoirs*].

Schellenberg died in 1952; what was published in this book is not a translation of the complete manuscript he left. Alan Bulloch, who wrote the introduction, cautioned that other omissions and additions may have been made between his death and the work's appearance in a publisher's office. Bulloch additionally cautions that it would be wise not to accept Schellenberg as a trustworthy witness of events unless there is corroboration. Others believe Schellenberg wrote a self-serving account of his life and of the intelligence and security case he treats; he is least reliable where he was not a participant or is not writing from first-hand knowledge.

It is wise to heed these warnings. One would have thought the man who headed the SD foreign intelligence department and later, with the removal of Admiral Canaris, was head of all German espionage would be reliable on the Scapa Flow matter and about the existence of the supposed German agent there; but we know that what he wrote of this and of Albert Oertel is false. Kahn in *Hitler's Spies* contests his claim that the material provided by the agent Cicero in Turkey helped break part of the British diplomatic code. And this, it must be kept in mind, was an SD operation. Bernard Newman, who studied the case of Lieutenant Colonel Sosnowski, stated that Schellenberg's record of it was "hopelessly inaccurate and in parts fantastic." There are, moreover, significant omissions and gaps. He has nothing to say of the important Czech penetration into German intelligence, Paul Thümmel, or A-54 as he was known to the Allies; there is no mention of how the Germans "burned" Colonel Sosnowski with his own service, as we learn from reading Leverkuehn's *German Military Intelligence.* There is less than a page on the agent Klatt—whom the Germans considered their most important agent of the eastern front, whose work Schellenberg called "masterly," and whose reports were "of special significance" and dealing with "large scale strategic plans as well as details of troop movements." He has nothing to say of German espionage in the United Kingdom during the war. Perhaps that is just as well, for he probably would have gotten it all wrong. On the other hand, his accounts of operations such as the Venlo incident in which he personally took part and his description, from personal knowledge, of Nazi intelligence and security personnel and of the bureaucratic jungle and jockeying for position within the Nazi regime and its services are accepted as useful additions to our knowledge. However, experts caution that the author's biases should be kept in mind even when he discusses the inner workings of the Nazi secret services. The chapter on Sorge provides one possible explanation of how Sorge managed to get to Japan as a journalist despite his communist past.

Schulze-Holthus, Bernard. DAYBREAK IN IRAN: A STORY OF THE GERMAN INTELLIGENCE SERVICE. London: Staples Press, 1954. 319 pp., no index.

The author served in Iran as the Abwehr man in Tabriz. This is the story of his experiences in that country and of his liaison with the pro-German Qashqai tribe during World War II. Schulze-Holthus was no Wassmuss. The role he played, as he describes it, was the passive one of prestige representative to the tribe and its khans and as a threat to the Allied position there. He provided no arms to the Qashqais and was not responsible for any sabotage. The Qashqais finally surrendered him to the British in 1944, an act that he felt was a bitter blow from erstwhile friends. There is nothing noteworthy in this book from an intelligence point of view except perhaps the lesson of the precariousness of relationships with groups whose support cannot be tangibly maintained. We do not learn from him of Abwehr and SD activities in Iran that played some part in provoking the invasion of the country by the British and the Soviets. See Roosevelt's *Countercoup* for the remarks of the Qashqai khans on their abandonment of the Germans and the Abwehr.

Schwarzwalder, John. WE CAUGHT SPIES. New York: Duell, Sloan and Pearce, 1946. 296 pp., no index.

The author was in the U.S. Army Counterintelligence Corps (CIC) in World War II, attaining the rank of major. He served in North Africa, Italy, France, Belgium, and finally Germany. Written right after the end of that war, the book is still a rarity in that it is by a CIC man about CIC operations. Schwarzwalder was motivated to write of the type of work done by CIC, from travel controls to interrogations, because he felt CIC men were not adequately appreciated despite their contribution to victory. He writes with fierce pride in CIC, its techniques, and its work but calls espionage a "distasteful trade." Another indication of his perspective is that he sees counterintelligence as the art of catching spies and denying the enemy information, a limited view of a subtle and more complicated intelligence activity. The author has a tendency to make sweeping opinions and judgments based on his own experience and on what he was told. A number of these and some facts he gives have not held up with time; his chapter entitled "Women Are Lousy Spies" does not contain proof that Schwarzwalder had the requisite experience, knowledge, and data to make such a broad pronouncement. Despite these shortcomings, this is still valuable as some record of CIC work. Note, too, that Schwarzwalder gives one of the first hints of the enormous success of Allied deception in the war. He concludes that the United States needs effective peacetime intelligence capabilities.

Scotland, A. P. THE LONDON CAGE. London: Evans Brothers, 1957. 195 pp., index.

Scotland headed the British prisoner-of-war interrogation system in World War II. Later, he was chief of the War Crimes Investigative Unit, which was tasked with pretrial interrogations of accused and production of evidence against those to be tried. Half this volume is on his latter work. For those interested in interrogating methods used to acquire intelligence from prisoners of war and hoping to learn details of what intelligence was acquired, this will prove disappointing; Scotland does not delve into these matters. The fact that he had experience in interrogation in World War I makes the disappointment greater. As if that were not enough, Scotland states he spent fifty years in intelligence but covers only the periods 1904–1915, 1915–1918, 1940–1945, and the war crimes trials years. He informs that he was recruited into British intelligence in 1904 to report on the Germans in Southwest Africa; during World War I he served in general headquarters as an intelligence expert on Germans and the German army. About the interwar years he says nothing directly but implies he was not officially involved in intelligence work. Scotland does clarify one matter, the subject of all sorts of apocryphal stories for years—the myth of the British intelligence penetration into the German General Staff in World War II. He explains that the story resulted from the disclosure at the war crimes trials that he had once served in the German army. Whitehall sent orders that he was not to comment on the resultant publicity and stories that he had been an agent in the German staff. Scotland actually served in the German army in Africa between 1904 and 1907; Whitehall's instruction to "let the story rip" was apparently designed to let British intelligence benefit from the myth.

Seale, Patrick, and McConville, Maureen. THE HILTON ASSIGNMENT. New York: Praeger, 1973. 235 pp., no index [London: Temple Smith].

"Hilton" refers to the jail near Tripoli in Libya in which opponents of Muammar Qaddafi, the Libyan officer who seized power in 1969, were imprisoned. In 1970–1971, say the authors, there was a plot afoot to attack the prison, free the opponents of the regime, and arm them as a means of overthrowing Qaddafi. It was to be accomplished by a hired group of mercenaries, recruited by the private British involved and largely French. Behind it all was a Libyan royalist refugee. Seale and McConville recount details of the plot, its planning, and its foiling by the secret services of a number of Western countries. It was truly, as they say, a "story of international intrigue." They were the first to tell the tale, and their very knowledge and intimacy with much that was not in the public domain at the time indicate that they had special access to those who were involved in the plot and to some of the secret services that worked to defeat it. Their sources are not exactly identified, needless to say. The authors are weak on some matters, such as when they discuss the "omniscience" of CIA and the exact motive of the United States for opposing the plot. Their perpetuation of the myth of General Gehlen is also a mark against their effort to bring to light this little-known incident in intelligence history.

Seale, Patrick, and McConville, Maureen. PHILBY: THE LONG ROAD TO MOSCOW. New York: Simon and Schuster, 1973. 277 pp., index [London: Hamish Hamilton].

The two journalists spent six years in researching their subject. In addition, they had the advantage of Seale's knowledge of Philby and access to details on Philby's life in Moscow from Philby's American wife. The focus is largely on Philby the man, his life and his motives. What he accomplished as a Soviet agent and also as a British intelligence officer is less their concern, probably because these are the questions hardest to answer. Although the reviewer of the *Times Literary Supplement* thought this the best book on the subject, others saw little in it to excite the experts. One will find mention of the British reading of Soviet traffic between New York and Moscow as the means by which Klaus Fuchs was identified as a Soviet agent. But the authors have Anthony Blunt all wrong (they write that his commitment to Marxism for the sake of Burgess was not real). They make assumptions on how Donald Maclean was warned of his impending interrogation, and they provide no evidence for the belief, most probably incorrect, that Philby was somehow the unwilling captive of Soviet intelligence after his initial recruitment. In fact, it was items such as the last that prompted some peoples' criticism that Seale and McConville went so far in trying to be impartial that they ended up coming close to sympathy for Philby. In light of later publicity given to the case of Sir Roger Hollis as a suspect Soviet agent while he was with MI5, the authors' brief speculation on his possible role in the raising of the Philby matter in Parliament assumes new interest. Boyle's *The Climate of Treason* supersedes this on many vital matters connected with Philby and his Cambridge friends who became Soviet agents, as does Pincher's *Their Trade is Treachery.*

Sellers, Charles Coleman. PATIENCE WRIGHT: AMERICAN ARTIST AND SPY IN GEORGE III'S LONDON. Middletown, Conn.: Wesleyan Univ. Press, 1976. 226 pp., notes, index.

Patience Wright was an American artist in wax sculpture who resided in London. This biography is concerned mostly with her social and artistic life. There is very little on any espionage she performed on behalf of the American revolutionary cause. As a matter of fact, the author has culled nothing from archives or from any other sources on what Patience Wright did as an agent. Patience did not disguise her sympathies, and as a result her effectiveness as a clandestine operative must have suffered. In one instance she is shown to have transmitted wrong information that the British obviously wished to pass on, raising the question of how frequently she may have unwittingly served in this way. The style of the writing is not felicitous. J. C. Long in an article on Wright in the *New Jersey Historical Society Proceedings* speculates that the British may have used her to pass deceptive material and concludes that the information she gave to Franklin had no effect on U.S. military and naval decisions.

Sergueiev, Lily. SECRET SERVICE RENDERED. London: William Kimber, 1968. 223 pp., no index.

Sergueiev or Sergeyev was the double agent of the Allies code-named Treasure whom Masterman in *The Double-Cross System* characterized as "intelligent but temperamental'' and ''troublesome'' but one who ''turned out not to belie her name.'' She was also in that category of double agents to be used for strategic deception of the Germans in conjunction with the invasion of France in 1944. Lily was the niece of the White Russian General de Miller who disappeared from Paris in 1937, presumably abducted by Soviet agents. Her personal memoir was originally published in French but was expanded in the English version. Her plan, which she fulfilled, was to volunteer to spy for the Germans as a means of working against them. According to her account, the lack of imagination and the poor tradecraft of the Abwehr contacts were balanced by her judgment of her British handlers and her rocky relations with them. There is no hiding her temperamental nature and her absorption in personal problems. Her detailed discussions of her personal relationships leave little room for anything concerning the most important aspect of her double agent role—the intelligence passed by the Allies up to D-Day designed to mislead the Germans. Her petulance contrasts mightily with her original motivation and with her role in and contribution to the deception of the Germans. Her version is instructive on the problems an intelligence service can encounter with agents that are difficult to deal with and handle. Farago in *The Game of the Foxes* has some additional facts on her but incorrectly calls her the single most important cog in the Allied deception plan for Normandy. The latest interesting item on Lily appeared in Deacon's *The British Connection,* which alleged that Sergueiev was a Soviet agent introduced into that service by her uncle (sic) Nicolai V. Skoblin. Deacon continued that she went to England under Soviet instructions. Deacon also claimed that Norman Pearson, the late Yale professor and OSS veteran (he wrote the foreword to the U.S. edition of Masterman's book), told him there were reports after the war that Lily had given the Soviets the most detailed plans of the U.S.-Britain operations in the closing stages of the war. Whatever the truth of her ultimate allegiance, it is unlikely she had access to Allied plans.

Seth, Ronald. THE ART OF SPYING. London: Peter Owen, 1957. 180 pp., index. [New York: Philosophical Library].

Herein are recounted five stories of modern-day spies; four are from World War II and one is from World War I. Two are women: Christine Granville and Ann-Marie Walters. The men are Isaac Trebitsch Lincoln, Alexander Foote, and Richard Sorge. Seth believed each of these illustrated one aspect of spying: Foote the inconspicuous, Sorge the flamboyant, Lincoln the international, Granville the bold lone wolf, and Walters the pedestrian team player.

The author acknowledges his indebtedness to Foote's and Walter's own books for his accounts of them and to two other books on Sorge. Consequently, he is prone to repeat the errors of his sources. For Foote, these are not inconsequential. In relying on Willoughby's *Sorge: Soviet Master Spy* he did not have the best book on Sorge, which appeared in 1966 (Deakin and Storry's *The Case of Richard Sorge*), but his version is acceptable. Without any full account of Lincoln and Granville, he relied on articles and books that mentioned them. He raises a point regarding Granville's saving the lives of Xan Fielding and Francis Cammaerts of SOE plus that of an OSS captain—that Fielding's is only one version of what happened, and the correct one is not known. Seth confuses Soviet legal and illegal networks when he declares that the Soviet resident always resides in a country other than the one that he is targeted against and "normally is not a Russian." Seth has been prolific in writing on intelligence and espionage over the years.

Seth, Ronald. ENCYCLOPEDIA OF ESPIONAGE. London: New English Library, 1972, 1975. 683 pp., no index [Garden City, N.Y.: Doubleday].

Seth wished to cover as wide a spectrum of espionage history as possible. This work encompasses names of agents, organizations, networks, prominent leaders of intelligence services, and cases, and the object is to make available to "espiomanes" a handy reference and to give the general reader information of interest. The expert will not be very happy with the results. First, the selection seems to have been determined by the availability of material rather than the intrinsic importance of each item. Seth devotes almost as much space to himself as to the Red Orchestra; the entry on a World War I agent by the name of McKenna is twice as large as that on Admiral Canaris and almost four times the size of the one on OSS. Allen Dulles is mentioned only in passing under the heading "CIA." Admiral Hall warrants less than half a page. There are strange omissions: no T. E. Lawrence, no Captain George Hill, and, above all, no Sidney Reilly, though Sir Paul Dukes is properly listed and recognized. The Cheka is inexcusably not included and only mentioned under Dzerzhinsky. The space given over to the obscure and unimportant is wasteful, and the long passages sometimes read as if they were rewrites of other writings. Errors are inevitable in a work of such scope. To cite a few: he makes mistakes about Wassmuss. He does not know the exact denouement of the Judith Coplon case or Rado's fate. He credits Gehlen with being responsible for all anti-Soviet espionage operations as head of Foreign Armies East and with obtaining the 1956 speech of Khrushchev denouncing Stalin; Colonel Nicolai he names director of the Abwehr. He seems to be unaware of the questions authorities raised about the Chevalier d'Eon and makes odd errors about CIA's organization, considering all that had been written about it. To his credit, Seth includes items such as that on Montgalliard or has some useful accounts (Gouzenko, Blake, Sorge, Lonsdale). The bibliographic references are of limited value and miss some works that would better serve the reader. An index is badly needed because of the peculiar system of subject categories—one searches to find the KGB, listed under "Russian Intelligence Organization," while the GRU warrants its own subject listing. The *Library Journal* review also found much to criticize in Seth's work, describing it as abounding in errors, poorly prepared, needing editing, and "cluttered with inane and trivial material."

Seth, Ronald. SECRET SERVANTS: A HISTORY OF JAPANESE ESPIONAGE. Farrar, Straus and Cudahy, 1957. 275 pp., bibliog., no index [London: Gollancz].

There are few books on Japanese intelligence and espionage despite the events and wars in which that country was involved in the last hundred years and the capture of some Japanese archives in 1945. Seth's book in no way fills the need—the DIS *Bibliography* is correct when it notes that *Secret Servants* is not particularly valuable or accurate. Seth has written what he calls a history of Japanese espionage based on Foreign Office material and other documents and on previous books on the subject without once indicating a source in the text or identifying the specific Japanese documents he has drawn from. The results are unacceptable to researchers, who cannot assess many of his statements and conclusions without knowing the documentary or other sources and support. One is constantly alerted to the book's poor quality by its failure to indicate sources and by excessive claims and errors. Colonel Nicolai, the German chief of military intelligence in World War I, is pictured as the man who was in contact with the Japanese to arrange intelligence cooperation in the 1930s and the man "who was later to become director of German military intelligence." Sorge is said to have advised Moscow that Japanese were to attack Pearl Harbor on 6 December 1941. He did no such thing—he only advised the Soviets in early October that it was safe to assume that war between the United States and Japan would start that month or the next. Seth calls the Japanese admiral in the 1904 war Tojo instead of Togo. He speaks of the fantastic Japanese system of espionage whose vastness in Manchuria and Russia, for illustration, made the purported forty thousand agents of the German Stieber in France in 1870 "pale into insignificance"—claims that are as unsupported as they are incredible. The amateurishness of some of the cases he describes should have alerted him, one would have thought, to the possibility that the Japanese were not as highly proficient as he makes them out to be.

It is only when he quotes from the newspaper accounts and trial papers on such espionage cases as those of the Americans Thompson and Farnsworth and the German Kühn family that we have something resembling the facts. As for the rest, Seth can be said to distort the reality of Japanese intelligence judging from what was learned of it after World War II unless he can better document his case. For the Pearl Harbor attack, the reader is refered to Wohlstetter's *Pearl Harbor,* which tells in clear terms the results of postwar interrogations of Japanese. These show them consistently playing down the role of foreign agents in the intelligence provided them for the attack.

Shackley, Theodore. THE THIRD OPTION: AN AMERICAN VIEW OF COUNTERINSURGENCY OPERATIONS. New York: Reader's Digest Press–McGraw-Hill, 1981. 168 pp., bibliog., index.

Ted Shackley rose to be the deputy chief of CIA's Clandestine Services. He was considered by many to be a possible future chief of that service and possibly of CIA itself. Among the other important positions he held before his retirement were those of chief of station, Laos and Saigon, South Vietnam. In this book, he discusses some of the concerns he and other foreign affairs specialists have about what the United States should do to meet the foreign policy challenges of the 1980s and how the United States can project its power abroad. The coming decade he foresees as one of irregular warfare used by the adversaries of the United States to threaten the balance of power. To counter this threat requires political warfare, covert action, and counterinsurgency; this last he calls the third option. The book concentrates on insurgency and counterinsurgency. Four current insurgencies are examined, and lessons from past conflicts are analyzed. Shackley, who spent a number of years in Vietnam, does not tap this conflict for many lessons as one would have expected him to do. The concepts and recommendations he outlines he believes "have been field-tested in the unforgiving school of two decades of practical experience." The work is unmistakably that of a man who has studied the problems as well as having faced them. There are some harsh words for the CIA stewardship of Admiral Stansfield Turner, some recommendations for restructuring the U.S. intelligence community, and a call for more emphasis on human collection activities to balance the technical. Some will question his precise calculations of what is needed to combat particular insurgencies and to train a new cadre of U.S. guerrilla warfare and counterinsurgency experts or his placing the blame only on Admiral Turner when others might similarly be accused of poor judgment. There is also insufficient discussion of the problems and difficulties involved once a nation is committed in a counterinsurgency effort: this seems essential so shortly after the Vietnam experience and U.S. wariness about the costs.

Shulman, David. AN ANNOTATED BIBLIOGRAPHY OF CRYPTOGRAPHY. New York: Garland, 1976. 325 pp., index.

This represents twenty-five years of effort on the part of Shulman, a cryptanalyst, member of the American Cryptogram Association, and contributor to various publications on the subject. He also coauthored the *Glossary of Cryptography* (1961). The *Annotated Bibliography* includes books, articles, manuscripts, pamphlets, and even advertising pamphlets. Its six sections are a chronological list of books and articles for the years 1518–1976; a chronological list of items relating indirectly to cryptography; a chronological list of manuscripts; an index of authors and translators; a chronological list of patents; and a list of books in various foreign languages. Shulman designed this for libraries, students of cryptography, and book collectors. His comments are for the benefit of students of ciphers who would wish to know if a book is of any value; he did not read all the titles, and many are in languages he does not know. He was thorough and assiduous in compiling titles, and when he feels strongly about a work, he does not hesitate to express his opinion—he calls one author an ignoramus. His evaluations are mostly technical; when he ventures to comment on a book on intelligence in the broad sense, he is not on familiar ground. Students of cryptography will probably wish the author had commented on more works rather than withholding comment to allow the reader to form his own judgment or because Shulman believed too many criticisms would be "pretentious, captious or boring." His technical comments occasionally fail to discuss the consequences of some cryptologic effort. For instance, Yardley's *The American Black Chamber* is brushed off from a cryptanalytical point of view, while no mention is made of the consequences abroad of its publication, especially in Japan.

Sigl, Rupert. IN THE CLAWS OF THE KGB: MEMOIRS OF A DOUBLE AGENT. Philadelphia: Dorrance, 1978. 247 pp., no index.

Sigl, a German, worked for the Soviet KGB for seventeen years until his defection to the Americans in 1969. He performed various duties as recruiter, case officer, and did general support work. This purports to be his story. The first half concerns his recruitment and training. This is the less interesting part of the book; his explanation that he was forced to work for the KGB is not that convincingly presented while details of his training in Russia are minute in all matters except the most pertinent—the tradecraft he was taught. The second half is a great improvement. Sigl provides information of some of the operations in which he was involved for the KGB and names some names. He is quite good on Soviet spotting and recruiting techniques and on Soviet/East German cooperation in these. He admits, however, that the concrete cases he divulged were only examples, given in brief, and that much had been left out. This is the case. Intelligence experts still regard this as a useful model of Soviet recruitment and use of agents and of how they can be converted from one function (CI) to another (illegal support).

Sihanouk, Prince Norodom, as related to Wilfred Burchett. MY WAR WITH CIA: THE MEMOIRS OF PRINCE NORODOM SIHANOUK. New York: Pantheon Books, 1972. 272 pp., no index [London: Penguin Books, 1974].

Prince Sihanouk, the former Cambodian leader, attempts to prove the "unceasing and determined intervention of the U.S. in the internal affairs of my country and particularly the role of the Central Intelligence Agency." The prince's known variability and his political interests at the time of the appearance of this book alone are reasons for caution as to his reliability on U.S. intelligence. When combined with the political biases of the Australian journalist Burchett, one-time resident of Moscow and consistent supporter of anti-U.S. policies, the results are predictable and unreliable.

Silber, Jules C. THE INVISIBLE WEAPONS. London: Hutchinson, 1932. 288 pp., no index.

Silber worked in British censorship in London and Liverpool throughout World War I. German-born, he was brought up in South Africa and lived in the United States. He was a self-recruited German agent who was never caught. His story tells how he passed secrets he learned to the Germans, working alone. The chapter entitled "The Terrrible Net" is interesting in that it describes the British censorship organization and methods; there are also other glimpses of that organization elsewhere in the book. Silber claims he learned many vital secrets; the problem is their verification. To date, no one, it seems, has researched these claims fully: advance knowledge of the Zeebrugge raid, of British foreknowledge of the Casement landing in Ireland, of German naval movements three days before the great naval battle of Jutland, and of Austrian peace feelers to the Allies. Silber contends he got word to Germany on the Q-boats and about the British tank in time to affect the situation. He also forwarded the Germans the British "Suspect List." An impressive and heady roll of accomplishments, any one of which would more than earn an agent's keep. But Silber's most spectacular claim is that he learned of the Russian salvaging of the German naval code book at the start of the war and its transfer to the British, facts that he passed on to the Germans. There is no independent confirmation for this or for any of the other accomplishments. Authors who have discussed Silber, such as Rowan or Seth, rely on his version and do not cite any German sources; as a matter of fact, Seth's write-up of Silber in his *Encyclopedia of Espionage* seemingly conflicts with Silber in stating that Silber refused to inform the Germans of which of the German safe addresses the British knew for fear of compromising himself. If Silber's account were accurate, he would have had to have been the most successful agent in that war.

Sillitoe, Percy. CLOAK WITHOUT DAGGER. London: Cassell, 1955. 200 pp., index [New York: Abelard-Schuman].

Most of this autobiography covers the author's long police career in the British colonies and in the United Kingdom. Only at the end is there anything dealing with Sir Percy's seven years as head of MI5, from 1946 to 1953. Little is said of his experience in the latter post; but this is not his fault. Cockerill in his biography *Sir Percy Sillitoe* explained that the Home Office gutted Sillitoe's first draft of his work, removing anything of any interest. The result is this bland account of his MI5 stewardship covering a period of dramatic events such as the Burgess and Maclean cases, postwar espionage (Sillitoe took over MI5 the day Allan Nunn May was charged), and the efforts to deal with communist infiltration into sensitive positions. Masterman in his autobiography *On the Chariot Wheel* told of the criticism Sillitoe was subjected to for publishing his memoirs. The consternation in the British establishment, let it be said, would have been greater had he included his strong and instinctive distrust of Kim Philby at a time when many thought otherwise.

Slater, Leonard. THE PLEDGE. New York: Simon and Schuster, 1970. 337 pp., index.

In anticipation of the British withdrawal from Palestine after World War II and of a war that would determine whether a Jewish state would be created, a large underground organization was created in the United States and elsewhere to procure arms and ship them to the Jews in Palestine. This is the story of that network, mainly in the United States and composed mostly of Jews, by a U.S. journalist who spent three years of investigative reporting on the subject. It also tells of the volunteers who went to fight in Palestine. Slater bases his account primarily on interviews with those involved in the smuggling of arms in violation of U.S. embargo laws; those interviewed, including the future mayor of Jerusalem Teddy Kollek, who played a key role in the United States, are named. *The Pledge* is an eye opener on a subject not often revealed—the formation and the work in one country of a well-financed, dedicated organization ultimately under the direction of foreign nationals supporting the national aspirations of these foreign people in technical violation of their own country's laws. The well-documented account of the underground exploits of this organized effort must be read, according to Leon Uris, to understand later Israeli feats such as the dash of the French gunboats from Cherbourg to Israel. Slater does not delve deeply into the questions of official U.S. knowledge of all this at the time and policy toward it. There may be a hint in the short episode of J. Edgar Hoover's being informed by the organization itself of the violation of U.S. embargo laws. Slater's work has opened up a subject for further research. A rare reference to specific U.S. intelligence reporting of illegal shipments of arms from U.S. bases to Palestine is contained in Thorpe's *East Wind Rain.*

Smith, Bradley F., and Agarossi, Elena. OPERATION SUNRISE: THE SECRET SURRENDER. New York: Basic Books, 1979. 192 pp., bibliog., notes, index [London: André Deutsch].

Sunrise was the covert effort to arrange the surrender of the Axis forces in Italy. Smith, a teacher of history and author of previous works on Himmler and the Nuremberg trials, and Agarossi, also a history teacher, have written a scholarly history of the surrender negotiations and the military and diplomatic context within which they were held. The authors were able to draw on previously classified documents and were the first historians given access to the Dulles papers. Agarossi wrote two chapters and portions of two others dealing with the Italian setting, Moscow's reactions to the negotiations, German changes of position, and the final negotiations at Caserta. There is a new perspective, the first since Dulles's *The Secret Surrender,* on the motives, the way negotiations were conducted, and the logic of it all. They support few, if any, of the contentions of the revisionist historians. They also view Dulles and his role in a new manner; he is not made to appear as perceptive or as shrewd as was once thought. They show Dulles as a man obsessed with the techniques of covert action, lacking the ability to see the political consequences of his acts. In this they go too far at times, as when they suggest that Dulles felt he needed a great coup, which Sunrise promised to provide, because he had accomplished nothing with OSS in Europe after three-and-a-half years. Thus, they speculate on his motives and will be challenged severely on their belief that Dulles both accomplished nothing with OSS and *knew* it. Similarly, Smith and Agarossi weaken the impact of their scholarly approach when they try to tie in the postwar actions of Dulles with events and experiences supposedly stemming from Sunrise. Nevertheless, they probe in a way Dulles in his book did not the practical, diplomatic, and other consequences and costs of the negotiations.

Smith, Joseph Burkholder. PORTRAIT OF A COLD WARRIOR. New York: Putnam's Sons, 1976. 436 pp., index.

"Little Joe," as he was known in CIA, served as an officer of that agency from 1950 until he resigned in 1973. He saw duty in a number of countries in the Far East and Latin America. He has produced a book on CIA operations as seen from the perspective of the case officer that gives the reader the feel and smell of operations that only an insider and veteran can impart. There are many operations and agents disclosed: covert operations involving propaganda, the influencing of elections, involvement in coups, the recruitment of journalists, the countering of Soviet and communist activities. Smith packs the book with details, indicating either amazing recall or the keeping of private notes over the years. Though he divulges secrets, he does not sympathize with the likes of Philip Agee; in fact, he remarks on "the treachery of Agee and his friends." In his view, CIA is needed, but a leaner, less bureaucratic CIA under greater Congressional control. So, too, does he see the need for some covert activities. Smith fails to clarify adequately his motives for publishing this autobiography, which the *New York Times* review felt contained a distastefully self-pitying quality. If he had explained himself, the reader would have been in a better position to judge the objectivity of his opinions. Those most familiar with his career thought he was accurate on the general outlines of the operations he describes; there was disagreement with the nuances and a feeling that he magnified his own role in certain instances.

Smith, Myron J., Jr. THE SECRET WARS: A GUIDE TO SOURCES IN ENGLISH. VOL. 1. INTELLIGENCE, PROPAGANDA AND PSYCHOLOGICAL WARFARE, RESISTANCE MOVEMENTS AND SECRET OPERATIONS, 1939–1945. War/Peace Bibliography Series, no. 12. Santa Barbara, Calif.: ABC-Clio, 1980. 222 pp., index.

Each issue in this series was designed to provide a comprehensive "working" bibliography rather than a definitive one on a relatively narrow theme, to quote the series' editor. Smith has compiled one of the most complete and useful references available to researchers and scholars, and used in conjunction with other bibliographies such as the DIS's *Bibliography of Intelligence Literature,* Blackstock and Schaf's *Intelligence, Espionage, Counterespionage and*

Covert Operations, and William R. Harris's *Intelligence and National Security,* it will direct the inquirer to the vast bulk of English-language books and many of the articles. Despite the claim of the series editor, however, this could have been still more comprehensive, even considering the workmanlike job already done in compiling more than two thousand citations. For instance, important books or books on significant individuals are missing—to name two, McLachlan's *Room 39* and Barker's work on Sidney Cotton, *Aviator Extraordinary.* There will also be some difference of opinion on Smith's selection of categories for certain works and his inclusion of all propaganda as one category in the secret war. Since there are virtually no annotations, it is the few errors in categorization that indicate absence of familiarity with the contents of certain works. Maskelyne's *Magic—Top Secret* is incorrectly put in the category of books on cryptography; Agar's *Baltic Episode* concerns post–World War I; the books listed in the section on personalities of the secret wars include those of Judith Listowel and Bernard Newman, as though these authors were themselves participants; Chester Wilmot's *The Struggle for Europe* most certainly belongs in the chapter on selected military campaigns rather than that on secret operations. Delmer's *The Counterfeit Spy* is not about his own war experiences but rather on the double agent Garbo. There are some mistakes in the "Selected Chronology" at the start of the book. The British did not learn of the upcoming German air raid on Coventry until the last moment; Lucy did not warn Moscow of the impending German invasion of Russia; Tricycle's purpose in arriving in New York was not exactly as described; the Gorgopotamos bridge in Greece was attacked by more than ELAS guerrillas in 1942; the role of decrypts in the sinking of the *Bismarck* as presented by Winterbotham and repeated here has been contested or expanded on in newer and better-informed works such as Beesly's and Calvocoressi's. Typographical errors appear to be responsible for the misspelling of Walter Schellenberg's name, as well as that of André Brissaud.

Smith, R. Harris. OSS: THE SECRET HISTORY OF AMERICA'S FIRST CENTRAL INTELLIGENCE AGENCY. Berkeley and Los Angeles: Univ. of California Press, 1972. 383 pp., bibliog., notes, index.

There was a mixed reception for Smith's book when it first appeared. Those critical of it cited such things as its pretentious subtitle for a book that was written without access to the classified OSS archives, its erroneous picture of the atmosphere of OSS operations in certain parts of the world, its many errors, its omissions, its particular political slant, its superficial treatment of some of the OSS operations, its image of the OSS as uncontrolled, and its tone. The last chapter was regarded as a political appendix containing debatable opinions of CIA's political makeup and preferences. There are grounds for these criticisms, but Smith wrote this before the classified material on OSS was released (including the OSS histories) and before other material became available. Inadequate in light of our present knowledge, it is still used as a reference because of its many merits. It was once the best single overall source on OSS. Smith improved the general quality of works on OSS and moved away from the postwar pattern of melodramatic accounts of derring-do; he read the material that was available and incorporated the results of interviews with some two hundred OSS and State Department veterans; he brought to light many matters not generally known and dealt with his subject in a broad way as well as bringing out interesting details. He tries to put events in the political and military context of the times, and the intrigues and disagreements in the political and bureaucratic arenas are strikingly drawn. With the publication of the OSS histories and works on specific aspects of OSS operations, the researcher will be in a better position to ascertain what portions of Smith's work can best be relied on. Predictably, too, its status as a virtually authoritative source on OSS will be diminished. The bibliography was at the time of publication one of the most complete of source material on OSS. The DIS's *Bibliography* found it to be the most complete story of the OSS to that date but advised that it be read with caution because of errors and some biases of the author. Note that *OSS* contained one of the earliest, if brief, revelations of operations of OSS into the German Reich.

Smith, Thomas Bell. THE ESSENTIAL CIA. Privately published, 1975. 204 pp., no index.

The author was in CIA between the years 1952 and 1963. His expertise was that of a Soviet documents specialist in the technical services section of the Clandestine Services. The book was written to illustrate the kinds of work CIA performs, as seen by a working-level insider. Attention is mainly given to the Clandestine Services, and Smith's purpose was to counter what he regarded as a distorted image of CIA and its work. The results are mixed, with the better aspects dominating. Smith's world in CIA was that of Soviet operations and more specifically technical support of such. His first-hand knowledge comes through very well; as does his feel for and knowledge of other sections of the Clandestine Services. His overall perspective is limited, however, and some judgments concerning events after he left the service do not have the same quality and touch. Even those who believe the book overdrawn will appreciate his witticism, "The bedroom is the soft underbelly of security." Smith feared the consequences of the criticisms of CIA because of the direction they were taking. The book was submitted to CIA for prepublication review.

Smith, Truman. AIR INTELLIGENCE ACTIVITIES: OFFICE OF THE MILITARY ATTACHÉ, AMERICAN EMBASSY, BERLIN, GERMANY: AUGUST 1935–APRIL 1939. New Haven, Conn.: Yale Univ. Library Holdings, 1954–1956. 158 pp., no index.

Colonel Smith was the U.S. military attaché in Berlin for the years covered in this report, prepared in 1953 at the request of army intelligence. The latter was interested in the history of Colonel Charles Lindbergh's connection with Smith's office in those prewar years; thus its additional title "With Special Reference to the Services of Colonel Charles A. Lindbergh." Smith clarifies he was the inspiration for the idea of using the American hero "as a sort of additional air assistant" to get entrée into the German Luftwaffe because the American hero had contacts and intelligence not available to regular attachés. He describes Lindbergh's trip to Germany, the intelligence he acquired, and the role he played in the preparation of a formal intelligence report to Washington in 1937. Further, Lindbergh's efforts to alert the U.S. authorities to the challenge posed by the growing German air force are recounted. Colonel Smith's assessment is that Lindbergh's intelligence and the reports were important in making accurate estimates of German air power. He never considers, however, the possibility that the Germans were using Lindbergh's visits for their own purposes. General Hans von Grieffenberg in his 1950 report to the U.S. War Department's Historical Division, *Deception and Cover,* tells of the Luftwaffe's prewar deception program designed to exaggerate its strength. Lindbergh's reports of German air strength to political leaders in Western Europe were believed to have affected their decisions and unwittingly served German purposes. Smith does provide a valuable account of nonclandestine collection by attaché systems before the war—the U.S. attaché's office in Germany had not a cent for espionage. Those experienced in intelligence collection and reporting will have a feeling of déjà vu when they read his account of how an important report sat in U.S. Army Air Force files unread by those who should have known of it. His report on Lindbergh was given to Yale University, which made it available to the general public in 1978. Four pages were changed in the released version for reasons of national security. Farago's *The Game of the Foxes* has further information on the Smith-Lindbergh tie and on Smith's activities on his return to Washington.

Snepp, Frank. DECENT INTERVAL: AN INSIDER'S ACCOUNT OF SAIGON'S INDECENT END; TOLD BY THE CIA'S CHIEF STRATEGY ANALYST IN VIETNAM. New York: Random House, 1977. 580 pp., index [London: Allen Lane, 1980].

A legal landmark in the history of works on intelligence. The U.S. judicial findings against Snepp for publishing this account of events in Vietnam without prior review by CIA and their implication for future works by former U.S. intelligence officers are matters for separate comment. Legal aspects have tended to distract attention from the contents of the work itself. This is partially due to CIA's legal strategy not to take action against Snepp because of his divulging of classified information; if CIA had done so, such violations would have been identified.

Snepp discusses much more than the performance of his service in Vietnam; the nonintelligence segments of the book are by far the principal ones. The author's Saigon position, interests, and outlook and his originating from the nonclandestine, analytical side of CIA are elements that went into his broader perspective of events. As to the performance of U.S. intelligence in Vietnam and particularly CIA, he has produced a well-written, detailed, largely eyewitness account that is also controversial. The picture he draws of the performance of the leaders of the CIA station in Vietnam is dismal, and his allegations on their competence, objectivity, and judgment are serious. These allegations include such things as being opinionated and inflexible, misreading enemy intentions, being easy targets for Soviet bloc and North Vietnamese deception, tailoring intelligence and intelligence appreciations to serve policy of the moment, cold-bloodedly abandoning agents and friends, and bungling the evacuation plan. Snepp says his own experiences in Vietnam are his primary references; his recollections are buttressed by interviews, a briefing notebook of the last two years of the war, congressional hearings, published works, and a personal diary. Intelligence events and personalities are drawn in sharp detail. Snepp is correct when he writes that enemy intentions were often misread and that the Soviets and North Vietnamese succeeded in deceiving the CIA leadership in Saigon at the late stages of the war. The other questions on the performance of that agency and the entire intelligence community remain to be studied to see how accurate Snepp's picture is.

Critics of Snepp's account, in the meanwhile, make the following points: Snepp's version of events leading to the book's publication is incomplete and not convincing. The fact that he kept a diary, contrary to regulations, indicates he may have had more than a future novel in mind. His portrayal of Thomas Polgar as virtually a villain is regarded as unfair. He is said to have exaggerated his own importance and his role in certain activities. For example, his critics contest some of his claimed operational work. They also contest certain other versions he has given. Then there are errors difficult to understand, such as certain purported personality conflicts. He does not make allowances for the improvisation that is inevitable under any evacuation plan. There is a serious analytical flaw, in the opinion of the *Economist* reviewer, in his asking the reader to take on faith that his way of preparing for the evacuation would have produced better results rather than the earlier panic. These criticisms or corrections still leave much of Snepp's story of CIA in Vietnam intact, though it must be remembered that this is one man's view and range of disclosure—even the author does not claim it is a definitive history. Though Snepp reveals certain operations and operational methods and capabilities, what he includes would hardly constitute a full history of CIA intelligence activities in that war.

Snow, John Howard. THE CASE OF TYLER KENT. New York and Chicago: Domestic and Foreign Affairs and Citizens Press, 1946. 59 pp., no index.

In 1940, the British arrested and tried Tyler Kent for violations of their Official Secrets Act after the U.S. dismissed him from his position of code clerk in the U.S. embassy. Kent was discovered to have passed telegrams from the embassy files to a pro-Axis group. This interesting case is mentioned in a number of works, including Kahn's *The Codebreakers* and Farago's *The Game of the Foxes.* No full treatment has ever been accorded it; and Snow's work does not alter this. It is a rambling, incoherent, and disconnected political tract that adds nothing relevant to our knowledge. The author is not concerned with providing any new facts; rather, he seems to call for a reinvestigation to determine the contents of the cables Kent copied. The implication given, and at times the allegation made, is that the Roosevelt administration had something to hide about its intentions on the war in progress. The only coherent segment is the reprint of the official 1944 State Department release on the case.

Stafford, David. BRITAIN AND EUROPEAN RESISTANCE, 1940–1945: A SURVEY OF THE SPECIAL OPERATIONS EXECUTIVE, WITH DOCUMENTS. London: Macmillan and Oxford: St. Anthony's, 1980. 259 pp., bibliog., notes, index [Toronto and Buffalo: Univ. of Toronto Press].

The reason for this, another book on SOE, is "to provide a general overview of the activities of SOE" in Europe and to try to ascertain how SOE and its activities related to British strategic and diplomatic objectives. Stafford contends his is the first general survey of SOE policy in Europe that tries to put SOE in context in "a general and provisional way." Stafford used previous writings on SOE and on British policy. He had no access to official SOE records, but this was partially compensated for by his use of "raw material" in Public Record Office documents (including SOE material contained in cabinet, Foreign Office, and Chiefs of Staff papers) and the recollections of some veterans. Stafford's work is commendable and requires close study. He defends SOE against most old charges and confronts the question of whether SOE was only a military organization or more—the instrument for political control of the resistance and of British policy to contain communism.

As much as he can, he tries to support his positions and his facts with some documentary citation or other source. He is well aware of the shortcomings of the sources available to him to tackle this task; only more access to official records will satisfy experts more fully on SOE's role in British policy and on certain issues and activities and events, e.g., the tug-of-war in Greece, the Rumanian operation, and the conduct of SOE in Cairo. Not all are ready to find SOE as blameless on some matters as Stafford does until the full record is available; but Stafford has set good standards for other surveys of this kind. There are also his contributions of interesting facts previously not well known—the 1940 agreement with the Jewish Agency by British intelligence for cooperation in underground activities, the dropping of Soviet agents into Western Europe via Allied planes, the near abolition of SOE-Cairo. M.R.D. Foot, in his 1981 review in *Journal of Strategic Studies,* calls attention to the Chiefs of Staff directive to SOE published herein. Auty and Clogg's *British Policy Towards Wartime Resistance* and Barker's *British Policy in South-East Europe in the Second World War* are two pertinent companions for this survey, as are the works of Foot, Davidson, Amery, Sweet-Escott, Howarth, and others.

Starr, Chester G. POLITICAL INTELLIGENCE IN CLASSICAL GREECE. Leiden, Holland: E. J. Brill, 1974. 48 pp., no index.

The author, a professor of history, declares it is his aim to show that problems of political intelligence really did exist in ancient Greece—as if there were any doubt that the supremely political Greeks, involved in shifting alliances and relations among the city-states and in wars among themselves and with non-Greeks, were concerned with political intelligence. Starr compiled examples of political and military intelligence from classical history and writings and copiously documented his research. We are given examples of intelligence collection by spies, deserters, and traitors and reports of ambassadors, merchants, and "aristocrats" with their intercity connections. Starr deals with the handling and evaluation of such information as was culled from the historical record. A most useful compilation, not only for scholars interested in intelligence. Starr reminds us of Euripides's words: "States whose policy is dark and cautious have their sight darkened by their carefulness."

Stead, Philip John. SECOND BUREAU. London: Evans Bros., 1959. 202 pp., index.

This effort to clarify the role of the French Secret Service of the Armies of the Armistice and of North Africa during World War II was written by a British writer who specialized in French subjects. Stead relied on French-language accounts and French sources, especially those of Colonel Paul Paillole, who made his files available. There is a strong bias in favor of the regular French intelligence of the armed forces, which continued to work against the Germans throughout the war, even under Vichy. Some experts felt the author's reliance on sources whose reputations were professionally at stake inevitably affected his conclusions and caused him to favor the military intelligence professionals against the "amateurs" under Jacques Soustelle. There is much of interest; comparatively little on French intelligence has been written in or translated into English. References to intelligence being sent by the French service to London by radio as early as September 1940 must refer principally to the communications intelligence being supplied by Bertrand's section; this and other references must be about this valuable source, although French work against German ciphers and Bertrand are not mentioned. See Bertrand's *Enigma*. Much will interest the counterintelligence specialist, especially because Stead regards the CI accomplishments of the French services as their primary success after France fell. The organizational buff will find much on the French services' structure to keep him happy if at times confused. Stead provides some interesting though brief looks into French positive and counterintelligence operations against the Germans and Italians before the war as well. For those studying the security of World War II Allied invasion plans, the claim of French counterespionage in Vichy that it knew for some days before the invasion of North Africa at what points and on what dates the Allied would land is worth investigating; another item to be researched is the contention that from 1936 on the German network for secret agents in France had virtually been eradicated. For OSS's relations with the French service dating back to Vichy days and for the U.S. high regard for it, see the U.S. War Department's *War Report of the OSS.*

Steele, Alexander. HOW TO SPY ON THE U.S. New Rochelle, N.Y.: Arlington House, 1974. 185 pp., no index.

Steele is a pseudonym, as are other names found in this story. It purports to be about a Polish defector taken in by the author and his family who proceeded to act in a manner that convinced his host he was a Polish or Soviet agent. Claiming he was coopted by CIA, the author concludes with exhortations and instructions smacking of vigilante fervor on how to spot spies and urges the reader to write to Congress on this matter. The reader will early conclude there is something wrong and strange about this book, and he will be correct. The best advice is to ignore it.

Stern, Philip Van Doren. SECRET MISSIONS OF THE CIVIL WAR: FIRST HAND ACCOUNTS BY MEN AND WOMEN WHO RISKED THEIR LIVES IN UNDERGROUND ACTIVITIES FOR THE NORTH AND THE SOUTH. Chicago: Rand McNally, 1959. 320 pp., no index.

The second subtitle contains information that the accounts were "woven into a continuous narrative." In 1953, the last of the secret service files of the Civil War were released by U.S. National Archives. Stern's great contribution is not in collecting some of these accounts but rather in his commentaries on each one and each year of the war. Not all the accounts deal with secret service or underground activities. After examining these records, Stern makes some very pertinent observations and helps put matters in perspective. The material was fragmentary, unsorted, and hard-to-read records; most of the vital Confederate records were destroyed, while many of the North's were destroyed and some important data were not committed to paper. He concludes he "touched only the outer edges of a vast, murky area which must always remain unexplored"; thus he warns that he could only sketch the outlines of the secret war. All the same, he concludes as well that most Civil War espionage was amateurish and raised questions about the reliability of personal accounts by Civil War figures such as Lafayette Baker. One must read Edwin C. Fischel's "The Mythology of Civil War Intelligence" in the December 1964 issue of the University of Iowa's *Civil War History* for a look at myths of intelligence operations in that conflict, an article called to greater public attention by Allen Dulles in *Great True Spy Stories.* The DIS *Bibliography*'s comment that the article was a starting point for more critical readings on Civil War intelligence is quite on target; the same could be said of some of Stern's comments in this book. Other historians have disagreed with Stern's agnosticism on the subject of a conspiracy to assassinate Lincoln. The *New York Times* review mentioned that Stern served up John Wise's story as true despite reservations of an expert such as Douglas S. Freeman and found that some background pieces occasionally erred.

Steven, Stewart. OPERATION SPLINTER FACTOR. Philadelphia: J. B. Lippincott, 1974. 238 pp., bibliog., index [London: Hodder and Stoughton].

The theme of this work by a British journalist is that Allen Dulles conceived an operation by the name of Splinter Factor to worsen dissent in the Soviet satellites after World War II and to foster a spirit of rebellion to roll back the Iron Curtain. These results would be accomplished by destroying satellite leaders who might become popular and thus assist rather than harm the Communist regimes in East Europe. The centerpiece was Noel Field, who would also be destroyed by being named as the supposed principal U.S. agent of the U.S. conspiracy. The channel was Joseph Swiatlo, the Polish intelligence official who defected to the West in 1953. So, Steven concludes, Dulles and Stalin were responsible for the Communist show trials, and Operation Splinter Factor led to the Korean War. Steven claims as sources some unidentified ex-CIA officers, Eastern European defectors formerly with security services and armies, and current employees of Western governments. The story is quite unreliable. The most penetrating and devastating review of the book was written by William Shawcross, who some might have expected to be receptive to its thesis, in the *New York Review of Books.* Shawcross brings out vital errors and other problems "that undermine confidence in his book"—the fact that nowhere are sources named; the lack of corroborative evidence; the failure of the author to interview Swiatlo, Hermann Field, and Erica Glasser and the incredible reason given by him for not doing so; the implausibility of his arguments; his failure to cite reports and facts that would go contrary to his thesis. *Operation Splinter Factor* is one of the worst books to appear in years in the field of intelligence; no time need be spent on it. For Dulles's view of the Fields, see his *Great True Spy Stories.*

Steven, Stewart. THE SPYMASTERS OF ISRAEL. New York: Macmillan, 1980. 318 pp., bibliog., index [London: Hodder and Stoughton, 1981].

In this book, as in *Operation Splinter Factor* (above), Steven does not name his sources. He claims he interviewed more than two hundred Israelis, some of whom he calls of sufficiently senior level in the Israeli intelligence community to make this an insider's but not an authorized book. Isser Harel, ex-head of Mossad; General Meir Amit of MI (Military Intelligence) and Mossad; generals Yehoshaphat Harkabi and Chaim Herzog, ex-chiefs of MI; and Wolfgang Lotz are among those mentioned. The focus is military and civilian intelligence, with deliberately little on internal security and counterintelligence. One of the principal themes is the struggle for supremacy between military and civilian intelligence, between MI and Mossad. His explanation of this conflict is better than any other in a popular source; he is fairly good on the strengths and weaknesses of various intelligence chiefs. There are good recaps of the Lavon affair, Operation Susannah, and the essence of the Lotz and Cohen operations in Egypt and Syria respectively. The internal political hothouse within which the struggle between Mossad and Military Intelligence takes place is well described. So is the intelligence failure of the 1973 war and many of the principal causes for it, including excellent Arab deception.

A number of important matters Steven reveals cannot be verified at this time because they have been closely held by Israelis and/or other parties. Examples are Steven's allegation of Mossad involvement in the Ben Barka affair and the Israeli claim that they were informed a week before the 1973 Arab attack of Arab intentions by a variety of sources. He seems to contradict the latter allegation when he writes that the chief of military intelligence wanted facts and was impatient with the uncertainties and options of intelligence estimates. Steven scooped up erroneous information along with the accurate: it is nonsense to say virtually all CIA men in the Middle East were working at second hand for the Israelis, that a CIA base was used as an intermediary point in the defection of an Iraqi MiG 21 plane and pilot, or that Americans assisted the Israelis in evacuating an Israeli illegal out of Beirut. He is in no position to judge that Israeli Military Intelligence is "the greatest military intelligence operation in the world," and he misses the significance of the case of Israel Beer (the Soviet agent). While there is much of which the accuracy cannot be determined and other items that are questionable, Steven at least has not repeated his disaster of *Operation*

Splinter Factor. Noninsiders can only speculate on a number of his revelations and contentions, as well as on the identities and motives of those he interviewed.

Stevenson, William. A MAN CALLED INTREPID: THE SECRET WAR. New York: Harcourt Brace Jovanovich, 1976. 472 pp., index [London: Macmillan].

"Intrepid" was the code name assigned to Sir William Stephenson, head of the British Security Coordination (BSC) in the United States during World War II; BSC was the British intelligence organization for the Western Hemisphere. Sir William in the foreword informs us the author had access to BSC papers and to himself but selected his own material and drew on many other sources as well. This became a U.S. best-seller and stimulated interest in the role of intelligence in that war. It also gave recognition for the contribution Sir William made to Allied intelligence and to U.S. intelligence's formative effort. Unfortunately, it does not fully represent a historically correct account of Stephenson's work and that of the BSC. Ronald Lewin in *RUSI* was unsparing, calling it "persistently inaccurate, ill-informed and ill written" and also a work with "gross exaggerations." Lewin also thought its endorsement by Stephenson was a tragedy. Hugh Trevor-Roper in the *New York Review of Books* regarded it as "utterly worthless" and said that any claims that Sir William was responsible for initiating or controlling strategic deception, cryptography, or special operations in Europe were "impertinent."

Of the many criticisms levelled at this book, the most serious is its picture of Stephenson as the most important figure or leader of British intelligence and its implication that the BSC was the center of British intelligence efforts worldwide. As Johns pointed out in *Within Two Cloaks,* the BSC was one of many SIS stations, and it was wrong to say that the BSC was unique, not in the chain of command, or over SOE. The errors and exaggeration do not end there. Stevenson's picture of BSC's cryptologic part in Torch is overdrawn, and BSC's role in the operation to assassinate Heydrich was tiny and inconsequential, not as great as the author shows it. Lewin discovered two photographs with the wrong captions. For a much more reliable work on the BSC and Sir William and for comments on the extent to which BSC activities have yet to be revealed, see this bibliography's entry on Hyde's *Room 3603.* See also comments on Hyde's *Cynthia* for reservations about that agent's accomplishments as a spy. Attention is directed to the preface to Stevenson's book by Charles Ellis, the BSC deputy, explaining the reasons for the British disclosures about BSC. See also Pincher's *Their Trade Is Treachery* for allegations about Ellis and consult Troy's *Donovan and the CIA* for a discussion of the extent of Sir William's influence on General Donovan.

Stockwell, John. IN SEARCH OF ENEMIES: A CIA STORY. New York: Norton, 1978. 285 pp., index [London: André Deutsch].

Stockwell's book did not have the overall impact and lasting effect that the former officer of CIA had hoped for. A twelve-year veteran of that organization, he had been chief of the CIA Angolan Task Force at one point. Most of his service, in fact, had been in Africa with the clandestine service. He resigned in 1977 and became one of the small group of disillusioned ex–CIA officers whose writings added to the antiintelligence atmosphere of the period. Stockwell declared himself opposed to the management of CIA; his purpose was to give a candid glimpse of the "clandestine mind behind the veils of secrecy." He revealed certain CIA operations, such as the one supporting Angolan groups, and provided a view of that agency's personnel, administration, and mental outlook that stemmed from first-hand experience. Unbiased observers thought that he made many valid observations about CIA but that his bias was revealed in others. The intensity of his disenchantment was shown in his view that the clandestine services were not essential to U.S. national security.

What Stockwell had to say was largely overshadowed

by court decisions and the legal precedent established stemming from the U.S. government's legal action against him for failing to submit the work for prepublication review. Among his more serious accusations were the allegations that CIA hired mercenaries, violated instructions forbidding agency officers from intruding into Angola, and lied to Congress; in the latter allegation Stockwell said unequivocally that William Colby fed Congress "patently false information about the ongoing Angolan operation, depriving them of the full information they needed to perform their constitutional role." The Senate intelligence committee completed its study of U.S. covert actions in Angola for 1975 and 1976 in May 1978 and forwarded its classified report to the president and the director of CIA for review and comment; no further public report had been issued as of 1981 nor further action taken on the charges that resulted. Snepp's *Decent Interval* contains snatches about Stockwell in Vietnam and about his disagreements with superiors on evacuation measures there. For another view of the situation in Angola from an insider of CIA, see Shackley's *The Third Option.*

Stratton, Roy Olin. SACO—THE RICE PADDY NAVY. Pleasantville, N.Y.: C. S. Palmer, 1950. 408 pp., no index.

A typical example of a unit history that would interest veterans of the organization more than it would scholars. Admiral Miles, the U.S. head of SACO, the joint intelligence organization in China in World War II, wrote in his own account, *A Different Kind of War,* that Stratton's was a carefully compiled and very detailed account to which many members of SACO contributed and that helped to give these men the credit they deserved. Stratton, a naval commander in SACO's supply department, was diligent in accumulating anecdotes of life in that particular organization and details of its many housekeeping, logistical, administrative, and personal activities. They compose the bulk of the book and tend to swamp any treatment of SACO's operational activities. His book should not be relied on as the main source for the latter as seen from the eyes of SACO personnel, though coast watching, intelligence, weather reporting, guerrilla, and raiding operations are discussed—for fuller coverage the reader must turn to Miles. Nevertheless, this book is of value since it is one of the few first-hand accounts of SACO published. Note the credit given to SACO for one of the spectacular intelligence successes of that organization, the sighting report of a Japanese carrier force en route to the Philippines in 1944; we now know this was a Japanese deception operation (see Holmes's *Double-Edged Secrets*).

Streetly, Martin. CONFOUND AND DESTROY: 100 GROUP AND THE BOMBER SUPPORT CAMPAIGN. London: Macdonald and Jane's, 1978. 270 pp., bibliog., index.

This history of the RAF group and its role in electronic warfare (EW) operations in support of RAF's bomber command in World War II was begun as a thesis. Finally given access to official material released, Streetly expanded it to this book. He claims no "definitive status" for the results because he did not have complete access to the available material and because many documents were lost. Deception tactics of spoofing, diversionary raids, false target marking, and deceptive routing are described along with the EW and ECM (electronics countermeasures) employed. These were the dual weapons of tactics and EW designed to shield the bombers. The group was given the task as well of airborne collection of intelligence, mostly elint (electronic intelligence). Streetly's language is often technical, and he presumes a minimum technical knowledge by his reader. He tries to analyze some effects of various tactics and items of equipment used and to show where success was greater in one instance or area than in others. On the last, the book is not very thorough, but this is not Streetly's fault because only one postwar study of the effectiveness of measures was conducted. He might have tried to provide more on how intelligence and other forms of deception were melded with EW; the author devotes only nine lines to Ultra and never makes a serious attempt to delve into other areas of intelligence collection to see how they contributed. The portion of the book containing photographs is especially valuable; according to the *RUSI* review, it has material that had not been previously available. Due to the importance of electronic warfare in modern combat, the experiences and lessons of this first of modern EW wars are necessary reading for the student of scientific intelligence, deception in warfare, or intelligence in the broad sense. Jones's *The Wizard War* and Clayton's *The Enemy Is Listening* provide more information on and a greater intimacy with the general subject tackled by Streetly.

Strik-Strikfeldt, Wilfred. AGAINST STALIN AND HITLER: MEMOIRS OF THE RUSSIAN LIBERATION MOVEMENT 1941–1945. New York: John Day, 1973. 263 pp., index [London: Macmillan, 1970].

It was fortunate for the Allied cause in World War II that Nazi doctrines made the adoption and pursuit of an intelligent policy on the Eastern Question impossible and contributed to Germany's defeat. The author was a minor official in Germany's overall structure dealing with the Soviet question but held the important position of liaison officer with General A. A. Vlasov, the Soviet officer who chose to throw in his lot with the Germans as the means of fighting Stalin and his regime. Strik-Strikfeldt has written a choppy account of the blindness and errors of German policy toward the Soviets and the various components in the Nazi regime that vied for power and influence in such policy, including the security services. A German Balt and former Russian officer, the author portrays Vlasov most sympathetically, and his admiration for the man is manifest; but he does not adequately answer the question of how Vlasov, knowing Hitler's basic philosophy toward the conquered Slavs, could have been as opposed to Hitler as the author contends, yet serve him. This is also a question applicable to the author, since a successful policy in the east, which he advocated, would have helped the regime he professes to have disliked. Pincher in *Their Trade Is Treachery* raises the possibility that the Soviets deceived the Germans on Vlasov's reliability via the Klatt operation from Sofia. Note the role of the intelligence services and the irony of Himmler's being the sponsor of a change in German policy in Russia.

Strong, Kenneth. INTELLIGENCE AT THE TOP: THE RECOLLECTIONS OF AN INTELLIGENCE OFFICER. London: Cassell, 1968. 257 pp., index [Garden City, N.Y.: Doubleday, 1969].

Few military men served as long in intelligence, especially in intelligence positions of great importance during crucial periods, as did General Strong. He became the first director general of intelligence at the British Ministry of Defense after World War II, but he is best known as the intelligence chief of General Eisenhower during that war, both in the Mediterranean phase and later at SHAEF. This account of his thirty years in intelligence work ending in 1966 is mostly devoted to his experiences with Eisenhower, which take up about sixty percent of the total. Naturally, he concludes that intelligence is vital for national survival and that it needs the personnel and organization "operating in close touch with the national decision-makers" to meet the demands of the postwar world. Strong describes this as a mainly autobiographical work that looks at the nature and role of military intelligence rather than intelligence as a whole (except for the final chapter).

What Strong has to say of his experiences and of the lessons he learned is of value. However, the following observations or reservations have been made about the book. First, some felt he was too discreet, unable to shed this professional turn of mind. This characteristic may account for his failure to mention deception plans for the invasion of France. Second, his account of his position on the question in 1945 of a possible German national redoubt is regarded by some as less complete and less revealing than it could have been. Third, more information now available raises new questions about the intelligence failure of the Ardennes in 1944 when the Germans caught SHAEF and the Allies by surprise; new facts make Strong's version less than the "modest and authoritative last word" on the matter the reviewer in *RUSI* thought it was. Fourth, the same British reviewer thought Strong underrated the contributions of certain individuals at SHAEF; he likewise does not speak of the contribution of deception plans such as Mincemeat to successful operations. There are those who feel he ascribed too modest a place to agents in the hierarchy of sources of military intelligence in the war. Most important of all, Strong was not able to write at that time about Ultra and its role in intelligence and operational successes or failures. For this input, see new works such as Lewin's *Ultra Goes to War,* Bennett's *Ultra in the West,* and Calvocoressi's *Top Secret Ultra.*

Strong, Kenneth. MEN OF INTELLIGENCE: A STUDY OF THE ROLES AND DECISIONS OF CHIEFS OF INTELLIGENCE FROM WORLD WAR I TO THE PRESENT DAY. London: Cassell, 1970. 170 pp., bibliog., index [New York: St. Martin's Press, 1971].

General Strong judges twelve intelligence officers of Britain, France, Germany, and the United States and the roles they played. In addition, he includes chapters on the relevance of spies and some thoughts on the relationship of intelligence to decision making in government and business. Of the intelligence officers he examines, the Germans are the largest number. Strong includes figures who are not too well known but who played important roles—one such is William Cavendish-Bentinck, chairman of the British Joint Intelligence Committee in World War II. The treatment is necessarily broad since the dozen are covered in some one hundred twenty-five pages of text and are seen from the vantage point of the military intelligence officer. The work contains some very interesting stories and valuable observations on those he knew. Strong regards and defines intelligence as the end product of a process of coordinating and evaluating information and as the structure for producing this product. He does not include the activity of collecting data as part of his definition; this is usually reflected in his approach to his subject and the emphasis in his writings. Ambrose in *Ike's Spies* criticized Strong for trying to place the blame on Allen Dulles for his own error on the National Redoubt question and characterized Strong's report in March 1945 on this as "one of the worst intelligence summaries of the war." All the same, Strong has some very perceptive observations about Dulles's personality. There may not be total agreement with his views on the value of spies (compare his opinion with that of R. V. Jones in *The Wizard War*) but his remarks on the success of Soviet espionage will meet with greater consensus. Readers will note that Strong said Gauché, the principal French officer concerned with estimating German strength from 1935 on, gave "extraordinarily accurate analyses." Yet in August 1939, on the edge of war, Gauché estimated there were between one hundred forty and one hundred fifty German divisions when actual German strength was ninety-eight. Strong's analysis of the reasons for German intelligence failures against the Soviets in World War II fails to consider the effectiveness of Soviet security and counterintelligence—despite Strong's repeating Stalin's remark, made to Air Marshal Tedder, that the identification and repression of the enemy's espionage apparatus was as essential to an attack as the accumulation of supplies. His belief that the Soviets misestimated when they invaded Czechoslovakia in 1968 has become less supportable with time.

Sullivan, William C., with Bill Brown. THE BUREAU: MY THIRTY YEARS IN HOOVER'S FBI. New York: Norton, 1979. 277 pp., index.

The Bureau was published after Sullivan's death and is based on his tape recordings and written notes, which Brown completed. Sullivan rose to be the third man in the FBI hierarchy before his split with Hoover in 1971.

He had been chief of the research and analysis section, supervisor of intelligence operations in Mexico and Central America after World War II, and for ten years assistant director of the intelligence division. In the latter position he had responsibility for espionage cases, giving him intimate, unsurpassed knowledge of how the FBI operated against foreign intelligence in this country and how it viewed this threat. The bulk of the book is not concerned with counterintelligence (CI) and counterespionage (CE); critics such as Anthony Morro in the *Washington Post* found Sullivan's criticisms of Hoover and the bureau conveyed "an intensity—almost an obsession—that was not apparent in the man himself." Though it is a minor portion of the book, what Sullivan reveals of foreign espionage, CI, and CE is, for those familiar with his work and thinking, pure Sullivan. He brings to light many things once considered inner secrets or whispered within the intelligence community—Hoover's lack of interest or real understanding of foreign espionage; his law-enforcement approach to CI and CE; the lack of suitable organization within the FBI to deal with the postwar espionage threat; the bureau's attitude toward informants; "second-story" operations; the use of sex operations by the bureau; the lack of proper equipment in the FBI; the problem of foreign illegals; Sullivan's suspicions of Soviet penetration of the FBI. Other revelations are his stories of Hoover's attitude toward CIA and the rest of the U.S. intelligence community and toward foreign intelligence and security services. Then there is the occasional operational gem such as the fact that Hayhanen, the Soviet agent, was under FBI surveillance long before anything was known of the illegal Abel. There is the tendency to blame bureau shortcomings in CI and CE on Hoover and the structure within the FBI, which many will consider valid as far as it goes but an incomplete explanation. The reader will also notice that Sullivan virtually ignores the bureau's work and successes against espionage in World War II and oddly describes the Harry Dexter White case as a "red herring" without explaining this break with conventional opinion of this case.

Sun Tzu. THE ART OF WAR. Oxford: Clarendon Press, 1963. 186 pp., bibliog., index [Oxford and New York: Oxford Univ. Press, 1971].

Though the authorship of this work is not proven conclusively, the maxims it expounds and its influence in other countries makes it compulsory reading for the intelligence officer. Sun Tzu has influenced the Chinese Communist leadership, and General Griffith, in his introduction, believes his ideas were transmitted to Russia via the Mongol-Tartar route. The vital importance of intelligence is shown in passages where the author underlines the role "foreknowledge" plays in the conquest of an enemy and tells why leaders "surpass . . . ordinary men" in achievement. For students of deception there is the famous maxim that "all warfare is based on deception." The chapter on the employment of spies delves into agent motivation with insights that are timeless. Here, too, one notices the importance assigned to double agents for purposes of deception and disinformation.

Sutherland, Douglas. THE FOURTH MAN: THE STORY OF BLUNT, PHILBY, BURGESS AND MACLEAN. London: Secker and Warburg, 1980. 168 pp., bibliog., index [New York: Times Books. *The Great Betrayal: The Definitive Story of Blunt, Philby, Burgess and Maclean*].

The author's purpose in writing this journalistic account is to put into perspective the relative importance of all the characters involved in these cases of espionage on behalf of the Soviets. He says that he had known "with complete certainty" that Blunt was the "fourth man" at the time he coauthored a book on Burgess and Maclean in 1963; thus, while relying heavily on material gathered for the previous book, he was now able to use much that he could not earlier. He offers very little that is new, much speculation, and a number of mistakes. He recognizes in the introduction that without access to secret records in the United States, the United Kingdom, or the Soviet Union, "much must remain a matter for deduction and speculation." Consequently, he makes no pretense that it was possible to aspire to complete accuracy. He is inconsistent in attitude, complaining of writers who come up with unsubstantiated new facets while he leaves the impression of a high-level cover-up. He believes continued interest in the four known agents had driven spies of greater importance into obscurity yet can be considered guilty of such interest as well. And as Pincher shows in *Their Trade Is Treachery,* we cannot be certain, as he feels, that all the threads have been picked up in the case of the Cambridge spies.

Sweet-Escott, Bickham. BAKER STREET IRREGULAR. London: Methuen, 1965. 266 pp., index.

Sweet-Escott occupied a number of positions in SOE in London and in the field, and this book was the first to describe SOE from the inside. He called it a purely personal record of his experiences and one he hoped would correct misconceptions that had risen about SOE, even though he did not consider it in any way a history of that organization. The range of positions he held was large; in one period of nine months in 1943 he had four different assignments. These staff positions, whether in London, Cairo, Algiers, Washington, Italy, or the Far East, where he ended the war, gave him a good vantage point on SOE, its operations, personnel, and politics. Much of great intelligence interest is here though at times he is too brief on matters. This is understandable aside from any wish to be brief. The author waited ten years to get official approval for publication and then only got it after cuts were made. Not only interesting operations and well-known and lesser-known SOE figures inhabit this account, but also the organizational and bureaucratic gyrations of SOE as seen in the odyssey of this official. He was at one point in contact with the London respresentatives of Hagana and the Poles; his stay in Washington is valuable for a number of stories and for his description of Stephenson and the BSC and of OSS-SOE relations viewed from the British end in Washington. He also had a sharp eye for the ridiculous and for questionable security and other practices. Since this work was first drafted in 1954, we have learned much more of many of the things he touched on; but it remains a basic and necessary study of SOE and a rare continuous view from SOE headquarters.

Sykes, Christopher. WASSMUSS, 'THE GERMAN LAWRENCE': HIS ADVENTURES IN PERSIA DURING AND AFTER THE WAR. Leipzig: Bernhard Tauchnitz, 1937. 246 pp., no index [New York: Longmans, 1936].

Wassmuss has not had the attention paid him in the English literature of intelligence of World War I that he warrants. He carried out the most successful operations of the German mission sent to the Middle East to attempt to raise the Afghans, the Kurds, and the Persian tribes against the British. Sykes's biography has the distinction of being an early try in English to place Wassmuss's achievements and their significance in proper perspective and to relate the sad story of his efforts to make good after the war on the financial obligation to the Persian tribes that Germany had assumed. He also wished to correct British misconceptions of the man and the prejudices against him that had been carried over from the war and to correct some myths. That he did not fully succeed can be seen in the accounts of Wassmuss by Rowan in *The Story of Secret Service* and Seth's *Encyclopedia of Espionage.* Aside from his guerrilla and covert actions, Wassmuss is remembered in intelligence history as the man whose captured code book supposedly led to the British breaking of the German political and diplomatic codes. (See especially James's *The Eyes of the Navy*). Sykes does not mention this. Nor does he hint, if he knew, that the code may have been captured elsewhere though he mentions the arrest of the German consul general in the Persian Gulf and the capture of his files (see C. J. Edmond's article in the January 1960 *Royal Central Asian Journal*). Sykes, unhappily, did not indicate what his sources for this biography were except in rare instances, so we are left guessing at how thorough he was in his research. The *London Times* review was of the opinion that without Wassmuss's side of the story, what had been written about him had to be considered incomplete.

Szulc, Tad. COMPULSIVE SPY: THE STRANGE CAREER OF E. HOWARD HUNT. New York: Viking, 1974. 180 pp., no index.

Howard Hunt became well known because of his involvement in Watergate. An OSS veteran and CIA retiree, it was he who ran the operation on behalf of the Nixon White House that ended in disaster for all those connected with it. Szulc, a former *New York Times* staffer and frequent writer on national security and intelligence subjects, has written what he describes as the "incomplete story" of Hunt, reconstructed "from a distance." He attempts to show us Hunt from his OSS days to Watergate and to draw certain lessons from his life and career. Blackstock and Schaf's bibliography said the book's first section on "national security" measures that led to Watergate was excellent and made this book more a study of counter-intelligence and security of the period than a biography. Szulc managed to pull together much material that had reached the public domain, but questions have arisen about the rest of the book. These include the identity of sources (all he says is that he received help from past CIA, State Department, and other officials), their exact knowledge of Hunt, and their objectivity; there is no documentation. Certain items on CIA and its organization are quite wrong. These indicate that Szulc either misunderstood his sources or accepted information from individuals who did not have the knowledge they claimed. A CIA officer never refers to other CIA officers as "agents"; chief of station conferences are not presided over by outsiders. Szulc toys with the thesis that intelligence organizations and the work they undertake create individuals with certain similar values and a certain mentality; he also allows that not all former CIA officers end up being carbon copies of Hunt and concludes that Hunt only served himself. Had Szulc not done such a hasty job, he might have produced a more reliable portrait of his subject; he did capture portions of the man whom Richard Helms described as "a bit of a romantic" and William Colby referred to in his book *Honorable Men* as having a penchant for unnecessary intrigue. Phillips's *The Night Watch* has some closeups of Hunt and corrects Szulc's statement that Hunt was in Mexico when Lee Harvey Oswald visited there.

T

Taylor, Charles E. THE SIGNAL AND SECRET SERVICE OF THE CONFEDERATE STATES. Hamlet, N.C.: North Carolina Booklet, 1903. 24 pp., no index.

Most of the important records of Confederate secret service activities in the American Civil War were destroyed when Richmond was burned. Consequently, anything reliable and first-hand that survived of that side's intelligence and covert action activities is all the more to be cherished. The author stated this brief monograph was designed to give only a general idea of that service as it had been known to him forty years earlier. He ended up producing a skimpy work with a minimum of information that gave only a tantalizing peek into a couple of intelligence activities of the service, such as its cipher work and the functions of its courier service. Frustration with what he doled out is made all the greater by his statement that an entire volume would be needed to present an elaborate and consecutive account of the work of the Confederate secret service. For a brief treatment of Confederate cryptology, see Kahn's *The Codebreakers.* For a glimpse of the Union's efforts see Bates's *Lincoln in the Telegraph Office.*

Taylor, John W. R., and Mondey, David. SPIES IN THE SKY. New York: Scribner's, 1972. 128 pp., no index [London: Ian Allan].

Coauthor Taylor was one of the editors of the Jane's survey of ships and aircraft and was concerned with the missile sections of that publication. This brief survey of aerial reconnaissance and photography covers the period from the balloon to modern day: drones, specialized reconnaissance aircraft, and satellites. There are interesting chapters on the developments of aerial photography in both world wars, the U-2, the Cuban missile crisis, and the Vietnam War, and there are many photographs. There are a number of lapses and shortcomings, such as on the U-2. Too little credit is given for photo reconnaissance's role in the discovery of the work being performed at the German missile and rocket center at Peenemünde in World War II, and there is no discussion of any contribution of aerial reconnaissance in the French attack at the Marne in 1914—both events of strategic importance. Land, incidentally, did not develop the first U-2 camera, as the authors state. To summarize, experts found this a useful work but weakest where one might expect—where classified matters were touched upon.

Thomas, John Oram. THE GIANT KILLERS: THE STORY OF THE DANISH RESISTANCE MOVEMENT 1940–1945. New York: Taplinger, 1976. 313 pp., index [London: Michael Joseph].

Thomas, who was associated with Danish resistance at one point, describes this as the bare outline of Denmark's years of occupation and resistance. He makes no pretense that this is a full history of the times and of that particular movement. He is correct that it is one of the resistance movements least familiar to English-speaking people; whether it was one of the greatest or even second to none, as Field Marshal Montgomery is quoted as calling it, is another matter that should be debated. Thomas tries to tell stories of some who resisted the Germans and by doing so to pay tribute to the many who deserve it. The technique makes for an episodic, disconnected work wherein the author tells or lets individuals relate particular experiences. This is a journalistic work lacking source indications, with the verbatim conversations that researchers so often question. The main fault is that Thomas has unevenly and poorly distributed its contents; his account of one of the Danes' most important organizations, the Princes, made up of officers in the intelligence services, gets less space than the efforts of particular individuals, however heroic. This is an excellent companion to Petrow's *The Bitter Years* because it recounts details of particular individuals and operations that the other's more general treatment misses.

Note that the author received assistance in writing this from the expert on the Danish resistance, Jorgen Haestrup.

Thompson, James Westfall, and Padover, Saul K. SECRET DIPLOMACY: ESPIONAGE AND CRYPTOGRAPHY 1500–1815. New York: Frederick Ungar, 1963. 263 pp., bibliog., index.

This work by an expert on the Middle Ages and one on diplomatic history was first published in 1937 under the title *Secret Diplomacy, A Record of Espionage and Double Dealing: 1500–1815.* Two editions appeared before World War II. The 1963 edition includes an up-to-date bibliography by Padover. According to the latter, the "core data" came from manuals and guidebooks, government reports, police dossiers, memoranda of ministers, personal letters, memoirs, official correspondence, scholarly histories, and biographies or autobiographies of participants. The authors call this a "study of the development of a relatively neglected aspect of diplomacy, that of institutionalized spying and coded communication." It is more than that. It is a fascinating and engrossing work containing numerous examples of how secret diplomacy, espionage, covert action, and covert political action were conducted and became standard practices in Europe by the eighteenth century and were carried out until the fall of Napoleon. We are told of the use of subsidies, bribery, deception, and assassination by rulers and governments to achieve their aims in addition to classical espionage. While there is much on the practice of intercepting communications and codes and the use of black chambers to read and to decipher messages, the book's subtitle is a bit of an exaggeration on the cryptographic contents. The authors come nowhere near treating the three hundred years of cryptography; one must turn to Kahn's *The Codebreakers* for such a treatment. A book of this length could never cover all the most important instances or examples of covert and clandestine diplomacy over a period of three centuries. For instance, while we learn of the treachery of Queen Elizabeth's ambassador to

Paris, the work of Walsingham is barely touched upon. Though there are many stories and anecdotes of the period, we are not told of the French revolutionary counterespionage success against the British and the French royalists that was the predecessor to the Soviet Trust operation almost a century later. For this, consult Rowan's *The Story of Secret Service.* The 1937 edition of this book appeared the same year as Rowan's and contains many examples of clandestine and covert diplomacy and warfare the latter either missed or neglected to include. The reader's attention is called to the authors' reconstruction of how Canning and the British government may have learned the secret clauses of the Treaty of Tilsit.

Thomson, Basil. THE ALLIED SECRET SERVICE IN GREECE. London: Hutchinson, 1931. 284 pp., index.

The title is misleading. Thomson, who achieved fame in Scotland Yard during World War I, does not concern himself with all the Allied services; rather, he covers the French and in particular the activities of the French naval attaché and intelligence representative, Commander de Roquefeuil. It is a passionate, strongly biased work on the direction political and diplomatic events took in Greece between 1914 and 1922 because of the activities of that French representative, as Thomson tells it. The author is firm in his judgments but only general as to actual intelligence activities. The British are barely mentioned as involved in any intelligence activities and Compton Mackenzie is only named once; the British services in Greece are pictured as taking a back seat to the French and as under their influence. Thomson mentions as one of his sources the unpublished 1919 report of the French Chamber of Deputies' Naval Commission, whose summary he claims to have seen; otherwise, he does not say how he became an expert on this subject or what the sources were for much of his material. Mackenzie in *Greek Memories* struck hard at this work and at Thomson's credentials on Greek affairs. He pronounced it untrustworthy and condemned it for giving currency to the Greek royalist version of events. The title, "Director of Intelligence, 1919–1921," that the publisher accorded Thomson in this book is correctly clarified by Mackenzie: it described his police position, which was not connected with foreign intelligence and counterintelligence work abroad. For other British works on British intelligence activities in Greece during those years, see Lawson's *Tales of Aegean Intrigue* and the remainder of Mackenzie's World War I memoirs.

Thorpe, Elliott R. EAST WIND RAIN: THE INTIMATE ACCOUNT OF AN INTELLIGENCE OFFICER IN THE PACIFIC, 1939–1949. Boston: Gambit, 1969. 290 pp., index.

General Thorpe began his career as a U.S. military intelligence officer in 1939; he served as General Douglas MacArthur's head of counterintelligence and civil intelligence. This was a result of a strange split in that command's intelligence whereby General Willoughby was in charge of combat intelligence. Both sections were combined under the latter in June 1945. Despite the positions he occupied, Thorpe has relatively little of intelligence interest to tell in this personal narrative. The title of the book is the text of the Japanese message that is at the heart of the author's most significant and controversial revelation. He claims "east wind rain" was the Japanese signal of their upcoming attack in 1941 and that it was intercepted by the Dutch in Japan in early December and deciphered. He further insists he forwarded this intelligence to Washington and was ordered by the latter to send no more on the subject. We know "east wind rain" was a Japanese Foreign Office message to designate a crisis in relations with the United States and to warn Japanese diplomatic and consular offices to destroy codes and secret files. It was not the go signal for a Japanese attack in the Pacific including Hawaii, as Thorpe pictures it. Further, Holmes in *Double-Edged Secrets* states no actual "winds" message was ever intercepted by the United States, and Kahn's *Codebreakers* supports this contention. There are a few snippets on the attitude of

MacArthur and other senior officers of his command toward counterintelligence work. Thorpe was no admirer of Willoughby; according to Powe and Wilson in *The Evolution of American Military Intelligence,* Thorpe was critical of his work as G-2. Willoughby's criticism of Thorpe's testimony on Owen Lattimore is to be found in Willoughby's *Sorge: Soviet Master Spy.* One review thought Thorpe did not even leak open secrets. For a fuller discussion of the debate on whether the "winds execute" message was ever received, including the opinions of Roberta Wohlstetter and William Friedman, the reader is referred to Clark's *The Man Who Broke Purple.*

Thwaites, Michael. TRUTH WILL OUT: ASIO AND THE PETROVS. Sydney, Austral.: Collins, 1980. 207 pp., bibliog., index.

Thwaites was director of the counterespionage branch in Melbourne of the Australian Security Intelligence Organization (ASIO) at the time of the defection of Vladimir and Evdokia Petrov, the MVD resident in Australia and his wife, also an MVD officer. He served in ASIO until 1971. This book is devoted largely to the Petrov case with which he was intimately connected for some three-and-a-half years, part of which was spent as ghost writer for the Petrovs' book *Empire of Fear.* Besides confirming his literary role in the telling of the Petrovs' story, Thwaites discusses the defection case from the side of Australian counterespionage, his views of the work of the Royal Commission to examine Petrov's information, and the political controversy that resulted in Australia, which has echoes until today in works such as Hall's *The Secret State.* We are given further insights into the Petrovs, such as that they had phenomenal memories and remarkable powers of description; but Thwaites does not tell much new about their intelligence work. He explains the absence of details on the Petrovs' work in Australia in *Empire of Fear* as the result of the advice of legal experts to delete such material. Thwaites's book is of added significance because it is a glimpse into the early years of ASIO by one of its original staff members. A necessary companion piece to the works of the Petrovs and Hall and to Bialoguski's *The Case of Colonel Petrov.*

Tinnin, David B., with Dag Christensen. THE HIT TEAM. Boston: Little, Brown, 1976. 240 pp., no index [London: Weidenfeld and Nicolson].

Both Tinnin and Christensen were associated with *Time* magazine—the former as a staffer and the latter as its stringer in Oslo. They relate the story of the Israeli intelligence operation in Norway in 1973 that resulted in the death of a person the Israelis mistook for their target. The origin of this counterterror and retaliation operation is traced back to the killing of members of the Israeli Olympic team in Munich. Tinnin and Christensen tell a story of poor planning, bungling, amateurish and insecure methods of operating, and poor execution of plans by the Israeli team that was assigned the task of finding and executing the man who the Israelis believed was responsible for the Munich massacre. Also, they tell of the court trial of six members of the Israeli team who were caught by the Norwegians.

This journalistic account, while exciting, must be read with a certain amount of caution. The discussion of the Israeli intelligence services is superficial and somewhat inaccurate, according to those familiar with them. There are facts included that are seemingly sensational and difficult to verify, not to speak of the difficulty of visualizing how the authors could have acquired them. A good example is their statement that the Israelis had broken the KGB code. They presume, as did the Israelis, that Salameh of the Palestinian Black September organization was the planner of the Munich massacre, which is not a certainty. Despite its weak points, this is a rare instance of a counterterror effort and organization of an intelligence service that is available for study due to a mishap that led to its exposure, and consequently the book is of considerable historical and professional value.

Trenowden, Ian. OPERATIONS MOST SECRET: SOE, THE MALAYAN THEATRE. London: William Kimber, 1978. 214 pp., bibliog., index.

Designed to be a history of SOE's Force 136, Group B (Malaya) in World War II. The author was denied access to SOE's archives; we must presume he would have produced a much better and more interesting book had he been allowed access. What we have is a unit history loaded down with administrative and logistical matters. The first two-thirds is devoted almost entirely to the history of the organization and to minor details at the expense of matters of intelligence, policy, or political importance. We are not told of the objectives and plans of Force 136, Group B until we begin the final pages of the book, and then we are informed that the disbandment of that group's records makes it impossible to sketch the manner in which policy evolved. Trenowden had previously authored a history of a British submarine that operated in the Malaya area. This may explain why he devotes pages to the sub's trip to a landing area, with reams on the nautical conditions encountered, at the expense of other items of greater interest to the intelligence expert. While the author was deprived of access to SOE records, he did have the advantage of being advised by an important figure involved with SOE operations in Malaya; consequently, the choice of what to include was his, for he presumably learned more about SOE's operations than he tells here. The interesting story of Division D's (out of India) pretending to be taken in by a Japanese deception operation and turning it against them to mislead them on British plans is the sort of operational information Trenowden should have included in larger quantities.

Trepper, Leopold. THE GREAT GAME: MEMOIRS OF THE SPY HITLER COULDN'T SILENCE. New York: McGraw-Hill, 1977. 436 pp., index [London: Michael Joseph. *The Great Game: The Story of the Red Orchesta*].

Trepper was the "Grand Chef," the head of the Soviet military intelligence network in Western Europe that the Germans called the Red Orchestra. This autobiography of a Communist and a member of Soviet intelligence is devoted mainly to his work with the network, his capture by the Germans, the period under their control, and finally his imprisonment for ten years by the Soviets and efforts to win his freedom. It was written after Trepper was allowed to go to Copenhagen and after total solitude for three years as a "free prisoner" in Poland. He stated it was his intent to tell the truth about his fifty years as a militant. From what we learned from studies such as CIA's *The Rote Kapelle,* it would seem Trepper's account is a case of partial or selective presentation of the extent of the Rote Kapelle and of his role while in the hands of the Germans. As one review put it, his narrative verges on apologia when he defends himself against charges of collaborating with the Germans after his capture. More research into this phase seems in order, though we may never learn the full truth at the Soviet end. We know the Rote Kapelle had connections in Eastern Europe, Britain, Scandinavia, and elsewhere about which Trepper is silent; according to the CIA study, Trepper from 1940 to 1942 commanded seven networks, each active in its own field and subordinated to its chief. Trepper himself speaks of the Red Orchestra as only one of the Soviet networks but omits Britain and the United States as countries where such networks were located. With this in mind, we note with interest his chapters on the major intelligence coups of his networks and on the errors of Moscow's center, which "bears the major responsibility for the liquidation" of the Berlin, Belgian, and French groups. There are cameo, first-hand portraits of the important figures in Soviet military intelligence Richard Sorge and General Berzin (although

Trepper does not get the story right of Bruce Lockhart's relationship to the right Berzin in the plot against the Bolsheviks). There are some, albeit too few, important facts divulged about how intelligence dealing with the planned 1941 German attack was received by Soviet military intelligence chiefs and Stalin. Examples of intelligence tradecraft, from cover to interrogation techniques, are naturally to be found. Finally, this is a revealing story of one man's militancy and disillusionment and of a regime's exploitation of its agents and the strange rewards it gave them for dangerous work, particularly as a way of hiding headquarters' errors. Drew Middleton in the *New York Times* thought this one of the masterpieces of factual espionage writing of World War II.

Trevor-Roper, Hugh R. THE PHILBY AFFAIR: ESPIONAGE, TREASON AND SECRET SERVICES. London: William Kimber, 1968. 126 pp., no index.

There are actually two essays in this book—one on Philby and the other on Admiral Canaris, head of the German Abwehr. The author, a well-known British historian, served in British intelligence (SIS) in World War II where, he says, he found himself studying the SIS and the German intelligence service at the same time. Cave Brown, in his introduction to *The Secret War Report of the OSS,* said Trevor-Roper was a junior officer in SIS and privy to little. However, Cave Brown's opinions may have been affected by the Oxford historian's very critical review of *Bodyguard of Lies.* Philby and Canaris had one thing in common: they both worked against the authority to which they presumably owed loyalty, with Philby going to the extreme of becoming a controlled agent of a foreign power. The essay on Philby is the major one in every way—content, insight, analysis, and length—and is a first-class piece of work. But beyond the perceptive and sometimes brilliant observations on Philby, there are jewels to be found about SIS. The author reveals the breaking of the German Enigma machine some six years before Winterbotham's *The Ultra Secret;* he informs us that the British were reading Abwehr traffic in hand ciphers from the start of 1940 and machine ciphers from 1942; he tells of SIS inefficiencies disguised by that organization's possession and control of communications intelligence and contends that not one great intelligence triumph of the war was directly or exclusively due to SIS agents. He puts Canaris's work in perspective ("as ineffective in conspiracy as in intelligence") and insists that Canaris approached the SIS to meet with its director and to treat with the British but was rebuffed.

Troy, Thomas F. DONOVAN AND THE CIA: A HISTORY OF THE ESTABLISHMENT OF THE CENTRAL INTELLIGENCE AGENCY. Washington, D.C.: Central Intelligence Agency, Center for the Study of Intelligence, 1981. 478 pp., bibliog., notes, index [Frederick, Md.: University Publications of America].

When originally completed in 1975, this detailed and scholarly account of the origin of CIA was classified secret and designed for the needs of CIA employees. This declassified version deleted some six pages of material and received some reediting. Troy, taking full advantage of access to material not available to other researchers on the subject such as Corson, the author of *The Armies of Ignorance,* made the best possible use of it to produce a work of high standards in scholarship. His research was enormous and painstaking and he carefully documented all his sources, including the classified ones. U.S. classified documents, private papers (for example, some reports of the head of British intelligence in the United States and his deputy, William Stephenson and Charles Ellis respectively), interviews, and secondary sources compose the mine of information he tapped.

Troy gives a blow-by-blow account of the bureaucratic, political, and philosophical squabbles, skirmishes, and battles that accompanied the creation of OSS and then CIA. The principal organizations and actors involved, their positions on the concept of central intelligence, and the atmosphere of hostility to the idea, to Donovan, to OSS, and to COI are all laid out, sharply delineated, and analyzed, as are matters such as President Truman's 1963 claim that CIA had strayed from its original purpose and the U.S. government's intent regarding CIA and covert action at the time CIA was created. We learn of what Troy calls the "missing link" connection between Donovan and CIA and the name of the U.S. Army G-2 intelligence-collection organization set up in 1942 to compete with OSS. This organization (Grombach), mentioned but not named in Kirkpatrick's *The Real CIA,* has been little discussed or written about. The preface updates his research on the source of the leak to the press of the 1944 Donovan plan and on the role of Stephenson and the BSC on certain matters.

Troy's is the most authoritative and comprehensive study of the subject made to date. He could have made it even better by describing the world environment within which the main debates and bureaucratic battles took place rather than making it sound as if they took place largely in a vacuum. He was aware of the forces as well as the persons who played a role in the shaping of CIA in 1947 and said so. The appendixes contain a useful collection of the principal documents, executive and other orders, proposals, directives, and legislation beginning in 1941. On influences that molded Donovan's ideas and whether Sir William Stephenson has been given the credit he deserves, Troy's account, good as it is, must be considered subject for further research. OSS veterans also cite some gaps in the record found by Troy. Lastly, Troy reveals the name of another little-known U.S. intelligence effort, that of John Franklin Carter (Jay Franklin).

Tuchman, Barbara W. THE ZIMMERMANN TELEGRAM. New York: Viking, 1958. 244 pp., bibliog., notes, index [London: Constable, 1959].

The cryptanalytic achievement of the British in intercepting and deciphering the German Zimmermann telegrams was their greatest success in World War I and also one of the greatest and most significant cryptanalytic successes in history. Tuchman's account of how it was accomplished and exploited is based on a study of the pertinent literature and documents. She deals with the cryptographic problems, the historical and political context, and the political and operational problems of its exploitation by the British. Her book provides, as DIS's *Bibliography* commented, an outstanding example of the impact of intelligence on the course of history. In the 1966 Macmillan edition, Tuchman acknowledged new information had affected portions of her 1958 account of the cryptanalytic work. The declassification of Friedman and Mendelsohn's *The Zimmermann Telegram of January 16, 1917 and Its Cryptographic Background* modified her earlier account by disclosing the existence of a second German code. She also made reference to the article of C. J. Edmonds in the January 1960 issue of the *Royal Central Asian Journal* that raised the distinct possibility that the German cipher book reported as recovered from the German agent Wassmuss in Persia was acquired in the legally questionable arrest of the German consul in Bushire. Wisely, she decided not to make any changes in the Alexander Szek story as one possible explanation of the acquisition of the German diplomatic code, despite the perennial denials of British authorities and doubts of experts such as Yves Gylden that such an operation ever existed. The startling item in Roskill's 1981 *Admiral of the Fleet Earl Beatty* (New York: Atheneum, 1981) raises for the first time the serious possibility that the story of Szek and his stealing of the German code for the British was true. Tuchman is an accomplished writer who describes well German activities in the United States and Mexico as background to the event. And looking at her long bibliography, one is struck by the fact that despite the importance of the telegram in world events and its fame, the tale had not been told as fully in English until Tuchman. Kahn in *The Codebreakers* called her work "a masterly study of the political circumstances surrounding the telegram and its publication" but added that unfortunately it appeared before the 1965 declassification of the study of the cryptographic background of the telegram, done by Friedman and Mendelsohn in 1938. Friederich Katz's *The Secret War in Mexico* (Chicago and London: Univ. of Chicago Press, 1981) contains an up-to-date study of the cryptanalytical history of the Zimmermann Telegram.

Tully, Andrew. CIA: THE INSIDE STORY. New York: William Morrow, 1962. 268 pp., index [London: Arthur Barker].

Tully's book is important in the history of intelligence because it represented a break with the past by being a full-length, critical look at CIA and its activities by a writer not ideologically identified with the left or the Communist point of view. Tully declared it his intention to attempt a "balance sheet" of CIA. He concluded CIA had not always performed well and had made errors he regarded as serious enough to threaten world peace. Consequently, CIA's influence on U.S. foreign policy concerned him. Allen Dulles, then director of CIA, attacked this book for what he deemed its errors and distortions and felt Tully had not been careful about the sources and material he used. There is no question that the work is loaded with errors. Some are explainable by the fact that accurate information on CIA operations was not that easy to come by at that time, but other errors are indicative of sloppy research. Examples: he believes SOE was still in existence seventeen years after its dissolution and makes MI5 the British intelligence service. Although he supposedly knew many deep secrets of CIA, he was not aware Radio Free Europe (RFE) was then under CIA control, not one of the best-kept secrets. The real fault, however, lies in the author's failure to distinguish between justified criticism of CIA errors and criticisms of its allegedly uncontrolled operations. The latter he saw as resulting in the formulation of policy by the agency (operations Blackstock and others called covert operations). He confused the two and as an outsider was never in a position to know if and when CIA acted on its own. Questions that Tully raised about CIA's efficiency and the propriety of some of its activities presaged similar and even tougher queries in the future when the consensus on CIA and U.S. foreign and national security and intelligence matters had broken down. So, too, his criticisms appear mild in comparison to what appeared in other books and other places in the years to follow. This book helped usher in a transitional period in U.S. attitudes toward intelligence; but its many mistakes limit its significance to that. Blackstock's opinion was that it was "astringent, informed and well-meaning criticism" of U.S. political warfare policy and of specific CIA operations. Obviously, its errors and collection of facts and stories from the outside do not justify the title's "Inside."

Tully, Andrew. INSIDE THE FBI: FROM THE FILES OF THE FEDERAL BUREAU OF INVESTIGATION AND INDEPENDENT SOURCES. New York: McGraw-Hill, 1980. 278 pp., index.

The counterintelligence (CI) and counterespionage (CE) segment is only one of six in Tully's book and covers three cases. These are those of William Kampiles, the CIA employee, with emphasis on his role in the sale of the KH-11 manual to the Soviets (the manual on the satellite's reconnaissance capabilities); the arrest and conviction of David Truong and Ronald Humphrey for espionage and the theft of documents and their passing of such to the North Vietnamese; and the double agent case of the FBI against the Soviets using Lieutenant Commander Arthur Lindberg of the U.S. Navy. These are popular treatments of the cases. Tully is more descriptive than analytical in his approach and does not add anything of significance to our knowledge of these three instances of successful FBI work. To keep the reader from getting the wrong impression of the overall threat, Tully at one point does give some idea of the enormous CI problem the FBI faces in the United States, of which the three cases discussed are only representative. He acknowledges the encouragement of the director of the FBI and the assistance of an FBI man; certain passages were fictionalized by him to hide investigative techniques and to protect informants.

U

U.S., Army, Security Agency. THE HISTORY OF CODES AND CIPHERS IN THE UNITED STATES DURING WORLD WAR I. Laguna Hills, Calif.: Aegean Park Press, 1979. 234 pp., index.

The second volume of an Army Security Agency (ASA) study written in 1946 and entitled *Codes and Ciphers in World War I (1917–1919).* Aegean Park Press edited the work, a piece much superior to the first volume (below), which covers the period prior to World War I. It is better not only because much more material was obviously available for this period to the Historical Section of ASA; it appears more effort was put into this portion of the total. The editor, Wayne G. Barker (who also edited the first volume), contributed a number of comments and clarifications as footnotes and praised this piece as a well-written one. Still, there is no claim that it is comprehensive, for a large section of MI8's records of its cryptanalytic effort was missing or not available at the time of writing. This gap did not prevent the main outlines for the cryptanalytic effort against the Germans from being drawn. Aegean Park Press would have been better advised to have used the original ASA title for this volume. It does not merely concern codes and ciphers *in* the United States but is broader, covering their use abroad and U.S. cryptanalytic work against German codes and ciphers. One chapter on cryptanalysis was admittedly sanitized before its release. The editor believed it dealt with work against nonenemy systems. He is probably correct, for little in this category is included. What is more, there is no denial or contradiction of revelations in Yardley's *The American Black Chamber* of this kind of U.S. cryptanalysis. Yardley was not spared by the authors on other matters, where his reliability was questioned. Substance is provided for other more general criticisms of Yardley's work, and Barker, the editor, thought the authors had no sympathy for him at all. There is no effort made to resolve differences expressed on the question of the security of American Expeditionary Force cryptographic systems. See also Kahn's *The Codebreakers.*

U.S., Army, Security Agency. THE HISTORY OF CODES AND CIPHERS IN THE U.S. PRIOR TO WORLD WAR I. Laguna Hills, Calif.: Aegean Park Press, 1978. 148 pp., index.

The Historical Section of the Army Security Agency (ASA) originally wrote this draft study in 1946 and entitled it *A Historical Background of the Signal Security Agency.* Taking advantage of the release of such material by the U.S. government, Aegean Park Press edited and published it; despite the editing and the corrections, the editor still believed the study was deficient in its "coverage of certain cryptologic events during the period." Its deficiency is quite obvious from both the contents and the admissions of the original ASA authors. They allowed that little was really known of formal U.S. cryptographic systems used from the American Revolution to the invention of the telegraph and the laying of the Atlantic cable and that little information had survived on the use of cryptography during the Spanish-American War. They also confessed they did not search State Department files thoroughly on the subject. Much in the study will be of interest primarily to the professional cryptographer or cryptanalyst and the buff. Any reader, however, will be struck by the shallow quality of this draft study, even after being made aware that certain material was not available or researched. It is difficult to believe this is the best that could be done when one considers the enormous advantages enjoyed by government researchers with access to archives and classified material. The editor at Aegean Park Press wisely changed the title to better accommodate the contents; the work contains chapters on the U.S. diplomatic cryptographic system in the Civil War, the British system in the American Revolution, and a U.S. Navy cipher device. The editor should have corrected the statement that the U.S. War Department Code of 1885 was the only American code known to have been used between the Civil War and the Spanish-American War. There were other American codes, such as the U.S. Navy Secret Code of 1887, still in use in 1898. See Kahn's *The Codebreakers* on this point. See also Weber.

U.S., Army, Security Agency. THE ORIGIN AND DEVELOPMENT OF THE ARMY SECURITY AGENCY 1917–1947. Laguna Hills, Calif.: Aegean Park Press, 1978. 38 pp., index.

Originally a classified lecture given by the Army Security Agency (ASA), declassified and released in 1975. The publisher added indexes but no comments or clarifications, which were included in the other ASA studies published (above). Kahn in *The Codebreakers* makes reference to a work that sounds very much like this one, so it seems that some material contained in it was available prior to 1975. For those familiar with the genre, it reads like a typical government orientation lecture. It is almost a straight structural description, giving bare-boned facts on the various names, organization, and reorganizations of the army cryptologic service over a period of thirty years and two wars. The names of Friedman and Yardley are among the very few mentioned in this general approach to the subject, and there is nothing of the successes in cryptography or cryptanalysis except for some claims for the U.S. Army military codes in World War I. There is nothing of the record against Japanese systems in World War II. To illustrate how thin the contents can be, the Cipher Bureau is referred to, but there is no discussion of why the bureau's experienced personnel chose not to join the newly organized Signal Intelligence Service. To illustrate the occasional odd selection of matters, there is no mention of an important cryptographic machine (SIGABA) developed by Friedman and used in the late war, but the M-209, which served in units below corps, is named.

U.S., Central Intelligence Agency. SEE **Central Intelligence Agency.**

U.S., Counter Intelligence Corps School. COUNTER INTELLIGENCE CORPS HISTORY AND MISSION IN WORLD WAR II. Baltimore: CIC School, CIC Center [1951?]. 83 pp., no index.

It takes a government monograph to make an interesting subject and a period full of action and drama uninteresting. This one falls into that pattern and has all the faults of an official history obviously written by the bureaucracy. It is general in its approach, dry, and devoid of accounts of operational activity that give life to any such work. To illustrate, the Battle of the Bulge was one of the more interesting periods for CIC in Europe and presented special challenges to it; yet this study devotes only three short paragraphs to it that impart little of the flavor of the times. It is, needless to say, heavy on organizational and line-of-command matters. Accomplishments, except for some data on operations in Italy, are discussed in such generalized language that one is never sure if CIC successes were not due more to Axis incompetence than to CIC abilities and efficiency. One thing is well emphasized, however: the lack of available linguistic ability and area knowledge in CIC to meet the operational requirements due to policies adopted. Authorities should give thought to another try at a serious effort at a CIC history, if they have not done so. Schwarzwalder's *We Caught Spies* is one of the rare books by a CIC veteran that discusses specific operations and techniques.

U.S., Defense Intelligence School. SEE **Defense Intelligence School.**

U.S., Department of Defense. THE "MAGIC" BACKGROUND OF PEARL HARBOR. 8 vols. Washington, D.C.: Government Printing Office, 1978. 3010 pp., index.

This great compilation was first completed in 1944; for its release, it was sanitized to a small extent and edited. Five of the volumes contain paraphrases of Japanese intercepts, collectively called "Magic." Three volumes are appendixes and contain verbatim messages; Volume 5 contains an index. The introduction cautions that they do not necessarily compose a definitive history of the period but should be seen "as a compilation of historical source materials," many disclosed to the public for the first time. Diplomatic messages and diplomatic historical material form the bulk of the contents, but Japanese messages dealing with espionage are also to be found. Admiral Tolley in his review in the *USNI Proceedings* judged this a storehouse of highly useful material for the historian or war buff, one that presents only factual evidence and avoids discussions and conclusions. It is, he said, useful for an understanding of what the U.S. leaders' information was in 1941 for their decisions. But it is also, as he indicates elsewhere, more than that. It is a window into Japanese thinking and deliberations, Japanese information on Germany and the Axis war effort, and plans for the increase in Japanese intelligence in the United States. Along with Ultra material released by the British Public Record Office beginning in 1977, these volumes provide a source of material to the researcher that is hard to equal.

U.S., War Department, Strategic Services Unit. WAR REPORT OF THE OSS. 2 vols. New York: Walker and Co., 1976. Vol. 1: 258 pp., index. Vol. 2: 460 pp., no index.

At the end of World War II, the U.S. Joint Chiefs of Staff requested that the OSS unit assigned to the Pentagon and renamed SSU write a history of the OSS and its predecessor, the COI. This was undertaken in 1946–1947 by a staff under the direction of Kermit Roosevelt, an OSS veteran, who has supplied new introductions. Originally top secret, it was declassified in 1976 following a minimum of deletions. The first volume covers largely the story of the creation of COI and OSS and implementing directives and is devoted primarily to organizational matters. Cave Brown in his own edition of the history, *The Secret War Report of the OSS,* made the observation that the discussion of secret finances was one of its virtues and a first for such a subject. Volume 2 deals with operations.

The history was intended as an internal record of operational and organizational matters and lessons learned and was meant to give a run-down principally of the main operations. Only a few months were allowed for its completion; as a result, there was little in the way of interviewing, and many records were still not available in Washington. Understandably, it was not regarded at the time as a comprehensive or definitive history of COI/OSS. Similarly, no attempt was made to evaluate OSS's overall contribution and no large claims were made; only occasionally is a particular operation judged. Leaving to the future and to others the assessment of OSS's role in the war was a wise and deliberate decision. All the same, it is an indispensable source on OSS and a starting point for more comprehensive histories of that organization and of individual operations. Criticism of the security decision not to include names of most OSS personnel was foreseen by Roosevelt. This unfortunate practice, insisted on by the Pentagon, compounds faults in writing style, which Roosevelt described in his *Countercoup* as "most horrible officialese." There may be the feeling as well that as an official history, the book is too deferential to the organization's leaders. R. Harris Smith's *OSS,* Persico's *Piercing the Reich,* Dulles's *The Secret Surrender,* Bradley Smith and Elena Agarossi's *Operation Sunrise,* and Peers and Brelis's *Behind the Burma Road* are some of the works on OSS that the reader will also wish to refer to for the development of aspects of its work.

U.S., Library of Congress. SEE **Library of Congress.**

V

Van Deman, Ralph Henry. MEMOIRS OF MAJOR GENERAL R.H. VAN DEMAN. 3 vols. Ft. Holabird, Md.: CIC Center, 1950–1956. 165 pp., no index.

In *The Armies of Ignorance,* Corson paid tribute to Van Deman as a person who left a lasting mark on U.S. intelligence and "a prime example of the intelligence professional's contribution to the American intelligence heritage," whose contributions were enough to earn him the title of "Father of American Military Intelligence." Allen Dulles believed he deserved this title. These three volumes, with appendixes, were sent to CIC in 1950; as specified by Van Deman, they were not to be considered a personal history and not to be published. He wrote them (and especially the first segment) because few people connected with the early history of U.S. military intelligence were still alive.

The first volume is in the nature of a history of U.S. Army intelligence and includes his personal experiences over a period of years. Book 2 relates his experiences on a special intelligence mission to Europe during World War I and as a G-2 officer with the American Expeditionary Force (AEF). The third concerns his activities as a counterintelligence officer with the U.S. Peace Delegation after the war. Corson's book should be read for a synopsis of Van Deman's work, including his more controversial second career in intelligence following his retirement in 1929. See Voska and Irwin's *Spy and Counterspy* for glimpses of Van Deman's work.

Van Der Rhoer, Edward. DEADLY MAGIC: A PERSONAL ACCOUNT OF COMMUNICATIONS INTELLIGENCE IN WORLD WAR II IN THE PACIFIC. New York: Scribner's Sons, 1978. 215 pp., index [London: Robert Hale, 1979].

The personal reminiscences of the author, who served in the U.S. naval communications intelligence organization as a linguist. He studied Japanese on his own before the war and was then selected for Japanese language training by the Navy. He worked for OP-20-G as a language expert from the spring of 1942 until the end of the war; his section, OP-20-GZ, read Japanese codes and ciphers and made translations of the messages. The major part of the book is given over to his account of the strategic and tactical military situations or to details of a particular battle. He does not dwell as much as one would have liked on the cryptologic aspects, despite his intent to write from the naval communications point of view. Van Der Rhoer is the first of the U.S. Navy comint personnel of the war to write his personal story, so the reader is justified in feeling he should have given more from his own experiences and those of his organization, despite the lack of a diary and reliance on memory. Francis Raven's review in *Cryptologia* points out the errors in this book, feels it is best when discussing personal experiences and people the author knew, but opines it shows "a quite limited knowledge" of the naval communications organization elsewhere; in fact, Raven finds it hard to believe that Van Der Rhoer is as unknowledgeable in this respect as he appears. Holmes's *Double-Edged Secrets* covers the naval intelligence war in the Pacific from the first-hand view of a naval intelligence officer benefiting from the crucial communications intelligence provided.

Van Doren, Carl. SECRET HISTORY OF THE AMERICAN REVOLUTION. Garden City, N.Y.: Garden City Publishing Co., 1941. 534 pp., bibliog., notes, index.

The title page includes the description "an account of the conspiracies of Benedict Arnold and numerous others drawn from Secret Service papers of the British Headquarters in North America, now for the first time examined and made public." Van Doren expanded his study of Arnold and André to include other operations run by the British to subvert American patriots with the aid of their loyalist allies; the fuller story of the Arnold-André affair was made possible by access to the Clinton papers, which included the complete correspondence between Arnold and the British. At the time of its publication, this was rightly hailed as a solid and basic addition to the great books on the American Revolution. Commager, in his *New York Times* review, was of the view that Van Doren did not pretend that this was "the" secret history, since there was much more that was secret; he was certainly correct, for this book only touches one aspect of the clandestine and covert parts of the war. All of these combined with the secret diplomacy conducted on the American continent and abroad would constitute the full secret war of both sides. Even Van Doren's account of British and loyalist clandestine and covert actions against the revolutionary cause on the American continent is only a portion of their total effort. Just as Commager felt this work would contribute an interesting chapter in a full story of the American Revolution, so it would be an important segment of a full history of the intelligence or secret war. A vital new piece in the Arnold-British relationship may be contained in the 1977 work of Frank E. McKone, *General Sullivan: New Hampshire Patriot,* which identifies the British agent close to Arnold, John Hall, as a link in Arnold's defection. In retrospect, it can now be seen that one of the consequences of Van Doren's work was that it stimulated interest in the role of intelligence in the American Revolution and inspired the research of others.

Varner, Roy, and Collier, Wayne. A MATTER OF RISK: THE INCREDIBLE INSIDE STORY OF THE CIA'S HUGHES GLOMAR EXPLORER MISSION TO RAISE A RUSSIAN SUBMARINE. New York: Random House, 1978. 258 pp., no index [London: Hodder and Stoughton, 1979].

In contrast to Burleson, author of *The Jennifer Project,* who had no first-hand knowledge or connection with his subject, Collier and Varner had the former's association with the project as a firm base on which to try to write the story of the attempt to raise a sunken Soviet submarine. Collier was a contract employee of CIA in charge of recruiting personnel for the mission. He is thus able to give first-hand details on arrangements for cover, personnel selection, and training and on technical characteristics of the *Glomar Explorer.* He left CIA as the ship went to sea, so it is up to the point of its mission, covered in the first segment of the work, that Varner, the writer, can relate facts with greatest authority and confidence. Collier acquired details on what happened during the ship's mission from talking to certain crew members, which is not as trustworthy as personal knowledge. Collier also was not in a position to know or to speak with any authority on such matters as high-level finances, planning, and decision making, yet he has a tendency to make assumptions at times without making it clear they are only that. And in contrast to the cool objectivity of the rest of the work, the final chapter on conclusions is out of character and weakens the story with what is seemingly an attempt to accommodate to the prevalent opinion about intelligence activities of the time. Also detracting from it are some items that appear designed to be sensational—such things as alleged intercepts of crew members' mail, hiring of Jews, and financial arrangements. All this said, it is the best book on the subject until someone composes a better version based on either official records or first-hand knowledge of the project from start to finish (from a fairly high level hierarchically).

Vassall, John. VASSALL: THE AUTOBIOGRAPHY OF A SPY. London: Sidgwick and Jackson, 1975. 193 pp., index.

Vassall was the British Admiralty clerk who was discovered in 1962 to have been a Soviet agent, tried, and sentenced to prison. In writing this and trying to explain and rationalize his espionage work for the Soviets, he unintentionally gives an insight into his character and his weaknesses, which (aside from his homosexuality) were exploitable by Soviet intelligence. He reveals little of his espionage work and of what information he passed his Soviet handlers; in fact, his spy activities are presented as merely a brief and unpleasant interlude in his social and sex life. An air of unreality pervades the book—Vassall actually thought he should not be prosecuted because he "was the victim of circumstances." There are a number of things of value in it, nevertheless. His attitude toward his Soviet bosses and case officers is worthy of examination by experts on agent handling and the psychology of agent recruitment. It has instructional value on how blackmail operations are run (from both the defensive and offensive points of view) for intelligence ends, assuming Vassall's version of how he was recruited is correct. There are, after all, not many books by agents who profess recruitment by blackmail, a method more common than the layman assumes and one especially used by the Soviet services and their allies within their jurisdictions. Also important are the lessons to be derived on the security lapses of British authorities in light of the lifestyle of Vassall, the clues, and the signs. For this and for penetrating observations on Vassall, see West's *The Vassall Affair* and *The New Meaning of Treason.* See also Pincher's *Their Trade Is Treachery* for other views and allegations concerning the damage, discovery, and security implications of this case.

Voska, Emmanuel Victor, and Irwin, William Henry. SPY AND COUNTERSPY. New York: Doubleday, Doran, 1940. 322 pp., no index [London: Harrap, 1941].

One reason for the defeat of German intelligence efforts in the United States prior to the U.S. entry into the war in 1917 was the existence of Voska's counterespionage organization, made up of Czechs and Slovaks. Voska served as the principal agent and representative of Tomás Masaryk, the father of Czechoslovakia and its first president. He put his organization and its capabilities at the disposal of Sir William Wiseman and Commodore Guy Gaunt, both of British intelligence in the United States. William James in his *The Eyes of the Navy* tells of Gaunt's having succeeded in planting Czech agents in the Austrian consulate-general in New York and obtaining some German and Austrian correspondence to Europe; he is probably referring to Voska's men. Willert, also in a position to know, describes the vital role Voska played for the British in the United States in *The Road To Safety.* The work his organization did in antisabotage security, in penetrating German and Austrian diplomatic installations, and in uncovering hostile political action such as the Hindu secessionist activities is described. In 1915, Voska was contacted by the FBI and agreed to cooperate with them as well. As Sir William Wiseman was the model for Sir William Stephenson for British intelligence in the United States in World War II, we can assume that Voska's organization and its work served as the inspiration of organizations that cooperated with the British in that war because of anti-German motivation. Voska's story is primarily of historical interest when it deals with his counterespionage work prior to the U.S. entry into the war. There are, however, interesting glimpses of his G-2 association with Colonel Van Deman and Lieutenant Colonel Marlborough Churchill in Europe, as well as a sketchy picture of his work in Russia in 1917. Tuchman in *The Zimmermann Telegram* called Voska "the most valuable secret agent of the Allies in the U.S." Whether that is true or not, and whether all the accomplishments he lists for his group were exactly as pictured, the fact is that Voska has been largely neglected by most intelligence historians and researchers. Irwin, a journalist, served a short time with Voska during the war.

W

Wade, Alexander G. SPIES TO-DAY. London: Stanley Paul, 1939. 283 pp., index.

Another one of those books whose predictions history proved wrong and that is best forgotten except as a reminder to security and counterintelligence officers not to lose their perspective. Writing just before the start of World War II, the author (who also wrote a book entitled *Counterspy*) alerted his fellow British citizens to the threat of the peacetime spy, propagandist, saboteur, and agitator preparing the ground, as he visualized it, for operations in Britain in time of war. He cited no known cases to back his claims of enemy preparations and of spies lurking everywhere. As events were to prove, the British isles turned out to be much more secure from Axis agents than he figured, and he was far wide of the mark on everything concerning the Axis threat to security including the danger of refugees. Only where women were concerned was he modern in outlook—he regarded women as doing work in espionage equal to that of men.

Wagner, Arthur L. THE SERVICE OF SECURITY AND INFORMATION. Kansas City, Mo.: Hudson-Kimberly, 1903. 236 pp., index.

Wagner was head of the Bureau of Military Intelligence of the U.S. War Department in 1898. Van Deman, later to gain fame as the "father of American military intelligence," served under him at one point. He ran afoul of the secretary of war at the time of the confrontation of the United States and Spain that led to war, and he was removed from his post; his promotion was blocked for the rest of his career, and he was named a brigadier general only on his deathbed. This 1903 edition was the twelfth of a work that first appeared in 1893; it was officially made a manual of instruction by the U.S. War Department. Its title is misleading by modern-day meanings of the terms. It is a tactical military manual covering such military practices and methods as reconnaissance, patrols, and advance and rear guards. Only one chapter is devoted to classical espionage, but it is of interest because it probably mirrors the general attitude toward espionage in the U.S. Army at the time. Civilian spies, Wagner said, "often deserve all the obloquy so often cast upon spies in general," but they are indispensable to a general; those forced to spy by coercion should not be of the "superior classes" whose patriotism is of a higher order (he quotes from a French authority). War correspondents are an "unavoidable evil." But Wagner is more acute about deception and shows a finely developed sense for it and its controlled use in his brief discussion of how known double agents, foreign agents, and even friendly foreign journalists can serve this purpose. Wagner's view of intelligence was that it was an arm of military operations, and he restricts his thinking to that. Corson's *The Armies of Ignorance* contains brief sections on Wagner's work in connection with the Spanish-American War.

Walker, David E. LUNCH WITH A STRANGER. London: Allan Wingate, 1957. 223 pp., no index [New York: Norton].

In 1938, Walker, then a British journalist and foreign correspondent, was recruited to work for British intelligence. Despite the fact that he was "blown" in 1939 and had to leave Switzerland, he continued his intelligence work under the cover of newspaper correspondent in Rumania, Bulgaria, Yugoslavia, and Greece until 1941. He then joined SOE and was assigned to Lisbon as head of its oral deception unit until the summer of 1944. His job, as he put it, was to be "in charge of subversion and deceit from Portugal." The main weapon he employed was that of "sibs" or rumors, for which he recruited a network. How successful this deception device was is uncertain. The exact impact of organized planting of rumors on the enemy during the war has yet to be determined satisfactorily. Walker claims it was valuable and cites a number of British memoirs and captured enemy intelligence records as support. Dennis Wheatley, a member of LCS, the deception group in London, wrote in 1976 that deception means such as misleading table talk by British ambassadors really counted, while spectacular operations such as Mincemeat were only a minor part of the entire deception effort. Other personal memoirs and books of the war have mentioned and described the use of rumors as a deception weapon, but Walker's, short as it is on details, is unique in that it is by someone with prime responsibility for such at a particular intelligence station. There are some very general observations and remarks on the D-Day deception operations (Fortitude is mentioned), but otherwise there is not much to be learned about this subject from this personal memoir. Interesting to note is Walker's belief that he was not a successful agent ("no successful agent writes a book") and his commentary on his SIS training in 1938 as being "on a most prosaic plane."

Walters, Vernon A. SILENT MISSIONS. Garden City, N.Y.: Doubleday, 1978. 630 pp., index.

For those who have listened to this linguist and raconteur, *Silent Missions* is the next best thing to hearing his many stories and anecdotes. However, the title will mislead because General Walters's career was not one involving primarily secret missions and intelligence per se. His involvement during the Vietnam War in the secret talks between the United States and North Vietnam and the People's Republic of China, which he helped to set up in Paris, his chapter on Watergate, and his testimony as deputy director of CIA constitute the core of such subjects in the book. For most of his involvement with great events and figures, Walters was an observer rather than an active participant. The reader looking for items dealing with intelligence operations or history will have to be content with many anecdotes and descriptions that are of interest but mostly unrelated to those subjects. This need not have been the case had Walters elected to write more about his work at CIA and of his assignments as defense attaché.

Way, Peter. CODES AND CIPHERS. London: Aldus Books, 1977. 141 pp., index.

In a review in *Cryptologia,* David Kahn called *Codes and Ciphers* "the first illustrated history of codes and ciphers." He added that he considered the pictures in it as first-rate, with many shown for the first time. Kahn also observed that the text would remind people of his own *The Codebreakers* and of a rewrite of Winterbotham's *The Ultra Secret.* In his reliance on Winterbotham, Way repeats many errors first made by the earlier writer. He rehashes the old tale of a Polish worker in a German factory producing Enigma machines as the means by which the Poles acquired data on such machines and reproduced them; Winterbotham's version of the German raid on Coventry and the British handling of intelligence about the coming attack are repeated, as are the earlier claims of Ultra's contributions in the Battle of Britain. Winterbotham is elevated to the status of final judge of who was to have access to Ultra. The story of the Lucy ring in Switzerland is derived from Foote's account in *Handbook for Spies,* with all its errors and distortions. The discovery of Peenemünde and the V1 are made to appear as exclusively an Ultra success, while the breaking of the Kroger one-time pad (in the Portland spy case) is presented as accomplished entirely by cryptologic means assisted by human error. But, to quote Kahn again, the photographs are what make this book worth having.

Weber, Ralph E. UNITED STATES DIPLOMATIC CODES AND CIPHERS 1775–1938. Chicago: Precedent Publishing, 1979. 615 pp., bibliog., index.

In his lengthy review in *Cryptologia,* David Kahn called this work the first solid study of diplomatic codes and ciphers used by the United States and "the first quantum leap" in more than a decade in our knowledge of pre–World War II cryptology. In fact, Kahn thought Weber had done for early American cryptography "what Meitter did for Renaissance Italian and papal cryptography." The text and notes are only some two hundred sixty pages long; the remainder is the various codes used by the U.S. diplomatic service during the period covered. Weber the historian managed to uncover in his research some fascinating facts. The most astonishing is that during the Civil War, U.S. diplomats did not have codes or ciphers. This was the situation for nineteen years, between 1848 and 1867. Most intriguing was his discovery that Congress authorized during the Articles of Confederation the inspection of letters by the secretary of state when national "safety or interest" required it. We learn that a code first used in 1803 was not discarded until 1867; that the U.S. intercepted and inspected foreign and domestic dispatches until 1789; and the the U.S. diplomatic service used French and English couriers on occasion as late as the 1870s.

Kahn thought this work deserved the adjective "definitive." This opinion is strange, because he points out shortcomings in Weber's treatment. Among them are the following. First, the last chapter does not examine post–World War I cryptosystems in detail and is skimpy. Second, Weber heavily weights the book on the side of the American Revolution and the early years of the republic. Third, the volume misses a few areas in addition to the period after World War I, such as compromises of U.S. systems. Fourth, more background information to make clear the role of communications in U.S. diplomacy was needed. Fans of Allen Dulles will be interested to read of his 1925 lecture that too much was made of secrecy in diplomacy, which shows that even Dulles was affected by the Wilsonian concepts of his time. The book won one of the annual book awards given by the National Intelligence Study Center for "intelligent writing on intelligence."

Weinstein, Allen. PERJURY: THE HISS-CHAMBERS CASE. New York: Alfred A. Knopf, 1978. 589 pp., bibliog., notes, index [Toronto: Random House of Canada, 1978].

The most current and comprehensive of a long list of works on this case. Weinstein had unprecedented access to FBI, Justice Department, and other U.S. records on the case following a lawsuit and amendment of the FOIA. He also sought out new documentary and oral evidence, among which were the Hiss legal defense files and interviews with former Soviet intelligence operatives. U.S. records provided an inside look into U.S. security and counterintelligence against Soviet espionage at the time—their lack of coordination and bureaucratic rivalries. Such records and interviews throw additional light on Soviet operations in the United States. Certain CI matters, such as Adolf Berle's questionable handling of Chambers's specifics on Soviet espionage or governmental delays in pursuing leads, still remain instructive and hard to fathom despite the author's best efforts to explain or to uncover the reasons. Copious notes provide enriching comments as well as scholarly (if at times confusing) documentation. Some noncrucial factual errors have been cited by experts, while certain Hiss supporters have challenged the work's substance and handling of documentation. For example, see C. J. Smith's review in the June 1978 issue of *Harper's.*

Welch, Robert H. THE LIFE OF JOHN BIRCH: IN THE STORY OF ONE AMERICAN BOY, THE ORDEAL OF HIS AGE. Boston: Western Islands Publishers, 1960. 130 pp., index [Chicago: Henry Regnery, 1954].

Birch served with Fourteenth U.S. Air Force intelligence under General Chennault and was on loan to OSS from May 1945 on. The first segment of this book, some seventy-odd pages long, outlines Birch's work in China as an air force officer between 1942 and his death at the hands of the Chinese Communists in August 1945. It is based mostly on the record of OSS, or as much as OSS had, for even that record is not complete; it does not contain answers to questions about the exact nature of the operations Birch was involved in. There is only a general treatment of his intelligence and liaison work. Birch had an unsurpassed knowledge of China, its language, and its peoples' mentality. These advantages and his rapport with the natives must have been used successfully in his operational work; but if a record of this work exists, it can only be found elsewhere. The full story of his wartime work has yet to be written for much is still unknown, including the exact purpose of his mission at the time he was killed and who ordered it, knowing it would take Birch into Communist-held territory. The second segment of the book, which is the author's political message and political exploitation of Birch's death, can be skipped.

West, Rebecca. THE NEW MEANING OF TREASON. New York: Viking Press, 1964. 370 pp., index [Canada: Macmillan].

The revised edition of an earlier book that was concerned with traitors in World War II. Now expanded to include accounts of Soviet espionage into the early 1960s, it is marked by the penetrating analyses and writing ability for which the author is famous. The cases paraded before us—those of May, Fuchs, Pontecorvo, Vassall, Houghton, Blake, Burgess, Maclean, Philby, the Rosenbergs, and others—illustrate the size of the problem of Soviet espionage and provide a telling contrast to the treason for fascism represented by Joyce and Amery. It is a sad litany of the lax security that prevailed in the West, especially in Britain, where the quality of security oversight was shockingly bad. West provides many examples of this and discerning judgments on the traitors and their motives; at the same time she focuses our attention on the expanded security problem created by developments in science and the bureaucracy. There is some interesting speculation on Soviet motives in certain of these cases. She urges vigilance and the elimination of sentimentality about traitors by democratic societies; they must be viewed for what they are. Blackstock and Schaf's bibliography makes the point that while many books and articles are concerned with the harm to personal freedom resulting from the activities of security and counterespionage agencies, this one speaks of the harm to a nation by too little attention to the problem of traitors and the protection of secrets.

This work has been praised but has not been immune to certain criticisms or reservations. Some scholars complained of the lack of source notes and documentation. Some critics felt that West generalized a bit too freely about the meaning of the espionage she described, such as implying that persons in a particular category were prone to treason or suggesting that the extent of treason was symptomatic of the West's decline. And now we naturally know more about how certain Soviet agents were discovered and need not speculate as she did. We also know that Blake was not (as she thought was probable) a double agent with the knowledge of his British superiors. What is important is how well so much of this work stands up after so many years and how vivid her account remains. Dulles in *Great True Spy Stories* called West one of those knowledgeable and imaginative reporters versed in the lore of espionage and able to get close to the heart of the cases she studied.

West, Rebecca. THE VASSALL AFFAIR. London: Sunday Telegraph, 1963. 99 pp., no index.

West undertook to delve into issues raised by the Vassall case and the tribunal set up by the British government in its aftermath. Vassall was the clerk in the British Admiralty who was a Soviet agent from at least the time he served in the naval attaché's office in Moscow. West is incomparable and unsparing in her penetrating observations and comments on Vassall the agent and on the British security system as revealed by this case. Her conclusions are worth pondering, especially her view that one of the purposes of the Soviets is to destroy the self-confidence of their adversaries. So, too, are such thoughts as "the essence of security is the assessment of character." The focus of the work is on the Radcliffe Tribunal and an evaluation of its findings on responsibility on the British side rather than details of the Vassall operation itself. See also her thoughts on Vassall in *The New Meaning of Treason* and compare both with Vassall's apologia, *Vassall.*

Whaley, Barton. CODEWORD BARBAROSSA. Cambridge, Mass., and London: MIT Press, 1973. 272 pp., bibliog., notes, index.

Whaley is considered by many a U.S. academic authority on the subject of deception in warfare. He is a pioneer in the study of the history, concept, and application of strategem; see his *Strategem* (below). The central argument or thesis of *Codeword Barbarossa* is that Hitler did succeed in deceiving Stalin about his intentions in 1941. Whaley also concluded that Roberta Wohlstetter's theory on surprise was not applicable to the Barbarossa attack because it disregarded deception as an important element in the equation. According to one expert, Whaley's model, which singles out deception as the key to surprise, complements rather than competes with Wohlstetter's. Whaley is first-rate in research, and his industry and ability to relate diverse data are laudable. He understands intelligence, and his feel for deception is matched by his ease of exposition. Hinsley in the official *British Intelligence in the Second World War* uses Whaley's material from this book extensively, with some thirteen footnotes citing it. However, some experts have taken issue with Whaley's theory of Hitler's successful deception of Stalin. Specifically, the following have been cited. First, nowhere does he produce specific evidence that Stalin was directly or significantly influenced by the German deception operations. There is a dearth of reliable information from the Soviet side on what transpired in the Kremlin, the Soviet staff, and the intelligence services. One writer called this the basic weakness of the work. Second, Whaley mixes the information from the non-Soviet side, much of it from secondary sources. His sections on communications intelligence and the Rado net in Switzerland, to cite two examples, contain many errors. He did not know of Ultra's contribution, although he guessed at its possible importance after Malcolm Muggeridge broke silence on this source of intelligence. Third, a weak part of the book deals with specific examples of German deception operations, their follow-through, their channels, and their effect. What he has to say on this in support of his theory pales in the face of evidence he recounts of indications of German intentions. Even he admits the security measures for Barbarossa were unable to hide the plans from foreign intelligence. Whaley rejects another thesis: that Stalin was wrong about the Germans not because they succeeded in deceiving him but because he deceived himself. This would bring in a third element beyond secrecy and deception, i.e., what one writer refers to as "that less obvious one" of self-deception. The bibliography is lengthy and useful, though Whaley's evaluations of some of the works are debatable.

Whaley, Barton. STRATEGEM: DECEPTION AND SURPRISE IN WAR. 4 vols. Unpublished, 1969. 1246 pp., bibliog., index.

Whaley called this a study of surprise and deception in warfare, particularly as strategically applied; "strategem" is the term he uses for this form of strategic deception. He employs case studies of some sixty-eight instances of strategic deception in warfare between 1914 and 1968; in addition there are some forty-seven examples of tactical deception and of other cases where it was not employed. Whaley pioneered renewed interest in deception at a time when awareness of Soviet use of it both in war and peace (by the use of disinformation) had been heightened in the West. He touches on disinformation, but it is deception in warfare that captures his attention and that he documents. We find him saying that "the Soviets still have much to learn about the subtleties of strategem," an opinion that will be contested; so, too, will his failure to appreciate Soviet applications of *maskirovka* in their military campaigns and disinformation to serve their ends both in peace and in war. Whaley makes a noble effort to penetrate the secrets of the Allied deception organization in World War II, and though he makes a number of mistakes, he does rather well considering the access he had.

He must be given credit for this initial effort to deal with a subject of great importance not only in warfare but also to intelligence and national security. Some will wish to refine and expand his views on the relationship of counterintelligence and deception and of security and deception. He could have broadened his examples to show how deception can be used to place strains on a society and its economy in peacetime; Whaley himself recognized that deception is the cheapest means of manipulating a nation's military economy. His belief that the Germans showed talent for and were successful in deception from World War I continuously through World War II will arouse debate. It was the basis for his thesis of German success in fooling the Soviets in 1941 (see his *Codeword Barbarossa,* above). The reader may be confused by the author's criteria for assigning precedence to various books on deception or his failure to include some—Barkas's *The Camouflage Story* and James's *The Eyes of the Navy,* to cite two. For reasons that are not clear, this pathbreaking study was never published.

Wheatley, Dennis. THE DECEPTION PLANNERS: MY SECRET WAR. London: Hutchinson, 1980. 230 pp., index.

Until the publication of this work, Wingate's 1959 *Not in the Limelight* was the only work by a former member of the London Controlling Section (LCS) that said anything about this deception unit of World War II other than the author's own *Stranger Than Fiction* (below). *The Deception Planners* was one volume of Wheatley's memoirs and dealt exclusively with his work as a deception planner; it was published posthumously. It was based on material Wheatley wrote shortly after the war that was supplemented but never fully revised. Wheatley said that the history of the LCS that he began in 1943 but did not finish served as one source for this book. Although a good deal of this book is about personal matters, it is the only detailed first-hand account of the LCS and its personnel and work and must serve as a reference work on the organization until official histories of it and of Allied deception are released. Wheatley contributes good character sketches of his colleagues in LCS and clarifies boundaries of responsibility for deception operations between LCS and Dudley Clarke's A Force in the Mediterranean and the Middle East. He helps us to understand better the relationship between LCS and the deception unit set up under Colonel Wild in COSSAC and later in SHAEF. Wheatley gives credit to Flight Lieutenant Chumley of MI5 (spelled "Cholmondeley" in Montagu's *Beyond Top Secret Ultra*) for originating the idea for Operation Mincemeat. He corrects the erroneous version given in Butler's *Mason-Mac* that General Mason-MacFarlane's broadcast to his troops in Gibraltar was not part of the deception plan for the North African invasion. He gives the Soviets full marks for their cooperation in the deception plan for Overlord; but this interpretation has now been questioned by Cruickshank in *Deception in World War II.* We learn of the size of the security problem faced by planners: no fewer than seven hundred persons had access in 1943 to the minutes of the daily meetings of the British Chiefs of Staff. There is no mention of Ultra and its role in formulating and conducting deception operations, and the U.S. role in deception is barely mentioned.

Wheatley, Dennis. STRANGER THAN FICTION. London: Hutchinson, 1959. 353 pp., index.

Sir Dennis was one of the first members of the London Controlling Section (LCS), the British body that coordinated at the Chiefs of Staff level deception plans and operations during World War II. He joined this section at the end of 1941 and served as an RAF representative until the fall of 1944. This book, unfortunately, contains only one small segment on his association with deception work. What little he has to say on deception gives no specifics on any operations and the name LCS is not given. He does give names of the members of LCS (perhaps the first or one of the first times they had appeared) and a very brief account of LCS's formation, using the excuse that General Sir John Kennedy had let out the secret of the section's existence in his book *The Business of War.* Since first-hand accounts of LCS are rare, his article in the September 1976 issue of *RUSI,* "Deception in World War II," is another valuable peek at this organization by one of its original members. For a much fuller account of Wheatley's work in LCS and about that organization, see his *The Deception Planners* (above).

White, John Baker, THE BIG LIE. New York: Thomas Y. Crowell, 1955. 235 pp., no index [London: Evans Bros].

White served most of World War II in London and the Middle East as an officer in Political Warfare Executive, the British psychological warfare organization directed against the Axis and occupied countries. This work is unhappily a bad mixture of two approaches: the autobiographical or "what I did during the war" and the general (dealing with deception work against the Germans). The review in the *Times Literary Supplement* commented that this approach, the difficulty of which is apparent to the reader, must have presented some problems to the author. White's role in deception was obviously inconsequential; yet he tries to hitch his wagon to the deception role in such a way as to make himself and/or PWE central to such operations. This he does in a variety of ways; by preposterous connections, by intimation, and by the mere confusion in his mind of what was deception and what purely psychological warfare. The title of the book is used indiscriminately and often incorrectly in the text and must have infuriated veterans of PWE. Some deception operations he describes, such as Montagu's Mincemeat or Fortitude, are better dealt with elsewhere. His account of other deception operations have numerous errors as to results, means, or the role he and PWE played in them, and thus his version must not be relied on. Since his own experiences in deception are inflated as to effect and his inside knowledge of overall deception operations is incomplete, faulty, or confused, this book has no lasting value to the study of deception. The only thing that marks it is its early treatment of the subject. Note that his implications of a direct, on-the-spot Soviet complicity in the revolt of the Greek forces in the Middle East have not been substantiated.

Whitehouse, Arch. ESPIONAGE AND COUNTERESPIONAGE: ADVENTURES IN MILITARY INTELLIGENCE. Garden City, N.Y.: Doubleday, 1964. 288 pp., bibliog., index.

Whitehouse served as a war correspondent in Europe in World War II. He later wrote a number of popular war histories. This he called the story of military intelligence from the point of view of those involved and the record of "the everyday operations of agents." Aside from a couple of segments (on the incident of the loss of the courier near Spain just prior to the invasion of North Africa, the Australian coast watchers, and Landau's military intelligence operations in World War I), there is nothing to recommend this to the serious student of intelligence. Whitehouse has written a series of war stories in which military intelligence may or may not figure. His writing of the tactical moves at the Battle of Jutland and not including the crucial role of Room 40 and the errors in communicating intelligence is a case in point. Another is his putting the special sabotage operations of midget subs and frogmen or the work of the underwater demolitions men in the category of military intelligence when the long descriptions he gives barely mention any intelligence-collection work. He can mislead on the importance of particular events or agents: an instance that comes to mind is his magnifying out of proportion the work of the Japanese agents, the Kühns, on Pearl Harbor.

Whiteside, Thomas. AN AGENT IN PLACE: THE WENNERSTROM AFFAIR. New York: Viking Press, 1966. 150 pp., no index [Toronto: Macmillan].

The story of Stig Wennerstrom, the Swedish air force colonel who was a Soviet agent, this was originally a series in the *New Yorker.* Wennerstrom was an agent of the Soviets for at least fifteen years until his arrest by the Swedes in 1963; he was found guilty and given a life sentence. U.S. interest was heightened because he had served as an air attaché in Washington. Whiteside studied transcripts of the pretrial interrogation of Wennerstrom, which ran to more than three thousand typewritten pages; those he saw were censored by the Swedish authorities, so he did not get everything. He also interviewed U.S. and Swedish intelligence officials but advises he made it a point not to seek or accept any off-the-record information. Many familiar with the case consider this the best account available in English; DIS's *Bibliography* describes it thus. As good as Whiteside is in describing what he learned, he does not give a full explanation for Wennerstrom's decision and reasons for working for the Soviets because the full record was not made available; Wennerstrom's own account, published in 1972 in Swedish under the title *From Beginning to End,* is said to add little. For Wennerstrom's effect on the United States and NATO, based on his translated testimony, see *The Wennerstrom Case: How it Touched the U.S. and NATO* (U.S., Senate, Committee on the Judiciary, Subcommittee to Investigate the Administration of the Internal Security Act; Washington, D.C.: Government Printing Office, 1964). Refer also to Dulles's *Great True Spy Stories* for his opinion of Wennerstrom's account during his trial and interrogation.

Whiting, Charles. THE SPYMASTERS: THE TRUE STORY OF ANGLO-AMERICAN INTELLIGENCE OPERATIONS WITHIN NAZI GERMANY 1939–1945. New York: Saturday Review Press and E.P. Dutton, 1976. 232 pp., index [London: Leo Cooper, 1975. *The Battle of Twelveland*].

What purports to be the "true story" of Anglo-American operations with Nazi Germany turns out to be a potpourri of fact and fiction, actuality and myth, assumptions, sketchy versions of certain events, contrived tie-ins, and a certain confusion. Whiting acknowledges the assistance of certain well-known individuals, yet in the introduction he says the professionals were "not prepared to talk about their activities in Germany during the war"—he names four British officials in this category who are also included in his acknowledgment list. He does not usually identify his exact sources of so-called inside information, which is often off the mark but sometimes so accurate as to indicate access to well-informed sources or successful combining of certain versions. The story of the alleged SIS traitor in Holland, Hooper, can be found in Ladislav Farago's *The Game of the Foxes;* the story of the interrogation of the German officer who after the war fingered a German agent in SIS was probably the one told by Winterbotham in *The Nazi Connection.* Winterbotham seems to have been one of the sources relied on for matters like the work of Sidney Cotton, relations within the SIS, and the treatment of Winterbotham by that service at the end of the war. Though some details are wrong, Whiting did write more of OSS operations into Germany under William Casey than did R. Harris Smith in *OSS,* a subject that had to wait for Persico's *Piercing the Reich* and the release of the U.S. War Department's *War Report of the OSS* for adequate coverage. He tells of the important Czech and (subsequently) Allied agent A-54. There will be marked differences with his harsh judgments of the work of Allen Dulles and of his political motives. Representative of his penchant for transforming speculation to fact is his presenting as certain the SIS use of Foote and the Lucy ring in Switzerland to transmit disguised Ultra to the Soviets. There is a good segment on SIS's role and the basis of its intelligence successes against Germany.

Whitwell, John. BRITISH AGENT. London: William Kimber, 1966. 224 pp., no index.

In *The Infernal Grove,* Muggeridge describes his introduction into SIS and his first contact, Leslie Nicholson (Whitwell's true name). Muggeridge says Nicholson was agreeable with a gentle manner, "amiable and helpful"; he thought him more a Bertie Wooster than a spymaster.

Nicholson served in SIS from 1929 through World War II in posts such as Riga and Prague. He was sent temporarily to Spain and Portugal to handle intelligence defectors. Despite these assignments and his handling of Middle East and Balkan matters for SIS during the war, he has relatively little to tell, although the book earned the praise of Haldane in *The Hidden War.* Others, including Blackstock and Schaf, thought it cynical but allowed that it was one of the few insights available on SIS. Muggeridge introduced it as neither hair-raising nor breathtaking, only true. Sardonic it is, but there are some good lessons on poor practices by intelligence services, including his own, which failed to train him properly. Of added interest are his claims that he managed during the first months of the war to get the complete wireless code used by German agents in the Baltic, that a Gestapo officer who defected in Spain in March 1941 provided information on the German invasion plan for Russia, Barbarossa, and that the Germans deceived the British in Riga for a whole year via a double agent.

Wighton, Charles. PIN-STRIPE SABOTEUR: THE STORY OF "ROBIN"; BRITISH AGENT AND FRENCH RESISTANCE LEADER. London: Odhams Press, 1959. 256 pp., no index.

Wighton does not correctly identify "Robin," the Swiss industrialist and Jew who, he said, organized his own network in France against the Germans in World War II. He pictures Robin as later operating in Switzerland when the Prosper network, with which Robin was tied, was broken up by the Germans. Wighton credits Robin with all sorts of great feats, including the discovery of the key to the mystery of the German rocket research base at Peenemünde. According to Foot in *SOE in France,* Wighton is in error when he attributes to Jacques Weil the code name Robin and the position of another man. The real leader of the Juggler network was Jean Worms. Foot also called this wartime life of Weil one "with plenty of imaginative reconstruction" and added that the errors to be found were the kind that made it all too typical of many of the works about SOE in English written at that time.

Willert, Arthur. THE ROAD TO SAFETY: A STUDY IN ANGLO-AMERICAN RELATIONS. London: Derek Verschoyle, 1952. 181 pp., index [New York: Praeger, 1953].

The author was a correspondent for the *London Times* in Washington before, during, and after World War I. During that conflict he was secretary of the British War Mission and representative of the Ministry of Information in Washington. He also served at one time as head of the news department of the Foreign Office. He was thus in a good position to set forth the story of the extraordinary services of Sir William Wiseman. Wiseman was chief of British intelligence in Washington (Mackenzie in *Greek Memories* identifies him as the SIS representative in the United States). Hyde in *Room 3603* refers to him as the World War I predecessor of Sir William Stephenson and the man on whose experiences the latter was able to draw. The book deals with Wiseman's role in high-level diplomacy in the United States, but the second chapter provides information on his work as intelligence chief prior to his being introduced to the Americans as such. Willert based this on some of Wiseman's papers as well as on his own recollections. Here we see something of the British tie-in with Emmanuel Voska and his organization to penetrate German and Austro-Hungarian installations and operations in the United States and of political maneuvering within British intelligence organizations for primacy in dealing with the United States once that country had become a belligerent; we learn of the dispatch of Somerset Maugham to Russia to run the British-U.S. intelligence and propaganda organization in that country (and of Wiseman's lecturing Maugham on the advantages of clarity of expression). Willert wrote this book (whose title is ill chosen) to throw fresh light on Wiseman's role, which was a key one. It is far from an adequate treatment of Wiseman's intelligence role in the United States which has yet to be written. Wiseman is truly a neglected figure in intelligence history—Seth's *Encyclopedia of Espionage,* for all its attention to

World War I, does not list him. For more on Voska and his side of the story, see Voska and Irwin's *Spy and Counterspy.*

Willoughby, Charles A. SORGE: SOVIET MASTER SPY. London: William Kimber, 1952. 256 pp., no index [New York: Dutton. *Shanghai Conspiracy: The Sorge Ring*].

Based on the original report of the case of Richard Sorge (the Soviet agent in Japan) completed by the staff of General Willoughby of General MacArthur's G-2 in Japan. It was compiled from Japanese court records and other material. It also has a chapter on Agnes Smedley. In the introduction, Willoughby made the point that the Sorge case paralleled the Canadian espionage cases. Deakin and Storry in their far superior *The Case of Richard Sorge* make the points that: Willoughby reluctantly released the Sorge report; there were certain political and legal motives in his pursuit of his research into Communist activity in Shanghai; as a result of the Gouzenko disclosures of Soviet espionage in Canada, Willoughby redrafted the report on the Sorge case and forwarded it to Washington; U.S. authorities were oblivious to the Sorge ring when they first occupied Japan; the first clue had come from a Japanese official to Willoughby (a fact that has been verified). They conclude that Willoughby distorted the historical significance of the case by highlighting it as one episode in a conspiracy extending to the United States. Others criticize this book as poorly organized, containing interpretations that reflected Willoughby's political values, and drawing conclusions with less care than is paid to the facts of the case itself. The reader will do best by relying on Deakin and Storry.

Wingate, Ronald. NOT IN THE LIMELIGHT. London: Hutchinson, 1959. 232 pp., no index.

Sir Dennis Wheatley, a member of a group that planned and coordinated British deception in World War II, LSC

(London Controlling Section), wrote in 1976 that not one group member had published anything on its activities. Sir Dennis was not quite right; Sir Ronald Wingate did publish something in this book, albeit very circumspectly. *Not in the Limelight,* his autobiography, contains one chapter devoted to deception in World War II about which he knew or with which he was connected. He does not mention LCS by name or anyone else connected with it except John Bevan, the controller, whose deputy he was. The organization is only vaguely identified as an element or echelon of the planning staff of the Chiefs of Staff. Despite his careful presentation, what he provides is of significance to the history of deception for two principal reasons. First, as stated earlier, Wingate is the only member of the LCS until 1980 besides Wheatley to have published anything on its deception work. Second, this is an early disclosure of anything authoritative on this subject. He provides some principles that govern deception, examples in history, and descriptions of some operations in the war, covering Europe and the war against Japan (he was posted to Ceylon in the fall of 1944 to run deceptions there). Much of what he relates has become better known, but considering prevailing restrictions when he wrote, the book is still a good, concentrated exposition on deception. Cave Brown lists it, quotes from it, and interviewed Wingate for his *Bodyguard of Lies.* For a look at Wingate and the LCS by an insider, see Wheatley's *The Deception Planners.*

Winstone, H.V.F. CAPTAIN SHAKESPEAR: A PORTRAIT. London: Jonathan Cape, 1976. 326 pp., bibliog., index [New York: Quartet Books, 1978].

King Ibn Saud of Saudi Arabia thought Captain William Henry Shakespear the greatest European he had ever known. Shakespear is one of those big "ifs" of history; had he not been killed at the start of 1915 but lived to represent Ibn Saud's cause as Feisal's was by others, the course of events in the Middle East during and after World War I may very well have been different. Winstone has written a portrait rather than a biography of this captain in the Indian Army and later political agent in Kuwait (between 1909 and 1914). This is because official records of his service in Kuwait were destroyed or have disappeared, so what Winstone was able to find in other records such as Shakespear's own diaries and notebooks and Indian archives do not provide the full story of his work in the Middle East. Shakespear made surveys of the area for War Office maps, an intelligence assignment that officers like Kitchener had earlier performed in Palestine. So, too, does Winstone make references to secret funds and collateral duties of Shakespear but gives us little more on any intelligence duties, one of the gaps in this first full-length treatment of this imperial servant who sponsored Ibn Saud for leadership.

Winterbotham, Francis W. THE NAZI CONNECTION. New York: Harper and Row, 1978. 213 pp., index [London: Weidenfeld and Nicolson. Toronto: Fitzhenry and Whiteside].

This is more than a second account of what Winterbotham divulged in his *Secret and Personal* (below); it covers broader ground as well as new terrain. Following up on his best-seller *The Ultra Secret* (below), he included brief mentions of his work in connection with Ultra. His meetings and contacts with prominent Nazis for purposes of intelligence as an SIS officer are recounted again with new details added. So, too, is the part he and the French played in prewar aerial espionage over Germany; both subjects are treated in the first part of *Secret and Personal.* Brookes in *Photo Reconnaissance* confirms Winterbotham's role in providing impetus for prewar collaboration in aerial espionage, which led to cooperation with Sidney Cotton. However, Brookes gives the credit to Cotton for solving the problem of condensation on the camera lens. As for his Nazi contacts, Winterbotham's description of these is interesting; but he discounts more than he should the probability that the Germans suspected or were pretty much aware of whom they were dealing with and used this channel to Britain for their own purposes. Of greater intelligence interest are the SIS operations he divulges, which collected intelligence on the Luftwaffe and which transcended in importance his contacts with Nazi officials. So, too, is his chapter on the politics of British estimates of German air strength in the 1930s and on the differences between the collectors in SIS and the evaluators on the Air Staff. The reader will find that the story here of the traitor who sold the names of British agents to the Germans has features resembling that of the SIS traitor in Whiting's *The Spymasters* and Farago's *The Game of the Foxes.* Winterbotham persists in his errors on how the Poles made their breakthrough against the Enigma machine and tenaciously ignores any contribution by the French to this cryptanalytic success. For a start on the German perspective of Winterbotham's contacts with Nazi officials, see Farago's *The Game of the Foxes.*

Winterbotham, Francis William. SECRET AND PERSONAL. London: William Kimber, 1969. 188 pp., index.

This was, according to what Winterbotham wrote in his later *The Nazi Connection* (above), his first account of the years described in that later work. Because of constraints, he was not able to write in this book much that he revealed subsequently, especially in *The Ultra Secret* (below). One should not, however, get the impression that he need only read *The Nazi Connection,* written in 1978, to find the same subjects and ground covered more thoroughly. *Secret and Personal* is of interest in its own right because it deals with matters not found in the 1978 work. Also, anyone conscious of Ultra will find a number of clues pointing to the likely nature of this special source of intelligence available to Allied leaders in World War II and suggesting Winterbotham's role in its handling and distribution; Winterbotham did not let out the secret until 1974. The *Economist* review commented that *Secret and Personal* annoyed readers when it appeared by its knowing tone. For comments on

Winterbotham's contacts with Nazi leaders and how he and the French originated aerial espionage before the war, see *The Nazi Connection* (above).

Winterbotham, Francis W. THE ULTRA SECRET. New York: Harper and Row, 1974. 191 pp., index [London: Weidenfeld and Nicolson].

Certain books stand out because they are conceived of as the first to tell something, not because of how well or how accurately they tell it. *The Ultra Secret* falls into this category. It revealed the British successes against German military ciphers in World War II; more accurately, it used this important subject and development in the intelligence war as its central theme. Winterbotham, because of the details given and due to his position in SIS as special security officer who set up the system of distribution and control, lent the revelations the necessary authority. Allied successes against Enigma and German and Italian cryptographic systems had surfaced in some form in a number of works before Winterbotham: Bertrand, Trevor-Roper, Philby, Muggeridge, Farago, Deacon, and Hyde are some who mentioned this in one way or another; Hinsley in *British Intelligence in the Second World War* believed that a 1967 book in Polish by W. Kozaczuk, *The Battle of Secrets,* was the first to reveal details of the breaking of Enigma, the German cipher machine; it preceded Bertrand's *Enigma,* published in France.

David Kahn in his review in the *New York Times* gave one of the first warnings that *The Ultra Secret* had to be read with caution. Among Kahn's caveats were: it exaggerated the importance of Ultra as decisive in the war; there were errors because the author was writing from memory—for instance, U.S. solutions to Japanese systems were not factors in breaking Enigma, and the version of how the Poles made the first solution is incorrect. Since then, we have learned that many more things are wrong with Winterbotham's version. The technical explanations are sometimes all wrong or too elementary; his account of the British handling of the Coventry raid is incorrect (see R. V. Jones and others on this); he fails to give the Americans anything but passing references and does not give the French any credit or mention Bertrand; the accuracy of his accounts of the role of Ultra at certain stages of the war is questionable; he wrongly suggests that Enigma was synonymous with Ultra and that it was the only valuable or high-level German cipher. Winterbotham was wrong on some details of British organizational attitudes where he could be expected to be very reliable—see Montagu's explanation in *Beyond Top Secret Ultra* of the British Navy's position on the handling of special intelligence, which refutes Winterbotham's account. All the above comments should suffice to reinforce Kahn's advice that care should be taken in relying on this work as a dependable and accurate account of Ultra and the Allied cryptologic successes and how they were used to wage the war. *The Ultra Secret* has its niche in intelligence history for what it did in bringing to attention one of the most significant events of the war. But it has been superseded by subsequent works, such as those of Lewin, Calvocoressi, Bennett, Beesly, Montagu, R. V. Jones, and Johnson, that deal with technical, cryptologic, and operational aspects of Ultra in a more complete and more accurate way.

Wise, David, and Ross, Thomas B. THE ESPIONAGE ESTABLISHMENT. New York: Random House, 1967. 294 pp., index [London: Cape, 1968].

The authors, journalists with an interest in intelligence and espionage, declared this was written to present a portrait of international espionage as it then existed; it was not to be an encyclopedia of spying. They were a bit too ambitious. They never really cover the intelligence community of the United States, touching only on CIA with other agencies hardly mentioned (for example, NSA) or brought in peripherally in connection with an espionage case. Sections describing certain of the intelligence organizations of the Soviet Union and Great Britain are marked by some good material; there are two good chapters on Soviet illegal operations in the United States. The authors' analysis of the authenticity of the Penkovsky papers is fair, balanced, and quite discerning for its time. The DIS *Bibliography* thought the section on CIA weak though "not as error-ridden" as a previous study by these authors. One major mistake they made was to equate the sizes in manpower of CIA and the KGB, even with the latter's border guards excluded. The weakest portion deals with the People's Republic of China; here the authors must rely largely on guesswork about that country's clandestine collection activities abroad, although material is available on Chinese political action under Mao. Source notes, except for occasional items, are absent, and a bibliography would have been useful. There will be inevitable differences with the authors' view on the extent of the threat of "secret power" to open societies and with the advocacy journalism practiced; what cannot be denied is that much of their attitude in calling for intelligence oversight and control later became the prevailing mood in the United States. Farago's opinion that this was the "definitive book" on the subject was both excessive and wrong.

Wise, David, and Ross, Thomas B. THE U-2 AFFAIR. New York, Random House, 1962. 269 pp., no index [London: Cresset Press, 1963].

The ill-fated mission of the U-2 on May 1, 1960, the trial of the CIA pilot Francis Gary Powers, and his subsequent exchange are told by Wise and Ross, two journalists, in this instant history; the *Kirkus* reviewer thought it an important account but still a "quickie." Despite this and its occasionally overdone style of writing, it is a fairly good version of the mission. The authors, trailblazers in the call for greater accountability and control of secret activities of the U.S. government, claim they interviewed a hundred officials. However, no actual sources are named and almost no official records are cited. That the authors had access to persons with privileged information is obvious. The main developments and the outline of the whole U-2 affair are fairly well covered. It is only at the end, where they express their philosophical position on secret operations and draw conclusions not justified by the facts, that Wise and Ross weaken their work. The U-2 affair still needs a thorough study—much more than is given it here—to provide more answers and insights into matters such as the decision to undertake the mission and any planning for compromise. Wise and Ross observe that the U-2 broke with traditional collection methods; yet there was no evidence that the implications of this break were thought through. Sam Jaffe, the CBS correspondent in whom Powers's wife confided, was later alleged to have been a Soviet agent in an affidavit filed by the FBI. See also Powers's *Operation Overflight.*

Wohlstetter, Roberta. CUBA AND PEARL HARBOR: HINDSIGHT AND FORESIGHT. Rand Corp. Memorandum, no. RM 4328-ISA. Santa Monica, Calif: Rand Corp., April 1965. 41 pp., no index.

Produced for the U.S. Department of Defense, this short study is along the lines of the author's more comprehensive work on Pearl Harbor (below). The Cuba problem, like the case of Pearl Harbor, confronted the United States with the challenge of separating "signals" from "noise"; both were marked by the availability of much information, but information that was "ambiguous and incomplete." Wohlstetter concludes there is no chance of ever completely eliminating the "ambiguity of signals," only of reducing it. The study was based on open sources, which may limit its usefulness; it certainly circumscribes the author's range of vision, for she only had access to a portion of the facts and evidence available. Wohlstetter states that no articulate expert played the role of Cassandra in estimating Soviet intentions regarding Cuba. This is true by her definition of "Soviet expert," but she fails to mention the role of CIA director John McCone. Note that she found the

Kennedy administration made very little allowance for deception in Soviet statements and that one of her beliefs is that "in periods of high tension, it is commonly accepted that deception will be an enemy tactic."

Wohlstetter, Roberta. PEARL HARBOR, WARNING AND DECISION. Stanford, Calif.: Stanford Univ. Press, 1962. 410 pp., bibliog., index.

Much praise has been rightfully heaped on this work. It has been called the most complete study of events leading to the surprise attack, an excellent study of strategic warning, and a most valuable analysis of the questions of indicators, warning systems, estimates, and alerts. Thomas Schelling in the foreword used the adjective "superb." One writer called it the "vade-mecum for any serious student of the subject." It is an outstanding analysis of the Pearl Harbor hearings evidence done by a first-class mind and with a sensitive feel for an understanding of the human, organizational, geographic, bureaucratic, and other factors that influence perception in intelligence estimating. She presents them as affecting the identification of critical warning indicators. Wohlstetter provided the terms "signals" and "noise" borrowed from communications theory to denote the type of information analysts and decision makers must deal with. Her treatment of the methods of collection and the interplay of methods, information, and decisions is classic.

Critiques of her analysis have tried to show that it was not complete. Whaley, who called it a brilliant analysis and the "first explicit statement of a systematic hypothesis about the nature and cause of strategic surprise," pointed out in *Codeword Barbarossa* that Wohlstetter's model was useful but only when deception was not practiced. Others concerned with deception and surprise have also argued that Wohstetter did not give it sufficient weight or attention. William Harris, one of that school, in his bibliography *Intelligence and National Security,* added that she was prevented from analyzing the Japanese side because of language difficulties and her work must be considered incomplete until Japanese records are exhausted and the deception factor is adequately weighed. The reader should not miss other facts and observations she brings forth on intelligence and counterintelligence. As examples we are told (in 1962) that a copy of a Purple cryptographic machine was given to Great Britain in 1941 in return for keys and machines needed to decode German codes and ciphers and of the violation of legal norms by the U.S. Navy and the FBI in their prewar counterintelligence work in Hawaii. For one disagreement with her principal conclusion on the attacker's advantage, consult Michael Howard in the July 1963 issue of *World Politics.*

Woytak, Richard A. ON THE BORDER OF WAR AND PEACE: POLISH INTELLIGENCE AND DIPLOMACY IN 1937–39 AND THE ORIGINS OF THE ULTRA SECRET. Boulder, Colo., and New York: East European Quarterly and Columbia Univ. Press, 1979. 92 pp., bibliog., index.

The subtitle raises expectations of great revelations about Ultra. There is nothing very significant on this subject or on the Polish codebreaking role in this short work; most has been covered elsewhere in greater detail. The English-reading audience will find intriguing glimpses of Polish intelligence during the period under study. Woytak relied heavily on Stefan Mayer, former chief of Polish counterintelligence, and on Josef Smolenski, the last chief of Polish intelligence, both residing in Britain. Mayer provided his personal reminiscences and shared his three unpublished works dealing with the breaking of Enigma. Smolenski gave interviews. There is valuable information on the organization of Polish intelligence in prewar years and on some Polish positive, cryptologic, and counterintelligence operations against the Germans and the Soviets. We learn a bit about German and Polish clandestine support of Ukrainian and other nationalist movements in Russia and of the extensive Soviet espionage against Poland. As for claims of Polish intelligence successes against Russia, if these are correct the Poles were among the very few to succeed up to that time to the extent portrayed. This and a number of other interesting matters raised cry out for further research.

Wriston, Henry Merritt. EXECUTIVE AGENTS IN AMERICAN FOREIGN RELATIONS. Gloucester, Mass.: Peter Smith, 1967. 837 pp., index.

Originally delivered in 1923 in lectures on diplomatic history, this was first published in 1927. It is a classic study of the history of the executive agent method used by presidents of the United States to undertake missions of various kinds. Wriston stressed the development of the practice and studied political and constitutional questions raised before the method became a regular feature of U.S. diplomacy through World War I. Executive diplomatic agents he defined as executive appointees acting alone with powers and duties derived from and assigned by the executive and payment determined by him. The final chapter dealt primarily with the use of secret agents in diplomacy as well as of intelligence and propaganda agents. He allowed that there were many other secret agents used for collection of intelligence, secret diplomacy, and covert action besides those mentioned, but in 1923 U.S. archives past 1878 were not yet open. Also, though he dealt with the political and constitutional issues of secrecy and confidential funds and of practices dating back to the American Revolution, he apparently lacked access to confidential fund records, and thus he could not draw on the use of the Contingent Fund for specific purposes and objectives. For those interested in the early roots of U.S. intelligence or the early use of secrecy and secret funds and operations to further U.S. objectives and for an antidote to the commonly held belief that Americans historically did not undertake, show interest in, or have talent for clandestine or covert action, Wriston's scholarly but easy-to-read study is a must. DIS's *Bibliography* thought it essential for the proper comprehension of the historical and legal basis of

U.S. intelligence systems today. Natalie Summers in 1951 compiled an index for the U.S. National Archives entitled *List of Documents Relating To Special Agents of the Department of State 1789–1906.* No one has done a follow-up study of the use of executive agents for intelligence purposes since that of Wriston.

Wyden, Peter. BAY OF PIGS: THE UNTOLD STORY. New York: Simon and Schuster, 1979. 331 pp., bibliog., notes, index [London: Jonathan Cape].

The Bay of Pigs has been described as a rare thing in history—a perfect failure; this book's reviewer in the *Washington Post* also called it a watershed and an operation uniquely inept and "based on the grossest intelligence miscalculations." Wyden, a journalist, tells the story in the manner of Cornelius Ryan or Walter Lord, drawing the comment from Drew Middleton in the *New York Times,* that he did not include a single chapter on the overall plan of operations and that "the full sweep of events is lost in the welter of anecdotes." Wyden made use of FOIA material but relied mostly on knowledgeable individuals in CIA (this a first) and to Cuban and other U.S. government participants; he placed primary emphasis on first-hand sources, learning from experience, he said, to distrust research in libraries. He allocates blame and shows the inner workings of the U.S. government and national security decision-making process. The force of momentum in operations and of self-fulfillment in planning, flaws in security, and intelligence estimates are highlighted. Wyden brings out the extent of CIA combat involvement in the invasion, which was previously confined to sporadic and unnoticed articles or to what was uncovered by Haynes Johnson. The last chapter summarizes lessons and meanings and should have served as the model for writing and style for the rest of the book. Lyman Kirkpatrick is quoted as praising this as a great book—high and authoritative praise coming from one who was responsible for the CIA postmortem report. Many regard it as the best on the subject since

Haynes Johnson's 1964 book of the same name, which Wyden described as a masterful encyclopedic reconstruction of the exiles' involvement. (Whether it is a complete study is another matter.) Wyden complained that some material from U.S. files was not forthcoming, such as the full Taylor Report. Though there are good looks into CIA thinking, it cannot be said Wyden explored this aspect thoroughly; he could not as long as some official material was denied him. Since very few nonexile Cuban sources were available, he was not able to get what he wanted from those Cubans who really counted. See Kirkpatrick's *The Real CIA* for part of the story and for hints on his critical CIA postmortem findings as inspector general, still classified, in addition to Kirpatrick's 1972 article in the *Naval War College Review,* cited by Wyden. Phillips's *The Night Watch* contains primary source material.

Wynne, Barry. COUNT FIVE AND DIE. London: Souvenir Press, 1958. 179 pp., no index.

The preface speaks of this as a true story supposedly related by an aide of General Donovan of OSS. It purports to be the account of how OSS deceived the Germans into believing that Holland would be one of the Allied landing points in 1944. It reads like a movie script and was actually made into a British film. According to Foot in *SOE in France,* there was nothing in British files to show that this was anything but fiction. U.S. experts concur that this book is pure fantasy; they point out that there is no record anywhere of the operation the author describes or of individuals said to have been connected with it.

Wynne, Greville. CONTACT ON GORKY STREET. New York: Atheneum, 1968. 222 pp., no index [London: Hutchinson, 1967. *The Man from Moscow*].

Wynne was the British agent who was used as the contact with Soviet Colonel Oleg Penkovsky (see his *The Penkovsky Papers*). Part of this memoir is devoted to Wynne's trial and jail term which lasted for a year and a half until he was exchanged for Gordon Lonsdale (Konon Molodiy), the Soviet agent held by the British. The principal value of Wynne's account is, of course, that it is the only first-hand one on this most important espionage case. It contains examples of good tradecraft required for the secure handling of a sensitive agent in a hostile environment. Concurrently, he alleges instances of questionable security and tradecraft. Examples: Penkovsky met twenty Soviet defectors in London on his first trip there to assure himself; Wynne made an SIS apartment available to Penkovsky for a tryst with a woman from a Soviet embassy; a large number of persons were involved in the meeting in Paris and in the United Kingdom; Wynne was used only a few months after Penkovsky had managed to get him out of the USSR, where he was under suspicion. DIS's *Bibliography* considered Wynne's account somewhat colored. For one view of the suspicions that some have raised about the value of Penkovsky's intelligence, see Pincher's *Their Trade Is Treachery.* Since Wynne's account is ex parte, a fuller perspective would require further research.

X

Mr. X, with Bruce E. Henderson and C. C. Cyr. DOUBLE EAGLE: THE AUTOBIOGRAPHY OF A POLISH SPY WHO DEFECTED TO THE WEST. Indianapolis: Bobbs-Merrill, 1979. 219 pp., index.

The author, an officer with the UB, the Polish intelligence organization, was also a CIA penetration for two years while in Oslo. He defected in 1966 after having served in the UB for thirteen years. Mr. X has given the reader some interesting views of Polish intelligence: its practices and its relationships; the setting up of illegal nets abroad and their handling; the assassination by the UB of an illegal suspected of working for the West; the attitude of intelligence officers toward their organization and toward the Soviets. Also of interest are the things he makes known of the mentality and problems of the defector. His story varies from the usual pattern in that he is openly critical of his handling by the U.S. service after his defection and does not disguise his low opinion of certain types of CIA officers. And not many defectors have told openly of providing cryptographic material as one of the services performed against their own service. Still, there are a number of things about his story that will not satisfy the discerning reader: He does not discuss his operations in sufficient length or detail to make them interesting; he tends to treat his intelligence work for the UB in too general a fashion; he does not tell why he was declared persona non grata while in Sweden. Even the 1960 defection of the senior UB officer Colonel Goleniewski is covered in only one short paragraph saying only that it "caused an uproar" in the UB. One will wonder, as did critics, why the author went the dramatic route of hiding his identity, which is known to the Polish service, when the declared principal reason for writing the book was to get his son out of Poland.

Y

Yardley, Herbert O. THE AMERICAN BLACK CHAMBER. London: Faber and Faber, 1931. 265 pp., no index [Indianapolis: Bobbs-Merrill].

In his own book on cryptology, *The Codebreakers,* Kahn gave his opinion that Yardley's book was "the most famous book on cryptology ever published" and that Yardley himself was "the most famous cryptologist in history." Kahn felt that Yardley owed his fame to his sensational book rather than to what he actually did but that his book, despite any faults and errors, captured public imagination and inspired interest in cryptology. Yardley described his experiences as head of MI8 during World War I and of the famous Black Chamber until 1929 when it was abolished by order of the secretary of state. The book caused a sensation, especially in Japan because of what it said of U.S. work against Japanese and other systems. One of its many consequences was the passage of the law in 1933 known popularly as the Yardley Law protecting cryptologic matters. See Kahn's discussion of the aftermath and the political and other fallouts from this book.

As Yardley's name faded from public awareness, so has the book's reputation for reliability, accuracy, and innovation. Galland in *An Historical and Analytical Bibliography of the Literature of Cryptology* in 1945 called Yardley's work "romantically exaggerated, somewhat inaccurate." Kahn regarded it as having not only faults but falsehoods as well. Shulman in *An Annotated Bibliography of Cryptography* opined that from a cryptanalytical point of view the book contributed nothing new and that the account of Yves Gylden of ciphers before and during World War I was more accurate and thorough. The U.S. Army Security Agency's *The History of Codes and Ciphers in the United States During World War I* spells out in some detail where Yardley was considered to be incorrect, unreliable, or exaggerated. This latter work, for example, called Yardley's three chapters on secret inks "untrustworthy" because the author was in no position to write on this matter from first-hand experience. There are aspects of Yardley's life and work yet to be explained adequately. The failure to continue the employment of this talented and experienced cryptologist after the Black Chamber was closed needs further inquiry. Farago's allegations in *The Broken Seal* of Yardley's later relations with the Japanese have been attacked by such experts as Shulman. Kahn felt Farago must be read "with extreme caution"; both views, however, should not close the subject to further research. If Farago were proven right, it would then be the case that the Japanese did not first learn of U.S. cryptanalytic successes from this book. Ballantine Books in 1981 issued a paperback edition with a short introduction by Kahn.

Young, Desmond. RUTLAND OF JUTLAND. London: Cassell, 1963. 186 pp., index.

This is about F. J. Rutland, the highly decorated pioneer of British naval aviation in World War I, a man who, Young says, had a raw deal; it is also an attack against potential abuses of British Regulation 18b, which gives the British government vast powers of detention. Rutland did important work and rendered great services to the British Navy and hastened the advent of the aircraft carrier. He was detained in England in December 1941 upon his return from the United States and held for two years without explanation and charges.

Young treats the subject of Rutland so emotionally, as he does the matter of Regulation 18b, that he never comes to grips with what Rutland may or may not have done to warrant such treatment. The book is heavy on speculation, forgetting the author's own advice that speculation is irritating to the reader and frustrating to the writer. Bulloch in *Akin to Treason* quotes from the review of Captain S. W. Roskill and from subsequent writings that make a strong case that Rutland was probably involved in selling secrets to the Japanese while still in British service and that he was asked to resign his commission rather than be prosecuted. Also, Bulloch quotes Roskill as saying that the "hostile associations" mentioned by the Home Office in connection with Rutland "had considerably more substance behind them than Brigadier Young realized when he wrote the book." Bulloch, citing no source, also says U.S. counterintelligence had established that Rutland was employed by Japanese intelligence to collect information by legal means rather than to purchase secrets or handle secret agents.

Young, Gordon. THE CAT WITH TWO FACES. New York: Coward-McCann, 1957. 223 pp., no index [London: Putnam].

Mathilde Carré gained notoriety as "The Cat," a triple agent during World War II who was involved in the destruction of an Allied network in France, Inter-Allié. This is a short history of this agent who was the mistress both of the head of Inter-Allié and of her Abwehr case officer, the well-known Hugo Bleicher. Foot in *SOE in France* described this book as accurate. Young, a journalist, traces the story of Mathilde's odyssey and tries to follow the complexities of her motives as seen by her colleagues and attested to by her actions. Writing in 1957, he was not in a position to know of the later experiences of Inter-Allié's chief, Armand. His chapter on how the Germans used the net's radio to pass deception that assisted the dash of the German Warships *Scharnhorst* and *Gneisenau* distorts what main factors were responsible for their escape to Germany (in which radar deception played an important role). For more on this event see works such as Beesly's *Very Special Intelligence,* which nowhere mentions this form of German agent deception; neither does McLachlan's *Room 39.* The security and tradecraft described would seem to have made the end of the network easy to predict. London's confused handling of warnings about Carré's loyalty is itself not likely to inspire confidence in intelligence services. For Bleicher's story of the network, but not really of Mathilde's role, see his *Colonel Henri's Story.*

Z

Zacharias, Ellis M. SECRET MISSIONS: THE STORY OF AN INTELLIGENCE OFFICER. New York: Putnam's Sons, 1946. 424 pp., index.

Zacharias's personal account is an indispensable record of ONI for the period he was associated with it and for the cryptologic and CI history of the prewar effort against Japan. His reminiscences are important for a number of reasons. He was one of the small band of Japanese-language students and country experts of the prewar era and a pioneer in the U.S. Navy's small language program. Second, he belonged to the small group involved in naval intercepts and cryptanalytic work in the Pacific in the 1920s. Third, he was one of those ONI officers who formed the cadre of that organization in World War II, rising to become deputy chief. Fourth, there are few accounts of U.S. counterintelligence against the Japanese in the prewar period or of U.S. Navy psychological warfare operations against Japan in the war.

Shortcomings to be found are Zacharias's overestimate of the Japanese intelligence threat (as well as the German) before and during the war. Some opinions and estimates of situations and people have a dated quality. But just as this is a valuable first-hand record of certain U.S. intelligence, counterintelligence, and psychological warfare operations and their organization, so it is a clear exposition of the crucial importance of intelligence and counterintelligence to a nation's security. According to Farago's *The Broken Seal,* he assisted Zacharias in writing this memoir, having been associated with him in the Special Warfare Branch, the secret psychological warfare unit of the U.S. Navy during the war.

Zeman, Z.A.B., and Scharlau, W. B. THE MERCHANT OF REVOLUTION: THE LIFE OF ALEXANDER ISRAEL HELP-

HAND (PARVUS), 1867–1924. Oxford and New York: Oxford Univ. Press, 1965. 281 pp., index.

A fascinating biography, the first in English, of Helphand (pen name Parvus), the brilliant and equally fascinating radical socialist who was a leading adviser to the Germans on revolutionary affairs in Russia in World War I and was used by the Germans to organize and finance efforts to bring about Russia's collapse via the Russian socialists. Helphand's role as a German political action agent was revealed by German foreign office archives captured after World War II. According to the authors, the archives show Helphand to have been the central figure in the conspiracy connecting the Germans and the Russian Social Democrat party, particularly Lenin's segment. Alan Moorehead in *The Russian Revolution* (New York: Harper and Bros., 1958) describes Helphand's agent role on behalf of the Germans and is based on these captured documents. This socialist, journalist, theoretician, writer, and publisher made a fortune in the war in business and as an agent; he plotted to bring a revolution to Russia, assisted Russian minorities' efforts to achieve independence, ran intelligence-collection operations, channeled funds to Lenin's faction, and subsidized other European socialists with German funds. He was also imaginative in conceiving economic warfare and propaganda schemes. The record of what he did is partial, first because Helphand destroyed his private papers and second because the Germans did not make a record of all their dealings with him. The critic for the *American Historical Review* stated that there was little about his life prior to the war and that the presentation of Helphand's association with the Russian Social Democrat party was "riddled with errors." Be that as it may, this work by a British and a German historian is a superior study of covert political, economic, and psychological warfare in time of war and in connection with some of the greatest and most far-reaching events in modern history; the same *American Historical Review* writer judged it the "best account available of German efforts to undermine the Czarist regime."

Zlotnick, Jack. NATIONAL INTELLIGENCE. Washington, D.C.: U.S. Industrial College of the Armed Forces, 1964. 67 pp., bibliog., index.

The author, formerly with CIA, wrote this study to describe "the design of the machinery, process and concepts of national intelligence." He divided this concise work into sections on, e.g., the U.S. intelligence community, the intelligence process, categories of national intelligence, and intelligence specializations (political, economic, military, etc). Organizational changes have naturally made this part of the work dated but useful for reference; the bulk still stands since it is concerned with categories of intelligence. It is well organized, precise, and commendably brief for a textbook touching on the basics. Judgments he makes that have not weathered the effects of time and greater experience are few, but one of these must be identified. We are now more aware of the impact and quality of many national intelligence estimates (NIEs), which are markedly different from his high rating.

Zuckerman, Solly. FROM APES TO WARLORDS: AUTOBIOGRAPHY (1904–1946). London: Hamish Hamilton, 1978. 447 pp., index.

Although by strict definition Zuckerman's book does not exactly meet this bibliography's criteria it is included for its symbolic lessons to the intelligence officer and because of the relevance of operations research in certain intelligence areas. Zuckerman was one of the pioneers in operations research in World War II and as the scientific adviser on planning to the Allied Expeditionary Air Force and to SHAEF was a working research scientist admitted into inner planning circles. He led the group arguing for air attacks on the enemy's railway system to paralyze its war-making machine instead of strategic bombing. Zuckerman's thesis is that a study of the facts should be the basis for action and for analyzing results of operations, not preconceived notions or a priori reasoning. The conclusions he draws on what bombing policy to pursue and the results of the applications of his theories in the invasion of France in 1944 contain lessons worth pondering when set against intelligence appreciations by the regular services. If Zuckerman's "transportation plan" was right, the question remains of why certain service estimates and decision makers who long opposed it or diluted it in practice were not. Zuckerman acknowledged the value of Ultra as his most important source in his postinvasion study of air attacks. Lewin in *Ultra Goes to War* was of the opinion that Zuckerman's version of the results of one phase of the railway interdiction strategy in Italy was rosier than the actuality. Still sobering is the author's accusation of the absence of any challenge to the uniformly negative appreciations of the intelligence agencies on the strategic significance of the program of attacks on transportation.

Glossary and Abbreviations

Abwehr: Intelligence and counterintelligence service of the German General Staff prior to and during most of World War II.

A Force: British deception organization in the Middle East and Mediterranean under Brigadier Dudley Clarke during World War II.

AIB: Allied Intelligence Bureau; combined Allied intelligence organization under General MacArthur in World War II.

ASA: U.S. Army Security Agency; the army's cryptologic service.

ASIO: Australian Security Intelligence Organization; Australian security service.

ASIS: Australian Secret Intelligence Service; Australian foreign intelligence service.

ASW: Antisubmarine warfare.

ATIS: Allied Translator and Interpreter Section.

Barbarossa: Code name for German 1941 invasion of the USSR.

B1A: Section of Britain's MI5 (security) responsible for double agents in World War II.

BCRA: Free French intelligence service during World War II.

B Dienst: German navy's intercept and cryptanalysis service prior to and during World War II.

BI: Dutch intelligence service during World War II; created November 1942.

Black Chamber: Organization for deciphering and reading intercepted messages.

Bletchley Park: Location of Britain's cryptologic service, the GC&CS (q.v.), during World War II.

BND: Foreign intelligence service of West Germany, organized by General Gehlen.

Bodyguard: Code name for Allied deception plan for the 1944 invasion of France.

BP: Bletchley Park (q.v.).

BSC: British Security Coordination; British intelligence security and special operations organization for the Western Hemisphere in World War II, headquartered in the U.S.

"C": Designation for the head of Britain's SIS (q.v.).
CE: Counterespionage.
Cheka: First Soviet security and secret service, the ancestor of the KGB (q.v.).
Chickenfeed: Information a service allows to be passed via double agents or via any other means controlled by it.
CI: Counterintelligence.
CIA: U.S. Central Intelligence Agency.
CIC: Counter Intelligence Corps; U.S. Army counter intelligence service.
Cicero: Code name of the German agent in the British embassy in Ankara in World War II.
CIG: Central Intelligence Group; created in 1946 and the predecessor of CIA.
Clandestine Services: Clandestine intelligence and covert operations directorate of CIA.
COI: Coordinator of Information, July 1941–June 1942; predecessor of OSS (q.v.).
Comint: Communications intelligence.
CS: Clandestine Services of CIA (q.v.).

D Section: Special operations section of Britain's SIS; later incorporated into SOE (q.v.).
DCI: Director of Central Intelligence and head of CIA.
DDP: Deputy Directorate for Plans; the operations directorate of CIA.
DDI: Deputy Directorate for Intelligence; the research and analysis section of CIA.
DF: Direction finding. *See also* HF/DF.
DIA: U.S. Defense Intelligence Agency
DGI: Cuban General Directorate of Intelligence; the foreign intelligence service.
DIS: U.S. Defense Intelligence School.
DNI: Director of Naval Intelligence (British).
Double Cross Committee: *See* XX Committee.

E&E: Escape and evasion.
ECM: Electronics countermeasures.
Elint: Electronic intelligence.
Enigma: Cipher machine of the German armed forces and security services prior to and during World War II.
EW: Electronic warfare.

FBI: U.S. Federal Bureau of Investigation.
FOIA: U.S. Freedom of Information Act.
F Section: SOE section in charge of independent operations into French territories in World War II.

GC&CS: Government Code and Cipher School; British cryptologic service.
G-2: U.S. Army intelligence.
GRU: Soviet military intelligence service.

HF/DF: High frequency direction finding; the location of ships and transmitting stations from the bearings of their radio traffic. Also known as Huff Duff.
Humint: Intelligence collected by agents.

IC: Intelligence community (U.S.).
INR: Bureau of Intelligence and Research, U.S. State Department.

KGB: Soviet intelligence and security service.
Klatt: German intelligence operation against the USSR in World War II believed to be under Soviet control.

Lavon Affair: Israeli political controversy over responsibility for ordering Operation Susannah (q.v.).
LCS: London Controlling Section; committee in London 1942–1945 responsible for deception operations.
Lucy ring: Soviet intelligence network in Switzerland during World War II.

Magic: U.S. code name for deciphered Japanese diplomatic messages.
Meinertzhagen satchel ploy: Deliberate planting of false documents to deceive an enemy.
MGB: Forerunner of the KGB (q.v.).
MI8: U.S. military intelligence cryptologic service, created in 1917.

MI5: British security service.

Mincemeat: Code name for British deception operation 1943 involving the discovery of a body laden with deceptive documents.

MI9: British escape and evasion organization in World War II.

MI6: British foreign intelligence service. Also known as SIS.

MIS-X: U.S. escape and evasion section, World War II.

MO: Morale Operations; OSS's psychological warfare branch.

Mossad: Israel's foreign intelligence or secret service.

MVD: Forerunner of the KGB (q.v.).

National Redoubt: Area thought chosen by the Germans for a last stand in World War II.

NID: Naval Intelligence Division (British).

NIE: National Intelligence Estimate (U.S.).

NKVD: Predecessor of the KGB (q.v.).

Northern Department: British intelligence headquarters out of Canada during the American Revolution.

North Pole: German deception operation against the British in Holland in World War II.

NSA: National Security Agency; U.S. cryptologic service, formed in 1952.

NSC: U.S. National Security Council.

NTS: Russian émigré group opposed to Soviets.

OG: Operational Group; branch of OSS.

OGPU: Forerunner and predecessor of the NKVD, the MGB, and the KGB (q.v.).

OIC: Operational Intelligence Center of the British Admiralty in World War II.

ONE: Office of National Estimates, CIA.

ONI: Office of Naval Intelligence; U.S. naval intelligence service.

OSO: Office of Special Operations, CIA.

OSS: Office of Strategic Services; the U.S. intelligence and special operations service in World War II.

Overlord: Code name for the Allied invasion of northwest France, 1944.

OWI: Office of War Information; U.S. propaganda and information agency in World War II.

PFIAB: President's Foreign Intelligence Advisory Board (U.S.).
PI: Photographic interpretation or photo interpreter.
PR: Photographic reconnaissance.
PRO: Public Record Office (British).
Purple: Japanese cipher machine of the 1930s and World War II.
PWE: Political Warfare Executive; the British political and psychological warfare organization in World War II.

RAF: Royal Air Force (British).
RCMP: Royal Canadian Mounted Police.
RF: SOE section for operations into France in cooperation with the Free French during World War II.
RFE: Radio Free Europe; U.S. radio beamed to Communist Eastern Europe after World War II.
Room 40: British naval cryptanalysis section in World War I.
RUSI: Journal of the Royal United Services Institute for Defense Studies (London).

SACO: Sino-American Cooperative Organization; U.S.–Nationalist Chinese intelligence and special operations organization in China during World War II.
SD: Sicherheitsdienst; the Nazi party security and secret service.
SDECE: French secret service.
SHAEF: Supreme Headquarters Allied Expeditionary Forces.
SI: Secret Intelligence; branch of OSS.
SIM: Servizio Informazione Militare; the Italian military intelligence and security service.
SIS: **1.** Britain's Secret Intelligence Service. Also known as MI6. **2.** Servizio Informazione Segreto; the Italian naval intelligence and security service.
SLU: Special Liaison Unit; responsible for Allied security of Ultra messages in World War II.
Smersh: Special Soviet counterintelligence and security organization in World War II.
SO: Special Operations; branch of OSS.
SOE: Special Operations Executive; the British resistance and sabotage organization in World War II.
Susannah: Israeli 1954 provocation sabotage plan in Egypt.

Szek, A.: Reputed World War I British agent employed by the Germans in Brussels.

Torch: Code name for the U.S.-British landing in North Africa, 1942.

Trust: Soviet-controlled organization and deception operation in the 1920s against Russian émigrés and Western intelligence services.

Twenty Committee: Also known as the Double Cross or XX Committee (q.v.).

UB: Polish intelligence organization.

Ultra: U.S.-British security designation for intelligence derived from deciphered high-system enemy traffic.

USIB: U.S. Intelligence Board.

USNI: U.S. Naval Institute.

Venlo incident: Enticement and kidnapping of two British intelligence officers by the Germans in 1939.

WIN: Polish Communist deception operation of the late 1940s and early 1950s. Also, the name of the controlled organization in Poland.

XX Committee: British interservice committee in World War II controlling intelligence sent by and the buildup of double agents.

X-2: Counterintelligence branch of OSS.

Y Service: British radio intercept, direction finding, traffic analysis, and lower-grade cryptanalysis service.

Zimmermann Telegram: German telegram sent in 1917 offering Mexico an alliance and U.S. territory.

Zinoviev Letter: Instructions purportedly sent by the Soviets to British Communists prior to British elections of 1924.

Title Index

Subject and Author Index